Power, Politics, and the Olympic Games

Alfred Erich Senn

Human Kinetics

Library of Congress Cataloging-in-Publication Data

Senn, Alfred Erich.
Power, politics, and the Olympic Games / Alfred Erich Senn.
p. cm.
Includes bibliographical references and index.
ISBN 0-88011-958-6
1. Olympics--Political aspects--History. 2. Sports and state--History. 3. Brundage, Avery. 4. International Olympic Committee--History. I. Title.
GV721.5.S443 1999
796.48--dc21 98-48879
CIP

ISBN-10: 0-88011-958-6
ISBN-13: 978-0-88011-958-0

Acquisitions Editor: Steven W. Pope, PhD; **Developmental Editor:** C.E. Petit, JD; **Assistant Editors:** Cassandra Mitchell, Phil Natividad; **Copyeditor:** Bonnie Pettifor; **Proofreader:** Pamela S. Johnson; **Indexer:** Craig Brown; **Graphic Designer:** Robert Reuther; **Graphic Artist:** Kathleen Boudreau-Fuoss; **Photo Editors:** Amy Outland, Clark Brooks; **Cover Designer:** Jack Davis; **Photographer:** Photos on pages 35 and 65 by Tom Roberts; **Printer:** United Graphics

Printed in the United States of America 10 9 8 7 6 5 4

Human Kinetics
Web site: www.HumanKinetics.com

United States: Human Kinetics
P.O. Box 5076, Champaign, IL 61825-5076
800-747-4457
e-mail: humank@hkusa.com

Canada: Human Kinetics
475 Devonshire Road Unit 100, Windsor, ON N8Y 2L5
800-465-7301 (in Canada only)
e-mail: orders@hkcanada.com

Europe: Human Kinetics
107 Bradford Road, Stanningley, Leeds LS28 6AT, United Kingdom
+44 (0) 113 255 5665
e-mail: hk@hkeurope.com

Australia: Human Kinetics
57A Price Avenue, Lower Mitcham, South Australia 5062
08 8372 0999
e-mail: liaw@hkaustralia.com

New Zealand: Human Kinetics
Division of Sports Distributors NZ Ltd.
P.O. Box 300 226 Albany, North Shore City, Auckland
0064 9 448 1207
e-mail: info@humankinetics.co.nz

Dedication

To John J. Brandabur and Paramjeet Chopra:
Without their help I could not have written this book.

Contents

Preface

This study arose out of my own specialization as a historian of Eastern Europe. When United States President Jimmy Carter announced the American boycott of the 1980 Olympic Games scheduled for Moscow, I was living in Moscow, and I read the slogans "Keep politics out of sports" and "Sports free of politics" almost every day in the Soviet press. Then one day I walked into the Academy of Sciences Library, where I was working, and was confronted with an announcement of a lecture entitled "The XXIInd Olympic Games and the Struggle Against Bourgeois Ideology." The idea of this sort of study immediately began to form in my mind. Since 1975, I had been helping Bob Johnson, then the hockey coach at the University of Wisconsin and later coach of the Stanley Cup champion Pittsburgh Penguins, host visiting Soviet hockey teams. As a result, I had begun studying the Soviet sport system. In 1980, the politics of the Olympic Games, that clash of myth and reality, began to interest me, and for 15 years I have taught a course on "The Political History of the Modern Olympics." In the spring of 1996, the University of Wisconsin granted me a sabbatical semester so I could develop this book.

Acknowledgments

This book comes from a course I have taught for fifteen years, and a course or a book, like a river, arises from many springs and creeks. I owe a great deal to all the people who have written about the Olympic Games before me, but since much of the material falls in the category of "contemporary history," I had to look for living sources in addition to the documents and publications a historian might usually use. Here, unfortunately, I have space to mention only a few of these living sources.

When I became interested in this topic, I found sport administrators and journalists more than willing to explain their work. I have to start with the memory of Bob Johnson, "Badger Bob," who was always ready to answer questions. Gennady Shibaev explained the Soviet sports system from Moscow's point of view, and then Vytas Nenius gave me a Lithuanian perspective on "The Big Red Machine." Ollan Cassel and his staff at The Athletics Congress instructed me on the politics of international track and field, and John Dustin explained the organization of the Goodwill Games of 1986. Bill Wohl was my first instructor in the politics of international basketball. I am especially grateful to Richard Pound, Vice President of the International Olympic Committee, who spent a goodly amount of time explaining some of the nuances in Olympic affairs that had eluded me.

Then there were former Olympians who helped me. In particular I want to mention Frank Lubin, or Pranas Lubinas as the Lithuanians call him, the captain of the 1936 US basketball team, and Šarunas Marčiulionis, who gave me access to the world of professional basketball. In addition, a number of athletes and coaches from my hometown of Madison, Wisconsin, have even come in to speak to my classes.

My students provided me with an unending flow of material, and their enthusiasms encouraged me to push further. Former students still write to me from around the world, sending publications and newspaper articles. One former student, stationed with the US Army in Korea at the time of the Seoul Games, collected local publications for me.

There remains, of course, the academic side of the topic, the "documents" and the historiography. Here I want to express my thanks to the University of Illinois at Urbana-Champaign's summer program for Slavic studies, which gave me the opportunity to work in those rich materials at the university library and especially in the library's archival section. Maynard Brichford provided me with invaluable instruction and help in using the massive archive assembled by Avery Brundage, the president of the IOC from 1952 to 1972. Without the materials in that archive, I could not have written this book.

Other help came from a variety of sources. In 1984, the Ban the Soviets Coalition, which was active before the Los Angeles Games, provided me with copies of their archive of newspaper clippings and video recordings. (I have donated these materials to the Lithuanian State Archives.) I also must mention the newspaper archive of the Welt Wirtschaftsarchiv in Hamburg, Germany. I want to express special thanks to the University of Wisconsin for the sabbatical semester that I received for the purpose of putting all these experiences into my computer's memory. Finally, I want to thank the staff at Human Kinetics for the energy and expertise they have put into transforming my computer's bytes into this book.

My intellectual debts are enormous. None of the people and institutions I have mentioned can of course be held responsible for anything I say. I just hope that they all will feel that their efforts were worthwhile.

Introduction

The Olympic Games are now the largest, regularly scheduled international gathering in the world, and as such they constitute a major political showplace. The International Olympic Committee (IOC), the master of the Games, plans the presentation of "theater" replete with "sacred" rituals. Television, the Games' basic means of communicating with the world, plans its broadcasts as entertainment, aiming at the broadest possible audience. Together these efforts command the world's attention like no other event. At this competition, appearing before a worldwide audience, large states have the opportunity to demonstrate their power, small states can win recognition for special achievements, and new states, participating in the introductory Parade of Nations, receive worldwide validation as members of the international community. For the political leaders of the participating countries, and for a great many of their citizens, every appearance of the national flag at the Games is a magic moment.

For some devotees, the Games can evoke almost religious feelings. The founder of the modern Games, the Baron Pierre de Coubertin (1979), who spoke of *religio atletae* ("religion of the athlete"), called sport a "religion with its church, dogmas, service . . . but above all a religious feeling." Juan Antonio Samaranch, the current President of the IOC, aroused considerable controversy before the Atlanta Games when he declared in a television interview, "We are more important than the Catholic religion." Explaining this statement to the Lithuanian newspaper *Lietuvos rytas* (April 5, 1997), he elaborated, "I was misunderstood. Some say that the Olympic Movement is almost a religion, but we do not say that. But the Olympic Movement is more universal than any religion."

Although many sport fans consider "politics" an unwelcome intruder in the Olympic Games, politics are in fact an integral part of the Games. The glamour and attractiveness of the Olympic Games and the fact people care give Olympic performances great political significance and weight. Lord Killanin, the head of the IOC in the 1970s, confirmed this, writing, "Ninety-five percent of my problems as president of the IOC involved national and international politics" (1983). In practice, the political dimensions of the Games are diverse and complicated, ranging from the certification of national teams, through the interplay and intrigues of the various international sports organizations, to the infighting of the IOC. Governments have tried to exploit the Games for their own ends, and at times the IOC has itself put pressure on governments. It is no surprise, then, that the Games have served as a focus for national rivalries and ideological rivalries between states.

At the same time, both participants and nonparticipants may be seeking to exploit the Games for their own purposes. Rules violations by athletes range from actions as innocent as smuggling a friend into the Olympic Village to using performance-enhancing drugs, the detection of which has deprived more than one would-be champion of a gold medal. The athletes, moreover, may engage in openly political demonstrations. When two American runners delivered the black power salute at Mexico City in 1968, they were taking advantage of the opportunity to hold the world's attention. The IOC disapproved of this action, but it did not protest when George Foreman waved American flags after his boxing victory in Mexico City. Whether "political," "apolitical," or "antipolitical," all such demonstrations have political significance in the eyes of a great number of spectators.

The majestic Olympic stage also appears very inviting to nonathletic groups. In the summer of 1996, the Olympic torch relay, symbolically carrying the news of the Games in Atlanta to the far corners of the United States, had to consider the possibilities of protests when planning to cross territories ruled by Indian tribes or territories that had adopted legislation discriminating against gays. During the Atlanta Games, Amnesty International condemned the way in which the Georgia justice system applied the death penalty. In the midst of the preparations for the 2000 Games in Sydney, Australian aborigine groups are debating how to publicize their protests against the Australian government's land policies. In all these instances, individuals and groups see the Olympics as a stage from which they may send out their own messages.

Outside intrusions into the Games even carry the threat of bloodshed. At the 1972 Munich Games, terrorists seized Israeli hostages to win publicity for demands against the Israeli government; in the end, all the hostages died. Lord Killanin has quoted a terrorist as having explained that his comrades chose to win attention by attacking the Games because they constituted the "most sacred ceremony" of the "modern religion of the western world" (1983). Yet, one must also remember that in the history of political assassinations, attacks carried out in seemingly neutral territory are not unusual. Indeed, even independently of the elaborate Olympic ritual, merely the visibility of the Games makes them an attractive target for political and social causes.

Since the terrible experience in Munich in 1972, Olympic officials have had to pay increasing attention to the possibility of terrorists' actions at the Games. In the last weeks before the Olympic Games of 1996 in Atlanta, the memories of the bombing of the federal courthouse in Oklahoma City, a gas attack in a Tokyo subway, a bomb attack on American soldiers in Saudi Arabia, and random bombings in Moscow public transportation all combined to put the security forces in Atlanta on highest alert. The crash of a TWA plane leaving New York three nights before the opening ceremonies intensified the concern, although investigators have never pinpointed the cause of the explosion that destroyed the plane. In Atlanta, the number of security personnel was reportedly triple the number of athletes competing in the Games, but even so, a bomb explosion disrupted the celebration. Officials have yet to identify the motivation for that bombing. On the eve of the Nagano Games of 1998, Japanese radicals shot several mortars into Tokyo's Narita airport, apparently simply to challenge Olympic security. As the Games grow, Olympic organizers have to prepare for more such peripheral occurrences that perhaps are not even aiming at the Games.

Rather than being an autonomous institution into which politics creep uninvited, the Games and international sport themselves play a significant role in international politics as they embody conflict and tension. Sport lore is full of stories of prisoners playing captors, in both wartime and peacetime, and of colonial peoples challenging the colonial masters in a game the masters consider their own—as in the case of former British colonies' playing cricket. In 1940, Polish prisoners of war defied their German captors by secretly staging their own "Prisoners' Olympics." The symbolism of the victories over the captors and masters, or ex-masters, is obvious, and of course very political. One scholar called the Games "metaphoric war between national-states" (Moragas Spa, Rivenburgh, and Larson 1995).

Americans long tried to ignore the politics of the Games, often attributing political tensions in the Games to the evil influence of American conflicts with the Soviet Union in the "Cold War." In their time, Soviet commentators accused the Americans of subterfuge for insisting ignorance of the relationship of politics and sport. A Soviet member of the IOC, Aleksei Romanov, declared that "as a mass social movement, international sport is in our time an arena of sharp political and ideological struggle" (1963). On another occasion, he complained about western hypocrisy on this topic: "At present there is a characteristic effort by bourgeois spokesmen to propagandize by any means possible the slogan 'sport outside of politics.'. . . The propagation of apoliticalness . . . is nothing but another method of ideological diversion on the part of imperialist circles, directed against the lands of the socialist camp" (1973). Now that the Cold War has ended and passed from the Olympic scene, American commentators must recognize that there are other, even deeper political considerations at play in the Games.

Some commentators view sport as a "transnational" rather than "international" phenomenon, suggesting the competition brings together nongovernmental groups and organizations independently of the governments of the world. In fact, Games organizers set quotas for participation by political entities. In turn, most governments support their national teams financially. Many governments include sport ministries that supervise their national sport programs; all cheer the triumphs of their champions.

The rules for admission seem quirky at times. The membership in the Olympic family outnumbers the membership in the United Nations. Puerto Rico is a member of the family; Scotland, which is a member of FIFA, the football federation, is not. In 1992, Spain, following a U.N. directive, refused Yugoslavia admission to the Games as a team but, at the IOC's insistence, allowed Yugoslav athletes to compete as individuals. At Atlanta in 1996, Eritrea had the dubious honor of being the only United Nations member not admitted to the Games, because the IOC had not yet recognized an Eritrean Olympic Committee. In any case, the IOC exercises considerable power in recognizing or not recognizing participants.

Likewise, governments frequently use sport as a weapon of their foreign policy or as a channel to communicate special messages. In the 1960s, East Germany, the German Democratic Republic, insisted its athletes carry East German passports in order to force signs of recognition from western states. "Sporting achievements of the GDR constitute worthy international representation of our socialist state," wrote one East German author (*Sportsmeny* 1974). The "Ping-Pong" diplomacy of 1971 that brought American table tennis players to China testified to China's interest in reestablishing political contacts with the United States. When black African states withdrew their athletes from Montreal in 1976, they wanted to strike a blow against apartheid in South Africa. But when facing an international boycott, South Africa responded by advocating the obviously political slogan "sports without politics."

Sport competition can also contribute to international tension by providing the occasion for incidents or expressing greater conflicts. The "soccer war" between Guatemala and El Salvador is well-known, as is the Hungarian-Soviet water polo match at Melbourne in 1956 in the aftermath of the Soviets' suppression of revolution in Hungary. Lesser known events include the Uruguayan diplomatic protest to the Dutch concerning the behavior of German soccer players at the Amsterdam Olympics of 1928 and the Czech-Soviet hockey matches in the late 1960s and early 1970s in the aftermath of the Warsaw Pact's invasion of Czechoslovakia in 1968. One can also point to controversy over national flags in London in 1908, the exclusion of Germany from the post–World War I Olympics in Antwerp and Paris, and the calls to boycott the Games scheduled for Berlin in 1936.

Victory in international sport competition can influence the development of national consciousness. The Greek royal family wanted to use the very first Olympic Games in Athens to enhance their own national image, as in 1995-1996 when Nelson Mandela, the President of postapartheid

South Africa, found the international victories of the country's rugby and soccer teams helpful in trying to forge a new identity for his country. Minority groups may also find messages: The protest of American blacks at the Mexico City Games electrified the world, and Jim Thorpe became an icon of native American grievances in American life after he lost his medals won at the Stockholm Games.

To be sure, what appears to one observer as politics may not seem so to another observer. Many commentators point to the waving of national flags at the Games as an example of undesirable national passions. But when a West German official proposed doing away with national flags in Munich in 1972, an East German official asserted this represented a West German effort to deny East Germany its recognition at the Games. In 1980, when British athletes participated in the Moscow Games under the Olympic flag, some westerners called this progress, but the Soviet hosts, wanting to enjoy their moment as host to the world, called it a violation of sacred Olympic traditions. To add to the tensions, fans in each country tend to think the sports in which their champions are best are the most important. Determining the role of politics in sport or of sport in politics, establishing the distinctions between healthy and unhealthy national feelings—all are subject to different perceptions.

Each branch of the Olympic structure approaches the Games from a different perspective. A member of the IOC, for example, could see his or her role as serving humanity, helping world peace. Some members of the IOC participated in the Games themselves; others feel only a sense of duty or a thrill of participation. When Avery Brundage, a former participant in the Games, was President of the IOC, he drew no income from the organization; in fact, he paid some $75,000 annually out of his own pocket to cover his own expenses as President. Since his time, members of the IOC have received repayment of their expenses, but IOC spokespersons frequently picture the Games as an idealistic, perhaps even quixotic, effort to improve the human condition in an unappreciative world.

The actual organizers and administrators of the competition—the International Sports Federations (IFs), the National Olympic Committees (NOCs), and the specific Games Organizing Committees (OCOGs)—have their own special interests, not to mention jobs. The Games are expensive, and the organizers must be professionals. Like administrators in other branches of sport, they include idealists, but the "bottom line" is financial. They must find the money to send athletes to the competition, organize and stage the competition, and of course support themselves. Although their public and private assessments of the nature of the Games may differ, as a whole, they represent specific interests in the continuation and development of the Olympic Games while jealously protecting their own turf.

Some authors complain the athletes are actually the forgotten element in the history of the Olympic Games. The athletes find their places in the Games as part of an official contingent, representing a political entity recognized by the IOC. Yet, there is sometimes some room for maneuvering. Zola Budd, excluded from the Games as a South African, found a place—albeit with considerable controversy—as a British citizen. In contrast, Jonty Skinner, arguably the fastest swimmer of his time, could not participate in the Montreal Olympics because he would not renounce his South African citizenship. In 1996, Wilson Kipketer, world champion in the 800 meters, did not want to run for his native Kenya, but the IOC would not permit him to participate as an individual. Bart Veldkamp, a speed skater who had objected to the Dutch qualification system, became a Belgian citizen and won third place in the 5,000-meter race in Nagano. In short, citizenship is the first factor in an athlete's hopes of finding a place in the Olympic Games.

The athlete then has to compete for that place. Ironically, because of the quota system of entries, although the large states of the world win most of the medals, all other things being equal, a world class athlete has a better chance of getting to the Games if he or she can represent a smaller country—with the exception of unique specializations such as the cases of runners in Kenya or skiers in Austria. (Austria would have no place for "Eddie the Eagle," the unlikely English skier at the Calgary Games.) On the victory stand a champion may feel he or she is representing only him- or herself or may feel transformed as the representative of a country, society, or cause. The great Finnish runner, Paavo Nurmi, declared, "I run for myself, not for Finland" (Phillips 1996); another Finnish runner, Hannes Kolehmainen, regretted that a Russian flag flew at his victory ceremony in 1912 (Noel-Baker 1978a). In a sport that does not have further financial rewards, glory, together with a sense of accomplishment, may be the ultimate reward; however, in figure skating, boxing, or track and field, money may well surpass fleeting glory as the ultimate reward.

The struggle for a place and then for honors and awards can be the occasion for negative phenomena: An intruder attacks a figure skater with a metal bar, obviously wanting to incapacitate her for the Games in Lillehammer; a sprinter in Seoul loses his gold medal after he fails a drug test; a fencer in Montreal wires his weapon illegally. Weight lifters in Seoul fail drug tests and lose their medals. In Rome in 1960, a Danish cyclist dies from a drug overdose. The practice of many countries in giving financial rewards to Olympic medal winners, while welcomed by many, actually increases the pressure to look for a "competitive edge." Thus the question remains "What did the coaches and the sport administrators know about each of these cases?"

This study is more concerned about team involvement in such behavior, particularly in regard to drug scandals, than in individuals' or even coaches' maneuvering. In April 1997, *Sports Illustrated* suggested most Olympic medalists probably use performance-enhancing substances and that "drug testing is serving as no deterrent" (Bamberger and Yaeger 1997). This in turn became a major topic of discussion at a special Olympic conference on drug abuse in Lausanne. The IOC's Medical Commission promised more efficient testing at the Sydney Games. The Director General of the IOC, François Carrard, wrote a letter to *SI* complaining that the magazine had targeted the Olympic Games rather than "those competitions in which antidrug measures are not taken" (*SI*, May 19, 1997). The IOC went on to sponsor a world conference on drugs in 1999. These exchanges nevertheless presented the question as being drug use by individuals rather than by team officials. The use of drugs may well have broader political motives.

The East German sport program serves as a major example. Since the German Democratic Republic (GDR) no longer exists, there have been myriad exposés of its use of drugs in producing champions. In its heyday, the GDR won considerable renown for the achievements of its athletes, especially its women, and enthusiasts such as Douglas Gilbert (1980) held the program up as an admirable model. Since the collapse of the GDR, scandals have abounded, and there has been discussion of revoking the medals of athletes who could be shown to have used drugs. Track and field officials have refused to consider withdrawing the medals won by GDR athletes, insisting the athletes passed the requisite drug tests. In 1998, when the Americans pressed for a reconsideration of swimming medals in the 1970s and 1980s, the IOC, over the protest of German Olympic officials, agreed to review the matter.

In turn, journalists and other commentators have to be cautious in making specific charges about currently functioning programs. In the fall of 1996, NBC apologized for its commentator's having raised such issues when talking about the Chinese swimming program. At the World Swimming Championship in Perth, Australia, in January 1998, the international swimming federation, FINA, stripped a German coach of his accreditation and then had to reaccredit him in the face of a court order. The American sprinter Butch Reynolds greatly embarrassed international track and field officials by winning court judgments in the United States against his being banned based on the results of a drug test. At Atlanta, the Court for Arbitration in Sport (CAS) overruled the IOC's suspension of several Russian athletes. The decision of the CAS at Nagano reinstating a champion snowboarder who had been disqualified after testing positive for marijuana cast another threatening shadow over the IOC's rules and practices.

Drug abuse may occur without the athlete's government approval, but governments can act forcefully when they want. Before the Seoul Games of 1988, Mikhail Gorbachev, then leader of the Soviet Union, warned Soviet sport officials that no Soviet athletes must fail drug testing. None did, and the Soviet team reaped a harvest of extra medals when athletes from other East European states failed their tests at the Games. As the rewards for Olympic triumph grow and drug use becomes more sophisticated, Olympic officials, who have to fear court cases and their costs, will undoubtedly face increasing problems in both defining and enforcing drug rules.

Commentators have both welcomed and bemoaned the improved economic conditions of the athletes. Authors commonly scorn the 19th-century English concept of "amateurism" as an expression of upper class snobbery and privilege, yet at the same time, a number of authors have defended the idea of amateurism as protection against "commercial infiltration" of sport (Lekarska 1973). The first amateur code, drawn up in 1866, defined an amateur as a "gentleman" who did not compete for money and who, moreover, did not compete with professionals. As established in "Bulletin no. 1" of the International Olympic Committee in 1894, an amateur was "any person who has never participated in a competition open to all comers, or competed for a cash prize or a sum of money from whatever source, in particular entry to the grounds—or with professionals—and who has never at any time in his life been a paid teacher or instructor of physical education." The sport societies taking part in the Games could repay the expenses of participants, but nothing else. Moreover, betting was to be discouraged by all possible means.

In practice, the concept of amateurism proved to be elusive. Before World War I, British authorities charged that American Olympic competitors were really professionals. In the 1930s, the British looked askance at German training methods and practices. In the 1950s and 1960s, Americans called Soviet athletes "shamateurs," not "true" amateurs. Amateurism, as observed in the Olympic Games, made sense only when defined as "eligibility," and the coming of professionals into the Games was almost inevitable. One might even argue the sooner the better, so as to end the hypocrisy of enforcing the ever-changing standard of amateurism.

The opening up of the Olympic Games to professionals has intensified the competition and to some extent changed sport geography. FIFA, the ruling body of international soccer, admitted professionals to Olympic competition after 1980 but imposed age limits so as to maintain the World Cup as its premier competition. In contrast, the entrance of professionals has radically changed Olympic basketball and Olympic ice hockey. For example, the number of European players now playing in the NHL produced a new level of international competition in Nagano's hockey competition. In basketball, however, the United States had won the gold only twice in the five Olympic Games from 1972 to 1988, but the domination of the NBA's "Dream Teams" in 1992 and 1996 has aroused some agonized discussion as to whether there can be too much professionalism. Yet, professional athletes seem to be in the Olympics to stay.

The media, especially television networks, which have provided the exposure that has produced much of the athletes' growing income, constitute another major controversial factor in the politics of the Olympic Games. Yet, television has played a major role in the development of the Games; Bert Sugar (1978), a television executive, boasted that if the Olympics had not existed, television would have invented them. Some call the Games a "media-constructed reality" (Moragas Spa, Rivenburgh, and Larson 1995). But when American television offered a challenge in the form of the Goodwill Games, TBS had to compensate advertisers after the Nielsen ratings proved to be well below promises and expectations. In contrast, the Olympic Games have their own mystique independent of television, but television and the Games have grown together in a symbiotic relationship.

Before the television age, the Olympic stage was relatively small. In the 1950s, some members of the IOC were considering the possibility of levying a worldwide tax on sporting events to pay for the Games. Beginning in the 1960s, however, television brought ever-growing wealth and attention; and Olympic officials have had to make concessions to the medium. According to press reports from Atlanta, IOC officials were demanding that the modern pentathlon, the one sport invented by the "Great Founder of the Games," Pierre de Coubertin himself, make its competition more exciting for television or face elimination from the Games. (Just before the Nagano Games the IOC decided to add women's competition in the pentathlon.) Olympic officials claim that 90 percent of the world's television sets tuned in for some part of the 1996 Olympic Games in Atlanta. Television rights, especially in the American market, are now a major factor in the Games' budgets.

Not surprisingly, television also made the Olympic stage more inviting for protest demonstrations; indeed, the cameras serve as weapons. A demonstration without a watching camera can evaporate, while a good picture can be more effective than a written protest. For example, the terrorists who seized Israeli athletes in Munich explicitly demanded access to world press and television; today, one probably remembers the images carried by television rather than the incoherent documents the terrorists passed out to the German authorities besieging them. Television reporters, in turn, might even participate in the story they are covering, as did the ABC reporter who helped American athletes formulate their protest against the presence of the Rhodesians in Munich in 1972.

Of course, television continues an old theme in the history of the Games—collecting money from spectators and sponsors to cover costs. Even in the 19th century, when sport competition began to attract more spectators, it quickly became dependent on them. Certainly, sporting events—even the most modest—involve costs. Originally these could be covered by the personal expenditure of the competitors, then perhaps by sponsors, and certainly by contributions from the spectators, systematized into "gate receipts." When print journalism began to cover sporting events, it was responding to popular interest, but in turn, by advertising the athletic competition, it helped build gate receipts. In the 1920s and 1930s, radio broadened the sport audience, and when the Germans provided local television coverage of the Berlin Olympics, the die was cast. The East Coast American television audience now plays a key role in television's considerations. And in 1996, even *The New York Times* considered it worth editorial space to complain about NBC's presentation of the Games.

Yet another player in today's "Big-Time Sports" are the equipment manufacturers. Regardless of how many times commentators insist "It is only a game," the sport industry is big business, and the competition is keen. The struggles between Puma and Adidas to shoe the feet of runners in Mexico City, the role of ski manufacturers in underwriting various national skiing federations, the competition by Nike, Adidas, and Reebok in the 1990s to have teams wear their brands of clothing and shoes—all testify to the growing dimensions of the sport business. This is nothing new, however: The official British report for the 1924 Paris Games carried a full-page advertisement for Bell's Running Shoes, "as worn by Eric Liddell." Nagano saw a new twist in this story: The network logo on the Nike-made jackets of CBS commentators could not display the Olympic rings because Nike was not an official sponsor of the Games. The activity and contributions of equipment manufacturers may be encompassed under the category of sponsors, but the "commercialization" of the Olympics, decried by myriad observers, is only a part of a greater picture of the growth of the sport business.

As the focus of these many financial, economic, political, and cultural considerations, the Olympic Games still produce a distinctive mystique that draws attention and commands respect. Some commentators want to concentrate on Olympic ideals, and they object to focusing on profane matters such as problems and politics. In 1957, Avery Brundage, who frequently complained about "lurid headlines," wrote, "In the materialistic world in which we live, the public and the press have overemphasized the competition and record breaking, overstressed national rivalries, and to a great extent ignored the moral, social and education values of amateur sport" (Brundage Archive). John Lucas has since spoken more forcefully: "There is that veritable army of nincompoops who, over the decades, have served up an undirected and inflammatory mishmash against the whole Olympic concept" (1980). In real life, the Olympic Games have developed as a dialectical clash between the ideals of their many supporters and the practices of their many participants.

A basic, fundamental definition of the modern Olympic Games identifies them as a quadrennial, multisport competition that travels the world. The competition at the Olympic Games represents the apex of elite sports, and as such, the Games have become the largest regularly scheduled international gathering of participants and spectators. The mass appeal of the elite competition in the Olympic Games gives the Games unique significance in world politics, culture, and even economic life; the purpose of this study is to trace the development of that significance.

Part I

The Formative Years

Baron Pierre de Coubertin led the modern Olympics through their first quarter-century.

The modern Olympic Games began as the brainchild of a French nobleman, the Baron Pierre de Coubertin. Other contemporaries entertained ideas of reviving the ancient celebrations of the Olympic Games, and entrepreneurs were already organizing international sport competitions, but the baron conceived of an international, multisport competition that would take place in a different region every four years. The seed of the idea lay in the sense of national shame he felt as a result of France's inglorious defeat in the Franco-Prussian War of 1871. He first conceived of physical education as a means of restoring the vigor of French youth and grandeur of France. Eventually, as his vision grew, he recognized the possibility of organizing international competition, so he then directed the establishment and early development of the modern Olympics.

From the start, Coubertin had no illusions about the political realities involved in his project as political intrigues, antagonisms, and conflicts abounded. He had to persuade officials in different sports to work together in a multisport festival. Then he had to bring athletes of different countries together; he had particular trouble persuading French and Germans to compete against each other. At the very first Games in Athens in 1896, he feared the Greeks were trying to take over his creation. When the Games became more firmly established, national rivalries arose, as between the English and the Americans, and governments raised questions about the flags that represented the nationalities involved in the competition. "The Games," Coubertin sighed in 1908, "have become an affair of state."

Indeed, the Games had become a focal point of state policies and national ambitions. Ultimately, participation in the Games became a public affirmation of international recognition, and the possibility that some governments might even object to Games' practices arose, as the Russians did to the flying of the Finnish flag at the London Games of 1908. In 1936, the Nazi regime in Germany, which was challenging the world order with both its domestic and foreign policies, used the Berlin Games as evidence the world appreciated the accomplishments of this new order. Buffeted by such political intrigues, the Olympic Games has seemed at times something like a disabled boat adrift in stormy international waters.

Over the years, buffeted as it was, the apparatus of the Games, their bureaucracy, grew slowly from uncertain, unstable beginnings to an elaborate system of established procedures. The tidy records of those Games, established later by historians, belie the confusion and uncertainty inherent in those early competitions. For example, some early winners learned only years later they were Olympic champions. The 1896 Games in Athens went smoothly enough, but the 1900 Games in Paris and the 1904 Games in St. Louis, Missouri fell far short of Coubertin's vision and dreams of an international festival. In both cases, the Games took place as part of major fairs and failed to produce a firm identity of their own. The 1908 Games in London finally provided a stable foundation, involving National Olympic Committees, certified entries, and clear rules for competition. The 1912 Games in Stockholm constituted an enormous success, although the troubles of the American athlete Jim Thorpe, who lost his gold medal for having played baseball for money, served as a harbinger of problems to come in determining athletes' eligibility.

Even in 1908 and 1912, however, some objected to the multisport character of the Games. The American sport czar James E. Sullivan, for example, argued that track and field constituted the most important sport and that most of those other types of competition should be excluded. Coubertin vigorously rejected this thought, insisting the Games should consist of many different types of competition. Not surprisingly, the baron took care that Sullivan did not become a member of the IOC.

The outbreak of war in 1914 brought the first phase of the Olympic Games to a sudden end. The conflict enveloped Europe for the next four years, and there could be no Games in 1916. When the Games resumed in 1920, Coubertin came forth with new rituals and symbols, most notably a special flag, displaying the five interlocking rings. He kept his Games separate from the new League of Nations organization, but at the same time, Games administrators shared the passions of the victorious Allied Powers. The victors had declared Germany "guilty" of having started "The Great War," as it was called then, and the IOC excluded the Germans from the 1920 Games in Antwerp and the 1924 Games in Paris.

Olympic historians sometimes speak of the period from 1920 to 1932 as the "Golden Age" of the Games. The "Olympic Movement," as many like to call it, expanded to Latin America and Asia; Germany reentered the Games in 1928; and although every Games saw some sort of national rivalry, even antagonism, there seemed to be no problems threatening the existence and enjoyment of this elite athletic competition. In 1924, the IOC also initiated Winter Games, but it kept this competition as something of a sideshow, maintaining the Summer Games as the main focus of Olympic activity. The Los Angeles Games of 1932, a success in the middle of a world wracked by the Great Depression, appeared to be the epitome of sport competition as an escape from the dismal realities of life and perhaps even an expression of hope for better times.

The Berlin Games of 1936 ended this idyllic image. Most commentators agree the Berlin Games constituted a milestone in Olympic history, but they do not necessarily agree as to why and how. Adolf Hitler's Nazi regime exploited the Games as a means of presenting its new order to the world in a favorable light, and members of the IOC found their platitudes about sport and politics put to a test. Individuals and groups abroad, shocked by the Nazis' openly anti-Jewish policies, called for withdrawing the Games from Berlin, but the IOC refused to reconsider its decision. American sport officials heatedly debated whether they should boycott the Games. In the end, the Games took place as scheduled and the Americans attended.

The Germans considered the Berlin Games a great success, as did IOC members. Opponents of the Nazi regime had failed to block the celebration, and most athletes spoke of having had a good time in Germany. (The Germans, many visitors declared, had thrown excellent parties.) Americans tend to claim that Jesse Owens's victories in the track and field competition exploded the German myths of racial superiority, but Jews, who represented the real target of German racial policies, had no corresponding successes to hail. The Germans themselves took considerable pride in the accomplishments of their athletes, who won more medals than did the athletes of any other country. IOC members, moreover, delighted in the ceremonial grandeur the Germans provided, and they were to keep many of the innovations the Germans had introduced in Berlin.

The first phase of this account of the Games' political history ends rather naturally with the closing of the Berlin Games, and the death of Coubertin in 1937 provides an additional sense of closure. After controlling the development of the Games over their first quarter-century, Coubertin had withdrawn from the IOC leadership in 1925, but he left behind an institutional apparatus that could succeed him and perpetuate the Games. By the time of his death, the Olympics had become a grand spectacle supported by ambitious hosts who often had motives other than the sheer joy of sport competition.

At the end of the decade, however, the Olympic structure would face the destruction of war a second time. Specifically, the German invasion of Poland in September 1939 started World War II, making peaceful international sport competition impossible for almost a decade.

Chapter 1

The Olympic Family

© Corbis-Bettmann

The ceremonies at the Athens Games drew heavily on the images of ancient Greece.

To examine politics, it is necessary first to establish the boundaries and crosscurrents of the political arena. In the words of Lord Killanin (1983), a former IOC President, "One of the greatest mysteries surrounding the Olympic Games is their operation: how it works, who does what, and why." The organization of the competition requires elaborate preparation and painstaking execution, and a complicated network of institutions provides the basic framework of the Games. The structure—replete with acronyms such as IOC, IF, NOC, IAAF, and FIFA—is itself a product of the Games' history, but it is useful to begin with a description of the present form of that structure to better understand how it evolved.

At the summit stands the International Olympic Committee (IOC), a group that at the beginning of 1998 consisted of 118 members and comprised a "private international organization" that in theory is responsible to no one but themselves. Lord Killanin called its members the "custodians of a trust" (1983) established by the Baron Pierre de Coubertin. Until relatively recently, the Committee was a male preserve, but admitted its first two female members in 1981; in 1986 it added its first American woman, Anita DeFrantz, a former Olympic rower. The IOC proudly advertises itself as a self-selecting, self-perpetuating body, and Killanin has called it the "most exclusive club in the world," in which membership is by invitation only.

The founder of the modern Games, Pierre de Coubertin, organized the first IOC in 1894, designating its members as "ambassadors" of the IOC to their respective countries or regions rather than as representatives of those regions in the IOC itself. He chose men of substantial means and influence whom he knew and trusted personally, and he claimed his choices represented "sports geography," rather than political geography. He wanted to keep the IOC free of governmental controls, but he had no illusions of keeping the committee free of politics. Indeed, he fully recognized the closed, oligarchical character of the result of this process, and he spoke freely about his distrust of democratic principles whereby the majority might out-vote him.

Sympathetic writers have acclaimed Coubertin's foresight, insisting that the IOC has avoided the political disputes that would accompany an open forum in which each country or each National Olympic Committee (NOC), regardless of size or strength, would have an equal vote. Critics have denounced it as a moribund institution devoid of any understanding for the modern world, existing only to serve the self-gratification of its members. Even members of the committee have occasionally expressed similar concerns. In his memoirs, Killanin wondered how liberals like himself and "above all, members of the Communist bloc countries" could tolerate "such a system" that openly defied "democratic principles" (1983).

The Committee's practices have undergone considerable modification since World War II. With the inclusion of the Soviet Union and the newly emerging countries of the Third World, the Committee came to tolerate a much more active role on the part of governments. It has also recognized that its members work basically in states, rather than regions. Although it still refuses to give a seat to every state, it makes an effort to represent the various parts of the world. It rejects thoughts that any country has the "right" to be represented or even the right to name its own representative; but it has often accepted official nominees. The Old Guard in the IOC long insisted that they were freely electing their colleagues, but in 1951, for example, when the Soviet Union demanded a seat and nominated its own candidate, the IOC simply yielded. In dealing with the United States, in contrast, it has shown considerably more independence in choosing its membership.

The Committee's fundamental task is to supervise the regular celebration of the Olympic Games, and toward that end, it speaks of promoting the "development of those physical and moral qualities which are the basis of sport" and of propagating the "Olympic ideal" so as to create "international goodwill." Centered in Lausanne, Switzerland, it now finances itself mainly through money from the sale of television rights and

The IOC Executive Board, 1998

President:	Juan Antonio Samaranch (1980) – Spain
Vice Presidents:	Kéba Mbaye (1994) – Senegal
	Pál Schmitt (1995) – Hungary
	Richard W. Pound (1996) – Canada
	Anita DeFrantz (1997) – United States of America
Members:	Richard Kevan Gosper, A.O. (1995) – Australia
	Thomas Bach (1996) – Germany
	Chiharu Igaya (1996) – Japan
	Un-Yong Kim (1997) – Republic of Korea
	Marc Hodler (1998) – Switzerland
	Jacques Rogge (1998) – Belgium

The President of the IOC is elected for an initial term of eight years and may be re-elected for successive four-year terms. The four Vice Presidents and the six other members serve a four-year mandate.

its own marketing programs. Its budget for 1997 totaled almost 37 million Swiss francs, about 25 million American dollars.

Since the IOC usually meets only once a year, an Executive Board, created by Coubertin in 1921, handles business and makes recommendations in the interim. Currently consisting of 11 members, the Board usually meets two or three times a year, and its decisions are subject to final confirmation by the entire Committee. The Board thereby brings together the most powerful members of the Committee into an inner circle, and from this group comes the leadership of the Committee and the Games.

The most important post in the IOC is that of President, elected by the Committee for an eight-year term with the possibility of reelection (see table 1.1). The President has always had considerable power in determining the general course that the IOC should follow. In the early years, Coubertin gave the position its prestige and power. The current President, Juan Antonio Samaranch of Spain, has served since 1980. In contrast to his predecessors, who directed the Committee's work more or less as a sideline to their careers, Samaranch, who is independently wealthy, moved to Lausanne in order to take a direct role in administering Olympic affairs. He now exerts more authority over a more powerful and financially strong network than any of his predecessors could have dreamed of.

According to the IOC's self-definition, its major task is the celebration of the great quadrennial "festival of sport." The intervening four years between Games is known officially as an *Olympiad.* Athens (1896) witnessed the Games of the Ist Olympiad; Moscow (1980), the Games of the XXIInd Olympiad; Los Angeles (1984), the Games of the XXIIIrd Olympiad; and Atlanta (1996), the Games of the XXVIth Olympiad. (The Winter Games follow a separate numbering system, simply numbering the

Table 1.1

Presidents of the IOC	
Demetrius Vikelas, Greece	1894-1896
Pierre de Coubertin, France	1896-1925
Henri Baillet-Latour, Belgium	1925-1942
J. Sigfrid Edstrøm, Sweden	1942-1946 (acting)
	1946-1952
Avery Brundage, USA	1952-1972
Lord Killanin, Ireland	1972-1980
Juan Antonio Samaranch, Spain	1980-(Current term will expire 2001)

Games sequentially—the Ist Winter Olympics, the XVIIIth Winter Olympics, and so on; and since 1994, they have taken place in the alternate even-numbered year to the Summer Games.) The IOC's *Charter*, its current code of principles and administrative statements, stipulates there must be no discrimination "against any country or person on grounds of race, religion or politics." The IOC has the power to amend the *Charter* at any time.

The IOC itself does not organize the competition in the various sports; instead, it works with two basic networks of sport organizations: the International Sports Federations (IFs) and the National Olympic Committees (NOCs). The IOC decides which sports are to be admitted to the Games, and it may set limits for the number of medals to be awarded in any sport. The IFs stage the competition, for which the NOCs provide the athletes. Although the interlacing networks may at times experience tension, they must interact harmoniously for the competition in all sports to be successful.

Coubertin had dreamed of the Olympic competition as constituting the world championship of every participating sport. Thus, the IOC long hoped that each federation would make the Olympic competition its world championship, at least for that particular year, and it preferred that at most a federation hold only one separate championship in the course of an Olympiad. In practice, however, few of the IFs have observed this ideal, and in the age of vast television revenues, the IFs have indeed become more independent and demanding.

The first major sports federation to challenge the IOC's mandates and then to break away from the Olympic structure was FIFA, the international soccer federation, and it made its move long before the age of television. There had been no soccer at the Ist Olympic Games in Athens, because Coubertin actually disapproved of admitting team sports to the Games. Soccer, however, which had been systematized by the English in the 1860s, was rapidly growing in popularity throughout the world, and it made its appearance in the 1900 Games in Paris, where the English easily won the gold medal. When FIFA came into existence in 1904, however, the English were not among the founding members.

As the game spread around the world, the amateur rules developed by English gentlemen in the 19th century posed intolerable conditions for participants who did not have independent sources of income. The English Brahmins argued that an amateur athlete should receive no financial gain from competition; this concept of "amateurism" faced challenges wherever soccer began to attract the interest of spectators as a popular sport for the working classes. By 1920, the English themselves had trouble fielding a strong amateur team because of the professionals' ravaging of the available pool of talent. As a result, England, the birthplace of modern soccer, did not even send a team to the 1928 Olympic Games in Amsterdam.

FIFA tried to resolve the problem of amateurism, that is, eligibility, by seeking "broken-time payments" for athletes, payments to athletes to make up for income lost from their regular jobs by taking time to participate in international competition. The IOC rejected FIFA's proposal and dropped the sport from the program of the Games scheduled for Los Angeles in 1932. (The IOC had already rejected an effort by tennis authorities to provide more money for athletes, and as a result, tennis left the Olympic fold after the Paris Games of 1924.) FIFA members responded by organizing their own championship tournament, the World Cup, staged for the first time in 1930 in Uruguay. The World Cup proved to be such a success that when soccer returned to the Olympic Games in 1936, the level of amateur play clearly suffered from the absence of both European and South American teams. Ever since that time the World Cup soccer tournament has meant more to FIFA members than the Olympic Games.

After World War II, the face of international soccer changed again. The Soviet Union and its allies sent state-supported teams that they called "amateur" to both the World Cup and the Olympics. FIFA eventually resolved the imbalance by broadening eligibility rules for the Olympic Games: In 1984, taking advantage of changes in IOC regulations on eligibility, FIFA officially ruled that "contract players," that is, professionals, who had not competed in a final World Cup tournament could play for their countries' teams in Los Angeles. At the same time, permitting an Olympic Team to have only two players over the age of 23, FIFA reconfirmed its decision to maintain the World Cup as a competition superior to the Olympics.

In contrast, basketball, another sport that now offers lucrative professional careers, has not in general been so controversial. Invented in the early 1890s in the United States and carried throughout the world by the YMCA, basketball spread far more slowly than soccer. Although the St. Louis Games of 1904, the Paris Games of 1924, and the Amsterdam Games of 1928 presented it as an exhibition sport, the Americans showed their own lack of interest in propagating the sport to the world when they ignored it as an exhibition sport at Los Angeles in 1932. Instead, the Los Angeles Games featured lacrosse and American football as exhibition sports.

FIBA, the International Amateur Basketball Federation, came into being in 1932—without the participation of the United States—and basketball became an official sport at the Berlin Games of 1936. After World War II, basketball became more popular throughout Europe, and by the 1980s, FIBA was winking at the income of European basketball players as it declared that only the American NBA created professionals. In 1986, FIBA took a giant step in a new direction when it dropped the word "Amateur" from its name—the "A" in its acronym now represented the second letter of the word "basketball." In 1989, it agreed to allow professionals into the World Championships and the Olympic Games, resulting in the United States' sending the "Dream Team," made up mostly of professional stars, to capture the gold medal in Barcelona in 1992 and Atlanta in 1996.

Historically, the most influential IF in the Games has been the IAAF, the international track and field federation. Coubertin's three successors—Baillet-Latour, Edstrøm, and Brundage—all had backgrounds in track and field, and for a country that wanted to take a place in the Olympic family, admission to membership in the IAAF long constituted a vital preliminary step. In the clash between FIFA and the IOC in the 1920s, the IAAF provided the strongest and probably the decisive opposition to the demands of the soccer federation for "broken-time payments." But after the liberalization of eligibility rules in 1973 and 1981, the IAAF took the lead in legitimizing payments to athletes, first in the form of contributions to a trust and subsequently in outright payments. IAAF officials still consider their sport the heart of the Games, and in recent years, IAAF president Primo Nebiolo has pressed the IOC to give a bigger share of television revenues to his federation.

In order to provide athletes for the quadrennial celebrations, the IOC and the IFs rely on the NOCs, the National Olympic Committees, in each country. The IOC proclaims its Games open to the youth of the world, but it admits only athletes certified by member NOCs. By IOC standards, there should be only one NOC per country, but again in recent years the Committee has blurred these distinctions, as, for example, in its admission of Palestinian athletes to the Atlanta Games in 1996. In turn, only the NOC can certify athletes, who must also meet the eligibility rules of the appropriate sports federations, for Olympic competition. In principle, an NOC should be independent of its government, although the IOC recognizes that an NOC may receive its funding from its government. In practice, many governments play prominent roles in the work of their NOCs.

The NOCs represent the basic building blocks in the structure of the Olympic Games. They recruit, supervise, and certify the athletes. Without certification from an NOC, no athlete can compete. When the question was raised in 1980 in the face of the American boycott of Moscow, the IOC would not allow individual athletes to enter the Games. The IOC's decision to allow individual Yugoslav athletes into the Barcelona Games of 1992 while enforcing the U.N.-ordered boycott of the Yugoslav NOC constituted an unusual deviation from this policy, but then, the IOC can change its own rules at will. Individual IOC members may on occasion speak of the Games' existing for the athletes, but in practice, the Games rest on the political entities that the IOC has recognized.

The NOCs are supposedly independent of the governments of their countries, but one of the most notable examples of governmental intervention occurred in the United States in the 1970s. The Americans had long invested most of their sport dollars in baseball and American football, neither of which was an Olympic sport, and their participation in international sport competition had been episodic. During Olympic years, they had mobilized their energies for the Games, but in the intervening four years public interest in international sport tended to lag. As a result, when challenged by the Soviet Union, which prepared seriously and systematically, the Americans seemed to be losing ground on this highly visible stage of international sport competition by the early 1970s. After a remarkable series of misfortunes at the Munich Games in 1972, the White House demanded changes that would improve the performances of American athletes.

Disturbed by the conflict between the Amateur Athletic Union (AAU), which had dominated American amateur sport for many years, and the NCAA, the athletic association of American colleges and universities, the United States government, by act of Congress, forced the dissolution of the AAU and the vesting of control of American participation in international sport in the United States Olympic Committee (USOC). The USOC itself would include representatives of the national governing bodies (NGBs) of the sports federations. In some sports, such as wrestling, the Old Guard resisted the changes, even seeking support from the IF, but the will of the United States government prevailed. The United States government then completed this show of power by forcing the USOC to keep American athletes away from Moscow in 1980.

The question then arises: How independent of its government can an NOC be? In the age of Olympic boycotts proclaimed by this or that government, could an NOC oppose its government's decision? Shows of independence on the part of NOCs are rare. In 1935, desperately trying to avoid a boycott of the Berlin Games by the ruling AAU, Avery Brundage had investigated the possibilities of athletes' attending the Games with certification by the United States Olympic Committee if not the AAU (Guttmann 1984); the American government stayed out of that controversy altogether. In 1980, the USOC accepted the United States government's demand to boycott the Games in Moscow. The British Olympic Committee, however, defied its government in 1980, and with the blessings of the IOC it dispatched its athletes to Moscow to compete (BOC 1981). The Soviet announcement of its boycott of Los Angeles in 1984, in contrast, came in the name of the Soviet NOC, although the Politburo of the Communist Party of the Soviet Union had really made the decision.

The interests of the NOCs also dominate the ritual of the Games. In the opening ceremonies, the athletes march in by country—not, say, by sport—behind their national flags. In the eyes of some, this parade emphasizes nationalist feelings, and individual IOC members have occasionally suggested abolishing this glorification of national units. When the British used the Olympic flag in Moscow rather than the Union Jack, Lord Killanin called their move a step forward for reducing "nationalism" in the Games, but the Soviets, who supported the rituals of the Games as expressions of "patriotism" and "internationalism," criticized it. Most NOCs, partly out of personal preference and partly as the result of fund-raising imperatives, would probably endorse the Soviet position of favoring the continued use of flags and the playing of national anthems to salute victors rather than the practice of the British in Moscow.

In the 1960s, both the IFs and the NOCs began to demand a greater voice in policy making as well as a greater share of the Games' income. Some NOCs demanded seats on the IOC or else a separate organization for the NOCs: This resulted in the formation of the Assembly of NOCs (originally GANOC, now ANOC). The IFs organized the General Assembly of International Sports Federations (GAIF). Both groups met with hostility from IOC leaders when they first began to function, but in the 1970s, they became an established part of the Olympic bureaucracy. The two groups, to be sure, were not of equal strength. Although each recognized NOC has the right to attend the Games, not all IFs have such assured tenure in the Olympic family: Sports are continually being added to the Games, and a few have been dropped. Nevertheless, under the leadership of the strong federations such as the IAAF, the GAIF has wielded considerable power.

After Lord Killanin became IOC President in 1972, he expanded the central Olympic structure by reviving the practice of holding Olympic Congresses, mass gatherings of IOC members together with representatives of the NOCs and the IFs. Such meetings had taken place fairly regularly in the time of Coubertin and Baillet-Latour, but after the IXth Congress in 1930, there had been none for more than 40 years. In 1973, Killanin convened the Xth Congress, under the title "The Olympic Movement and Its Future," at Varna, Bulgaria. Although some feared that the Congress might challenge the power of the IOC, Killanin preserved the primacy of the IOC in the Olympic structure. Since 1973, Congresses have met every seven or eight years, and the Centennial Congress met in Paris in 1994.

With the support of the Congresses, Killanin's IOC carried out a major reform in the question of eligibility for competition in the Games. The Xth Congress recommended eliminating the term "amateur" and legalizing the payment of athletes for "broken time," that is, the income they would lose because of the time required for international athletic competition. The XIth Congress, held in 1981, recommended that the IFs, in consultation with the IOC, determine their own rules of eligibility. As a result, athletes in some sports, such as track and field or skiing, could then amass considerable amounts of money while still remaining eligible for international competition. Some federations, such as the wrestlers whose federation was dominated by East Europeans, maintained stricter rules of eligibility, but eventually, under Samaranch's determined leadership, the IOC basically accepted the principle of "open" competition, that is, Games open to all comers, professional or not.

Another vital, albeit ephemeral, institution in the Olympic structure is the Olympic Organizing Committee for the particular Games (OCOG). Coubertin established the principle that the Olympic Games should take place at a new site every four years. The IOC awards the Games, now seven years in advance, to a city, although it is of course understood that the national government and other local governments must be involved. The various contestants for hosting the Games make presentations, some more lavish, some more vague, many both. Cities usually have to reckon with losing once or twice before being chosen; for example, Montreal, Moscow, and Los Angeles were all unsuccessful candidates before being chosen respectively for the 1976, 1980, and 1984 Games. Atlanta, the site of the 1996 Games, was the first city to win the Games on its first application.

When the IOC awards the Games, the new OCOG has to prepare the locale for both the competition and the visitors. This means working with the IOC, the NOCs, the IFs, and local authorities and other important people. Each OCOG exists for perhaps only eight years: six or seven years of preparation and a year or two after the Games to clean up the books and make its final reports to the IOC and other appropriate institutions. Yet the OCOG sets the character of a given Olympics, and the history of the Games themselves is to a great extent the sum of the work of these ephemeral groups. As of 1998, four OCOGs were functioning, wrapping up work on the Nagano Games and preparing for the Summer Games of 2000 in Sydney, the Winter Games of 2002 in Salt Lake City, and the Summer Games of 2004 in Athens.

In the background of the competition to host the Games stands the occasional campaign of the Greek government, launched seriously in the midst of the debates in 1980 over the American boycott of the Moscow Games, to be designated as the permanent home of the Games. The IOC thus far has declined this suggestion, preferring to maintain the Games' itinerant character. Athens was a major candidate, perhaps even a sentimental favorite, to host the 1996 Games, but Atlanta's startling success left the Greek authorities resentful. At present there seems to be no serious movement toward establishing a permanent home for the Games; indeed, critics question whether it would be in Greece's interest to host the Games on a permanent basis (Senn 1988). The awarding of the Games of 2004 to Athens, however, will undoubtedly revive the discussion of a permanent home for the Games, although the IOC will probably show little interest in any such proposals.

Discussion of Olympic institutions would be incomplete without considering the way in which the role of television, especially the American television networks, has grown. When television first entered the Games in the 1960s, it played only a minor role, but the money it brought quickly gave it more importance (table 1.2). In the beginning, OCOGs could sell the rights; then the IOC stepped in to assert its authority and, of course, control over the money. In 1997, the IOC signed an agreement with NBC, selling exclusive United States television rights to the Games of 2004, 2006, and 2008 for $2.3 billion. The IOC now has the television money assured before it has to choose the hosts of those Games, but, in turn, NBC occupies a place in the Olympic hierarchy rather ahead of the as yet not established OCOGs for those Games. The consequences of this arrangement have yet to be seen.

In the 1960s, the formative years of the relationship between television and the Games, the American Broadcasting Company (ABC) proclaimed itself the "Network of the Olympics," owing greatly to the work of its sports director, Roone Arledge. Arledge honed the coverage of a wide variety of sports and through clever negotiating obtained the television contracts for a total of 10 Winter and Summer Olympic Games. One might find many of his techniques—slow motion, focusing on the crowd, special angles—in Leni Riefenstahl's film of the 1936 Games, *Olympia*, but Arledge brought them into American sports telecasting. And sports telecasting had tremendous success. As a *Sports Illustrated* commentator, Steve Rushin (1994), put it succinctly, "Sometime in the second half of this century, sports became an axis on which the world turns." The distinctive relationship between television and the Olympics was no small part of this development.

The American television networks, the big spenders in Olympic budgets, cover the Games as entertainment for the American market. Thus, broadcasters would prefer sports popular in the United States to be played in hours appropriate for reaching the prime-time audience on the East Coast of the United States. The organizers of the 1988 Games in Seoul discovered this when the bids for the television rights to the Games were considerably below what they had hoped for. Television contributed greatly to the popularity of women's gymnastics, but when NBC offered a taped replay of women's gymnastics competition in the Atlanta Games, critics complained that the network was deceiving the public for the sake of melodrama. In broadcasting the Nagano Games of 1998, CBS also offered taped programming in what could have been live-time broadcasting, and critics again declared that the television networks were offering entertainment and not news. What one observer calls the theater and

Table 1.2

American Television Payments for Olympic Broadcast Rights

Year	Winter Games	Payment ($US)	Summer Games	Payment ($US)
1960	Squaw Valley, CA (CBS)	50,000	Rome, Italy (CBS)	394,000
1964	Innsbruck, Austria (ABC)	597,000	Tokyo, Japan (NBC)	1,500,000
1968	Grenoble, France (ABC)	2,500,000	Mexico City, Mexico (ABC)	4,500,000
1972	Sapporo, Japan (NBC)	6,400,000	Munich, FRG (ABC)	7,500,000
1976	Innsbruck, Austria (ABC)	10,000,000	Montreal, Canada (ABC)	25,000,000
1980	Lake Placid, NY (ABC)	15,500,000	Moscow, USSR (NBC)	87,000,000
1984	Sarajevo, Yugoslavia (ABC)	91,500,000	Los Angeles, CA (ABC)	223,000,000
1988	Calgary, Alberta, Canada (ABC)	309,000,000	Seoul, Republic of Korea (NBC)	300,000,000
1992	Albertville, France (CBS)	243,000,000	Barcelona, Spain (NBC)	401,000,000
1994	Lillehammer, Norway (CBS)	300,000,000		
1996			Atlanta, GA (NBC)	456,000,000
1998	Nagano, Japan (CBS)	375,000,000		
2000			Sydney, Australia (NBC)	705,000,000
2002	Salt Lake City, Utah (NBC)	545,000,000		
2004			Athens, Greece (NBC)	793,000,000
2006	TBA (NBC)	613,000,000		
2008			TBA (NBC)	894,000,000

drama of the Olympic Games, another may denounce as show business, but the cooperation between television and the Games is an overpowering fact of Olympic life.

Olympic organizers are only beginning to comprehend the enormous power of the television cameras, which can project images that are very different from what the spectators at the Games see. In remembering the Los Angeles Games of 1984, most Americans probably have stronger images in their minds of the pictures of the American flags carried by ABC than they do of the muted pastel colors with which the LAOOC decorated the venues. Television can create heroes and promote careers, as it did in 1972 for the Soviet gymnast Olga Korbut or, for that matter, for Jim McKay, the ABC anchorman who covered the terrorist seizure of Israeli athletes as hostages.

The IOC declares that its policy is to ensure the broadest possible television coverage for the Games. Samaranch has declared his determination to keep the Games away from "pay television." Still, the relationship between television and the Olympic Games has probably more than one crisis to go through yet.

The experiences of Atlanta 1996, as a matter of fact, will probably intensify television's role in the Games. A generation or two earlier, the IOC, as the "owner" of the Games, had struggled to maximize gate receipts. In 1960, before television's impact became clear, the Rome Organizing Committee moved track and field events from their regular schedule early in the Games to a later block of time so as to ensure greater attendance at the Games in general. In Atlanta, disturbed by the problems of handling so many visitors, some IOC officials were welcoming the thought that Sydney, the host of the Games in the year 2000, would sell fewer tickets, have fewer visitors, and rely more on television coverage.

In 1985, having decided that its dependence on American television receipts was too constricting and, of course, seeking more money for itself, the IOC decided to seek out its own sponsors. The success of the Los Angeles organizers in tapping sponsor money also undoubtedly contributed to this decision. In June 1985, at its meeting in East Berlin, the IOC signed an exclusive merchandising contract with International Sports, Culture, and Leisure Marketing (ISL) of Luzern. Dubbed TOP for The Olympic Programme, the IOC's plan offered worldwide sponsorships to multinational corporations: TOP I (1985-1988) attracted 9 sponsors, who contributed $95 million; TOP II (1989-1992), 12 for $175 million; and TOP III (1993-1996), 10 for more than $300 million. TOP IV (1997-2000) already had 11 sponsors as of this writing.

In the IOC's listing of TOP III sponsors, the companies explained their relationships to the Games in a variety of ways. Five specialized in documentation of the Games, as establishing a history is a vital part of the

Games mystique. Kodak dated its "involvement with the Olympic Movement" back to 1896. *Time/Sports Illustrated*, an Official Sponsor since 1980, was the "exclusive worldwide publishing sponsor." Xerox, "at the very heart of the action" for the "past 30 years" declared, "During the Centennial Olympic quadrennial, Xerox will deliver its 1 billionth document in support of the Olympic Movement." Matsushita, makers of Panasonic equipment and a sponsor since 1987, promised the "latest state-of-the-art broadcast equipment to the host broadcaster." IBM, a TOP sponsor since 1993, had provided "information technology solutions" since 1960.

The other sponsors included financial and technical support as well as consumer products. Coca-Cola dated its support of the Games back to 1928. VISA called itself the "sole provider of financial payment systems at the Olympic Games since 1988." Bausch & Lomb, a sponsor since 1989, was carrying out a "long-range study of the critical relationship between vision and sports performance." United Parcel Service, "providing state-of-the-art package delivery services to the Olympic family," joined the program in 1994. John Hancock, "prior to becoming a TOP Sponsor . . . was a supplier to the International Olympic Committee." The IOC's supplier program included Mercedes, Lufthansa, and Ricoh (the Olympic fax network).

All in all, the Games and the IOC itself have undergone significant changes since their founding, but the structure has proved to be flexible, and the IOC itself durable. Of course, a strength may on occasion be a weakness, and vice versa. Yet the IOC's institutional relationships have grown, broadened, and deepened, resulting in a complicated intertwining network of organizations administering the various aspects of elite sport competition. As the Games have grown and expanded, the IOC has beaten back some challenges and preempted others. For example, the workers' sports festivals of the 1930s, GANEFO in the 1960s, and the Goodwill Games in 1986 were all efforts by others to organize competing international competition. In the 1970s, UNESCO, the United Nations Education and Social Commission, revealed designs on the Olympic Games. Under the leadership of Brundage, Killanin, and now Samaranch, however, the IOC has beaten off these challenges. At present, there seem to be no serious "hostile" takeover bids on the horizon, and the IOC will rule the Games for the foreseeable future.

Chapter **2**

Coubertin's Creation

© Archive Photos

Images of the London Games.

The Olympic Games grew from a sense of patriotic duty on the part of a French nobleman, Baron Pierre de Coubertin. Born on January 1, 1863, he grew up in the shadow of France's military defeat at the hands of the Germans in 1870-1871, and like other patriotic young Frenchmen he felt the need of doing something to expunge that blot on his country's honor. Forsaking a career in law, diplomacy, or the military, he decided to devote his efforts to improving French education, particularly physical education. Here, he thought, he could best help bring new life and strength to his country, primarily to French youth, the hope of today and the leaders of tomorrow.

On visits to Rugby School in England, he became fascinated by the role of sport in British education, and he concluded that "muscular Christianity," "athleticism," constituted a fundamental part of British imperial greatness. Sports, or "games," infused the "moral discipline" that built "character," producing the future leaders of the empire. Sports, moreover, constituted a major British cultural export in the 19th century and bonded people to the British empire: Peoples of the British empire learned cricket, and football (soccer) eventually became the most popular sport in the world. Coubertin concluded that competitive sport could serve as a vehicle for a "great pedagogical reform" in France (MacAloon 1981). Thus, improving physical education would strengthen all aspects of physical, moral, and intellectual growth.

From the start he found his path plagued by problems. For example, when he advocated including competitive sports in the French school system, he ran into opposition from the physical educators who advocated individual fitness rather than elitist competition and also from Frenchmen who disapproved of his enthusiasm for things English. He discovered that specialists in one sport tended to oppose communicating and cooperating with specialists in another. Nevertheless, Coubertin succeeded in establishing a French "Union of Athletic Sports" in 1888, bringing together sport specialists to develop a multisport program within France.

By the early 1890s, his vision had expanded: looking at Europe, North America, and the world, he dreamed of directing international sport competition. Concurrently, the states of Europe were deepening cultural contacts as they experienced ever greater economic independence. The industrialization of Western Europe was now providing leisure time for an urban population, and sport activities were growing rapidly to fill that space. Then, too, Europeans were fascinated by stories of the life of Classical Greece, stimulated by the excavations of ancient Greek sites. In seizing on the image of the ancient Greek Olympics, Coubertin invented neither the idea of recreating the ancient Games nor the thought of staging international sports competition. His accomplishment, then, was the establishment of an international, quadrennial, multisport competition that for reasons of expediency he robed in the garb of Classical Greece. Even more significantly, he created the organization that could continue the Games after he had left the scene.

At first he found it difficult to sell his dream to others, despite that fact that reenactment of the glories of ancient Greece was a vogue of the time, and excavations of the ruins at Troy had excited many imaginations. Coubertin's vision, however, involved modern competitive athletics, not a sterile imitation of the styles and forms of the ancients. When he first issued his call for organizing new Olympic Games, he found it difficult to explain the new wine he wanted to put in this old bottle. As he wrote in his memoirs, "Naturally I had foreseen every eventuality except what actually happened"—namely, incomprehension (1979). In short, no one seemed to understand what he was talking about.

In 1894, he used the occasion of an international congress on problems of amateurism in athletics to present his idea for organizing international competition in modern sports under the name of the "Olympic Games." The group responded with such enthusiasm that it renamed itself an Olympic Congress and voted to hold the first Games in Greece in 1896. Coubertin had favored starting the Games in Paris in the year 1900, but, seizing the moment, he went along with the group's decision.

The Congress established an International Olympic Committee (IOC), the 14 members of which Coubertin nominated. As he later reminisced, "Nobody seemed to have noticed that I had chosen almost exclusively absentee members. . . . I needed elbow room at the start, for many conflicts were bound to rise" (1979). Coubertin indeed controlled fundamental decision making throughout these crucial early years of the Games. In his view, the IOC was a "self-recruiting body," working within "three concentric circles . . . a small nucleus of dedicated active members; a nursery of willing members capable of being educated along the right lines; and finally, a facade of people of varying degrees of usefulness, whose presence would serve to satisfy national pretensions while lending prestige to the whole" (1979). Leadership would radiate out from the center. "As the best means of safeguarding liberty and serving democracy, it is not always best to abandon ourselves to the popular will," Coubertin explained, "Rather we must maintain, in the midst of the vast electoral ocean, strong islands that will ensure independence and stability."

The individuals with whom Coubertin chose to work were persons of substance, means, and influence in their respective countries, whom he could count on to share his enthusiasm for sport: General Aleksandr Butovsky of Russia, Count Lucchesi Palli of Italy, Count Max de Bousies of Belgium, and Lord Ampthill of England. He also recruited academics such as Professor William Sloane of Princeton University. Each member of the IOC had to consider himself the representative of the IOC to his own country and not as his country's representative in the IOC. To maintain this relationship, Coubertin insisted the IOC must exercise its own free choice in coopting members.

The members of the IOC, of course, had the task of publicizing the Games in their respective homelands, but staging the competition required the cooperation of other sport authorities, because Coubertin preferred not to draw up and administer rules for each sport. International competition in sport was already no novelty: An international swimming championship had taken place in Australia in 1858, and the Wimbledon tennis tournament had become international in 1877. IFs already existed for gymnastics, rowing, and speed skating. Soccer adopted international rules in 1895, although an IF, FIFA, came into being only in 1904. Besides bringing the athletes of different nations together, Coubertin had to bring officials from different sports together under one sponsorship on a basis of equality.

In preparing for these first Games, Coubertin experienced a stern baptism of fire in the delicate nuances of sport's actual and potential roles in international relations. Not yet having any established apparatus for staging the Games, he had to rely on local organizers to do the job. The founding Olympic Congress had expressed no doubts in choosing Athens as the host for the first modern Olympic Games, but when Coubertin perceived trouble with the Greek government, he toyed with the idea of possibly moving the Games to Budapest. But with the strong support of the Greek Crown Prince Constantine, the pro-Olympic forces in Athens did their work, and the Games could go ahead as first conceived.

But Coubertin also had to find the athletes as well as sponsors to send them to the competition. Although he could count on strong support for his idea from the Americans and the Hungarians, the British objected to using the metric system for measuring running distances. As mentioned, he even had trouble in winning support for his Olympic dream from his fellow Frenchmen. His biggest problem came in persuading the Germans to come, however: Without them, these Olympics would have only a pale international character, but many Germans distrusted him and his ideas because he was, after all, French.

It was France's defeat in the war with Prussia in 1870-1871 that had spurred the young Coubertin to consider how he could contribute to the reestablishment of French grandeur, and he himself had stronger anti-German feelings than he cared to admit. He denied any significance to the fact that no German sat in the original membership of the International Olympic Committee; when a French newspaper quoted the baron as having called the absence of the Germans from the founding Congress a small loss, he expressed surprise that Germans should have misunderstood his meaning. He repeatedly told his German colleagues that they were too sensitive to perceived insults—even when one German complained, in Paris in 1900, of having found feces in his bed.

Fortunately for Coubertin's dream, he had an important German ally in Willibald Gebhardt, a chemist by training. Coubertin made Gebhardt's self-assumed task of winning German support for the Olympic Games extremely difficult, but Gebhardt nevertheless won over German gymnasts, who in principle opposed the idea of competition, as contrasted to individual training. Thus, through his determined efforts, a German team showed up in Athens, thereby making a significant contribution to the international character of the gathering. Even so, the Germans did not feel welcome, and they returned home resentful about their treatment.

The Games in Athens, held in April 1896, were a great success anyway. Of the 311 participants, representing 13 countries and for the most part paying their own expenses, 230 were Greeks. The Greeks had found a "sponsor," a wealthy businessman, Georgios Averoff, who contributed a considerable sum to rebuild the Panathenean stadium; and as part of the Opening Ceremonies, the organizers unveiled a statue honoring Averoff. Organizers received additional income from the sale of medals, coins, and admission tickets. Not the least of the trappings was an eight-page daily Olympic supplement to the local French-language newspaper *Le Messager d'Athènes.*

When a Greek runner, Spiridon Louis, won the marathon on the last day, Greek nationalism exploded with pride (12 of the event's 16 entrants were Greeks). As the spectators celebrated, the Crown Prince and his brother first ran beside the victor and then carried him on their shoulders. "It was," Coubertin later recalled, "as if the spirit of Ancient Greece had entered with him into the arena" (1979). No one seemed much concerned about the fact that the marathon had no place in the ancient Games: A Greek had bested the rest of the world in a competition that invoked Greek national pride, and this event by itself established a link with the idealized glories of Classical Greece. This meant not only that the Greek flag waved over his awards ceremony but also that the Greeks, like many subsequent Olympic hosts, felt that the Games now belonged to them.

The Greek royal family, actually imposed on the Greeks by the Great Powers of Europe, claimed that modern Greece was the heir and successor of Classical Greece. "Mother and wet nurse of Olympic Games in antiquity," the king declaimed at the final banquet, "Greece, having undertaken to celebrate them again today under the eyes of Europe and the New World, can, now that success has surpassed every expectation, hope that the foreigners who have honored her with their presence will appoint our country the peaceful meeting-place of the nations and their permanent and stable home of the Olympic Games." Coubertin chose to ignore the king's invitation and reemphasized his determination to hold

The Marathon in the Early Games

A French scholar, Michel Bréa, had suggested running a race honoring the legendary Greek victory over the Persians in 490 B.C., and Coubertin had endorsed the idea. Spiridon Louis's dramatic victory established this as a Greek crown jewel in the Games. The modern distance of 26 miles and 385 yards was set in the London Olympics of 1908—this constituted the distance from Windsor Castle to the Olympic Stadium in Shepherd's Bush.

The staging of an event over such a long distance could lead to eccentric controversy. In 1900, Americans accused the winner, Michel Theato, a Frenchman, of having taken shortcuts. In St. Louis in 1904, Fred Lorz, an American, entered the stadium as the seeming victor, but, after he had been photographed with President Theodore Roosevelt's daughter, it was learned that he had ridden in a car for about half the course. The real winner, Thomas Hicks, completed the course only after taking several doses of strychnine and some brandy. In 1908, an Italian, Dorando Pietri, entered the stadium and collapsed; British officials helped him over the finish line. An American, Johnny Hayes, came in second and protested the help that Pietri had received. Officials then declared Hayes the winner; Pietri vehemently denied rumors that he had taken strychnine.

A number of athletes apparently tried using strychnine as a performance-enhancing drug. It is, of course, a stimulant, and too much can kill. But it was in fact ineffective. Since it strongly affected certain facial muscles, it gave the athlete the image of straining himself, but in fact it did little for performance.

the Games of the IInd Olympiad in Paris four years hence, in 1900 (Coubertin 1979).

Confusion surrounds the exact nature of Coubertin's dispute with the Greeks. Coubertin (1979) complained that the Greeks accused him of stealing their heritage and that they refused to give him credit for having organized the first modern Olympic Games. Did the Greeks demand that Athens be the permanent home of the Games or did they only propose "intercalary" competition between the formal Olympics (Young 1996)? Have Coubertin's memoirs actually misled generations of historians in considering the Games' origins? Whatever the answers to these questions, Coubertin's insistence that the Games be a quadrennial movable feast, passing from country to country, gave the modern Olympic Games a distinctive stamp.

In preparing for the 1900 Games in Paris, Coubertin learned more cautionary lessons that forced him to revise the fundamental hierarchy of the Games. He had originally conceived of the presidency of the IOC as rotating every four years, passing to a representative of the next host of the Games. This person would accordingly direct the preparations for the Games. A Greek, Demetrius Vikelas, therefore served as President of the IOC until the Athens Games. Coubertin had taken for himself the post of Secretary-General, in his words a "position of greater interest than most presidencies" (Coubertin 1979). Coubertin then assumed the presidency in preparation for the Paris Games. When trouble arose in organizing the Games in France, Coubertin dissolved the preparatory commission and then had to deal with rumors that the IOC itself had been disbanded. Deploring the lack of understanding of the Olympic "spirit" among the public and the French civil service, Coubertin drew two important conclusions from the experience: He kept the title of President in his own hands for the next quarter of a century, and he also decided that the IOC must divorce itself from the actual organization of a specific set of Games.

The Paris Games of 1900 disappointed Coubertin. He did not receive the support he had expected from the state and local authorities, and the athletic competition stretched over six months in association with a world's fair. Coubertin quoted a friend as saying, "Our idea had been used, but it had been torn to shreds in the process" (Coubertin 1979). In the confusion, no one could be sure what were "official Olympic events," and some athletes were even unaware that they were competing in "Olympic Games." A French runner, Michel Theato, won the marathon, but he learned only 12 years later that he was an Olympic champion when Olympic historians tried to systematize the records of the Games. In Coubertin's words, the Games had served as a "humiliated vassal" to the World's Fair. A lesson to be drawn was "never to allow the Games to become dependent on or be taken over by a big fair where their philosophical value vanishes into thin air and their educational merit becomes nil" (Coubertin 1979). Only in 1912, however, could he put this lesson fully into practice.

If Paris was a disappointment, European historians of the Games have considered the 1904 Games in St. Louis truly a fiasco. According to Coubertin, participants in the founding Congress of 1894 had already thought of holding the IIIrd Games in the United States, and the IOC enthusiastically chose Chicago as the site. Problems arose when St. Louis demanded the Games as part of its centenary celebration of the Louisiana Purchase (which had occurred in 1803). With Coubertin's approval, United States President Theodore Roosevelt resolved the dispute by approving transfer of the Games to St. Louis. The actual idea of traveling to the United States, however, did not appeal to the authorities of

European sport: Coubertin himself chose not to go to St. Louis and instead called an IOC meeting in London.

Although apparently well-organized, the St. Louis Games represented a step back from the Paris competition. Europeans were conspicuous for their scarcity. Only 617 athletes participated, and of these, 525 were Americans and 41, Canadians. The American athletes easily dominated the competition. The so-called "anthropology days," featuring competition between representatives of various nonwestern peoples, left the historical accounts of these Games with indelible, negative impressions of American culture (Pope 1997). "The St. Louis Games were completely lacking in attraction," declared Coubertin (1979). "I had a sort of presentiment that the Olympiad would match the mediocrity of the town."

After the problems in Paris and St. Louis, Greece's readiness to host a celebration of the Games' 10th anniversary was welcome, but Coubertin still feared the ambitions of the Greek royal house. The Olympic Games themselves were by no means firmly established. Coubertin had argued with the Greeks in 1896; at the Paris Games he had felt ignored; then the American sport leader James Sullivan angered Coubertin by suggesting the separation of the "Olympic Games proper," meaning "footrace, jumping and throwing events," from the "other sports." Some Olympic historians even speak of Coubertin's "antagonists" within the IOC (Lucas 1980).

Coubertin chose not to attend the Games of 1906 in Athens. In his memoirs, he bitterly criticized the IOC members who attended them and who "voted a sort of resolution advocating an early reorganization of the IOC and had even offered the honorary presidency to the Crown Prince. . . . An absurd gesture on their part for, by Hellenising the committee in this way, they were depriving it of all international independence" (1979). The IOC President, Coubertin tersely reported, "naturally rejected it all." Coubertin was determined to keep the Olympic Games under his own direction as a moveable feast. He subsequently excluded the Athens Games from his official Olympic count, leaving them to be known as the "Interim Games."

Coubertin exploited the image of the ancient Greek Olympics, but he gave his creation a character different from the ancient Games. The name "Olympic" carried with it the idea of a quadrennial competition—this is perhaps the most basic of Coubertin's arrangements—and it carried a desirable aura of idealized athletic competition, infrequent enough to be special but not so infrequent as to be forgotten. Coubertin filled in this concept with modern substance—modern sports with the competition open to athletes from all countries, not only Greeks (table 2.1).

Primary among the modern practices that had no place in the ancient Games was the concept of "amateurism." The athletes in classical times

Table 2.1

The Growth of the Early Olympic Games

		Number of Sports	Number of Nations	Male Competitiors	Female Competitors
1896	Athens	9	13	311	0
1900	Paris	17	22	1,319	11
1904	St. Louis	14	12	681	6
1906	Athens	11	20	877	7
1908	London	21	23	1,999	36
1912	Stockholm	13	28	2,490	57

were professionals and expected considerable personal profit from Olympic victories. In the modern Games, the concept of amateurism arose from the situation of the 19th century English gentleman athlete, who thought of sport as the pastime of the upper class. Even at this early point in the development of the Games, however, the rules could not be universally applied. Coubertin and the IOC had to allow equestrian competition, shooting, and yachting to have special regulations of their own; rules for eligibility in these sports even demanded professional standing—a military man in equestrianship had to be an officer; a common soldier was ineligible. In an effort to maintain a semblance of uniformity in these rules, the IOC decreed that no competitor could be a professional in one sport and an amateur in another.

Coubertin himself did not have strong feelings about amateurism. Although some authors place amateurism high in his vision of the Games, in his memoirs he called the concept an "admirable mummy" (1979). Personally, he asserted, "I wasn't particularly concerned. Today I can admit it; the question never really bothered me. . . . Realizing the importance attached to it in sports circles, I always showed the necessary enthusiasm, but it was an enthusiasm without real conviction." Like many other contemporaries, he considered this ideal preferable to what appeared to be the brutality and corruption of professional sports. In his later years, Coubertin went so far as to call the Games' rules of amateurism "wicked." Games administrators nevertheless continued to wear the genteel but shabby cloak of amateurism until the 1970s.

Team sports constituted another element in the modern Games that was unknown in the ancient Games—unless one wanted to consider Roman chariot-racing. Coubertin idealized the competition between individuals, and he frequently declared that he was opposed to team sports—this despite his avowed admiration for the English style in sports—but with the playing of soccer in Paris, team sports entered the modern Games to stay. Would-be reformers argue that team sports encourage stronger nationalistic feelings than individual sports do, but the prevailing tendency of the IOC has been to expand team sports.

Yet a third question in the modern Games that had no place in the ancient festivals concerned the participation of women. Women could not even attend the ancient Games, and Coubertin, wanting to establish the Olympic Games as an elite competition of the very best with only one class of champions, opposed separate competition for women or, for that matter, for children. He only grudgingly gave women a place in his Games, although certainly not in the IOC itself. In Athens there were no women competitors, and there were only 11 in Paris in 1900. Coubertin acknowledged that sport activities could have a salutary effect on women, but to the end he insisted that it would be best if the women did not perform in front of spectators. Coubertin, moreover, was not alone in his resistance to admitting women into the Games; the IOC did not admit women into its ranks until almost half a century after his death.

An aspect of the ancient Games that deviously left its own mark on the modern Games was the worship of Zeus. The ancient Games had evolved from religious rituals, and Coubertin viewed sport as a form of religion: In his mind, sport should serve as a means of seeking perfection. He worked at developing an elaborate ritual in which, in fact, using national symbols replaced Zeus with the loyalty to one's country: "If the image of God were replaced for each athlete by the flag of his country, the grandeur of the ceremony could surely not fail to be enhanced and the appropriateness of this modernization is so obvious that there is no need to insist upon it" (Coubertin 1979). He came to see the Olympics, his own creation, as the foundation of a new world order.

These various parts of the Olympic structure came together in a dramatic way in the Games of the IVth Olympiad, held in London in 1908, in which some 2,000 athletes competed. These Games had first been awarded to Rome, but in 1906, after the eruption of Mt. Vesuvius, the Italians announced they could not handle them. The British agreed to bring the Games to London, and the IOC gratefully accepted. A British Organizing Committee took control of the Games, and British sports federations undertook the publication of rules and the selection of officials for the various sports. For the first time, moreover, the hosts limited the number of entries that could come from any one country. Among other things, the British established the standard distance of the marathon—the distance from Windsor Castle to the Olympic Stadium in Shepherd's Bush. The British also took pride in being supported "by private enterprise, and without help of any sort from the government" (Cook 1908). Even though the Games were again a part of a fair, and even though attendance at first lagged, Coubertin was delighted with the results. Ultimately, the arrangements set the tone and form for future Games.

At the same time as the British formalized the sport structure of the Games, they also had to make fundamental decisions as to the political structure. In the words of Lord Desborough of Taplow, the head of the Organizing Committee, "The definition of the word 'country' also presented questions of no small difficulty" (Cook 1908). This related specifically to British colonies, Finland, which was a part of the Russian empire, and Bohemia, a part of the Hapsburg empire. The Organizing Committee finally decided that a "'country' is 'any territory having separate representation on the International Olympic Committee.'" Participants accepted the separate participation of regions such as Canada and South Africa, but both the Russian and the Austro-Hungarian governments objected to the Committee's readiness to recognize Finland and Bohemia.

The rivalry that flared between the British and the Americans in London proved to be a harbinger of future international conflicts at the Games. The British, who had provided a model for international sport in the 19th century, tended to view the Americans as uncouth and demanding, and they charged that the upstarts from the New World were overemphasizing athletic prowess, spending far too much money on training athletes, and even using athletic accomplishments for political purposes. The Americans, in turn, wanted to challenge the British, their former imperial rulers, and conquer them on the athletic field.

Naturally, then, the two sides clashed on many issues. British organizers objected to the demands of the American Amateur Athletic Union (AAU) that the deadline for entries be made as late as possible, so that the Americans could hold tryouts. "The interval of four years gives ample time for the discovery and development of fresh talent that may have appeared since the last meeting," the official report of the Games sniffed (Cook 1908). The Americans were enraged when their flag did not wave at the Opening Ceremonies, and the American standard bearer refused to dip his banner to the British sovereign. In the competition, the Americans protested what they considered biased officiating that favored the British. They protested when officials allowed British firemen to wear their work boots in the tug-of-war and when an official called a foul against one of their runners. They were convinced that skullduggery lay in the confusion at the conclusion of the marathon when British officials, in violation of the rules, helped an Italian, Dorando Pietri, over the finish line ahead of an American, Johnny Hayes. The British, of course, claimed there were no grounds for controversy, but the Anglo-American clashes stimulated the development of the IAAF as the IF for track and field.

As this "nationalist Olympic discourse" (Pope 1997) took form, Coubertin sympathized with the British. King Edward, he noted, took exception to the "American athletes because of their behavior and their barbaric shouts that resounded through the stadium" (1979) (in 1896, Greek observers had considered American college cheers quaint). Coubertin himself objected to the AAU chief James Sullivan's drive for American "athletic supremacy of the world" and to Sullivan's campaign to become a member of the IOC. He dismissed Sullivan's complaints about "biased" anti-American judges, but the IOC decided that the IFs, and not the host country, should select the officials for the competition in the future. "The Olympic Games were becoming an affair of State," Coubertin sighed, but he argued that such conflict had given the Games "added interest" (1979).

The problem of national teams' participation in the Games became acute in Stockholm in 1912. Finnish athletes now had to compete under the Russian flag, topped by a Finnish pennant, and the Czechs had to compete under the Austrian flag. (Hungarians, as a sovereign part of the Dual Monarchy, maintained their separate identity.) On the winner's stand in Stockholm, a Finnish runner, Hannes Kolehmainen, pointing to the Russian flag waving in his honor, reportedly told an English friend, "I would almost rather not have won, than see that flag up there" (Noel-Baker 1978a). But the IOC accepted its place within the international system of states.

Despite such problems, however, the Vth Olympic Games in Stockholm in 1912, which assembled over 2,500 athletes, essentially represented the realization of Coubertin's ideals (see table 2.2). These Games were the first to use electric timing devices, photography to help in determining close finishes, and a public address system. The Swedes had banned boxing as a sport, and the IOC agreeably omitted it from the program. Coubertin even introduced a sport of his own design, the modern pentathlon, which combined five activities of a military courier: horseback riding, shooting, running, swimming, and fencing. (Until 1948 this was the only sport that the IOC itself supervised directly.) In addition, the Stockholm Games gave Coubertin special satisfaction by awarding a literary prize to his "Ode to Sport," which he had submitted for consideration under a pseudonym.

Scandal, however, arose after the Games when Olympic authorities enforced rules on amateur status against an Olympic champion for the first time. They had, to be sure, already banned an Austrian swimmer, Francis Beaurepaire, on the grounds that he had given lifeguarding and swimming lessons, but the history books, especially the American books, pay more attention to the case of Jim Thorpe. Thorpe had won the gold medal in

Table 2.2

Results of Early Olympic Competition

		Gold	Silver	Bronze	Total
1896 Athens	Greece	10	19	17	46
	United States	11	7	1	19
	Germany	7	5	2	14
1900 Paris	France	26	36	33	95
	United States	20	15	16	51
	Great Britain	17	8	12	37
1904 St. Louis	United States	70	75	64	209
	Germany	4	4	5	13
	Cuba	5	2	3	10
1908 London	Great Britain	56	50	39	145
	United States	23	12	12	47
	Sweden	8	6	11	25
1912 Stockholm	Sweden	24	24	16	64
	United States	23	19	19	61
	Great Britain	10	15	16	41

the decathlon and the traditional pentathlon in Stockholm, and the King of Sweden had given him a silver model Viking boat in recognition of his prowess. After the American press had revealed that Thorpe, an American Indian, had played baseball for pay, the American authorities, the AAU, demanded that his medals be withdrawn. The President of the newly formed IAAF, J. Sigfrid Edstrøm, hesitated, but at the demand of the Americans he finally complied. While this scandal lingered on as an open sore in American sport, Coubertin approved this enforcement of Olympic standards.

The VIth Olympic Games, scheduled for Berlin in 1916, were to mark the 20th anniversary of the first Games as well as heal Coubertin's uneasy relations with the Germans. The Germans threw themselves into the preparations with great enthusiasm. Despite some opposition in the German Parliament, the government funded the construction of a new Olympic Stadium in Berlin. The secretary of the Berlin Organizing Committee, Carl Diem, a professional journalist and sport administrator, breathed new life into the German sport program by beginning to reorganize athletic training along the model of the Americans. He pushed for a broader program of physical education to produce world class athletes, and he imported American coaches to help with training. The Germans

Jim Thorpe, a native American, won the decathlon at the Stockholm Games (1912), but Olympic authorities took away his medals and awards because he had previously played semiprofessional baseball.

looked forward to being a successful host; in turn, Coubertin welcomed such a broadly based athletic program.

When Europe went to war in 1914, however, this opening period of Olympic history came to an abrupt halt. To be sure, statesmen commonly thought that this would be a short war, and at first it was not clear that there would be no Games in 1916. Nevertheless, strong anti-German feelings immediately arose within the IOC, leading to demands that the 1916 Games be taken away from Berlin and German members of the Committee be expelled. Coubertin refused to take any precipitate action. In 1915, he removed the International Olympic Committee from its rather awkward base in Paris, transferring its headquarters to Lausanne, Switzerland, where it could enjoy a more neutral atmosphere under the supervision of his friend Baron Godefroy de Blonay. Nothing, however, could be done to save the Games of the VIth Olympiad.

The five official sets of Olympic Games before World War I had gone through a perilous process of birth, childhood problems, and early growth, and as a result of this process, Coubertin's vision had changed significantly. He had first seen sport as a means of moral regeneration for French youth, but in his later years, he saw them as inspiring mankind with the spirit of "Olympism," a "religion of sport" (1979). Historians do not all agree with his exultant picture. Dietrich Quanz (1993) has called the Games the "first international peace movement," but Manfred Blödern (1984), in contrast, has called politics an "Olympic original sin" and has asserted that one could see the "metamorphosis of sport into surrogate war" in Athens in 1896.

For Coubertin, however, there was no doubt. When he finally accepted the fact that it would be impossible to hold the Olympic Games in 1916 as scheduled, he added a new twist to his Olympic imagery: "An Olympiad may fail to be celebrated," he declared, "but its number remains." The Games of the VIth Olympiad would not take place; it remained to look forward to the Games of the VIIth Olympiad, to be held in 1920—if the Games could survive the flames of war.

Chapter 3

Starting Anew

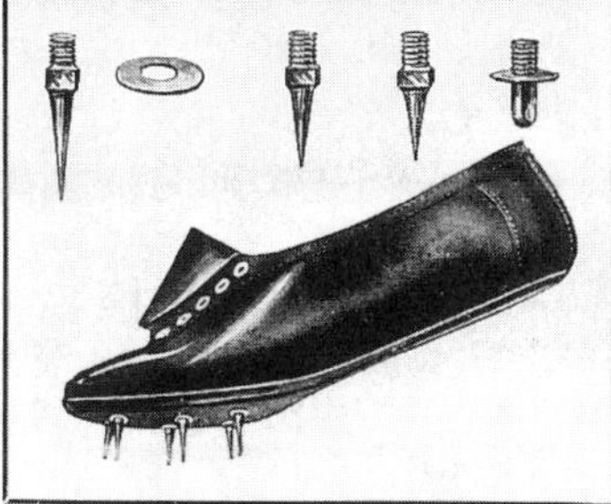

As shown by this advertisement (reprinted from the official British report of the Antwerp Games of 1924), today's "equipment wars" exploiting Olympic performances and athletes are not new.

One of the grand myths in the modern memory of the ancient Olympic Games is that warring states would suspend hostilities so that the Games could take place. In fact, the ancient Games witnessed exclusion of participants and even armed intervention. The Greek historian Thucydides (V, 49), for example, noted, "The Lacedaemonians were excluded from the temple by the Eleans and thus prevented from sacrificing or contending"; the Eleans then mounted a guard for fear of a Lacedaemonian attack. In Herodotus's *Persian Wars* (VI, 127), we find a description of "Pheidon, king of the Argives, who . . . was the most insolent of all the Grecians—the same who drove out the Elean directors of the games and himself presided over the contests at Olympia." Certainly, the ancient Games witnessed their share of political intervention, including efforts to control the Games.

In 1920, when the modern Olympic Games resumed, Olympic officials revealed their own dependence on the state system by agreeing to hold their celebration in Antwerp, Belgium and excluding Germany from the temple. In 1914, before the war, Budapest and Antwerp had been the leading contestants to host the 1920 Games. According to Coubertin's soundings, Budapest had at that time even enjoyed a small edge in the sympathies of IOC members. The passions of war, however, altered the picture drastically, and at the end of the war, the victorious Allied Powers welcomed the thought of meeting in Belgium as a reaffirmation of Germany's guilt for having started the Great War by invading Belgium in 1914. In this context, Antwerp was a natural choice. In addition, as a major European port, with secure railway communications reaching to Northern Italy, the city had economic ties extending to the Americas and even to East Asia.

In 1919, the victorious armies had already staged "Inter-Allied Games" in Paris as part of their victory celebrations, thereby offering their own statement on the relationship of sport to political and military affairs. The Americans, who had not entered the war until 1917, easily dominated the competition, but the political side of international sport showed some new twists. The Czechs, ruled by the Austrians before 1914, reveled in the recognition given the new state of Czechoslovakia. The Serbs, now garbed as Yugoslavs, enjoyed favored status as having been victims of Austrian "aggression" in 1914, while the former King Nikita of Montenegro found little sympathy as he vainly tried to use the occasion to protest Serbia's takeover of his small land in the latter stages of the Great War. Likewise, the victors interpreted justice in their own ways. Coubertin endorsed the Games, seeing them as an affirmation of the values of international sport; for the organizers, however, the Games advertised the vigor and virility of the conquering armies.

The Antwerp Games took place in a similar spirit. Faced with the question of whether to invite the former Central Powers, the losers in the

Great War, the IOC chose the path of least resistance, agreeing that the Organizing Committee, representing the city of Antwerp, had the final decision on sending out invitations. Neither Germany nor Hungary received invitations. Also absent were the Russians, then in the midst of the agonies of the communist revolution: The IOC ignored the new Soviet regime and kept the representative of the old order, Prince Urusov, in his seat, although the Committee would not allow emigrés to compete in the Games. The Games welcomed the victorious Allies and also teams from states that had remained neutral.

These Games of the VIIth Olympiad celebrated the western victory and the restoration of the Belgian state. "The Antwerp games furnished a remarkable demonstration of the Olympic spirit conquering tremendous handicaps," wrote an American journalist (Henry 1948), but the memorials for the athletes who had died in the war emphasized the winners' cause. In a publication coedited by Lord Killanin, Philip Noel-Baker (1978b) declared, "The decision [to hold the games in Antwerp] was, of course, intended as a tribute of honour to the gallant Belgians, who had been the victims of unprovoked aggression five years before; it was universally popular throughout the world." Such a view of course presumed that Germany, Soviet Russia, and other outcast nations were not a part of "the world."

Coubertin came to these Games determined as ever, now armed with a new set of symbols, slogans, and practices. His aim was to create a "religious ceremony" that would be "sufficiently neutral in character to rise above all differences in doctrine" (Coubertin 1979). As the visual symbol of the Games, he unfurled an Olympic flag depicting five interlocking rings of different colors, at least one of which was in every national flag in the world. Olympic lore calls this "The Antwerp Flag," although Coubertin had first introduced it in 1914. In the Opening Ceremonies, an athlete, selected by the hosts, delivered an oath on behalf of all the participants: "In the name of all athletes, I promise that we shall participate in these Olympic Games respecting and observing the rules of the Games in the true sporting spirit, in the name of the sport and for the honor of our countries." As the theme of the Games, Coubertin offered the thought, "The importance of life is not the triumph, but the struggle." As the motto for the competition, in contrast, he proclaimed, *Citius, altius, fortius*, "Faster, Higher, Stronger."

The leaders of the IOC and the participants themselves hailed the Games in Antwerp as a success. Almost all the athletes, officials, and visitors recognized that the Belgians had little time to prepare—less than a year and a half—and they all expressed profound respect and admiration for what the Belgians had in fact accomplished. Even so, the organizers complained of poor attendance and financial problems. The Games had their share of disputes and complaints by the athletes, especially the Americans who objected to the housing, but Coubertin was satisfied that his dream was again on track.

For the Americans, the Antwerp Games were the occasion for a significant revamping of their Olympic program. James E. Sullivan had died in 1914, and the American Olympic Committee had remained inactive for the duration of the war. Then in November 1919, it began to organize its team and raise money, but its specific goals remained unclear until February 1920 when it finally received a copy of the program for the Antwerp Games. Since Antwerp was a key port in the United States military's supply lines to its occupation force in Germany, a Joint Resolution of Congress empowered the Olympians to travel in the free space on military ships. The accommodations were frequently uncomfortable and unclean, but the athletes got to the Games and back on time and within budget.

In the years of the VIIth Olympiad, 1920-1923, Coubertin worked feverishly to set the Games on a course to follow after his departure. In his memoirs, he spoke of this as a period of uncertainty: There was talk of turning the Games over to the League of Nations; the societies of Europe were slowly recovering from the ravages of war; and even within the Olympic family, factions seemed to be pulling in opposite directions. "The situation called above all for a declaration of unity," Coubertin wrote, "and that is why the pilot at the helm felt that everyone was looking to him to steer a steady course" (1979). The American Olympic Committee (n.d.) complained of his "petulance and misunderstanding," but Coubertin insisted that he did only what he had to do: "The IOC does not look upon its authority as an exclusive right; it would gladly share it, were it not for the conviction that it would be seriously endangering the future of a progressive institution by giving any part over to those who eagerly covet it" (Coubertin 1979).

The first question that had to be settled, of course, concerned the site for the 1924 Games. Coubertin favored Paris, arguing that this would mark the 30th anniversary of the formation of the IOC, but opposition arose within the Committee when the so-called "League of Neutrals" argued that this would only consolidate the image of the Games as being the toy of the victors and that therefore the Games should take place on a "neutral" site. In what he himself called "a masterly coup d'état," Coubertin (1979), evoking sympathy by announcing that he would soon retire, won the 1924 Games for Paris. Amsterdam—the Netherlands had been neutral in the recent war—would host the 1928 Games.

At the same time, preparing for an orderly succession, Coubertin established an Executive Board for the IOC, consisting of five men who would share the responsibilities of the organization. The Committee itself

The Work of the Executive Board

The Executive Board manages the affairs of the IOC. In particular, the Board

- attends to the observance of the Olympic *Charter*;
- assumes the ultimate responsibility for the administration of the IOC;
- approves the IOC's international organization, its organization chart, and all internal regulations relating to its organization;
- is responsible for the management of the IOC's finances and prepares an annual report;
- presents a report to the Session on any proposed change of rule or by-law;
- submits to the IOC Session the names of the persons it recommends for election to the IOC;
- establishes the agenda for the IOC Sessions;
- upon proposal from the President it appoints the Director General and Secretary General;
- keeps the records of the IOC; and
- enacts, in the form it deems most appropriate (codes, rulings, norms, guidelines, guides, instructions), all regulations necessary to ensure the proper implementation of the Olympic *Charter* and the organization of the Olympic Games.

was becoming too big and unwieldy; therefore, he created this new "small nucleus of dedicated active members," (Coubertin 1979) adding a new inner ring in his pattern of concentric circles. Coubertin looked to the Executive Board as the group to follow the path he had laid out and provide leadership in the years to come. All subsequent Presidents of the IOC were already serving on the Executive Board at the time of their elections.

The IOC also decided to experiment with organizing winter competition. Ancient Greece, of course, had not indulged in winter sports, but the modern Games had already included the sports of figure skating and ice hockey. The development of Alpine skiing, invented by an Englishman, led to new winter sports programs in Austria, Switzerland, and Canada, but the Scandinavians had long opposed any initiatives by the IOC in this direction, insisting that their "Nordic Games," held every four years, fully served the needs of winter sports. The IOC now decided, however, to try its hand at winter sports.

Coubertin had his doubts about the venture, although in his memoirs he described winter sports as being "so truly amateur, so frank and so pure in their sporting dignity, that their complete exclusion from the Olympic programme deprived it of much force and value" (1979). (This judgment must have tormented Avery Brundage in later years.) Since it was impossible to stage a full program of winter sports at the same time and place as the regular Olympic Games, the IOC arranged for them to be structured as a separate competition, held at a separate site in the wintertime (table 3.1). Because of the uncertainty of the venture, the IOC declared that the first Winter Games, to be held in Chamonix, France, preceding the Summer Games in Paris, were only an experiment.

Coubertin's preparations for his glorious and emotional exit from the Olympic Movement still almost ran afoul of French politics. Struggling with problems of reconstruction, in 1923 the French government sent troops into the Ruhr to enforce reparations claims on Germany, and war and revolution threatened. Parisian authorities could not agree on the financial arrangements and the responsibilities for holding the Games. Therefore, as a precaution, Coubertin privately reached an understanding with an American entrepreneur, William Garland, establishing the possibility of shifting the 1924 Games, on short notice, to Los Angeles. Eventually, however, the French resolved their controversies, and the preparations for Paris went ahead. Coubertin rewarded his American ally by persuading the IOC, in an unprecedented early decision, to commit itself to staging the 1932 Games in Los Angeles.

Fortunately for all concerned, the first Winter Games, held in February 1924 and called simply an "International Sports Week" under the patronage of the IOC, were a success. Subsequently the IOC retroactively changed the name to the Olympic Winter Games but refused to include

Table 3.1

Growth of the Winter Olympics

		Nations	Events	Sports	Male Competitors	Female Competitors
1924	Chamonix	16	13	5	281	13
1928	St. Moritz	25	13	6	468	27
1932	Lake Placid	17	14	5	274	32
1936	Garmisch-Partenkirchen	28	17	5	675	80

them in the mystical numbering system of the Summer Games. "The prizes, medals, and diplomas," the IOC decreed, "must be different from those of the Olympic Summer Games, and the term 'Olympiad' shall not be used in this connection" (Coubertin 1979). Olympic officials later occasionally regretted this odd discrimination, but the form remained.

The Summer Games of 1924, held in Paris, also passed without major controversy, although there were complaints about low attendance, discourteous behavior on the part of the fans, and a lingering deficit that plagued the hosts. When a British referee disqualified an Italian boxer, the crowd pelted him. Some British writers thought they were hearing the death knell of the Olympics, and *The Times* of London recommended that the Games be abolished. A letter to *The Times* suggested that some "fiery contests" not be held "before temperamental audiences" (Kanin 1981). The British Olympic Association (1924), in contrast, called talk of withdrawing from the Games "ridiculous" and urged the IOC to assert its authority over the sports federations more vigorously.

As Coubertin now fulfilled his last official duties at an Olympic Games, he could see that his dream had grown beyond what anyone could have expected 30 years earlier (table 3.2). Success, however, rather naturally brought up new types of problems, not the least of which arose from the fact that these athletes came as members of national teams: 13 in Athens,

Table 3.2

Growth of the Summer Olympics

		Sports	Nations	Male Competitors	Female Competitors
1896	Athens	9	13	311	0
1900	Paris	17	22	1,319	11
1904	St. Louis	14	12	681	6
1906	Athens	11	20	877	7
1908	London	21	23	1,999	36
1912	Stockholm	13	28	2,490	57
1920	Antwerp	21	29	2,543	64
1924	Paris	18	44	2,956	136
1928	Amsterdam	14	46	2,724	290
1932	Los Angeles	14	37	1,281	127
1936	Berlin	19	49	3,738	328

29 in Antwerp, and 44 in Paris. For many, and especially the Americans, success at the Olympic Games became a measure of the system from which the athletes had come.

In 1919, Coubertin had decreed, "No general point score by country will be established, but only a score for each sport." In the years before World War I, although there had been considerable rivalry between nations—Germans and French, British and Americans—the host team always won the most medals. After World War I, American athletes began to dominate the Games. At Antwerp, they scored 203.5 points to the Swedes' 121.5. In Paris, the Americans again claimed victory with 625.55 points while the French stood in second place with 277.5. Flushed by these successes, the Americans, charging that some other countries were devising their own scoring systems so as to minimize the achievements of American athletes, demanded that the IOC adopt an official point system to identify a national team championship in the Olympic Games.

Coubertin himself presided over a meeting in Paris to discuss the question (Grombach 1975). The two most popular systems under consideration offered points for six places, differing as to whether first place should be greater than second and third combined or less than the two combined: 7-5-4-3-2-1 or 10-5-4-3-2-1. The official report of the French Organizing Committee (Comité Olympique Français 1924) used the 10-5 system. According to this system, in the track and field competition, the Americans totaled 255.5 points, the Finns (led by the legendary Paavo Nurmi) 166, and the British 85.5. Yet another system, commonly attributed to Douglas MacArthur, later the hero of the American war in the Pacific, proposed to relate a country's point score to its population so as to establish a ratio of points per million inhabitants. Under MacArthur's proposal, the weight lifter from Luxembourg who won a gold medal in Antwerp could have claimed the Olympic "team" championship; at the Atlanta Olympics of 1996, the Tongan silver medalist in boxing won the team championship for his country of some 100,000 inhabitants. In 1924, after heated discussion, the IOC refused to designate any system of team scoring as "official," but journalists persisted in calculating unofficial team scores, according to their own systems.

The Paris Games completed, Coubertin carried out his promise to retire, and meeting in Prague in 1925, the IOC selected Count Henri de Baillet-Latour, a Belgian, as the baron's successor. Born in 1876, Baillet-Latour had been a member of the IOC since 1903, and he had directed the work of the Organizing Committee for the Antwerp Games in 1920. Considered the IOC's "Olympic apostle" to South America, he had watched over the Latin American Games of 1922, the first regional games to be staged under the Olympic umbrella, and he had also handled the delicate questions of relations between the IOC and the IFs. When Coubertin departed the stage, not the least of his accomplishments was his having arranged an orderly succession to the office of the presidency.

Baillet-Latour's tenure in office was marked first of all by the controversial expansion of women's participation in Olympic "light athletics," as track and field, "the queen of sports," is known in most European languages. Disgruntled by the IOC's refusal to introduce women's track and field events at the Antwerp Games, a Frenchwoman, Alice Milliat, together with five representatives of other lands, had organized the International Women's Sports Federation (FSFI). Coubertin showed little sympathy for her efforts, proposing instead that women's events be dropped from the Games altogether. In 1922, Milliat prepared the first "Women's Olympic Games" in Paris. Under pressure from the IOC, she eventually changed the name to "Women's World Games," but the games were successful enough to warrant being scheduled ahead for 1926, 1930, and 1934.

The IAAF and the IOC quickly moved to control this development. In 1924, the IAAF took charge of women's "athletics," and the IOC scheduled a limited women's program of five track and field events for the Amsterdam Games (Phillips 1996). British women chose to boycott the Amsterdam Games in protest over the limitations on their competition. After the completion of the 1928 Games, Milliat and the FSFI demanded that the IOC accept a "complete" program of 11 events for women in track and field, but the IOC argued that women's physiques were unfit for athletic competition and voted to eliminate women's track and field altogether. Pressure from the organizers of the Los Angeles Games of 1932 forced the Committee to reinstate the women's competition, although the IOC, claiming medical documentation for its position, ruled out the 800-meter run.

While the IOC fussed, countervailing forces among feminists themselves questioned whether women should participate in the Games. A strong current of thought in the United States, for example, argued that women should not engage in competitive sport at all. But many European feminists felt that the Americans' ideas were in fact retarding the development of women's sports. Members of the FSFI, in turn, wanted their organization to be the exclusive organizer of women's athletics, and they asserted that the IOC should give up any thought of holding women's competition. The IOC settled for gradually expanding the women's program, and eventually the FSFI dissolved. By way of contrast to the resistance of the IAAF to women's competition, other sports federations expanded women's competition more rapidly. For example, in 1924, FINA, the swimming federation, had nine events for men and seven for women. Women's fencing entered the Games in 1924, and in 1928 women's gymnastics entered, albeit only as a team sport. At Antwerp in

1920, women participants made up less than 3 percent of the contestants; in Paris, 136 women constituted 4.4 percent of the contestants; and in Amsterdam in 1928, the 290 women present made up 9.6 percent of the contestants, competing in 11.5 percent of the events.

The 1928 Winter Games in St. Moritz and Summer Games in Amsterdam were the first, apart from the St. Louis fiasco, to take place in Coubertin's absence. In a message to the "athletes and all those taking part in the Games" in Amsterdam, the baron urged all concerned "strongly and faithfully to keep ever alive the flame of the revived Olympic spirit and maintain its necessary principles." Referring to his own ill health, he melodramatically commented, "I should be wise to take the present opportunity of bidding you farewell," and he concluded, "Once again, I beg to thank those who have followed me and helped me to fight a forty-year war, not often easy and not always cleanly fought." His was now, however, a voice from the past; he had become a relic and an object in the politics of the Games, not a principal player.

American Women Resist Participation

In the 1920s and early 1930s, to the dismay of European women activists, there was resistance among American women to participating in the Olympic Games. From a statement of the Women's Division of the National Amateur Athletic Federation, sent to Henri Baillet-Latour before the Olympic Congress of 1930:

WHEREAS, The Women's Division, National Amateur Athletic Federation, believes wholeheartedly in competition and believes that competition is the soul of athletics and of sports and Games, and that without it, they could not exist . . .

And, WHEREAS, Participation in the Olympic Games, particularly participation in the Track and Field Events,

(1) Entails the specialized training of the few,
(2) Offers opportunity for exploitation and commercialization,
(3) Stresses individual accomplishment and winning of championships,
(4) Places men in immediate charge of athletic activities for girls and women,
(5) Offers opportunity for possible overstrain in preparation for and during the Games themselves

. . . *Therefore*, The Women's Division, National Amateur Athletic Federation, petitions this International Olympic Congress to vote to omit track and field events for women from the 1932 program.

Alice Ailene Setton, *The Women's Division National Amateur Athletic Federation: Sixteen Years of Progress in Athletics for Girls and Women, 1923-1939* (Stanford: Stanford Univ. Press, 1941), pp. 83-84.

The 1928 Games marked the first appearance of the Germans since before the Great War. Admitted to the League of Nations in 1926, they were now acceptable Olympic company. German newspapers reported that in St. Moritz their athletes "were greeted with enthusiastic applause." In Amsterdam, the Dutch fans greeted them generally in friendly fashion, but when a fight broke out on the field in the German-Uruguayan soccer match, the situation quickly escalated into a diplomatic incident, leading to a formal Uruguayan protest to the Dutch Foreign Ministry. (The Uruguayan soccer team went on to win the gold medal.) The Germans went home believing that their presence had lent a special grace to the Olympics, and sport authorities almost immediately began planning to invite the Olympics to Berlin in 1936.

In contrast, after the Amsterdam Games, the Americans had cause to reflect on their own bad Olympic image. The head of the American delegation, Douglas MacArthur, confined his forces to the ship on which they had come, the *President Roosevelt*, letting them go ashore only for competition; the Europeans, he insisted, were spying on them. The American athletes subsequently put on their worst show in track and field since the war. As they went off licking their wounds, wondering whether their representatives had suffered more from bad attitudes or overeating, Europeans rejoiced in the victories of the Finns, led by the great distance runner Paavo Nurmi. The British in particular welcomed their amateur Davids' dispatching the American professional Goliaths (Kanin 1981).

The problem of "amateurism" in fact took a new twist after the Amsterdam Games when soccer, which had been the first team sport to be admitted to the Olympics, broke away to establish its own professional world championship. (The IOC had already dropped tennis because of problems of "amateurism," but the row with soccer had more worldwide significance.) Soccer had spread rapidly from its origins in 19th century Britain to become the most popular sport in the world. With its popularity came professionalism, especially when it took root in South America. In protest against creeping professionalism, the British authorities withdrew from Olympic soccer competition after 1920. In their absence, FIFA officials attempted to broaden the rules of eligibility. Even so, because of problems in meeting Olympic standards of "amateurism," there were only 17 teams competing in Amsterdam as opposed to 22 in Paris four years earlier.

The IOC found itself caught between FIFA and the IAAF. FIFA endorsed the principle of broken-time payments, which would allow the athletes to receive their regular salaries while competing. The IAAF, however, approved of vacations with pay but opposed broken-time payments. Since soccer produced one-third of the total gate receipts in Amsterdam, FIFA

IOC Decisions on Broken-Time Payments

From the IOC Resolution on August 3, 1928:

The IOC having fully considered all the facts which have arisen since the meeting at Monaco regrets—

That the FIFA has modified its views of amateurism in such a way that they are not in accordance with the Olympic rules.

It hopes that the said Federation will realize that, unless it alters its rules so as to conform with the principles of qualification of the IOC voted by the Congress of Prague, or permit such of its members as do comply with its rules to compete, its sport cannot be included in the Olympic programme.

---

had a strong bargaining position, but the IAAF had stronger support among the members of the IOC. Thus, the Committee rejected the idea of broken-time payments.

FIFA went on to organize its own World Cup competition in which all soccer players, professional or amateur, could compete. Because Uruguay had won the last two Olympic competitions, it hosted the first World Cup tournament in 1930, and it became the first World Cup champion. The success of the World Cup tournament relegated the Olympic Games to the role of a secondary competition for soccer, and professionalism spread even more rapidly. In effect, it was no longer necessary or even desirable in soccer to "save oneself" for the Olympics. The IOC responded by dropping soccer from the schedule for the 1932 Games in Los Angeles. Since soccer, however, had great spectator appeal, the IOC restored the sport in 1936.

Even without such controversy, the worldwide depression of the early 1930s signified trouble for international sport, but both the Winter and the Summer Games of 1932, held in the United States, turned out well. The IIIrd Winter Games took place in Lake Placid, New York in February, with 17 nations participating. Warm weather had threatened to disrupt the Winter Games, but at virtually the last possible moment a frost set in, and the competition proceeded as planned. Americans won the most medals, dominating the speed skating and bobsled events, while Norway dominated the skiing events.

As the winter of 1932 passed into history, however, there were still doubts about the feasibility of holding the Summer Games in Los Angeles, because it was unclear whether many foreign teams could afford to travel in this time of austerity. Apart from the St. Louis Games, to which few Europeans came, this would mark the first time European athletes had left their own continent to compete in the Summer Olympics. Thus, the Los

Angeles Games were by no means assured of success, and lagging ticket sales seemed to foretell financial problems.

The fact that the Games were being staged in Los Angeles was a result of the work of William May Garland. In 1920, Garland had attended the Antwerp Games and attempted to persuade the IOC to hold the 1924 Games in Los Angeles, but the Committee chose Paris. When it then committed itself to Amsterdam in 1928, the Californians complained they had not received a fair hearing. Somewhat to Garland's surprise, the Committee then turned around and elected him a member. He became a confidante of Coubertin, and of course he had provided the baron an alternative in the face of troubles in organizing the Paris Games of 1924. The baron reciprocated by helping Los Angeles win the 1932 Games. Garland's election to the IOC, however, shocked the American sport establishment, which considered him a newcomer Californian. In the ensuing conflict, the Games seemed threatened until Avery Brundage, a Chicago businessman, replaced Douglas MacArthur as the President of the American Olympic Committee in 1929. Under Brundage's careful guidance, the contending parties made peace, and preparations for the Los Angeles Games moved ahead.

To the surprise and joy of all concerned, the Los Angeles organizers worked out arrangements whereby athletes from Europe were able to make the 30-day round-trip to the Games for about $500—no small sum, but one-third what had been expected. Once in Los Angeles, the male athletes enjoyed residence in the first Olympic Village, made up of two-room cottages and guarded by cowboys on horseback; the 127 women stayed in a hotel for the same price of two dollars per day. Final reckoning showed that the Los Angeles Games made a profit of almost one million dollars.

Many western historians of the Olympic Games, who like to think of the Games from Antwerp to Los Angeles as the "golden era of the Olympics," revel in stories of sportsmanship at these "last innocent" Games. David Lord Burghley, defending champion in the 400-meter hurdles (and the prototype of the nobleman in the English film *Chariots of Fire*), had intended to stay away from the opening parade in order to rest, but he felt obliged to march when he discovered that his major rival, Morgan Taylor, would carry the American flag. (The winner in the race in question was Bob Tisdall, an Irishman.) In the 5000-meter run, a Finn, Lauri Lehtinen, defeated Ralph Hill of Oregon after what the crowd considered several fouls. But when Bill Henry, the Los Angeles journalist who was manning the public address system, intoned "Remember, please, these people are our guests," the spectators responded with cheers.

Critics, however, had their own views: Athletes complained the venues for competition were scattered from Long Beach to Pasadena; Finns threatened a boycott when the authorities ruled Paavo Nurmi ineligible on a charge of professionalism. The IOC itself angered the Japanese by rejecting an application from the Japanese puppet state of Manchukuo to be admitted to the Games. Nevertheless, after the strains of "Aloha" and "Taps" had died away at the closing ceremonies, American journalists wrote eloquently about the success of the Games.

American performances in Los Angeles were marked by the remarkable accomplishments of black runners and a woman, Babe Didricksen. Eddie Tolan and Ralph Metcalfe took gold and silver in the 100-meter dash; Tolan then went on to win the 200-meter dash. Didricksen, who had previously won the women's United States national team championship all by herself, set world records while winning the 80-meter hurdles and the javelin, and she broke the old world's record while finishing second in the high jump.

The success of the black athletes in Los Angeles seemed a bolt from the blue, but it was in fact a natural development of black participation in American sport. While there had been outstanding black athletes throughout the history of American sport, they had a difficult time in finding a place in elite sport. The ones who were most successful were the ones who participated in individual sports that involved direct combat, like boxing, or clear measurement with a stopwatch or tape measure. The coach of a team sport could easily exclude a superior athlete in the name of the team's "chemistry," as it came to be called, but the man who could jump higher or run faster could prove his superiority regardless of such judgments. The fact that the 1932 Games were in the United States also broadened the possibilities for blacks' participation in the competition, and the track and field contenders took advantage of it.

As the IOC now looked forward to celebrating the Games of the XIth Olympiad in Berlin four years hence, it was by no means "innocent" of politics, but as yet few politicians understood the political potential of the Games and the possibilities of exploiting the Games for political ends. In 1896, the Greek royal family had considered it desirable to sponsor the Olympic Games, and President Theodore Roosevelt had played a major role in assigning the 1904 Games to St. Louis, but President Hoover considered himself too busy with his campaign for reelection to attend the 1932 Summer Games. Instead he sent his Vice President to the opening ceremonies. It remained for the host of the next Games to remind the world of the political usefulness of associating oneself with this mass gathering of the youth of the world.

Chapter 4

The Berlin Games

The Olympic torch first burned at the Amsterdam Games (1928). For the Berlin Games (1936), the Germans initiated the torch relay beginning with the lighting of the torch in Greece.

The Games of 1936 in Berlin completed the formative period in the history of the modern Olympics. Frustrated in the early years of the Games and excluded from the Games of 1920 and 1924, Germans now wanted to show the sport world what it had failed to appreciate. In addition, a new government, headed by Adolf Hitler, had come to power in Germany in 1933. Having withdrawn from the League of Nations, this Germany chose to use the Games as a stage for showing the world the strength and vigor of its new order. When anti-Nazi forces objected and demanded that the IOC withdraw the Games from Berlin, the IOC had to redefine its own standards. In practice, in 1920 the IOC had excluded Germany at the Allies' insistence; now, it moved to broaden its international base and essentially validated Hitler's regime.

The IOC had awarded the Games of the XIth Olympiad to Berlin in 1931. When it met in Barcelona in July of that year to discuss the question, the Spanish Civil War that was to continue through the decade was already moving into the streets. With only about one-third of its members present—not even its Spanish members were there—the Committee had to choose between Berlin and this same Barcelona. IOC President Baillet-Latour sealed the ballots, unread, and then asked the missing members of the Committee to mail in their votes to IOC headquarters in Lausanne. Two and a half weeks later, he announced that Berlin had won by a vote of 43-16. As was the custom, the Germans had first call on the Winter Games, and they accepted, naming the resort of Garmisch-Partenkirchen as their site.

The Germans had only returned to the Olympic family three years earlier, but they had claimed second place at the Amsterdam Games, bowing only to the Americans in the number of medals won. The IOC had further awarded them an Olympic Cup for a gymnastics display in the main stadium. The Germans had expected to host the 1916 Games, which would have marked the 20th anniversary of the Games. The IOC's award now put the Germans in charge of the celebration of the 40th anniversary of the modern Games, and IOC members quietly hoped that this would heal the lingering wounds of the Great War and the succeeding years.

In the midst of the celebration of the Xth Games in Los Angeles, however, sounds of trouble were rising. The Nazis (the National Socialists), an extremist nationalist German party, denounced the Olympic Games as an "infamous festival dominated by Jews" (Mandell 1971). The *Völkischer Beobachter*, the party's official newspaper, denounced the successes of American blacks in Los Angeles: "Negroes have no business at the Olympics. Today we witness that free white men have to compete with the unfree Negro. This is a debasement of the Olympic idea beyond comparison. . . . The next Olympics will be held in Berlin in 1936. We hope

Germany at the Olympic Games

After having been excluded from the Games of 1920 and 1924, Germany returned to the Olympic Games in 1928. The performance of their athletes won increasing respect at each succeeding competition.

Olympiad		Pts Rank	Medals	Strongest Events
1928	San Moritz	13	1 (1 bronze)	Bobsled
	Amsterdam	2	31 (10 gold, 7 silver, 14 bronze)	Greco-Roman wrestling, men's track and field, swimming, weight lifting
1932	Lake Placid	6	3 (3 bronze)	Bobsled, hockey
	Los Angeles	3	21 (4 gold, 12 silver, 5 bronze)	Greco-Roman wrestling, men's track and field, weight lifting
1936	Garmisch-Partenkirchen	2	6 (3 gold, 3 bronze)	
	Berlin	1	89 (33 gold, 26 silver, 30 bronze)	Boxing, Greco-Roman wrestling, men's gymnastics, rowing, equestrian, men's track and field, men's and women's swimming, weight lifting

Khavin 1979.

that the responsible men know what will be their duty. The blacks have to be expelled. We demand it!"

Independent of Nazi propaganda, there was broad opposition to the Olympic Games that crossed ideological boundaries in Germany, ranging from the extreme right to the extreme left. Conservative circles in Germany had long considered the Olympic Games a foreign intrusion into their native culture. For example, in February 1933 the *Deutscher Kampfring gegen die Olympischen Spiele* (*German Circle for Struggle Against the Olympic Games*) complained, "German sport leaders are demanding millions for the organization of the Olympic Games. A sensational show, such as the world has never yet seen, is to be constructed on the back of the German people. While our youth hunger, peoples of all colors and races, who keep us down, are to compete with us for honor in an arena to be built with German money." On the left wing of German politics, both the German Communist Party and the German Social Democrats opposed hosting the Games. Communist deputies in the Reichstag, the German national legislature, argued that the government should put no money into the Games, as the Games would serve only nationalist pride and passion for triumph.

On January 24, 1933, the Organizing Committee of the XIth Games held its first meeting in Berlin without incident, but within a week, Adolf Hitler received the call to power as Chancellor of the state. In February, as the new regime began to take form, Paul von Hindenburg, the President of Germany, accepted the title of patron of the Games. In March, only a few days after Hitler had won a majority in elections to the Reichstag, Dr. Theodor Lewald, the President of the Berlin Organizing Committee, visited the new Chancellor to explain the Games to him.

At first doubtful, Hitler finally agreed that these Games could be useful to himself and the German state. As his Minister for Propaganda, Joseph Goebbels, put it, the Olympics should not be only a *Sportwettkampf* (sports competition), but also a *Wettkampf des Geistes* (a competition of the spirit). The Nazis' moves against Germany's Jews were already arousing international controversy. At the end of March 1933, the regime proclaimed a national boycott of Jewish business, and it then began purging Jews from public office and public institutions. Following this lead, the German boxing federation declared it would no longer tolerate Jewish fighters or referees. In June, the Ministry of Education announced that all gymnastic organizations were henceforth closed to Jews, and after July, Jews could not be lifeguards. Then in the summer of 1933, Hitler took Germany out of the League of Nations. The Olympic Games, as a grand cultural festival where style and spirit predominated, could turn the world's attention away from international political conflicts. Thus Berlin viewed hosting the Olympics as an opportunity to offset foreign criticism of its domestic policies.

Nevertheless, the German government had to negotiate carefully with Olympic officials. The first conflict between the Nazi regime and the IOC came over Lewald's position as head of the Organizing Committee for the Berlin Games. The Nazis declared him unfit to serve the Third Reich, the new order being constructed in Germany. Although he had formerly worked as Secretary of State in the German Ministry of the Interior and was a long-time member of the IOC, his grandmother had been born a Jew. When the IOC protested, the Nazis relented and reinstated him, although the Ministry of the Interior took over supervision of the Games. Baillet-Latour and other members of the IOC rejoiced in having won this particular battle and convinced themselves they could deal with Hitler and his government.

Under pressure especially from the Americans, the IOC also considered the impact of the Nazis' racial policies on athletes from other countries. In May 1933, Baillet-Latour warned his German colleagues on the Committee that there was great concern as to how Jews from other lands would be received in Berlin. Lewald accordingly warned Hitler there was significant sentiment within the IOC for withdrawing the Games from Berlin, and Berlin in turn empowered him to promise that Germany would observe all Olympic rules and that, in principle, Jews would not be excluded from German teams. Again the IOC was convinced that it had achieved a meaningful victory.

In their determination to proceed with the Games, IOC leaders forged several important links in their "chain of myths" about the Games. Defending themselves against charges of sympathizing with the Hitler regime, they insisted they had awarded the Games to the city of Berlin, not to the Third Reich. They also conjured up an extraterritorial image of the Games. As Baillet-Latour reportedly told Hitler, "When the five-circled Olympic flag is raised over the stadium, it becomes sacred Olympic territory and for all practical purposes, the Games are held in ancient Olympia. There, I am the master" (Constable 1996). This image of Olympic sovereignty bespoke volumes about the sense of power that Baillet-Latour and his successors felt as Presidents of the IOC.

Baillet-Latour privately urged the Americans to keep pressure on Berlin. "I am not personally fond of the Jews and of the Jewish influence," he admitted in a letter to Avery Brundage (Brundage Archive), but he wanted the American Olympic Committee to press its German counterpart to live up to all agreements, even, if necessary, to the point of threatening boycott: "*La crainte*, as we say in French, *est le commencement de la sagesse*" [Fear is the beginning of wisdom]. The Americans, who were among the most outspoken opponents of the Nazis' racial policies, needed little encouragement to pursue such a policy. In November 1933, the AAU voted not to attend the Games in Germany if there would be any discrimination against Jews; the Americans demanded assurances that Jewish athletes would be treated like all others at the Olympics and would be included on German teams.

The Germans again made a concession. In June 1934, they announced that 21 Jewish athletes had been nominated to participate in training camps for the German Olympic team. (The Germans eventually accepted onto the team only two Jews, one of whom, a woman, had been living in the United States.) Confused and suspicious, the American Olympic Committee sent Avery Brundage to Germany to investigate the situation, and upon his return, Brundage declared the Germans were indeed observing the rules of the IOC. Henceforth, Brundage unwaveringly supported American participation in the Games as scheduled.

Brundage's position in the controversy has aroused considerable hostile comment over the years. Although he had supported the AAU's resolution threatening to boycott the Berlin Games, many observers insisted he was not an impartial observer when he visited Germany and his subsequent enthusiasm for the Berlin Games indicated either shocking naiveté or warm sympathy for the Nazi regime. Brundage indeed displayed no sympathy toward Jewish complaints about persecution by the Nazis, but whatever his personal feelings, he was probably primarily motivated by a desire to protect the image of the Olympic Games. For him, the "Olympic Movement" was becoming the focus of his life and even a mission: he would not consider making concessions to what he considered extraneous passions.

Brundage had found in Germany a man in whom he placed considerable trust, Karl Ritter von Halt, and the friendship of these two men deeply influenced the Olympic Movement for the next 20 years. Like Brundage, Halt, a member of the IOC since 1929 and now head of the Garmisch Organizing Committee, had come into the Olympic family through the IAAF; thus, the two men shared a common background in track and field. Halt, however, was an avowed Nazi, who probably served as a channel for direct communication between Hitler and Baillet-Latour, bypassing Lewald. Obviously, he influenced Brundage to accept German explanations uncritically.

Despite Brundage's support of the Berlin Games, opposition continued within the AAU. In 1935, when Brundage had retired as President of the AAU to concentrate on his work as President of the American Olympic Committee, his successor, Jeremiah T. Mahoney, a New York judge, insisted that the United States should not send athletes to Berlin. "This whole thing is not a question of politics," declared Mahoney, "It is a question of humanity" (Mahoney 1935). In an open letter to Lewald, published as a leaflet under the title "Germany Has Violated the Olympic Code!" he advised the German to resign rather than serve as a figurehead for the Nazis' inhuman policies (Mahoney 1935).

Mahoney received no support from the IOC. Instead, satisfied with the concessions offered by the Nazi regime, Baillet-Latour leaned toward Brundage's view that foreigners were now demanding too much of the Germans. The IOC did not want to intervene into the internal affairs of a member country, and therefore, so long as the Germans indicated their

Mahoney's Protest

As a result of my investigation, I am convinced, and I do not see how you can deny, that the German Jews are being excluded from the possibility of participating in the Olympic Games merely because they are Jews . . . ; that the present German Government has injected race, religion and politics into sports in general and into the Olympics in particular, and has destroyed their free and independent character. . . .

I believe that participation in the games under the Swastika implies the tacit approval of all that the Swastika symbolizes. Surely, it does not imply the disapproval and abhorrence which so many Americans feel. I believe that for America to participate in the Olympics in Germany means giving American moral and financial support to the Nazi regime, which is opposed to all that Americans hold dearest. Therefore I hope that all Americans will join with me in opposing American participation in the Olympic games and aid me in having the games transferred to another country.

Jeremiah T. Mahoney. 1935. "Germany Has Violated the Olympic Code!" Pamphlet. New York: The Committee on Fair Play in Sports.

readiness to observe Olympic rules, the Committee wanted to raise no further challenges. When an American member of the IOC, Ernest Lee Jahncke, spoke out against keeping the Games in Berlin, Baillet-Latour arranged for his ouster from the Committee on the charge of having missed two consecutive meetings.

The German press, operating under tight governmental controls, strongly supported the Games and incorporated Germany's hosting the festival into its picture of the new order under Nazi leadership. It reported extensively on the anti-Olympic moves in other countries and denounced those calling for boycott as being hostile to the idea that the youth of the world should gather together in a festival of friendship and learn the "truth" about the New Germany. Berlin's hosting the Games, insisted the *Kölner Zeitung*, struck a serious blow at all those who for "transparent reasons" hated Germany. In response to charges that Germany was politicizing the Games, the Reichskommissar for Sport, Hans von Tschammer und Osten, agreed that indeed it was, and he added that this politicization constituted a positive contribution to the Games.

In December 1935, the question of American participation in the Games came to a head at the AAU's annual convention. Brundage complained of attacks against his stand on principle: "Because I have pointed out that amateur sport and the Olympic Games are above political, racial and religious considerations, I am being denounced and threatened with great violence." The proponents of boycott, he argued, had "no right to invade the sphere of athletics in the first place, but when they spent thousands

Letter Sent by Ernest Lee Jahncke to Henri Baillet-Latour, November 25, 1935:

I shall urge upon my countrymen that they should not participate in the Games in Nazi Germany because it is my opinion that under the domination of the Nazi Government the German sports authorities have violated and are continuing to violate every requirement of fair play in the conduct of sports in Germany and in the selection of the German team, and are exploiting the Games for the political and financial profit of the Nazi regime. . . .

I am convinced, moreover, that to hold the Games in Nazi Germany will be to deal a severe blow to the Olympic idea. And, tragically enough, it will have been damaged by the International Olympic Committee which is its custodian and to which it was given in sacred trust more than a generation ago by those fine sportsmen who revived the Olympics. . . .

It is plainly your duty to hold the Nazi sports authorities accountable for the violation of their pledges. I simply cannot understand why, instead of doing that, you are engaged in formulating and in spreading "arguments" to show why those of us who still believe in the Olympic idea should take part in the Games in Nazi Germany.

Brundage Archives, University of Illinois.

---

and thousands of dollars in the effort to sway the Amateur Athletic Union meeting, they showed an egregious disregard for *all* the proprieties." On the chance that the AAU would vote down his demand, he had already been investigating the manner in which the United States Olympic Committee might send a team without the approval of the AAU; after the fact, he wrote, "Regardless of any action taken by the AAU convention, American athletes would have been sent to Germany." After complicated parliamentary maneuvering, the assembled delegates at the AAU convention agreed to send the athletes to Germany.

The IVth Winter Olympic Games, held in Garmisch-Partenkirchen February 6-16, 1936, provided a dress rehearsal for the Berlin Games, and the Germans claimed success. Noting that 28 countries intended to come to the Winter Games and 49 to the Summer Games, the *Frankfurter Zeitung* crowed that the efforts to deny Germany its due had failed; Germany would have its chance to present itself to the youth of the world. Halt declared, "We Germans want to show the world that we, true to the order of our Führer and Reichskanzler, will make these Olympic Games into a true festival of peace and of true understanding between peoples." German authorities noted which foreign correspondents filed "poisonous reports," and at the Winter Games Nazi officials carefully separated hostile journalists such as Paul Gallico, Westbrook Pegler, and William Shirer from the more sympathetic or more pliable foreign correspondents.

From Avery Brundage's Summary of the AAU Meeting in December 1935:

Few of the delegates who attended, let alone the general public, realize how close amateur sport in this country came to being "sold down the river." The proponents of the German boycott had no right to invade the sphere of athletics in the first place, but when they spent thousands and thousands of dollars in the effort to sway the Amateur Athletic Union meeting, they showed an egregious disregard for all the proprieties. . . .

It was clearly evident that a considerable proportion of the delegates attending the recent convention did not have the interests of the AAU foremost in their thoughts. It was rumored that the expenses of many of these strangers who had had no previous connection with the AAU, were paid by organizations which had never displayed any interest in amateur sport. . . . We must be on our guard against invasions of this kind in the future.

It is a strange thing that in all of the arguments against participation the rights of the athletes were completely forgotten yet the athletes in the last analysis are the reason for the existence of the AAU.

Brundage Archive, University of Illinois.

There were no signs of tension between the Olympic officials and the Nazi authorities; quite to the contrary, the two parties rejoiced at the success of the proceedings. Baillet-Latour saw no signs of discrimination against Jews—the Nazis had only recently and temporarily taken down signs forbidding Jews from entering Garmisch (Holmes 1971)—and Brundage of course saw no discrimination either. At a banquet honoring the Games, Joseph Goebbels proclaimed, "It is true that the Olympic Games are not political in spirit or in idea, but this gathering of men and women of all countries sounds a political note in a higher sense. Here there is afforded an opportunity for all, above all political differences and differentiations, to learn to know one another and thus to promote understanding among nations." Baillet-Latour responded in kind, declaring that "all who participated in the Games will bear testimony to the splendid spirit in which German sport realized the Olympic idea." "Nowhere," added Brundage, "can one find a more true Olympic atmosphere than here in Garmisch-Partenkirchen" (WWA Hamburg). The Germans were pleased. As the Nazi organ *Völkischer Beobachter* commented, "This recognition from our guests is the finest reward for our people and especially for the men who had to organize the Winter Games."

For many other people, however, the struggle over the Berlin Olympics was barely beginning. In the course of 1935, "committees for the defense of the Olympic idea" had formed in a number of European countries, and in March 1936, they developed new energy when Hitler announced German remilitarization of the Rhineland, which the Treaty of Versailles had neutralized in 1919. The French government postponed allocating money to send its athletes to Berlin, and the President of the French National Sports Committee, Louis Rimet, declared, “One is a Frenchman before one is an Olympic competitor.” After considerable debate, however, both French and British authorities agreed to send teams. Baillet-Latour declared that only war could prevent the Games from taking place as scheduled.

Socialist and communist sport leaders offered the most determined and consistent opposition to the celebration in Berlin. Even before Hitler's accession to power, to be sure, they had shown little sympathy for the ideals of the IOC. In the 1920s, socialists, united in the International Workers' Association for Sport and Physical Culture, better known as the Luzern Sports International (LSI), had sharply criticized individualistic “recordmania.” In 1925, it had staged a “Workers' Olympiad” in Germany, replete with banners proclaiming “Down With Imperialist War,” “Struggle for the Eight-Hour Day,” and “Avoid Alcohol.” The Communist Red Sports International (RSI) had staged a “Spartakiad” in Moscow in 1928, which they proclaimed a “powerful demonstration of proletarian class sport against bourgeois-fascist sport—especially against the Amsterdam Olympiad.” In 1932, the chairman of the USSR All-Union Council on Physical Culture, N.K. Antipov, denounced the Los Angeles Olympics as representing the efforts of the bourgeoisie to train the youth of the world to fight against the proletarian revolutionary movement, and American radicals organized “Counter-Olympics” in Chicago as a challenge to the Los Angeles Games (Steinberg 1979).

After Hitler's rise to power, the Nazis quickly crushed the workers' sport movement in Germany. Since the Germans had constituted the strongest section of the Socialist Workers' Sports International (the SWSI, as the LSI was now called) this dealt a terrible blow to the organization. The RSI, still based in the Soviet Union, then proposed that the two organizations, bitter enemies in the past, form a united front against the Nazis. In August 1934, in a show of workers' unity, they staged a joint festival in Paris, which in fact marked a first step in creating the Popular Front, uniting the parties of the left wherever possible against fascism. Meeting in Prague in September 1935, representatives of the two sport organizations called on the “athletes and gymnasts of the entire world to boycott the Berlin Olympics” (Steinberg 1979). In February 1936, the Communist Red International of Labor Unions directed all its members to join anti-Olympic committees, and in March a conference of the RSI, which had now formally changed its name to International Union of Workers' and Peasants' Sports Associations, called on all workers' sport organizations to join anti-Olympic committees.

In the spring of 1936, when the idea of holding alternative games in protest against the Berlin Olympics arose, both the communists and socialists responded enthusiastically, choosing Barcelona as the ideal site for the competition. A Popular Front government had come to power in Spain in February 1936; Spain had no diplomatic relations with Germany; and Barcelona itself had been a contender to host the 1936 Summer Olympics. The city had a stadium that could hold 72,000 spectators and a modern natatorium that could seat 5,000. When the organizers of these alternative games began to receive entries, they estimated their festival would draw some 4,000 Spanish participants and 3,500 foreigners from 22 nations.

The controversy over the Berlin Olympic Games now became part of the internal political tension in Spain, where conservative opposition to the Popular Front government was mounting. A pamphlet distributed among soldiers in the Barcelona garrison complained, "Soldiers of Spain! The scum of humanity is coming to Barcelona for the Olympic Games. Is it right that they take away our beds so that the socialist and communist scum can sleep well?" The President of Catalonia cautiously banned the display of revolutionary or political flags in connection with the alternative games and directed that there should be no singing of the revolutionary anthem *The Internationale.* Even so, preparations went ahead amid the considerable controversy.

On July 17, the counterrevolution in Spain struck: Francisco Franco began his revolt against the republican government in Madrid. Fighting broke out in Barcelona the next day, and many athletes who had already arrived for the alternative games threw themselves into the fray. Fascists charged that the "People's Olympics" had in fact been a cover for smuggling communist military forces into Catalonia. At any rate, the fighting prevented the holding of the alternative games in Barcelona; instead, the opponents of the Berlin Olympics concentrated their attention on a sport festival held in Prague, Czechoslovakia, at the beginning of August.

Ignoring the activity of the workers' internationals, the Berlin Olympics went ahead on schedule. German spokesmen waxed enthusiastic about how the new social order was enhancing the performance of German athletes. In June, when Max Schmeling defeated the American Joe Louis in a heavyweight boxing match, German officials attributed his success to the inspiration that Schmeling had derived from a personal phone conversation with Hitler. Foreign critics nevertheless continued to object: the British *Manchester Guardian,* which had earlier called for boycott, warned that the Germans were seizing ideological control of the Games; an "authoritarian government," it declared, was leading the Olympics into "yet another stage of transformation" where the "crowds and their emotions are part of the new phase."

The Germans prepared an elaborate stage. They spared no expense in building a comfortable Olympic Village, which would subsequently be converted into officers' quarters. Berlin itself got a face-lift; stores stocked up on scarce items such as eggs. Special hotel rates were set for Olympic visitors, and 900 students were trained as guides. An experimental television network was set up to transmit pictures of the competition to a paying audience around the city. (There had been some experimentation with television in Amsterdam, but Los Angeles had nothing of the sort in 1932.) An *Olympia-Zug* (Olympic train), consisting of four diesel trucks, toured the country to tell how the New Germany would host the youth of the world in a grand celebration of peace and friendship.

The choreographer of the Games' ceremonies was Carl Diem, who was General Secretary of the Organizing Committee. A member of the German sport establishment since 1912, he had made some outspoken nationalistic statements during the period of Germany's exclusion from the Olympics in the 1920s, insisting that Germany should not participate in any international competition so long as foreign troops stood on German soil. When the door for international competition reopened, he toned down his rhetoric and now created a new ritual for the Games. Probably his greatest innovation was the introduction of a torch relay to carry the Olympic flame by hand from Olympia in Greece to the site of the Games in Berlin.

At the opening ceremonies on August 1, Richard Strauss directed an orchestra of over 100 pieces together with a chorus of 3,000 voices. Coubertin, because of ill health, could not be present, but a phonograph record carried his welcoming speech over the loudspeaker system to the crowd. After the formal arrival of the Olympic flame, Spiridon Louis, the legendary victor of the first Olympic marathon in 1896, presented Hitler with an olive branch from the Sacred Grove of Zeus in Olympia. In the evening, 10,000 dancers performed a festival play written by Diem, and a chorus of 1,500 voices sang Schiller's "Ode to Joy" from Beethoven's *Ninth Symphony*. The German press reported Hitler's greeting to the athletes as a "world event of incomparable historical meaning" (Mandell 1971).

American writers usually center their discussion of the Berlin Games on the achievements of the black American track and field competitors, who won six gold medals, three silver, and two bronze. Jesse Owens took three individual gold medals and participated in a winning relay. Still, according to the traditional but unofficial system of reckoning team points, the Germans dominated the Games. Winning 33 gold medals, 26 silver, and 30 bronze, the Germans earned 573.7 points to the United States' 403.3. The American victories were concentrated in their traditional sports, track and field and men's and women's swimming, where they received about 70 percent of their points. But the German women outscored the American women in track and field, and the Germans did well in men's gymnastics, rowing, kayaks and canoes, equestrian sports, men's track and field, and weight lifting. The German athletes were obviously excited and aroused for the competition to do so well.

British commentators, who had previously expressed unhappiness with the enthusiasm and training of American athletes, now looked upon German methods as even more threatening. Describing a confrontation with German athletes in 1939, Jack Crump, an English sport administrator, exclaimed, "We had the impression that we were competing against a scientifically organized machine. For example, after each event the German athletes were taken into a room and their blood pressure and other tests taken. It was all very serious and highly planned and to my mind the antithesis of amateur sport" (1966). The ideas that Crump and others decried as Nazi mobilization of their athletes would in fact become common in sport a few years later.

The Americans also had their share of controversies. Administrators were not sure until almost the last minute they would have enough money to send the entire team: Brundage reportedly refused an offer of a hundred thousand dollars from a breakfast food company (Constable 1996). Once at sea, Brundage dismissed the swimmer Eleanor Holm from the team for having broken disciplinary rules. At the Games, the American track coach, Lawson Robertson, benched two Jewish sprinters, Marty Glickman and Sam Stoller, scheduled to run in the 400-meter relay in favor of two blacks, Owens and Ralph Metcalfe, who had already won medals. Rumor had it that the American officials, perhaps at Brundage's urging, had wanted to make a concession to the sensitivity of the Nazis. (The only American Jew to win a medal in any sport was Sam Balder, a basketball player, who had himself come to Berlin against the wishes of his employers, Universal Pictures in Los Angeles.) Brundage subsequently faced criticism from many quarters, but he argued that Glickman and Stoller had finished only fifth and sixth in the United States tryouts (American Olympic Committee n.d.).

As far as the Nazi government was concerned, the Games brought a period of international good feeling. Visitors left with memories of grand parties; in the words of the suspended Eleanor Holm, "It was a fantastic Olympics, spectacular! I had such fun!" (Constable 1996). According to Hitler's translator, Paul Schmidt (1949), all the Chancellor's conversations during the Summer Games were favorable. "These days seemed to me then," Schmidt later reminisced, "a sort of apotheosis for Hitler and the Third Reich." The Olympics, he declared, had been a "fantastic show and a production of the highest order, which all who experienced, whether they were friend or foe, will still remember today" (1949). The German government was satisfied with the results of the Games.

After the fact, the International Olympic Committee never had any doubts about its decision to hold the Games in Berlin. When the Germans nominated Coubertin for the Nobel Peace Prize, the Committee expressed delight, and it was overjoyed by the German announcement that profits from the Games would be used to continue archaeological excavations at Olympia. The Committee hailed the official German film of the Games, *Olympia*, made by Leni Riefenstahl, as a great achievement. In 1938, the IOC awarded the Olympic Coubertin Cup to the German sport organization *Kraft Durch Freude* (Strength Through Joy), and it barely acknowledged Lewald's resignation from its ranks.

For Avery Brundage the Berlin Games constituted his ticket into the ranks and soon the inner circle of the IOC. He joined the Committee as the replacement for Jahncke, the American who had advocated boycotting Berlin; then he almost immediately joined the IOC's Executive Board. He himself had no doubts about the success of the Berlin Games. "Germany," he told a German-American group in New York, "has progressed as a nation out of her discouragement of five years ago into a spirit of confidence in herself. . . . No country since ancient Greece has displayed a more truly national interest in the Olympic spirit than you find in Germany today" (WWA). In his official report on the Games, he was equally outspoken: "The Games of the XIth Olympiad at Berlin, Germany, was the greatest and most glorious athletic festival ever conducted—the most spectacular and colossal of all time" (American Olympic Committee, n.d.). This, he rhapsodized, had been "far more than a mere athletic spectacle." As to the opposition he had faced, he suggested that there had been some sort of conspiracy, saying that "probably more money was spent in this futile endeavor to keep the United States out of the Games than was needed to send the American team to Berlin."

Certainly, not all American sport authorities shared Brundage's enthusiasm. In 1937, with Mahoney again in charge, the AAU displayed renewed hostility toward the German authorities. In the summer of 1937, American athletes touring Europe demonstratively boycotted Germany, and Halt complained to Brundage that the Germans were saddened and displeased by this action. The American protests, however, had no impact on the policies and attitudes of the IOC.

Most contemporary observers tended to agree that the Nazi regime had produced a remarkable model for the political exploitation of international athletic competition in general and of the Olympic Games in particular. A report in *The New York Times* (August 16, 1936) spoke in rapturous terms: "Visitors will especially carry away from Berlin an impression of cleanliness, tidiness and orderliness unapproached by any other capital." The reporter then added, "But the strongest impression that visitors will carry away is the sense of having experienced exceeding courtesy, extreme consideration and hospitality organized to the last degree." The American correspondent William L. Shirer later wrote, "Hitler and his Nazi thugs had succeeded in making the XIth Olympiad the most colorful in history and, what was more important, had used the Olympics to fool the world into believing that Nazi Germany was a peaceful, civilized and contented nation" (Shirer 1941). As the Hungarian historian Laszlo Kun put it, "Pedantism and nostalgia, taken together, cannot obviate the fact that the Winter Games of 1936 in Garmisch-Partenkirchen and the Summer Games in Berlin were converted in Hitler's hands into a means of political manipulation" (1982). Thus, the Nazis had secured a firm, unique place for themselves in the history of the Olympic Games.

Did the Berlin Games constitute a perversion of the ideals of the Olympic Games? Probably only in the abstract, one might conclude. In practice, the forceful intervention of the government might be considered something new, but only as a matter of degree, not as a new feature of the Games. In 1896, for example, the Greek government had understood the usefulness of harnessing the appeal of this type of athletic competition; the Belgians and the Allied Powers had certainly used the Antwerp Games for their own purposes. Yet, the hopes of IOC leaders that the Games might have a civilizing influence on Nazi racial policies were fanciful, because the Nazis exploited the Games for their own uses. Once the Games were over, Olympic officials ignored the policies of the German government, even when it brought about the destruction of Jewish communities throughout Europe, and Olympic enthusiasts worked to incorporate their positive memories of Berlin into their own networks of myths.

Part II

The Brundage Era

Baillet-Latour, Brundage, and Edstrøm met in Chicago in 1935 when Baillet-Latour passed through on a fact-finding trip to Tokyo. In 1936 the IOC awarded the 1940 Games to Tokyo, but the outbreak of the Second World War suspended the Games for twelve years.

Avery Brundage served as President of the IOC for 20 years, from 1952 to 1972, but the "Brundage Era" actually began 20 year earlier, during the preparations for the Berlin Games in 1936. Brundage had been a key figure, if not the definitive one, in the Americans' decision to attend the Games in Berlin despite the calls for boycott. For this the IOC rewarded him with membership and then added him to the Executive Board, the IOC's own inner circle. When, after the Berlin Games, German members of the IOC, carrying out the will of their government in Berlin, played a major role in the Committee's work, Brundage seemed accommodating toward them, welcoming their declarations of belief in the power and significance of sport.

In September 1939, war returned to Europe and again interrupted the Olympic Games. After Nazi Germany and the Soviet Union had signed a nonaggression pact in August 1939, Germany attacked Poland. The Soviet Union subsequently sent troops to occupy Eastern Poland, and by the late summer of 1940, the political mosaic of European states had changed drastically. Germany and the Soviet Union had divided Poland. Germany had broken up Czechoslovakia and occupied Denmark and Norway. German troops stood as conquerors in Paris. The Soviet Union had occupied and annexed the Baltic republics of Latvia, Lithuania, and Estonia and had forced Romania to surrender territory. In June 1941, German troops attacked the Soviet Union, and only after another four years of conflict could the "Grand Alliance," as Winston Churchill called the cooperation of Great Britain, the United States, and the USSR, defeat the German-led Axis Powers. At war's end, much of Europe was in ruins, millions had died as a result of the conflict—including six million Jews—and the Soviet Union stood as the strongest state in Europe.

There was no space for the Olympic Games in this titanic clash, and no Games were held in 1940 or 1944. During the war, while the Germans dominated the continent, authorities in Berlin gave signs of wanting to take over the Olympic structure, but after the German surrender in 1945, the IOC painfully reassembled itself without its German component. As at Antwerp in 1920, there could be no talk of inviting the Germans to the revival of the Games in 1948, this time because the celebration was to take place in the victorious Allied capital of London, which had undergone considerable devastation from German bombs.

Avery Brundage had been a rising star in the Olympic realm in the 1930s, and he played a major role in reconstructing the Olympic apparatus after the war. In 1946, the reconstituted IOC elected him as its Vice President. In 1952, he became IOC President, and, as mentioned, he held that post for the next 20 years, leading the Olympic Games through the maelstrom of Cold War politics and tensions.

Brundage did not draw personal profit from his work for the Olympic Committee; in fact, the post cost him an estimated $75,000 a year out of his own pocket. He dedicated himself to his own ideals of international sport, concepts that he could not always clearly articulate himself. Sport for him constituted an activity more uplifting than crude politics, and it seemed to promise uplifting spiritual guidance. Moreover, sport, he believed, offered a means of resolving political, ideological, and ethnic conflicts. He welcomed the cooperation of those who seemed to endorse his sentiments and fought bitterly against those who criticized him.

Brundage's passions and concerns displayed themselves perhaps most graphically in his dealings with the Soviet Union. Essentially an ally of Nazi Germany in 1939-1940, the Soviet Union had then played a major role in the destruction of Hitler's regime, and it emerged from the conflict as one of the world's two superpowers. For the members of the IOC, the key question was "What would the Soviet attitude toward the Olympic Games be?" Between the wars, the IOC had ignored the USSR, but now IOC leaders had to win its cooperation if they wanted their organization to encompass the entire world. But how should they go about it? What should they do?

Brundage, who wanted to help the Germans return to the Games, deeply resented the Soviets' past scorn for the Olympic Games. He remembered only too well the Soviet efforts to discredit the Los Angeles Games and their support for the unsuccessful Counter-Olympics in Barcelona. Nevertheless, in accordance with his belief in international sport, he went along with the efforts of his colleagues to bring the Soviet Union into the Olympic family.

Soviet officials, however, responded coolly to invitations to open talks on joining the Games, refusing to be put in the position of suppliants, but finally in 1951, the IOC welcomed the USSR and installed a Soviet representative as one of its members. In the framework of the Games, athletic competition became one of the most visible battlegrounds of the Cold War, the Great Powers' ideological and political struggle for power and influence around the world. The role of the Nazis in the IOC in the 1930s had given its members a taste of ideological conflict. In the 1950s, as Brundage took over the Committee's leadership, the ideological conflict promised to be both sharper and more enduring.

Even so, Brundage struggled to ignore the ideological and political struggles of the Cold War, vainly arguing the Olympic Games did not constitute a competition between states, but journalists and national team leaders alike ignored his protestations. The competition, to be sure, focused more clearly on the Summer Games than the Winter Games, perhaps because the United States traditionally did not fare as well in the Winter Games. Brundage nevertheless had to contend with Great Power politics on almost a daily basis.

Then the decolonization of Africa in the 1950s and 1960s brought a flood of new members to the Olympic family and with them new tests for the IOC. Most leaders of the new states chose to participate in the Olympics, but the Games of the Newly Emerging Forces, GANEFO, held in 1963, briefly posed a challenge to the appeal of the Olympics in the Third World. Even so, by the end of the 1960s, strengthened by the money accruing from the sale of television rights, the IOC had more trouble with its internal squabbles over the distribution of that money than it had from outside challenges.

Brundage insisted sport competition must be free of political considerations, but frequently he went on to argue that Olympic officials such as himself understood the issues and problems of world peace better than the diplomats did. He spoke of keeping the Olympic Games independent of the passions of the Cold War, and he steadfastly refused to put his Games at the service of one or the other side. For example, Americans criticized him for his readiness to accept a "two-Chinas" policy. Although he openly admired the Soviets' program for mass physical culture, he steadfastly rejected Soviet proposals to reform the Olympic structure.

Many of Brundage's critics considered him outdated. They ridiculed his almost fanatical dedication to the idea of "amateur" athletic competition even as the athletes continued to set world records and the IOC began collecting revenues from the sale of television rights to the Games. His authoritarian practices in directing the IOC frequently angered even his sympathizers. Yet, he did much to maintain the Games' identity in the midst of the Cold War.

One nagging question for even his most avid supporters is whether Brundage stayed in office for too long—shouldn't he have retired in 1968 at the latest? He won reelection in 1968 only with considerable difficulty, and that at the cost of promising his retirement in 1972. By the time of the Munich Games of 1972, battles over apartheid in Africa, struggles over the Rhodesian question, continuing conflict with commercialism in the Winter Games, increasing intrusion of political protests into his beloved Games, and finally the terrorist action and killing of the Israeli athletes in Munich all cost him heavily. No matter how much he tried to prove the contrary, he was unable to control the further development of the Olympic Games.

The Munich Games constituted a sad ending to Brundage's years of dedication and effort on behalf of the Olympics. He had been a member of the IOC for 36 years. His opponents insisted that at best he had outlived his time; certainly, he was out of tune with the imperatives of the modern world. His supporters argued he had served the Olympic Movement well in keeping it out of the focus of the Cold War and the rivalry between the superpowers of the world, but even his most ardent sympathizers had trouble presenting him in a positive light at the time of his retirement. Still, for better or worse, he left his mark on the Games, and his successors inherited a lively and growing organization, albeit one troubled by outside threats and internal dissension.

Chapter 5

Another War

© Archive Photos

The London Games (1948) tried to avoid the nationalistic pageantry of the Berlin Games (1936), but accepted certain ceremonial innovations that the Germans had created. Like the Antwerp Games (1920), however, this was a celebration of the victors of the recent war.

By the late 1930s, the Olympic Games were rapidly growing in importance as an arena of international politics. The Games were reaching out to the world, and the world was coming to the Games, which also meant sharing in the destruction and disruption of war. When Baillet-Latour, speaking over a worldwide radio hookup through the Columbia Broadcasting System, announced that the IOC had chosen Tokyo as the site for the 1940 Games, Committee members could not know that world conflict would prevent them from celebrating another Olympic Games for more than a decade and that in the midst of wartime devastation, they would lose their President.

The choice of Tokyo as the host for 1940 itself symbolized both the growth of the Games and their growing importance in international affairs. London had been a competitor for the 1936 Games and had at first advanced its candidacy again for 1940. The British Foreign Office, however, hoped to win the goodwill of the Japanese, so London then withdrew its candidacy, saying that it would hold back and apply only for the 1944 Games. German authorities in turn looked warily at this diplomatic maneuvering, which they suspected was aimed against them. In a few years, however, Tokyo and London were at war with each other.

The Japanese were the first Asian nation to become an Olympic power (table 5.1). Like many other non-European nations, they chose to participate in this international sport festival, in spite of their own rich tradition of native sports. The Japanese Olympic Committee came into being in 1911; the Japanese won their first medals at Antwerp and their first gold medals at Amsterdam. In the 1930s, Japan emerged as a major swimming power, amassing more points in men's events than the

Table 5.1

Japan's Growth as an Olympic Power

		Points Rank	Medals
1912	Stockholm		Failed to place in top six in any event
1920	Antwerp	17	2 silver medals in tennis
1924	Paris	21	1 bronze medal
1928	Amsterdam	16	2 gold, 2 bronze
1932	Los Angeles	6	7 gold, 7 silver, 4 bronze
1936	Berlin	7	6 gold, 4 silver, 8 bronze

Khavin 1979, p. 525.

Americans did in Los Angeles (72-62) and barely trailing the Americans in Berlin (68-71). In Los Angeles, the Japanese ranked sixth in the unofficial point count, in Berlin, seventh.

As the first Asian host of the Olympic Games, the Japanese promised the best possible hospitality. "Europe should find time," said a Japanese spokesperson in Berlin, "for the journey that the countries outside Europe make at each Olympic Games."

Tokyo organizers made lavish promises, but they soon discovered that they could not live up to them. Even before the start of the European war in 1939, the Japanese had to withdraw their commitment. In 1937, when the Japanese invaded China, a chorus of voices demanded that the IOC withdraw its award to Tokyo, but the IOC refused to consider such a step, insisting that politics and sport must be kept separate. As late as January 1938, despite rumors that the Japanese military wanted to cancel the Games, the Tokyo Organizing Committee insisted it would fulfill its promises. On July 16, 1938, the Tokyo Olympic Committee finally gave up; Japan surrendered both the Winter and the Summer Games: "Although the [Japanese] government has been desirous of holding the Olympic Games, there seems to be no alternative but to forfeit the right to celebrate the XIIth Olympic Games to be held in Tokyo under the present circumstances when the nation is confronted with the necessity of requiring both spiritual and material mobilization in order to realize the ultimate object of the present incident" (Tokyo Organizing Committee 1940). Having delivered this message to the IOC, the Japanese representative resigned from the Committee.

The IOC thereupon accepted an invitation to come to Helsinki for the Summer Games, but the Winter Games presented a more difficult problem. The Norwegians had already offered Oslo as an alternative site for the 1940 Winter Games even before the Japanese had withdrawn their invitation, and at first the IOC wavered between choosing Oslo or St. Moritz. Eventually talks failed with both cities, and meeting in London in 1939, the IOC agreed to give the Winter Games back to Garmisch-Partenkirchen, the host of the 1936 Games.

The decision to return to Germany reflected the very strong position of the three German members of the IOC. The senior German member was Adolf Friedrich zu Mecklenburg, a relative of the Queen of the Netherlands. Officially designated as a Dutch representative, Mecklenburg would play a key role in providing the continuity for reconstructing the German Olympic Committee after 1945. The second German member was Karl Ritter von Halt, who became the head of all German sport. Arrested by occupying Soviet forces in 1945, he made his way to West Germany in 1950 and succeeded Mecklenburg as the President of the German NOC, albeit not without controversy. The third German member of the IOC in the late

1930s was General Walter von Reichenau, who had played a major role in the building of the Olympic Village in 1936. Named to the IOC as Lewald's replacement in 1938, he died in 1942 on the Russian front.

The German contingent in the IOC assumed the role of "Patron of the Olympic Movement": As mentioned, they dedicated the "profits" of the Berlin Games to the reconstruction of Olympic sites in Greece; and upon hearing that Coubertin, now living in isolated retirement in Switzerland, was impoverished, they sent him a check for 10,000 RM. (Norway and Sweden also sent Coubertin financial aid.) The Games' founder, to be sure, no longer played any influential role in Olympic politics, but his image was still important. (After his death in September 1937, his heart was removed and sent to be buried at Olympia in accordance with his wishes.) For the Germans, association with Coubertin constituted a major propaganda asset.

Despite the Germans' position of strength, however, the decision to award the 1940 Winter Games to Garmisch-Partenkirchen raised a number of delicate political problems: Czechoslovakia had vanished from maps of Europe; Austria was now a part of the Third Reich; and tensions were rising on the German-Polish frontier. Yet Halt and Reichenau, who were presumably in personal contact with Hitler, promised to permit Czechoslovakia, which officially did not exist but which had a rich Olympic tradition, to have its own athletes at the Winter Games. But all this became moot in November 1939 when the German Organizing Committee finally gave up its commission to stage the Winter Games, ending this peculiar story. When the Olympic Games resumed in 1948, there was no trace left of the Germans' erstwhile position in the IOC.

Helsinki clung to tenuous hopes for holding the Summer Games into the spring of 1940. The Finns tried to ignore the explosion of conflict in

---

Letter From Sigfrid Edstrøm to Avery Brundage, March 27, 1940:

Have been in connection with Baillet-Latour about the Ol-Games in Finland. The Finns wish to hold them if USA will participate. How do you feel about it? There are good ocean liners plying between N.Y. and Swedish and Norwegian ports and there are even American steamers going to Bergen. They are however only for a limited number of passengers.

Everything prepared for the Games in Helsingfors is in great order—thus technically the Games can be held....

They would be a great impetus for Finland and of great help to the country. Therefore we should give the Finns this assistance. Polignac and Aberdare are against the Games on account of the war. France and England would not compete. But Germany will.

Brundage Archive, University of Illinois.

Eastern Europe when the Nazis invaded Poland in the fall of 1939, but then the Soviet Union, at this point virtually an ally of Germany, sent its troops into Finland in the winter of 1939-1940. In this predicament, the Olympic Games represented a means of winning international attention. Thus, Finnish authorities insisted the Games would go on, they were cutting back on expenses for the Games, and as late as March 1940 they were still printing tickets. In April 1940, however, they finally admitted they would have to yield; and the Olympics became dormant for the duration of the war.

World War II forced the general suspension of international sport competition in Europe, although some regional competitions took place in other parts of the world. The International Olympic Committee, dominated by Europeans, ceased to function; its members generally rallied to the flags of their respective nations. Each warring power, to be sure, developed its own domestic sport program. In the United States, the Roosevelt administration gave its blessings to the continuation of professional baseball, and the colleges maintained their athletic programs with 16-year-olds and service personnel on special assignments. The Soviet government held no national championships, but it recognized that physical training helped the people fight and work and that broadcasting local soccer matches could be good for public morale. England organized "Special Cup" competitions for service soccer teams. Both the Germans and the Japanese, in contrast, staged national athletic competitions they advertised as filling the void left by the breakdown of traditional international gatherings.

The workers' sports internationals, the RSI and the SWSI, fared no better. In 1937, the two internationals cooperated in staging a Workers' Olympiad in Antwerp, which was dominated by athletes from the Soviet Union. This left some Socialists muttering darkly about professionalism in Soviet athletics, but the two internationals could not follow up this successful gathering. They were soon forgotten as war swept across Europe, and unlike the Olympics, they could not reestablish themselves in the postwar world.

The IOC suffered a wartime loss at the very core of its structure: its President, Henri Baillet-Latour, died in 1942. The war had brought only grief to Baillet-Latour. In 1940, German troops overran his native Belgium for the second time in just over a quarter of a century, and he found himself isolated in occupied Brussels, unable to communicate with his former colleagues outside of the German sphere of control. In 1941, he received word that his son, an air attaché in the Belgian embassy in Washington, had died in a plane crash. The IOC had no possibility of meeting to consider replacing Baillet-Latour, but in any case, he had already lost control of the scattered pieces of the Olympic Movement.

Baillet-Latour had provided leadership of a very different sort from Coubertin's: He could never play the forceful, creative role that Coubertin had, although he won considerable respect for his administrative abilities and especially for his negotiations with Hitler. When he was being led into his celebrated first meeting with the German Chancellor in November 1935, he was allegedly told he should not discuss the "Jewish problem" and he should not smoke. To show his independence, once seated, he immediately lit up a cigar, declaring, "In such talks I am always accustomed to smoke" (Mandell 1971). Baillet-Latour insisted Hitler had to accept all Olympic regulations and not insult any particular group. At the Games themselves, Baillet-Latour persuaded Hitler not to congratulate German victors publicly, arguing that he would have to congratulate all if he insisted on congratulating any.

Throughout the 1930s, Baillet-Latour also had to deal continuously with the twin problems of professionalism and commercialism. The arguments over broken-time payments to soccer players constituted only the tip of the commercial iceberg; athletes were finding increasing opportunities to convert Olympic victories into cash profits. Athletes like the figure skater Sonja Henie or the swimmers Johnny Weissmuller and Eleanor Holm enjoyed lucrative film careers. When sanctions struck at popular national heroes, like Paavo Nurmi of Finland, the IOC faced sharp criticism, and Baillet-Latour had found it difficult to plug the holes in the dike of "amateurism."

Meanwhile, other problems were slowly appearing on the horizon. Medical questions were dragging the deliberations of the IOC into previously unconsidered areas. For example, a report by the Belgian Medical Society for Physical Education and Sports in 1937 expressed grave concern about the use of stimulants by cyclists. The IOC began to worry about the use of performance-enhancing medication, but they had little understanding of such practices by the athletes and their coaches. A generation later, the group would learn of problems that it had not even suspected in the 1930s. Stanislawa Walasiewicz of Poland won a gold medal in the 100-meter sprint in 1932 and a silver medal in the same event in 1936. Known as Stella Walsh, she won over 40 United States titles. In 1946, she again represented Poland at the European championships in Oslo, but when she died in the early 1980s, medical examination of her body raised questions as to whether she should not have been considered a man. Another competitor in 1936, the German Dora Rantjen, who took sixth place in the women's high jump, was discovered living as a man in Hamburg in the 1950s. Baillet-Latour had probably had no inkling of such problems.

Historians have generally paid special attention to Baillet-Latour's dealings with the IFs; he made cautious concessions to assure their

Stella Walsh

After Stella Walsh's death in 1981, an autopsy revealed what were called "genetic anomalies." The following is a commentary written soon thereafter by a member of the IOC Medical Commission:

> In cases of sexual differentiation problems, care must be taken for the result to be kept secret, and the athlete prevented from participating in a competition for which unfortunately because of the anomaly with which she has been born, she is ineligible.... The athlete Stella Walsh took part in the competitions in 1932 and 1936. At that time, cases of hermaphroditism were scarcely known from the medical point of view....
>
> Returning to the unfortunate case of Stella Walsh, it is obvious that she would not have been allowed to participate nowadays, since she would have undergone and failed the femininity control of the IOC's Medical Commission.

Eduardo Hay, "The Stella Walsh Case," *Olympic Review*, 1981, pp. 221-222.

cooperation. To some critics he seemed to be abandoning the powers that Coubertin had carefully reserved for the IOC and, more importantly, for the IOC's Executive Board and its President. Baillet-Latour, however, better represented the spirit of the '20s and '30s when opportunities for athletic activity were significantly broader than they had been in the elite years before World War I. Overall, his style of administration was considerably more open and democratic than Coubertin's had been. Coubertin had thought of himself as the helmsman, the captain of the ship, with the obligation of charting the way for others. Baillet-Latour, however, would not be around for the test of reviving the Games after a war as Coubertin had done in 1920.

Stepping into Baillet-Latour's shoes in this time of confusion was a Swede, J. Sigfrid Edstrøm, who directed the Olympic Games in Stockholm in 1912. Born in 1870, Edstrøm had worked in his youth as an electrical engineer in both Switzerland and in the United States. A world class sprinter in the early 1890s, he founded and then became President of the IAAF. He became a member of the IOC in 1920, officially the Committee's 101st member, and the following year Coubertin invited him to join the Executive Board. From 1920 to 1936, he was the leader of the Swedish delegation to each Olympic Games. As Vice President of the IOC since 1931, he seemed the logical person to become Acting President until some formal institutional action could be taken, but especially important was his nationality. Since Sweden maintained its neutrality throughout the war, Edstrøm, as a well-known businessman, enjoyed the freedom of corresponding with individuals in both warring camps and even of visiting both Germany and the United States during the war.

At heart Edstrøm was a pacifist who believed that sport could offer the world a new and better moral code. When the war began, he tried to organize a petition summoning athletes throughout the world to refuse to take up arms, but he found little support. Nevertheless, he maintained his friendships in both camps. When von Tschammer und Osten, the Nazi sport leader, died in 1943, Edstrøm lamented, "He was in many ways a splendid and nice man" (Brundage Archive). Edstrøm provided a fundamental link of continuity for the IOC in the midst of destruction, serving as a center for communications between otherwise hostile parties and in turn putting out periodical bulletins summarizing sport news from around the world.

At the same time, Edstrøm had to deal with German efforts to take over key parts of the Olympic movement. When the Germans first moved into Belgium, Halt, who was Edstrøm's main contact in the lands under German control, assured the Swede that Baillet-Latour was safe and well and that he, Halt, would look after the Belgian. In another move, Carl Diem attempted to take control of Olympic headquarters in Lausanne, apparently with the intention of moving them to Berlin. "I hid the most important documents in the cellar," the IOC secretary Madame L. Zanchi later told John Lucas, "and convinced the community that Diem was a spy. I alerted Mr. Edstrøm of Sweden" (Lucas 1980). In 1942, Edstrøm visited Switzerland and put the IOC's archives in a bank vault. Short of a complete triumph by Nazi Germany in the war, Diem and Halt could not replace Edstrøm.

Edstrøm's contact in the United States was Avery Brundage. In the 1930s Brundage, justifiably, was considered friendly to the Germans. When war threatened, he called the impending conflict the "suicide of a culture," and he warned that the United States was showing too much favor toward the English and the French. Japan and Germany, he complained, had been needlessly insulted on "every possible occasion by our public officials" (Guttmann 1984). Once the war in Europe had begun, he took an isolationist and somewhat pacifist position (Guttmann 1984). In 1944, he angered many people by suggesting that when war ended and the Olympic Games resumed, the Germans and the Japanese should take part. He then insisted he had been misquoted: "All I said was that if a country is politically and commercially recognized by this government, I supposed naturally, it will be recognized athletically as well." But his statement was not to be forgotten. With his fanatical dedication to the Olympic Games, compounded by his ideological naiveté, Brundage was to remain a controversial figure in peace, war, and Cold War.

When the war finally ground to its end in the summer of 1945, Edstrøm, still officially only the Vice President of the IOC, began to pull the shattered pieces of the International Olympic Committee back together again. On August 21, 1945, one short week after V-J Day, he met in London with Brundage and Lord Aberdare, a British member of the IOC since 1929. The three men called themselves the Executive Board of the IOC. Agreeing that the Olympic Games should resume in 1948, they decided to award them to London and then began contacting the other surviving members of the IOC in order to gain ratification of their decision.

As the IOC slowly reassembled, the members found their ranks severely depleted. Some members, like Reichenau, had died fighting; Baillet-Latour had died of more or less natural causes. The Polish and Hungarian representatives were now stateless, uprooted by the new order in their homelands. Brundage and Edstrøm were personally distressed by the news that the Soviets had arrested Halt. Despite these losses, the Executive Board of the IOC brought the remnants of the group back together and restructured it to meet the new demands of the postwar world. In September 1946, the reconstituted IOC met in Lausanne to elect Edstrøm President. With Edstrøm's strong support, Brundage became Vice President.

Edstrøm's move to the office of the presidency resulted in his surrendering his post as head of the IAAF, and Lord Burghley succeeded him there. The English welcomed this change; unlike Brundage, they resented some of Edstrøm's actions during the war, considering him to have been too friendly toward the Germans. "The feeling existed amongst most of the Allied Countries," wrote Jack Crump, "that during the war period the association between the IAAF headquarters and the Nazi-controlled German Federation had been less neutral than Sweden's position in the international set-up justified" (1966). Certainly, British track and field officials thought it high time that Edstrøm surrender his post in the IAAF.

Meeting in September 1946, the IOC also approved the decision to stage the Games of the XIVth Olympiad in London in 1948. Spokespersons liked to say this constituted simply a renewal of a tentative prewar agreement to give London the Games in 1944—not simply another example of the war victors' taking the spoils. (Edstrøm personally rejected Brundage's proposal that the Games be awarded to Los Angeles.) The IOC awarded the Winter Games of 1948 to St. Moritz. The Swiss, neutral during the war, were eager to revive their tourist trade. The IOC was preparing for business as usual.

The preparations for both the Winter and the Summer Games of 1948 went ahead surprisingly well, considering the ravages of war. When the Winter Games opened in St. Moritz on January 30, 1948, 713 athletes were present, as compared to 491 in 1928, when the Games were last held in this Swiss resort. There were also 10 times as many journalists and correspondents covering the Games as there had been in 1928. As evidence of the ravages of war, however, the Norwegians, who had endured Nazi occupation during the war, were dethroned as Nordic skiing champions, and the Swedes, who had remained neutral in the war, swept the medals in that sport. The Norwegians, however, still dominated the speed skating.

The Games experienced a particularly heated jurisdictional controversy concerning the United States hockey team or, in this case, one should say "teams." Two American hockey teams showed up in St. Moritz, each claiming to represent the United States. In the confusion, which had been brewing for several years, one team, formed by the AAU, had the certification of the American Olympic Committee. The other, formed by a group called the Amateur Hockey Association (AHA), had the certification of the International Ice Hockey Federation. The Swiss Organizing Committee, wanting to keep its peace with the international federation, recognized its authority; but the IOC hemmed and hawed before finally ruling the AHA team ineligible for awards.

The issue was not soon forgotten; in the long run, the AHA won, later becoming the Amateur Hockey Association of the United States (AHAUS). At the height of the controversy, Edstrøm wanted to compromise, but Brundage vigorously backed the AAU. As far as Brundage was concerned, the issue concerned the "purity of the Games." He considered his opponents to be engaging in politics and legalistic quibbling, and he even threatened to pull the American athletes out of the Games. The dispute stuck in Brundage's craw for years; in his official report on the Games, he argued that hockey should be dropped from the Olympic program "until

---

London in 1948

There was considerable resentment among the English about the sacrifices demanded by the effort to host the 1948 Games:

> Sane opinion will marvel at the colossal thickness of hide which permits its owners, at this time of crisis in the nation's serious affairs, to indulge in grandiose and luxurious schemes for an international weight-lifting and basketball jamboree. . . . A people which had its housing program and its food imports cut and which is preparing for a winter battle of survival may be forgiven for thinking that a full year of expensive preparations for the reception of an army of foreign athletes verges on the borders of the excessive. It is still not too late for invitations, in view of altered conditions, to be politely withdrawn.

London Evening Standard (Brundage Archive, University of Illinois).

---

there is an international housecleaning in this sport" (Guttmann 1984). Although others did not share Brundage's sense of urgency—Europeans tended to consider this "a purely internal American conflict" (*Olympia* 1948)—Brundage was launching a running conflict that would haunt the Winter Olympics for a quarter of a century.

The London Games of the summer of 1948 promised to be controversial in their own way. Not the least was the question of London's capacity even for hosting its athletic visitors. Ignoring the destruction of World War II, the IOC declared the English already had all the necessary construction in place before the war. In fact, the city was a shambles, and the British economy faced hard winters in the latter 1940s. Walter Jewell, an English sport official, recommended the Olympics be put off for 10 years. Jack Crump, another official, declared, "I personally thought it would be no bad thing to wait until 1952" (1966). Meanwhile, the Americans offered to provide food especially for the Games, but the British would have none of it. Lord Burghley served as President of the London Organizing Committee, and by anyone's standards he did a remarkable job.

Yet, the London Organizing Committee worked on, and the Games drew over 4,000 athletes from 59 countries (table 5.2). The British made this a Spartan festival, putting up no new stadiums and not even constructing an Olympic Village. Political questions, reflecting the political upheavals and disruptions left by the war, abounded, but somehow they did not threaten the basic flow of the Games. Arab states, objecting to the existence of the new state of Israel, threatened to boycott the Games if Israel should be admitted. The IOC avoided a crisis by deciding it had not yet recognized an NOC in Israel and therefore the Israelis could not attend.

Table 5.2

The Summer Olympic Games in the Brundage Era

		Sports	Nations	Male Competitors	Female Competitors
1948	London	17	59	3,714	385
1952	Helsinki	17	69	4,407	518
1956	Melbourne	17	67	2,958	384
1960	Rome	17	83	4,738	610
1964	Tokyo	19	93	4,457	683
1968	Mexico City	18	112	4,750	781
1972	Munich	21	122	5,848	1,299

Like Antwerp, this was again an Olympics of the western victors. The London Organizing Committee sent invitations to neither the Germans nor the Soviets; neither state had an NOC recognized by the International Olympic Committee. In the case of the Germans, the members of the IOC saw no problem with this arrangement as Germany had lost the war. The Soviet Union, however, presented a different problem. After being attacked by Germany in 1941, the Soviet Union had played a major role in crushing Nazi Germany. IOC leaders had expected the Soviets to apply to come to London. When Moscow remained silent, the members of the IOC, who did not feel ready to deal with the Soviets, breathed deeply in relief and looked to other problems. The IOC rejected out of hand the appeals of Eastern European emigrés, displaced by the upheavals in their homelands, for permission to compete in the Games as stateless persons. It would only admit athletes certified by recognized NOCs as citizens of their respective states.

In all, despite all the dark clouds, which included bad weather, the London Games were successful. Indeed, once begun, the Games again worked their magic. In the Games' rituals, the organizers paid silent tribute to the Berlin Olympics as they chose to keep the Germans' innovation of a torch relay from Greece and even took over the Nazis' call "I summon the youth of the world." They discreetly dropped the traditional Olympic salute, however, because it looked disturbingly like the Nazi salute. The athletes enjoyed the festival in their own ways: The French brought their own wine, the Americans, their own ice cream. The Italians, the only former Axis Power to attend the Games, exchanged some of their pasta and wine for quarters of Argentine beef, and both sides were happy. The United States dominated the competition, winning 38 gold medals and earning 70 percent of its 548 points in track and field, men's and women's swimming and diving, and weight lifting.

Letter From Otto Mayer, Chancellor of the IOC, to Tufton Beamish, of the Council of Europe, September 2, 1952:

It is quite correct that the first fundamental principle of our Charter is that the Olympic Games are held every four years and shall assemble amateurs of all Nations. . . .

If you consider this rule, you will find out that we speak about amateurs OF A NATION. By saying so, we mean that an athlete, to be able to take part in the Games, MUST be member of a National Sports Organisation, as well as he must be citizen of the country concerned. This is unfortunately not the fact with the refugees and exiled athletes.

Brundage Archive, University of Illinois.

Sweden placed a distant second, and France was third in the unofficial point count.

The individual star of the Games was a Dutch housewife, Fanny Blankers-Koen, who won gold medals in the 100- and 200-meter sprints, in the 80-meter hurdles, and also as a member of the winning relay team. Acclaimed as the "Queen of the Olympic Games, Wembley 1948," she imparted a new glamour and cachet to the women's competition, even though many male observers still considered women's events a secondary sideshow. A columnist for *The New York Times,* Arthur Daley, argued that women's events had no place in the modern Games—there had been no women's events in the ancient Games.

The athletes put up with the hardships of life in the British capital with generally good cheer and understanding, and the Olympic Games seemed to have regained and even strengthened their place in the sphere of international cultural relations. Gustavus Kirby, the head of the American contingent, epitomized the good feeling by announcing, "In no Olympic Games have we had a display of better sportsmanship or more camaraderie. We thank Great Britain for a fine display and we want to express to the world our appreciation of the courtesy, fine feeling, and international goodwill which the games brought to us at Wembley last week" (Crump 1966).

Once the Games had ended, the English looked back on them with pride. Jack Crump, the manager of the British Olympic team, had been one of the doubters about the feasibility of hosting the 1948 Games, but once the Games had finished, he was of a different mind: "When one looks back on the years of 1947 and 1948," he wrote, "a sense of really deep pride arises in the genius which we possess in this country for organized improvisation" (1966).

Although the leaders of the IOC had successfully brought their organization through the disruptions of war and the uncertainties of succession, more storm clouds remained on the horizon. The question of Germany's reentry into the Games promised considerable controversy, and the selection of Helsinki, Finland for the 1952 Summer Games served to remind everyone that the question of Soviet participation in the Games remained open. Indeed, Soviet observers had been very visible at the London Games, carrying cameras with them everywhere. The IOC would have to make its own peace with the Soviet Union before the Helsinki Games.

Chapter 6

Entry of the Soviets

The IOC had banned distance runner Paavo Nurmi at the Los Angeles Games (1932) for professionalism, but at Helsinki (1952), the Finns showed that they had neither forgotten nor forgiven as they gave Nurmi the honor of carrying the Olympic torch into the stadium.

Since the chaotic days at the end of World War I, the Soviet state had stood apart from the Olympic family, criticizing the Games as a plaything of international capitalism and expressing scorn for the 19th-century British ideal of the gentleman "amateur." The IOC, for its part, displayed little interest in having Soviet athletes participate in the Olympic Games throughout the 1920s and 1930s. Although the Soviets did indeed have some outstanding athletes, the IOC had not believed that the presence of Soviet competitors would add to the character or popularity of the Games. Thus, the two parties lived in isolation from each other, with the Soviets showing more interest in ridiculing Olympic ideals than the IOC did in responding to the attacks.

World War II changed this relationship drastically. Besides forcing the cancellation of the scheduled Games of 1940 and 1944, the war ravaged Europe, brought wholesale destruction to Germany, and elevated the Soviet Union and the United States to a confrontation as superpowers. The IOC had traditionally functioned as a West European and North American organization, gradually admitting new forces into its ranks on its own terms. Now, like other international organizations, the leaders of the IOC had to adjust their practices to accommodate the new balance of power in the world; this meant first of all reaching agreement with the Soviet Union.

Edstrøm and Brundage, who were shaping the IOC's policies at this time, distrusted the giant Eastern European superpower, but they both recognized they could no longer ignore it. Edstrøm believed the Soviet Red Army, which he had called "barbarian" in 1939 at the time of the Soviet-Finnish war, posed a serious threat to the security of Western Europe, but he also believed that international sport organizations should include the Soviet Union. For his part, Brundage could not forgive the Soviets their campaigns against the Los Angeles and Berlin Olympics; nevertheless, he agreed that the IAAF and the IOC had to open its doors to the Russians, albeit carefully.

In October 1945, Edstrøm, in the name of the IAAF, invited the Soviet Union to join its ranks. Membership in this organization constituted a key step in being admitted to the Olympic family, because the IAAF was the strongest and most important of the sport federations participating in the Olympic Games. The IAAF, however, normally entertained applications; it did not send out invitations. Edstrøm and Brundage, to be sure, had no idea what the Soviet response might be: As Brundage put it, the federation had "extended the hand of friendship," but the Soviets might feel unprepared, and they might not care for "fraternization with athletes of other nations." Brundage, for one, would seem to have been hoping that the Soviet authorities would not accept the invitation.

Soviet track and field officials did not immediately respond to Edstrøm's overture. In any case, the issue was not in their power to decide. In the centralized Soviet party-state, the Communist Party, and at this time ultimately Josef V. Stalin, controlled all decisions in international affairs. For party ideologists, mass sport served the purpose of producing better soldiers and workers for the state, while elite sport heralded the triumphs of the system. Even before Edstrøm's invitation arrived, Soviet officials announced a new system of cash rewards for athletes, ranging up to 15,000 rubles for breaking a national record and up to 25,000 rubles for breaking a world record. They also announced the establishment of special sport schools aimed at producing highly qualified athletes. The Olympic rules on amateurism seemed of no concern to them, and they certainly did not care about the IOC's disapproval of a government's, much less a party's, directing a country's athletic program. Thus, the IOC and the IAAF had to wait their turns while Stalin and other Soviet leaders defined their goals regarding Olympic competition.

Soviet soccer officials, in contrast, responded positively to an invitation to send a soccer team to England. Soviet historians subsequently insisted this tour opened the "window to the West," which the western powers had attempted to keep closed. The Soviet team, which the Soviets called a "club team," but which was in fact more of a national team, did well: After tying Chelsea 3-3, the Soviet team defeated Cardiff 10-1, Arsenal 3-2, and tied the Glasgow Rangers 2-2, for a record of two wins and two ties. This, the Soviets argued, showed that Soviet soccer had surpassed the level of play in the homeland of the sport (Peppard and Riordan 1993). Apparently their encounter with British culture and cuisine was more difficult than their encounters with British soccer, however: When the Soviet players returned home, they complained the English had failed to offer them flowers and had tried to poison them. At any rate, Soviet officials knew their soccer players could perform well on the international level.

In February 1946, when the London Olympic Organizing Committee sent out its invitations to the Games of the XIVth Olympiad, it ignored the Soviet Union: As mentioned earlier, the USSR had no National Olympic Committee, and in any case some "technicalities" had to be cleared up before the Soviets could participate in the Games. Brundage explained to reporters that the IOC would probably object to the Soviet practice of giving cash prizes to winning athletes. Edstrøm declared the Russians would have to prove their athletes were not professionals.

Soviet authorities remained silent until August 1946, when a planeload of Soviet athletes unexpectedly showed up at the European track and field championships in Oslo. Since they were not members of the IAAF, the Soviet athletes technically had no right to compete there. Edstrøm and Brundage painstakingly instructed them about athletic protocol, and Burghley, now the acting head of the IAAF, agreed to let them into the competition as an exception. "A wise decision, although quite contrary to the rules," wrote Jack Crump, and he quoted Lauie Miettenen, a Finn, as commenting, "So now Britannia waives the rules" (1966). The Soviet men won only one title, N. Karakulov's victory in the 200 meters, but the Soviet women made clear that in the future they were a force to be reckoned with. Edstrøm gave the Soviet delegation a letter to take home, again inviting the Soviet Union to join the IAAF.

On October 21, 1946, still not having received any answer, Edstrøm sent yet another letter to Nikolai Romanov, Chairman of the All-Union Committee of Physical Culture and Sports in the Soviet Union, inviting the USSR to join the IAAF and specifying the federation's standards of amateurism. No answer came, but a Soviet team showed up unannounced for an international weight lifting competition in Paris. By a vote of 8-7, the federation's council allowed the Soviets to compete. FIFA, the soccer federation, however, blocked scheduled games between the Soviets and Sweden and Norway on the grounds that the Soviets had not applied for membership in the federation. Faced by such considerations, the Soviets joined the IFs for soccer, basketball, weight lifting, and skiing, but IAAF and IOC officials still had to wait for word from Moscow.

On November 25, 1946, Edstrøm wrote again to Romanov, pointing out that the Soviet Union must join the IAAF and form an NOC before it could be invited to the London Games. He sent the letter, in both Russian and English, through both the Soviet legation in Stockholm and the Swedish legation in Moscow. On December 4, he complained to Brundage, "I have time upon time sent invitations to Mr. Romanoff, but he does not answer. Perhaps he does not care, but probably he does not know that one should answer a letter." Just before Christmas he tried again, this time, as he told Brundage, "through three channels," but with no more success (Brundage Archive).

Letter From S. Edstrøm to Mr. Romanov, November 25, 1946:

On the 21st of September, 1945, I wrote a letter as per enclosed copy addressed to the Athletic Association of the Soviet Union. . . . I received no reply from you but your athletes participated in Oslo. On that occasion I handed to your representatives . . . a letter of which I enclose a copy. . . .

Having had no reply to this letter, I sent you on October 21st this year . . . a letter, of which I also enclose a copy. . . .

Also this letter being without reply, I wish to point out to you that if Soviet athletes in field and track events want to compete at the Olympic Games in London 1948, your country's sports organisation must adhere to the International Amateur Athletic Federation and an Olympic Committee must be formed in Moscow.

As I have received no answers whatsoever on my previous letters to you, I wish to inform you that this is the last time I write to you until I hear from you.

Brundage Archive, University of Illinois.

Brundage did not share his Swedish colleague's dedication and determination to bring the Soviets into the Games. He assured Edstrøm the IAAF's overtures exceeded the "requirements of common courtesy," but in his view, Soviet sport policies posed a threat to some of the Olympics' most treasured standards: "If we are to prevent the machinery of international sport from breaking up and the high standards of amateur sport from collapsing," he wrote in October 1946, "we will have to watch things very carefully and stop all deviations from our regulations" (Brundage Archive).

In January 1947, the Soviet Union announced its readiness to join the International Wrestling Federation as well as the IAAF, but it posed its own set of conditions: It demanded the recognition of Russian as an official language of the federation, the installation of a Soviet representative on the executive board of each federation, and the ouster of Franco Spain from both federations. The Soviets' conditions enraged Olympic leaders. Over 20 years later Brundage still characterized them as "impudent" and "arrogant." In a letter of March 4, 1947, Brundage warned Edstrøm that the situation "is loaded with dynamite," and he predicted problems in the formation of an NOC in the Soviet Union. In the face of the "double barriers of language and iron curtain," he urged that all "fundamental questions be settled before admitting the Soviets into the IAAF and the Olympic Games. Otherwise the future would see only conflict and misunderstandings that

---

Letter From Avery Brundage to Sigfrid Edstrøm, January 21, 1947:

The overtures made by you on behalf of the IAAF and by other sport leaders to the USSR are unprecedented as you know. They exceed the requirements of common courtesy and no other country has ever been so favored. We have done more than our share and if there is no response why worry, we have gotten along very well without the Russians for 35 years since 1912. As a matter of fact, as I have indicated in my letter of October 25th . . . I do not see how, with their special treatment for athletes and their payments to winners, the Russians can possibly qualify under amateur rules and regulations. Furthermore their organization of sport is purely political and under their system must remain so. . . .

For the first time since their organization we have observed since the war[,] in amateur sport Federation meeting[s,] the operations of political blocs. This violates all Olympic principles and must be stopped before it is too late. . . .

If by any chance the USSR does apply for membership in any Federation, they must not be given any special consideration and their athletes must not be admitted to international or Olympic competition unless we are positively certain they are amateurs. Any other course will only invite disaster.

Brundage Archive, University of Illinois.

---

could ruin the "whole structure of amateur sport and the Olympic Games which we have labored so many years to create" (Brundage Archive).

In practice the IOC leaders took a more cautious tone. Burghley promised to bring the Soviet demands before the IAAF's governing council, but he dismissed the attack on Spain's membership in the organization, saying that the IAAF was "entirely nonpolitical." In April the Wrestling Federation formally admitted the Soviet Union, accepting a Soviet representative into the council but rejecting the proposal that Russian be made an official language by a vote of 13-6 and rejecting the Soviet demand to oust Spain by 12-7 (Norway supported the Soviet resolution). The leaders of the IAAF decided to follow the procedural example established by their wrestling cousins.

The council of the IAAF, in which Brundage was Vice President, prepared an elaborate scenario. At its meeting in May 1947, the Spanish delegate, by prearrangement, rose to ask that his language be made an official language of the federation. When the Egyptian delegate unexpectedly followed with a similar demand for Arabic, the language question was shelved. The admission of a Soviet representative to membership in the council posed no particular problem, but questions arose about "amateurism" in Soviet athletics. As Brundage exclaimed, "They may not even know what an amateur is," and the IAAF council requested an explanation of the Soviets' system of cash prizes. Burghley proposed extending an "amnesty" for all athletes as of a certain date, with no questions being asked about past payments, and the federation's leaders undertook their own investigation of conditions in the Soviet Union.

The Soviets now showed interest in joining the Olympic family. Soviet sport officials, long inaccessible, were suddenly willing to talk to foreign correspondents, although they apparently had trouble understanding what the issues were. When the chief of the United Press office in Moscow, Henry Shapiro (1976), spoke with Alexei Chikin, head of the international section of the All-Union Sports Committee, the Russian gave a confused explanation of the Soviet system. "Some of our athletes are students," said Chikin, "but most of them are workers. Since work in sport is as hard as any other kind, workers in sport are not prevented from participating with others on the same basis." On the question of payments to athletes, he declared, "For one or for many victories, nobody gets any money. But sometimes for an accumulation of victories an athlete gets prizes in money and awards, although this is not done regularly." In conclusion, Chikin confidently asserted that all Soviet athletes were amateurs, the system supported no professionals; "professionals" existed only in the capitalist system.

The IAAF specifically questioned the practice of cash awards to athletes, and Soviet authorities, obliging the peculiarities of these western gentlemen, announced a complete overhaul of the system to reward athletic achievement. In July 1947, a government decree entitled "On Remuneration of the Sports Achievements of Soviet Athletes" declared that henceforth prizes would consist only of medals and badges. The Soviet authorities went on to assure "master" athletes of adequate time for training without any threat of financial problems. At the same time, they specified that there were no "professional entertainers" in Soviet athletics: everyone was either working at another job, for which he or she received their sustenance, or else they were training (studying) for some future career (Riordan 1977). Although many athletes sought careers in physical education, athletes competing for an army club or for the Dinamo organization (the police sport club) might also have other careers in their future.

Soviet athletes were now stepping up their participation in other international competition. In the summer of 1947, they won the European basketball championship, and in the course of the year, in addition to joining the wrestling federation, they joined the IFs for chess, swimming, and skating. Nevertheless, they still aroused their share of controversy. For example, they failed to show up for a gymnastics competition in France at which they were expected. At best the Soviets were considered unreliable entries at international sporting events; it seemed increasingly clear they wanted only to enter events in which they were sure their athletes would perform well.

In the latter part of July 1947, Burghley visited Moscow, marking the first direct meeting of the Soviet leaders with a representative of the Olympic establishment. Together with other distinguished foreign guests, Burghley witnessed the festivities surrounding the celebration of the "Day of the Physical Culturist." Impressed by a mass parade of athletes, which he called a "remarkable spectacle of colour and precision movements," he took the occasion to lecture the Soviets on the niceties of international athletic protocol and on the forms to be followed. He returned to London optimistic: "As a result of these conversations," he informed Edstrøm and Brundage, "in so far as one can ever be sure of anything in that country, I feel that they will join the IAAF" (letter of July 31, 1947, Brundage Archive).

The Soviet Union finally joined the IAAF in December 1947. Its one concession had been to drop the system of cash awards for winning athletes. On the problem of the payment of athletes during the time of competition, so-called broken-time payments, Burghley had explained to them, "My understanding of it was that an athlete's 'pay' could continue from his employer while on holiday under normal business practices for holidays or leave, but the athlete could not receive payment from the promotor of the meeting or other outside body." The Soviet authorities, Burghley noted, "anticipated no difficulty under this item" (Brundage Archive).

Burghley had opened an important door for the Soviet authorities. His interpretation of broken-time payments and vacations had been far simpler than what Brundage might have offered. Burghley's explanations, moreover, committed the IOC to posing minimal demands on the Soviets and accepted their system of state-supported athletics. He had emphasized that the athletes must not receive payments or awards from promoters. The Soviet order was "socialist," meaning the government owned and controlled all economic enterprises and since there was no private enterprise, there were no legal private entrepreneurs. In the absence of the elements in the capitalist order that promoted professionalism in sport, the Soviets argued, there could be no professionals in Soviet athletics. Ten years later, as President of the IOC, Brundage was still inveighing against training camps and private coaches, and if he had been in Burghley's position in 1947, he might not have been so quick to accept Soviet arguments. Carl Diem (1952) later warned that in its dealing with the Soviets, the IOC had compromised its principle of amateurism for the idea of universality.

The Soviets nevertheless did not participate in the Winter or Summer Games of 1948. They made no move to organize the requisite NOC that should then apply for membership in the Olympic family. They chose to bide their time in order to prepare their forces. According to a memoir by Nikolai Romanov, Soviet authorities had considered joining the Olympic community immediately upon war's end, but they had then concluded, "Participation in the 1948 Olympic Games was out of the question because we did not have enough time to get ready for them" (1981). During the war Soviet athletes had no time for training at a world class level. In 1945, according to Romanov, there were 999 Masters of Sport in the Soviet Union, of whom only 312 were under the age of 30, 44 under the age of 25. The Soviets, he indicated, chose their international competitions carefully so as to show their athletes at their best.

Soviet sport officials watched western sport developments closely. They studied the results of all competitions where a stopwatch or tape measure determined the winner, giving them a good understanding of whether their own athletes would be competitive. In addition, at Oslo in 1946, they had noted that many western champions collapsed at the end of their events. (Western journalists commented extensively on this phenomenon.) This, they concluded, indicated western athletes were using performance-enhancing drugs, and Soviet authorities embarked on their own research into this subject. No matter what it took the Soviets wanted to be sure that their athletes would properly represent the Soviet system. As Soviet journalists frequently wrote, "Each new victory is a victory for the Soviet form of society and the socialist sports system; it provides irrefutable proof of the superiority of socialist culture over the decaying culture of the capitalist states."

In December 1948, the Central Committee of the Soviet Communist Party decided its athletes were ready and announced a campaign to expand mass participation in sport, raise the level of sport competition throughout the land, and achieve "world supremacy in the major sports in the immediate future" (Riordan 1977). The campaign focused specifically on Olympic sports and aimed at choosing an elite group from the broadest possible mobilization of the resources in the masses. Of course, this meant that sports not included in Olympic competition would have a more difficult time in finding state funds. To American observers, this posed a striking contrast to the American investments in football and baseball, which were not Olympic sports.

From this period of the late 1940s dated the development, for example, of Soviet ice hockey, a sport that had not previously been played much in the Soviet Union. Drawing on their extensive experience in the sport of bandy, a game on ice using a ball instead of a puck, they imported coaching help from Czechoslovakia, which had long had a strong hockey tradition, and they quickly produced world class players. In the wake of international success, the sport soon became second only to soccer in popularity, although many observers in the multinational Soviet Union considered it basically a "Russian sport." By 1956, the Soviets had unseated the Canadians as Olympic champions. The Canadians complained bitterly about the "state amateurs" playing in Soviet uniforms. When, in the 1960s, Soviet teams dared to play with Canadian professionals of the World Hockey Association (WHA), they surprised their North American rivals, showing that Soviet ice hockey teams were ready to challenge the world.

At the same time as the Soviet system invested heavily in its athletic program, however, the Stalinist order that ruled the Soviet Union also caused the program considerable damage. A new wave of purges erupted in the late 1940s, and the regime expressed suspicion of any athletes who had contact with the West. Athletes, praised one day for their achievements in international competition, could find themselves accused the next of having engaged in "counterrevolutionary activities" such as talking with foreigners. Even football (soccer) stars whose names had become household words suddenly had to settle "above the Arctic circle," as they would later euphemistically speak of their exile. The fact that many Soviet leaders were enthusiastic sport fans only added to the uncertainties on the Soviet sport stage in this authoritarian period.

Despite this new activity, the Soviets dallied in organizing a National Olympic Committee, and IOC leaders worried as the time for the 1952 Olympic Games approached. Brundage and Edstrøm feared that in 1952 the Soviets, as they had at Oslo in 1946, might again suddenly appear in Oslo or Helsinki and demand admission to the competition. The IOC had no direct contact with Soviet sport officials and therefore knew little of

Letter From Brundage to Edstrøm, December 7, 1950:

You remember what happened at the European Track and Field championships at Oslo four years ago when the Russians arrived without notice and without being members of the IAAF. . . .

It would not surprise me if they tried the same stunt at Helsinki in 1952. . . . They are likely to appear at Helsinki just as they did at Oslo without even making the proper entry.

From all reports the best Russian athletes are State proteges with all sorts of special concessions and rewards. They certainly are not amateurs. . . . According to Communist philosophy, every person and everything is subservient to the State. It is impossible, therefore, to find a NOC in any Communist country that is free and not under complete State control. If we conform to fundamental Olympic principles and follow our rules and regulations we cannot possibly recognize any Communist Olympic Committee.

Brundage Archive, University of Illinois.

what was happening. "It is possible that we will have a most serious problem confronting us in 1952," Brundage warned Edstrøm, "and I think we should be prepared" (Brundage Archive).

The Soviet authorities, however, had studied and learned their lessons in Olympic protocol. In April 1951, they announced the formation of a National Olympic Committee, and they formally requested admission into the Olympic family. Edstrøm brought the question to the IOC's meeting in Vienna the next month. While some members still questioned the amateur status of Soviet athletes, others countered that the "Olympic code of fair play and good sportsmanship" would have a beneficial effect on Soviet youth. After prolonged debate, the Committee recognized the Soviet NOC by a vote of 31 in favor with 3 abstentions, and it then elected Konstantin Andrianov, the Soviet nominee, to membership in the IOC by a vote of 24 for, 5 against, and 4 abstaining.

Andrianov's election itself marked a significant change in the work of the IOC. For the first time Committee members accepted a state appointee as a colleague without any pretense they had themselves selected the man. For the first time, moreover, they had to work with a man who spoke neither French nor English. In addition to tolerating the introduction of new ideological forces, the IOC would have to change the very nature of communication at its meetings. Even so, Andrianov became a significant force within the IOC, although he reached the inner circles only briefly, serving as a member of the Executive Board, 1962-1964 and Vice President, 1966-1970.

The Soviets treated their entry into the Olympic family as a recognition of their state's importance and its positive role in international affairs, and

---

Letter From Edstrøm to Brundage, April 25, 1951:

Yesterday occurred something very important. I received a long telegram from Moscow, telling me that a Russian Olympic Committee had been formed with Mr. Konstantin Andrianov as president and Mr. Sobolev as secretary. They want to be recognized to participate at Olympic Games. I answered that they were welcome to be present at the opening ceremony in Vienna. . . .

Karl von Halt and the Duke of Mecklenburg are not coming to Vienna. They are afraid of the Russians, as they both have been in trouble with them before. I have asked the Duke to remain as a member of the IOC until Helsinki in order to make it possible for him to say good-bye to us in a proper way.

Brundage Archive, University of Illinois.

---

they spoke of the IOC's having yielded to the pressure of world opinion in having invited the Soviet Union to join its company. As Sergei Popov later put it, the IOC's recognition of the newly formed Soviet NOC "showed appreciation of the Soviet Union's services in promoting physical education and sport" (Popov and Srebnitsky 1979). Indeed, the leaders of the IOC had made significant concessions to win Soviet participation. The invitation to join the IAAF, extended by Edstrøm in 1945, had obliged the IOC to follow the IAAF's lead. As Burghley, in a moment of frustration in March 1947 noted, the IOC was following a "street with no turning" (Brundage Archive). When the Soviets made the formal concession of revising their system of rewarding victorious athletes, the IAAF and the IOC simply yielded to political realities and accepted the Soviets without any further questions. The Soviets had won entry on their own terms.

For some time Brundage continued to disapprove of the Soviets' "state amateurs," and as a result, the Soviets and their East European allies opposed Brundage's candidacy for the presidency of the IOC in 1952. Instead they supported Burghley; Brundage won the election only after more than two dozen rounds of voting (Guttmann 1984). Angered by some of Brundage's complaints about state amateurs, the Soviets even threatened to withdraw from the Olympic family; "My dear Avery," wrote Edstrøm in November 1952 (Brundage Archive), "The Russians and Hungarians are after your scalp!!" Unflustered, Brundage responded, "If these people do not know Olympic rules and regulations, it is time they learned, and if they are not going to respect them, it is time we learned." He seemed to be on a collision course with all the East European states.

The Soviet sport authorities then decided to deal differently with Brundage. While arguing that in the postwar world socialist states would

Letter From Edstrøm to Otto Mayer, November 5, 1952:

One of the Swedish daily papers has today an article about Avery Brundage. It states that Avery has issued a circular letter in which he is against governmental training of athletes and having the athletes competing in the Olympic Games for the glory of their nations. That has caused reaction against Avery Brundage especially in the countries behind the iron curtain, who threaten to leave the Olympic Movement if Avery will remain President of the IOC. It is particularly the Hungarian papers that give this statement. It seems that our Soviet friends never can understand the idea of the Olympic Movement.

Brundage Archive, University of Illinois (with minor spelling corrections).

naturally develop strong athletic programs and of necessity direct them, they set about wooing the American, in 1954 inviting him to visit the USSR. (Stalin had died in 1953, and Soviet leaders now seemed more open to western contacts.) In order to affirm his own independence, Brundage insisted on paying his own airline ticket, but, just as Burghley had been, he was overwhelmed by the sight of a mass Soviet athletic demonstration celebrating the "Day of the Physical Culturist": "What a fantastic display was the superlative performance, faultlessly organized, that warm July afternoon in Moscow in 1954!" It was, he exclaimed, "like something out of the Arabian nights, far surpassing anything of its kind I had ever seen in any other part of the world both in magnitude and in beauty" (Brundage Archive). Brundage, like many other IOC officials, thrilled to the majesty of mass synchronized exercise, and he was now ready to pay the Soviet system considerably more respect.

As time went by, Brundage's views of the Soviet system mellowed considerably. He continually had trouble with Soviet proposals to "democratize" and restructure the IOC, but he welcomed the way in which the Soviet Union quickly became an enthusiastic advocate of the virtues of the Olympic Games, however they interpreted them. He received no reports from sources within the Soviet Union about abuses of the athletic program, and he became increasingly impatient with western complaints about Soviet practices. At first, when he read criticisms in the western press, he would turn to Andrianov for explanations; as time passed, he instead began to ask Andrianov for information with which he himself could respond.

Brundage considered the Soviet system of maintaining athletes no worse than the American system of financial support for collegiate athletics, of which he knew something and of which he strongly disapproved. The mass character of the Soviet sport program, moreover, captivated him. He very much approved of the balance he saw between mass participation and encouragement of excellence; and he dismissed American complaints about Soviet practices as "sour grapes." Always recalling the conditions of life when he was young "before the First World War," he argued that the very difficulty of daily life in the Soviet Union contributed to the prowess of their athletes. Americans, he declared in February 1956, had better worry about "our national complacency and the softness of life, brought on by too much prosperity"; like Coubertin, he saw athletics as a means of strengthening and ennobling youth (Brundage Archive).

In June 1962, when Brundage said of the Soviet Union, "No country applies more intensively the theory of the Baron de Coubertin that a national program of physical training and competitive sport will build stronger and healthier boys and girls and make better citizens" (Brundage Archive), the Soviet authorities were justifiably pleased. In Brundage's rhetorical treasury, there was no higher authority to be invoked than the name of the "Great Founder" of the modern Olympic Games. Brundage's critics, however, quickly pointed out that he had said essentially the same thing about Nazi Germany in 1936, and they were more than ever convinced that the man's political naiveté had addled his thinking.

The Soviets indeed shared many of Coubertin's original views on the usefulness and significance of physical education as preparation for military service and for work. In considering the principles of amateurism, they strongly supported the ideal, resolutely opposing opening up the Games to "professionals," but at the same time they considered the particular rules of eligibility, especially the IOC's attitude toward broken-time payments, to be ridiculous. Once the Soviets had entered the Olympic family, they systematically proposed their own interpretation of the ideals of the Olympic Movement.

The Soviet entry into the Olympic Games also opened a new era of Olympic politics as sport competition became a test of the two rival superpowers and the systems they each claimed to represent. Both sides accepted the image of the Olympic Games as surrogate warfare, whatever verbiage they clothed these thoughts in. Athletes might find personal means of communication, just as soldiers might under certain circumstances in warfare, but on the level of sponsoring organizations there were no doubts that the competition in sport constituted a single arena within a larger confrontation.

Chapter 7

The Cold War Arena

At the Melbourne Games (1956), after the Soviet invasion of Hungary, the water polo match between the USSR and Hungary served as a vivid example of Olympic competition as surrogate warfare.

With the Soviet entry into the Olympic family in 1951, the IOC became a Cold War arena in which the superpowers competed directly. The Committee's leaders continued to insist politics had no place in the Olympic Games, but Soviet representatives looked at the question differently. V.I. Lenin, the founder of the Soviet state, had dismissed claims of avoiding controversies as a "hidden polemic" (1961). Aleksei Romanov, whom the IOC soon accepted into its ranks, later insisted, "In a world seized by the class struggle, there is not and cannot be a classless or supraclass ideology. . . . The exposing of bourgeois ideology in the international sports movement, the struggle with it, was and will remain the most important tasks of the sports organization of the Soviet Union and of other socialist lands" (1973). However much it might protest its neutrality, the IOC had no place to hide. Superpower rivalry gave international athletic competition a sharp new edge, and, in turn, decisions of the IOC had an important place in the superpowers' struggles for position and prestige.

Even before the Soviet entry into the Olympic family, the IOC had to confront some key Cold War issues, first of all, the German question. At the end of the war, the victorious Allies had each taken occupation zones in the conquered land, and as the Cold War developed, the French, British, and Americans combined their zones, eventually nurturing the Federal Republic of Germany (FRG). The Soviets converted their zone into the German Democratic Republic (GDR). Both sides paid lip service to the thought of German unification, but the two German states embarked on divergent paths.

Naturally, this posed difficulties for the IOC. As mentioned, in its preparation for the London Games, the Committee did not consider admitting Germany. Many European NOCs opposed any thought of German participation in the Games at that time, and the IOC justified its inaction by pointing out there was no recognized NOC in the land. The West Germans organized an NOC in 1949, and in 1950 when Mecklenburg and Halt reclaimed their seats in the IOC, the western powers encouraged

---

Romanov and Ideology:

In all spheres of international life, including the Olympic Movement, there is a continuous struggle of the new with the old, of the progressive with the reactionary, and, as a mass social movement, international sport is in our time an arena of sharp political and ideological struggle. This struggle is not limited to the realm of theoretical and methodological problems of sport. It bears a political character even in those instances where at first glance one speaks of "purely technical" questions.

Romanov 1963, 11-12.

---

the IOC to bring the Germans, meaning in this case the FRG, back into its ranks. The IOC "provisionally" admitted them to its ranks and to the Games.

Soviet entry into the IOC in 1951 brought pressure to recognize the GDR, which organized its own NOC at the same time as the Soviets did. In line with the thought of Germany's eventually being reunified, the IOC encouraged cooperation between the two German states. Brundage, a shrewd negotiator, tried to arrange a settlement, but because of his celebrated role in the 1936 Games and his friendship with Halt, he found dealing with the East Germans enormously frustrating. More than once he decided the East Germans were openly insulting him. He persisted, however, and when he seemed to have finally arranged an agreement for uniting the two Germanies under one flag for the Helsinki Games, he proclaimed the IOC had succeeded where diplomats and politicians had failed: "In bringing about the sublimation of political protocol and rolling back the Iron Curtain, the International Olympic Committee has accomplished more with the Russians in pledging them to the Olympic idea than the United Nations has been able to achieve in the realm of international relations" (Brundage Archive). But to Brundage's dismay, the agreement disintegrated (Guttmann 1984), and the West Germans alone represented Germany at Helsinki in 1952.

Independently of the will of the Great Powers, the reentry of the Germans also raised the question of how the European countries that had only recently experienced Nazi occupation would react to the appearance of German athletes in the Olympic Games. The IOC chose not to invite the Germans to Oslo for the 1952 Winter Games because of the strong feelings still lingering in Norway from the years of German occupation during World War II. Norwegians even objected to Halt's attending the Oslo Games as an observer. Japan, however, reentered the Olympic family at Oslo without any untoward incidents.

The case of China posed a somewhat different problem for the IOC. The communist victory on the mainland in the fall of 1949, which drove the nationalist government of Chiang Kai-Shek off to the island of Formosa (Taiwan), created a dilemma. In contrast to the German situation, there could be no discussion of combining the two. Therefore, the IOC had to establish its own definition of "China"—whether to choose between the two contenders or to recognize them both.

The Chinese Communists angered Edstrøm at their very first meeting by paying no attention to the Committee's operating myths. When a Chinese diplomat spoke of politics as determining the policies of sport, Edstrøm indignantly rejected such an argument as a violation of the most sacred principles of the IOC, and the Chinese retired to contemplate the strange ways of this organization.

The Helsinki Organizing Committee sent invitations to both Chinese sport organizations, and both accepted. The IOC had yet to decide whether to accept both, one or the other, or neither; it could not hope to arrange a compromise between the two. Edstrøm personally wanted no part of the dispute. He favored admitting neither, but since he was planning to retire in 1952, he chose to do nothing. Brundage, Edstrøm's apparent successor, also favored recognizing neither, but he had to look for a compromise.

The IOC first considered recognizing whichever Chinese sport organization was in turn recognized by the appropriate IF; the Nationalist Chinese might compete in one sport and the Communist Chinese in another. By this action the Committee ran the risk of allowing athletes sent by an unrecognized NOC to compete in the Games, but this particular piece of legislation was soon forgotten. In protest against the decision, the Nationalist Chinese declared they would not come to Helsinki; the Communist Chinese, however, sent a delegation, but it arrived too late to enter any official competition. The IOC could look forward to more problems in connection with the 1956 Games.

As the time of the 1952 Games approached, the disputes over Germany and China took second place to the fundamental issue that gave the Olympic Games new visibility and controversy: the looming confrontation between the Soviets and Americans in the sport arena. The Soviets did not attend the Winter Games in Oslo—their hockey application arrived too late for acceptance—and therefore attention focused on Helsinki. The Finnish capital itself seemed the epitome of current international tensions. Finland had fought against the Soviets in World War II, but somehow it had emerged from that conflict a neutral state, under the Soviet shadow but outside the Soviet orbit. Finnish governments painstakingly struggled to maintain that neutrality, taking great care to avoid antagonizing their giant neighbor to the east, but in the eyes of many westerners, in the early 1950s Helsinki lived under a cloud of doom.

The preparations for the Games emphasized the Finns' geopolitical dependence on their giant neighbor. The Soviets refused permission for the Olympic torch relay to pass through its territory—the bitter armed resistance the Soviets still faced in Lithuania was undoubtedly a factor—and therefore the organizers had to arrange an elaborate roundabout route. When the British Olympic team flew to Helsinki for the Games, Soviet aircraft buzzed their plane. (The British had insured their athletes for £1,000 each [Bear 1952].) Soviet authorities then told the Finns the British had strayed from their defined corridor and the Soviet planes only permitted the British to continue their flight because their plane displayed Olympic symbols (Crump 1966).

Americans prepared their athletes and the American public for a great confrontation. In June Bob Hope induced Bing Crosby to make his television debut in a telethon to raise money for the team. Both NBC and

CBS donated time and space—over one million dollars were pledged and about a third of that amount was collected. Writing in *The New York Times*, Arthur Daley exclaimed, "The Communist propaganda machine must be silenced so that there can't be even one distorted bleat out of it in regard to the Olympics."

Soviet officials also saw the Games as a great political test, and at the same time they displayed great concern about their athletes. The Soviets wanted no part of a common Olympic Village, and at first they considered commuting from the Soviet side of the border each day. The Olympic authorities objected, and the Soviets then accepted separate housing in Helsinki, where they could live with their East European allies. (They posted a large picture of Stalin on the outside of their building.) Although many western critics insisted the Soviets feared uncontrolled contact between their athletes and westerners, some commentators attributed their behavior to other reasons. After first confronting Soviet athletes at Oslo in 1946, Jack Crump wrote, "The Russians were very difficult to approach and kept themselves very much to themselves, but on mature reflection, I now believe that the language difficulty was the greatest factor in producing this atmosphere of coldness and isolationism" (1966).

When the Games began, Cold War emotions immediately centered on the unofficial team scoring system. The IOC still refused to establish an official system, but journalists and the teams themselves had persisted in keeping unofficial counts, usually adding up points for the top six places in an event. When the Games were renewed in London in 1948, the Americans easily garnered the most medals and points. The Americans had presumed they would dominate these Games as they had the London Games, but to their dismay they discovered the Soviets were far better prepared for this type of competition than they were.

The American domination of past Games reflected mainly the concentration of American strength in only a few sports that produced high quantities of medals and points, namely men's track and field and men's and women's swimming. As Arthur Daley explained, "In the old days, the United States was usually so far ahead in everything that it hardly was worth bothering about from an IOC standpoint" (Kieran et al. 1977). The imbalance in the Americans' program, of course, reflected the peculiarities of the American sport scene, where the greatest financial investment, and many of the best athletes, concentrated on baseball and American football, neither of which were Olympic sports. Because track and field and swimming, based on strong programs in American colleges and universities, stood on a high enough competitive level to collect honors internationally, most American observers, particularly the journalists, believed that domination of these "major" sports more than compensated for the weak showing of the Americans in the "minor" sports.

The Soviets, in contrast, had structured their competitive program around the Olympic program, and when their athletes arrived in Helsinki, they were ready to compete in all but 1 of the 26 sports (they did not bring a field hockey team). They were particularly strong in the women's events. Daley complained, "Ordinarily no one pays much attention to women's track and field performances, especially reporters. But the dual meet overtones of this Olympic Games yanked the gals into the headlines" (Kieran et al. 1977). Like many other Americans, Daley did not know whether to focus his complaints on the point system or on the Olympic program itself. On the whole, American journalists had simply not considered the problem of the balance between the several sports in which their heroes excelled, and the Soviet successes shocked them.

With its tremendous strength in women's events, the Soviet team amassed great numbers of medals from the start. The Soviets set up a public scoreboard in the yard of their housing compound, offering a daily running score in their confrontation with the Americans. In the unofficial point counts, controversy immediately arose as to whether one should be using the 10-5-4-3-2-1 system or the 7-5-4-3-2-1 system. Daley—like many other Americans—insisted the Soviets had chosen their system for ulterior motives: "Just to be on the safe side and to give themselves a slightly better edge, [the Soviets] invented a point-scoring system of their own. Designed to counteract the big American first-place bulge, the Russians awarded only 7 points for a first instead of 10" (Kieran et al. 1977). The Soviets, in fact, were observing the same system British authorities had publicized in 1948.

Americans also argued the sports and awards should not be weighted equally. Daley wrote, "The Russian gal gymnasts suddenly bobbed up with 602 points to none for the United States. Ordinarily that feat would have caught no one's eye. This time it caught the headlines because it indicated to gullible readers that the Soviet was leading America in total points, 1372 to 115" (Kieran et al. 1977). Then he added, "It was an astounding and uncomfortable situation. America was winning with unprecedented success in the major leagues and the Reds were scoring in the minor leagues. A Kitty League team had become of equal importance to the Brooklyn Dodgers." Even State Department officials, Daley reported, were worried about the Soviet successes.

The IOC feared for the worst in this confrontation, and at Brundage's urging, it reaffirmed its opposition to reckoning team point scores: "The IOC deplores the practice in the newspapers of the world of attributing and publishing tables of points showing national placings in the Olympic Games. This is entirely contrary to the rules and spirit of the Olympic Games, which are contests between individuals with no points scored" (Brundage Archive) The resolution had no discernable effect on the nature of the reporting from Helsinki, however.

With a surge of American victories on the last two days of the competition, it seemed the United States had finally overhauled the impressive lead the Soviets had established. Suddenly, the scoreboard in the Soviet encampment went blank. The head of the Soviet NOC, Nikolai Romanov, told journalists "I do not have the score with me, I do not know how we stand" (Kieran et al. 1977). The Soviets finally announced the Games had ended in an exact tie: both the United States and the Soviet Union had 494 points. Kieran and other Americans claimed the United States had won by 614 to 532. The Soviets won 71 medals: 22 gold, 30 silver, and 19 bronze; the Americans won 76: 40-19-17. Neither side could claim a conclusive victory, and that in itself represented a major Soviet triumph (table 7.1).

Commentators from both the East and the West took special note of the number of world records broken in the competition at the Helsinki Games.

Table 7.1

The Soviet-American Confrontation in Helsinki, 1952

	POINTS (ACCORDING TO THE SOVIET SYSTEM) IN SELECTED SPORTS	
	USSR	**US**
Basketball	5	7
Boxing	24	35
Wrestling, Free style	28	33
Graeco-Roman	44	0
Gymnastics, men's	87	0
Gymnastics, women's	602	0
Rowing	17	18
Track and Field, men's	57	182
Track and Field, women's	64	8
Swimming, men's	0	49
Swimming, women's	15	1
Diving, men's	2	26
Diving, women's	5	27

Khavin 1979, 138-39.

The Soviet-American confrontation, together with the readmission of Germany into the Games, would seem to have stimulated performances, and, in John Lucas's words, this "marked the modern reemphasis on record-breaking, a Western, century-old tradition that placed infinitely greater value on the quantifiable mark than on the ritualistic or intrinsic value of the performance" (1980). Laszlo Kun, a Hungarian historian, commented, "At these Games this meant in practice that to win, one had to break Olympic records" (1982). As a result, future training of athletes would only be more intense as they struggled against each other and for new victories over the past.

The concern with setting records, at least in those sports in which the athlete's performance could be measured in time or space, disturbed many people. It seemed a continuation of the tendencies the British, with their concern for "amateurism," had decried in observing the Germans in the 1930s. Brundage warned that the new obsession with setting world records would intensify the problems of trying to maintain the principle of amateurism in the Olympic Games. Records, he declared, meant the "certain death of the amateur" because of the training and dedication they demanded (Brundage Archive). Workers' sport leaders had once bemoaned "recordmania" as destructive to athletics, especially mass athletics, and voices could still be heard echoing these thoughts. Yet, generally, observers quickly fell into the habit of judging the quality of Olympic competitions by considering the number of world records that had fallen, even though such records were necessarily limited to those sports in which results were measurable by time or distance.

The Soviets went home from Helsinki satisfied they had performed well and made an indelible mark in the sport world; their athletic achievements had definitely surprised westerners. Moreover, the performance of their women athletes undoubtedly stimulated greater attention for women athletes in western lands. Soviet ideologists also attributed far-reaching political significance to the victories in sport. As Aleksei Romanov, a Soviet member of the IOC, declared, Soviet participation in the Olympic Games "plays a large role in the propaganda of the achievements of the Soviet people and of socialist culture" (1963).

The Soviet leadership, to be sure, was not entirely happy with the results in Helsinki. Regardless of the publicity given other sports, soccer reigned as the most popular sport in the country, and when the Soviet soccer team lost to the ideologically heretic Yugoslavs in the preliminary round of the Olympic tournament, Soviet leader J.V. Stalin reacted strongly. In a move reminiscent of the action of tsarist authorities who, after the Russian Olympic soccer team had suffered a humiliating defeat in Stockholm in 1912, had dissolved the national team on the spot, Stalin ordered the dissolution of the Army 11 who had constituted the core of the Soviet team in Helsinki. Stalin could not tolerate such a failure even when it stood amid 22 gold medals.

The Cold War rhetoric and maneuvering greatly complicated Avery Brundage's job as President of the IOC when he took office after the Helsinki Games. He had visions of renewing the Games as he thought Coubertin would have wanted them, and he sought desperately to avoid taking sides in the Cold War. Neither side, however, showed much respect for his efforts at neutrality: The Soviets resented his criticisms of their financial support of athletes and the Americans thought he was leaning over backward to appease the Soviets. Nevertheless, Brundage continued to argue that sport, and more specifically the Olympic Games, could point the way out of international conflict.

When the IOC finally brought about a workable compromise between East and West Germans on forming a joint Olympic team, Brundage again crowed, "We have obtained in the field of sport what politicians have failed to achieve so far" (Guttmann 1984). In fact, the agreement between East and West Germans to compete together in the 1956 Olympics, to be staged in Melbourne, Australia, raised as many questions as it resolved. The two teams would join as one, under one flag that displayed the five Olympic rings superimposed on the black-red-gold tricolor that formed the basis for both German flags. In addition, German Olympic victors were to be saluted to the strains of Beethoven's music rather than either national anthem.

Brundage believed the Olympic ideal had wrought this compromise, but the two parties obviously had other considerations in mind. The West Germans (FRG), the stronger of the two parties in this arrangement, believed they would control the arrangement, and they welcomed the cooperation of the two teams as a step toward something more. The East Germans (GDR) were fighting for their place in the diplomatic sun, trying to emerge from under the heavy shadow cast by the West Germans. West Germany threatened to break off relations with any state, aside from the Soviet Union, that established diplomatic relations with the East Germans. Under this new arrangement, GDR athletes could enter lands that GDR diplomats could not—"diplomats in warm-up suits" some commentators called the athletes (Holzweissig 1981).

Brundage viewed the German compromise as a great achievement, but he was unable to duplicate it in the question of China. In 1954, the IOC tried to establish a "two-China" policy. Acting on a favorable report offered by the Soviet Union, it voted by a narrow margin to recognize the Chinese People's Republic (PRC) as the representative of China in the Olympic organization. Beijing still refused to participate in the Melbourne Games of 1956, however, because the IOC at the same time continued to recognize the Nationalist Chinese regime on the island of Formosa. In exasperation, Brundage later exclaimed that he "had not yet met a sportsman from Red China with whom

I could discuss athletic matters, but only diplomatic representatives" (Brundage Archive). The IOC could not bridge this gap.

As he struggled with the problems of the Cold War, Brundage expressed special concern about the intrusion of political alliances into the ranks of the IOC. He repeatedly spoke out against the emergence of "blocs" within the Committee. Richard Espy (1981) has recounted an IOC session at which the Soviet representative announced there was no East European bloc, and then his colleagues from other East European states followed with identical statements. Aleksei Romanov, however, explained the socialist states had naturally had to coordinate their policies: "The collective preparation of strategy and tactics of sports organizations of the socialist lands in the international sports movement has become an objective necessity and in practice displays a growing influence on the course of development of world sport" (1973). Although Brundage vigorously denounced the formation of blocs within the IOC, the Committee could not avoid becoming a parliament any more than the Games could avoid becoming an arena of Cold War conflict.

In the Olympic year of 1956 international tensions severely tested the IOC's capacity to survive the Cold War. The Winter Games in Cortina, Italy, to be sure, passed almost idyllically. The problems that arose belonged in the realm of sport: Poor conditions on the ski slopes caused a terrible spate of accidents; the Soviets complained about the judging, the Americans, about the housing. In the end, the Soviets, competing in their first Winter Olympic Games, took home the lion's share of the awards. "We came here expecting triumphs in our strong events," said Romanov, "and expecting

---

Circular Letter From Brundage to Members of the IOC, January 30, 1954:

It is only since the last world war that there has been talk of "an European Bloc," "a Latin Bloc," "a Bloc from behind the Iron Curtain," "a Western Hemisphere Bloc," "a British Empire Bloc," etc. in the membership of the IOC. Certainly this has not developed to any very serious extent as yet, but the very fact that such blocs have been mentioned indicates that something has gone awry. There must be no blocs and there must be no nationalism in the International Olympic Committee. . . .

Unless we adhere to the principles so wisely laid down by Baron de Coubertin, however, and unless the IOC is preserved as an "Olympic Family" composed of members who are entirely free from economic or political considerations, and devoted primarily to the Olympic Movement, the Committee will lose its strength, its power, its influence, and its usefulness. . . .

To allow countries to select their representatives on the Committee would be fatal. Political considerations would soon control and all the good work of the last sixty years would be destroyed.

Brundage Archive, University of Illinois.

---

to gain experience in others. We did both." The Soviets even upset the Canadians for the ice hockey championship.

The so-called Summer Games in Melbourne, Australia, by way of contrast, abounded with political problems. Since the Games were being held in the Southern Hemisphere, they had to be scheduled in November and December. (January might have been better, but on the one hand they could not compete with the Winter Games and on the other they had to take place in the Olympic year of 1956.) The Europeans complained, as was to be expected, about having to travel so far, and the Australians had their full share of problems in preparing, replete with arguments about financing and construction. Brundage more than once threatened to move the Games. The Australians, moreover, refused to lift their quarantine rules for horses, but in the end, the IOC scheduled the equestrian events for Sweden in the summertime, half a world and half a year away from the competition in Melbourne, which opened as scheduled.

In 1956, as a background to the organizational problems of the Melbourne Games, the international scene lurched from crisis to crisis. In February, the head of the Soviet Communist Party, Nikita Khrushchev, made an effort to de-Stalinize the Soviet Union, and the fallout from this intellectual upheaval led to challenges to the Soviet Union's position in Eastern Europe. Events in Poland, beginning with riots in June and culminating in a change of leadership in the fall, did not reach the point of violence and open warfare, but in the fall the Soviet authorities intervened with force in Hungary to restore the socialist order there. Other trouble erupted in the Middle East: Egyptian and Israeli forces clashed, the British and the French seized the Suez Canal, and the Soviet Union threatened to intervene in the conflict.

These controversies threatened the Games. Egypt, Lebanon, and Iraq withdrew in protest against the seizure of the Suez Canal. The Egyptians demanded all countries at war with them be excluded from the Games. Spain, the Netherlands, and Switzerland announced their withdrawal in protest against the Soviet intervention in Hungary. The Swiss then changed their minds, but it was too late to arrange transportation for their delegation: They had to stay home.

Despite the turmoil in Eastern Europe and in the Middle East, Brundage insisted the Olympic Games must go on:

> Every civilized person recoils in horror at the savage slaughter in Hungary, but that is no reason for destroying the nucleus of international cooperation. . . . The Olympic Games are contests between individuals and not between nations.
>
> In an imperfect world, if participation in sports is to be stopped every time the politicians violate the laws of humanity, there will never be any international contests. Is it not better to try to expand the sportsmanship of the athletic field into other areas?

The IOC censured all NOCs that had refused to participate in the Games: "The International Olympic Committee, an organization concerned only with sports, expresses its sadness and regret at the abstentions, which it considers contrary to Olympic ideals." The Games went ahead as scheduled.

Among the athletes who were arriving in Melbourne, the Hungarians initially drew the most attention. The Swiss government intervened with the authorities in Budapest to win travel permits for some Hungarian athletes to get to the Games. Another small group of Hungarians was traveling to Australia by ship, in the company of Soviet athletes, and they heard nothing of the trouble at home until Hungarian emigrés greeted them at the dock in Melbourne with stories of repression. Anti-Soviet demonstrations abounded in Melbourne, and the water polo match between the Hungarians and the Soviets became a legendary event. Eyewitnesses swore there was blood in the water when the game ended. The Hungarians won and went on to win the gold medal; many of them then refused to go home and were granted asylum in the West.

Overall the Soviets won the most medals at Melbourne: 37 gold, 29 silver, and 32 bronze. Soviet historians, ignoring most of the political controversy, speak of the Games as the Olympics of Vladimir Kuts, their winner in the 5,000- and 10,000-meter runs. Brundage continued to be uncomfortable with the tallying of team points. At the opening ceremonies in Melbourne, the scoreboard carried a message from the IOC: "Classification by points on a national basis is not recognized." The caution only drew laughs and ridicule from spectators and journalists, who went ahead as before. The Soviets reckoned they had won by a score of 622-497 over

---

IOC Resolution on Point Scoring in the Olympic Games of 1952:

The Olympic Games are a contest between individuals. They are designed to be a joyous festival of the youth of the world. . . .

The Games are not, and must not become, a contest between nations, which would be entirely contrary to the spirit of the Olympic Movement and would surely lead to disaster. For this reason there is no official score and tables of points are really misinformation because they are entirely inaccurate. . . .

Normal national pride is perfectly legitimate, but neither the Olympic Games nor any other sport contest can be said to indicate the superiority of one political system over another, or of one country over another. One of the objects of the Olympic Games is to build international good will, and efforts made to pit one nation against another in this or any other manner must be severely censured.

Brundage Archive, University of Illinois.

---

the Americans, while American journalists calculated the Soviet win at 722-593. "The myth of US superiority in sports" had been "dissipated completely," the Soviets crowed (Shteinbakh 1980), and they particularly relished their country's gold medal in soccer.

Despite the uncertainties in the preparations for the Games, most everyone felt that the Melbourne Olympics had been a success. In the actual fervor and joy of competition, most of the political struggles receded into the background. The Australians had insisted the Soviets could not have a separate Olympic Village such as they had enjoyed in Helsinki, and the Soviet athletes found the Village in Melbourne so much to their liking that the Soviet press complained of the western powers' having introduced "Mata Haris" into the Village with the intention of leading the Soviet competitors astray and interfering with their training. (Soviet police officials ordered their athletes not to dance to decadent western rock and roll; the IOC received several complaints that male and female athletes were being housed too near each other.) Those looking for symbols of international friendship in the Olympic Games pointed to the romance that developed between the American gold medalist in the hammer throw, Harold Connolly, and the female discus champion from Czechoslovakia, Olga Fikotova. The two were married, and Olga Connolly was the flag carrier for the United States team at Munich in 1972.

Most important for the IOC and Brundage, the Olympic Games had survived the challenge of international politics in the Games of both 1952 and 1956. These were formative Olympics, establishing the bases for the confrontation and competition between the two superpowers who had different economic systems and different sport systems. The Olympic Games survived the challenge, absorbing the superpowers' rivalry into the fabric of the competition. The Cold War had moved into the Games, the Games had merged into the Cold War, but the Cold War did not co-opt the Games.

Chapter **8**

The Idealist at the Helm

Avery Brundage, an American businessman and former track athlete, dominated the Olympics for almost a quarter-century of Cold War. His inflexibility and high-handed approach helped maintain consistency in Olympic practices, but also alienated many world and sport leaders.

Once he had brought his first Games as President of the IOC to a successful conclusion, Avery Brundage turned his thoughts to the problem of reconciling traditional Olympic ideals—as he understood them—with the demands and trends of modern society. The Games were growing rapidly, in his judgment perhaps too rapidly: New countries were joining the Olympic family, new sports federations wanted to be a part of the Games, and established federations wanted to stage more events. Brundage feared the Games could lose their idealistic character, but to protect and guide the Games, he had to do battle with the modern world.

Above all, he wanted the IOC to reaffirm the principles of amateurism. The Olympic Games, he explained in April 1954, "are an idealistic enterprise confined by their charter to amateurs. This is one of the fundamental principles governing the Olympic movement, that participants should be amateurs who take part for love of sport and not for any mercenary ends." Although the IOC's rules were clear enough, the "Olympic philosophy is not thoroughly comprehended" because of the

---

Circular Letter to IOC Members, April 12, 1954:

The Olympic Games are an idealistic enterprise confined by their charter to amateurs. This is one of the fundamental principles governing the Olympic movement, that participants should be amateurs who take part for love of sport and not for any mercenary ends. The Games are intended to be non-commercial; sport and not business or work. . . .

The world today is filled with queer ideas, strange political and philosophical doctrines, and curious aberrations. Words have been given distorted meanings, far from their real sense, and fundamental principles are being forgotten or ignored. This is so also in the world of sport. . . .

Since amateurism is a thing of the spirit, it is not a simple matter to draft rules on such a delicate subject to cover all cases. . . . An amateur sportsman may be rich or poor; he may be uneducated or a doctor of philosophy; he may be a beginner, or he may have had years of experience; he may be a champion or he may be a dud; but he must be a good sportsman. . . . Amateurism is an inflexible, an absolute and universal thing. . . . An athlete is an amateur only so long as he is competing for the love of the sport. The minute that financial, commercial, or political considerations intrude he is no longer an amateur. The Olympic Games can be thrown open to professionals (God forbid) but no one, not even the International Olympic Committee can change the definition of amateur. . . .

If the creation of national prestige is to be made the main objective of our sport program, if athletes are to be considered as soldiers defending their countries' reputation, if special regulations are to be adopted so that "no one shall be prevented by financial reasons from representing his country," then we shall be abandoning amateurism.

Brundage Archive, University of Illinois.

"numerous languages and varying customs in different parts of the world." Sport, he continually argued, was play: "Amateur sport is fun, diversion, amusement, recreation, and only that" while professional sport constitutes a "branch of the entertainment business." Like others in sport, he glorified winners, but he decried the insidious effect of specialized training given elite athletes. He strongly endorsed the IOC's ban on broken-time payments, insisting the Baron de Coubertin had not meant the Games simply to glorify an elite, "a small class of super-athletes to entertain the populace," but rather "to develop participants, not spectators," by encouraging the development of mass sports.

Brundage considered the confrontation of the superpowers the greatest external threat to the Games at this time, and he pointedly attacked the practice of reckoning national team points in the quadrennial competition. "In a world engaged in a titanic all[-]out struggle between political philosophies, it is not easy to keep aloof," he solemnly declared, insisting, "The Olympic Games are contests between individuals and teams and not between nations." In 1936, when he was President of the American Olympic Committee, his organization had emphasized patriotism in its appeal for public money, but as President of the IOC he now advocated different values.

As part of his campaign to tone down nationalist rivalries, Brundage emphasized his opposition to the presence of team sports in the Games, arguing that Coubertin, the Games' "Worthy Founder," had fought "to his dying day" against including team sports in the festivities. Sports such as soccer, basketball, and hockey not only aroused national passions, they also fed into strong professional programs. Edstrøm, moreover, had

---

Fundraising Advertisement of the American Olympic Committee, 1936:

Picture one of Uncle Sam's boys at the Olympic Games of 1936.

Boy? He's budding manhood personified! Proudly he stands at attention, with the outlines of a sculptured hero, but with warm, living character in his face. In the set lines of his jaw and the glint in his eye he shows he means to prove his right to wear the red, white, and blue shield blazoned on his chest. . . .

Our 100 athletes against 5000 rivals out to beat us.

In 116 individual and team contests in 19 sports.

How many of the 267 victory medals will our boys and girls bring home?

Every patriotic American may share in the glory of their conquest.

How? By contributions, large or small[,] to the American Olympic Fund being raised to equip, transport, feed and house, coach and manage the American team.

Brundage Archive, University of Illinois.

Circular Letter to IOC Members, August 26, 1957:

Referring to the item on the agenda for the Sofia meeting suggesting dropping team games from the Olympic program, the Baron de Coubertin was vehement in his argument about admitting team events to the Games; the Worthy Founder's eyes were so firmly fixed on the welfare of the individual, that, to his dying day, he fought to preserve the individuals' rights and was wholeheartedly against the introduction into the Games of team sports. Unfortunately, he could not prevent their participation, but he never ceased to protest. I quote from a letter of our Dutch colleague, Peter Scharoo, who served on the Executive Board for many years:

"Exaggerated nationalism is one of the greatest dangers of our society. We must confess that this phenomenon is also manifested in the Olympic Movement. . . .

"You will remember that during the years that I was a member of the Executive Committee, I urged again and again the necessity of *eliminating all team sports*. This will inevitably have the great advantage of preventing the promotion of national interests, because in team sports the competition is obviously between countries and not between athletes."

Brundage Archive, University of Illinois.

shared these views, warning Brundage, "I fully believe that the only way to save amateurism and the Olympic Games is to eliminate team sports" (Brundage Archive).

Brundage recognized his mission had a certain quixotic flavor. "The world today," he complained, "is filled with queer ideas, strange political and philosophical doctrines and curious aberrations." Nevertheless, he considered international sport competition a powerful force for establishing peace in the world regardless of ideological conflicts. As a step toward reducing national passions, he tried unsuccessfully to do away with the awards ceremonies in Melbourne; he did arrange for the bands to play shortened versions of the national anthems of the victorious athletes. (In 1963, he unsuccessfully attempted to do away altogether with the playing of national anthems.) In the final ceremonies in Melbourne, only a token group of some 500 out of the 4,000 competitors walked in, as individuals rather than as national units. These piecemeal moves had little impact on general sentiment, however.

When the IOC met in Sofia, Bulgaria, in the fall of 1957, Brundage's ideals crashed against the reefs of political realities. He offered a number of suggestions for streamlining the Games: reducing the number of events, limiting the number of entries permitted in each event, and even eliminating some sports, especially team sports. The Games, he warned, were "suffering from giganticism and the costs are growing in an alarming fashion" (Brundage Archive). He shuddered at the thought of staging an

800-meter run with three entries each from 80 countries. He himself favored sports that used a tape measure or stopwatch and not human judgment to determine the winner, and he objected strongly to the number of gold medals awarded in some sports, especially in gymnastics in which one person could win as many as eight medals.

While most IOC members agreed on the desirability of limiting the size of the Games, they chose not to eliminate any sport, noting that the program for the 1960 Games in Rome had already been announced. The Committee instead asked the federations to reduce the number of entrants and events. Team sports remained in the Games, although the Committee voted to eliminate "artificial team sports" (i.e., "those depending on the addition of the scores in individual competition"), meaning the team events in modern pentathlon, equestrian sports, and gymnastics. Brundage's efforts to do away with the national identification of athletes made little headway, and the Rome Games in 1960, as might be expected with the return to Europe, entertained 60 percent more competitors than Melbourne had.

Leading the charge against Brundage's proposals were the Soviet representatives on the IOC, who offered their own interpretation of the ideals of the Olympics and put forth their own program for reform of the Games. The efforts to reduce the size and scope of the Olympic Games, they declared, came from "reactionaries" and "promoters," who feared the successes of "progressive forces" and who wanted to "introduce discrimination against athletes and some sports in the Olympic movement and to deprive them of their main objective—to be a sport festival for the youth of all countries, to serve the noble cause of consolidating friendship among sportsmen and peoples." No IF or NOC, the Soviets argued, had called for cuts in the program. The Soviets opposed any reduction in team sports, they urged the expansion of the program of women's sports and the inclusion of all events approved by the participating sport federations, and they calculated the number of participants at a given Olympics could easily be raised to 10,000 (Romanov 1963).

The Soviets expressed sympathy for Brundage's concerns about professionalism and commercialism, but they declared he was fighting his battle on the wrong field. Whereas he worried about restraining the influence of commercial interests, they insisted the capitalist system had created the malignant institutions that brought professionalism and commercialism into sport. Only fundamental economic and social change could alter this situation, but for the moment, they loudly endorsed Brundage's ideal of amateur athletics. The Soviet NOC even proposed its own definition of amateurism: "An amateur is a person who has always engaged and is engaging in sport for his own physical and spiritual development and improvement, thereby contributing to the social good and not obtaining any material advantages for himself personally. For the amateur, activity in sport is not the source of his existence." Even so, they wished the IOC would accept the principle of broken-time payments.

The Soviets clearly wanted to strengthen their position in the Games' organization and competition. They opposed reducing the program because they expected sports in which they were dominant to be the targets of any cutbacks. They could claim to have no professionalism so long as this was defined as purely a concomitant of the capitalist economic order. They favored broken-time payments because that is what they were in fact doing, but they opposed "open competition" in the Games (meaning admitting professionals).

In March 1959, the Soviets offered a plan for reorganizing the Olympic Movement, essentially proposing to destroy the IOC's historic character as a self-selecting private international organization. Declaring the Committee needed a more democratic structure that better represented the different social systems and different cultures around the world, the Soviet memorandum called for adding representatives of 35 IFs and 115 NOCs to the 64 current members of the IOC, thereby creating a "broad representative international organization, consisting of 210-215 persons" (Brundage Archive). The IOC would then have a general assembly, meeting every four years, together with an Executive Committee of 50 to 55 persons, a Bureau, and a Chancery. This, the Soviets argued, would put the Olympics on a firm and secure path into the future.

Brundage reacted negatively to this plan. The independence of the IOC, he argued, lay at the heart of the Games' success. The IOC had the responsibility of directing the Olympic structure as a whole, but NOC and IF Presidents would represent first of all their own particular constituencies. Representatives of the IFs and the NOCs, he insisted, had full opportunity to present their views to the IOC. "These views are carefully considered by the IOC, whose members represent solely the Olympic Movement rather than their countries or their sport." The IOC, he admitted, "is hardly a perfect organization and it can probably be improved, but any changes made that disturb its independence and its impartiality would result in disaster" (Brundage Archive). At Brundage's urging, the IOC tabled the Soviet proposals until after the 1960 Olympic Games.

Brundage also won an unexpected reprieve in his struggles with the question of Chinese participation in the Games when the Chinese Communists turned their backs on the Olympic organization. Andrianov, the Soviet representative in the IOC, had been urging the Committee to recognize the PRC (Communist China) as the sole Chinese representative, while the United States backed Nationalist China, located on the island of Formosa (Taiwan). The IOC's effort at a "two-China" policy aroused only protest from both sides. After an extended series of exchanges with Brundage, Tung Shou-yi, a Communist Chinese member of the IOC,

Circular Letter to IOC, NOC, and IF Members, June 3, 1959:

At our meeting in Munich it was pointed out that if the Peking Committee has no authority in Taiwan, it is equally true that the Formosa Committee has no authority in China. It was for this reason that the following action was taken in Munich:

"The Chinese National Olympic Committee having its seat in Taipei (Taiwan) will be notified by the International Olympic Committee chancellor that it cannot continue to be recognized under that name since it does not control sport in the country of China, and its name will be removed from the official list.

"If an application for recognition under a different name is made it will be considered by the International Olympic Committee."

There was no "Pressure" from anyone—the action was practically unanimous and it was a purely common sense decision, not political in any sense of the word. We cannot recognize a Chinese Committee in Taiwan any more than we could recognize an Italian Committee in Sicily or a Canadian Committee in Newfoundland.

Furthermore there is nothing new about this action since already for the 3rd Asian Games in Tokyo last year, the athletes from Taiwan were notified that they could only participate as from Formosa and not from China and they did so participate. The International Olympic Committee does not deal with Governments and does not propose to become involved in political controversies. Its Executive Board had therefore recommended that its rules indicate more clearly that Olympic Committees represent the geographical areas in which they operate, about which there can be no dispute, and not Governments.

Brundage Archive, University of Illinois.

denounced the IOC's President as an "imperialist" who was trampling on Olympic ideals and a "faithful menial of the US imperialists bent on serving their plot of creating 'two Chinas'" (Guttmann 1984). Tung thereupon resigned from the IOC, and the Communist Chinese withdrew from a number of other international sport organizations.

The IOC nevertheless decided to disassociate itself from the Nationalist claims to the mainland. In 1959, it withdrew its recognition of the Nationalist regime's name, the Republic of China, and it ordered the Nationalists to apply for recognition under another name. A storm of protest erupted in the United States, where many commentators interpreted this decision as meaning the exclusion of the Nationalists from the Olympic family, and Brundage explained that the IOC "does not deal with Governments" but rather with geographical areas.

In May 1959, under fire from all sides, from all parts of the world, Brundage took a moment to expound on his own philosophy and contemplate the difficulty of being an apostle of sport. Exhibiting a selective historical memory, he recalled how in 1936 "certain individuals and groups did not approve of the German Government at that time, although the German Government had nothing to do with the organization or control of the Games," and he repeated his own words in defending the Melbourne Games: "The Olympic Games are contests between individuals and not between nations." Decrying the obstacles posed by the outside world, he declared, "The marvel is, considering political conditions and the materialism of our time, that there are any Olympic Games at all." A few days later he added the thought that in light of the "continuous effort since the war to involve the International Olympic Committee in politics," the Baron de Coubertin had displayed remarkable foresight in having been so "careful to arrange that [the IOC] should always be completely free, independent and autonomous, and to insure its impartiality" (Brundage Archive).

At the same time as controversy raged around the IOC, however, Brundage argued athletic competition was providing a new medium for cultural communication between the states of the world. In 1956 at Melbourne, when Dan Ferris, President of the American AAU, reached agreement with Soviet representatives on the holding of dual US-USSR track meets, many saw this as a positive sign for the development of better relations between the two states. This agreement was soon followed by agreements for competition in hockey, boxing, and wrestling. Could sport create a better atmosphere for the politicians and diplomats, enabling them to accomplish better things? Or did sport only serve as another arena for the clash of foreign policies?

Brundage, of course, looked at Olympic sport as a realm in which he was the sovereign, but he had to recognize that this same competition was also becoming an important instrument of national policies around the world. For example, leaders of the new states of Africa and Asia quickly recognized the usefulness of sport as a quick and effective way to establish national identity and feelings of national loyalty. While some anticolonialists objected to the popularity of the sports of the former imperial masters, a victory over a soccer team from a neighboring country could create all sorts of good feelings. As a result, these new governments were quite likely to have sport ministries, sport councils, and articulated sport policies, which, however, were aimed at identifying promising talents of world class athletes more than at encouraging mass participation as such.

Although the IOC basically welcomed the eagerness of the new states of Africa and Asia to participate in the Olympic Games, this participation also carried with it the potential for disrupting the festival of youth. Beginning with the Olympics of 1948, the Arab states objected to any competition with the Israelis. To play together would be construed as a form of cooperation, and the Arab states objected to the very existence of the Jewish state. A generation later, the Soviet Union strongly supported

India's refusal to invite Israel to the Asian Games of 1982 as a protest against "Israel's policy of genocide and the racist philosophy of Zionism practiced against the Arab world" ("India Hosts the Asian Games" 1983). Boycotts were also a well-used part of the arsenals of both Chinese teams.

In the late 1950s, boycott emerged as an important weapon against the policy of apartheid, the system of racial discrimination practiced in South Africa. In 1956, the ruling National Party enforced apartheid by banning interracial sport, including with foreign athletes. Norway brought the issue to the IOC in 1958, and in 1959, Andrianov proposed the exclusion of the Union of South Africa from the IOC. After some discussion, Brundage insisted the Committee had to take the statements of the South African representative at face value, as indeed the IOC did the statements of all its other members, and therefore the IOC had no cause to act. The question, however, would obviously return in the future.

Sport competition had also become a weapon both for resisting a boycott and winning recognition. Just as the South Africans would appeal to the principle of keeping politics out of sport as a means of breaking the boycott established against their athletes, in the late 1950s, the East Germans began using their athletes as a wedge to open doors that had been shut to their diplomats. The members of the North Atlantic Treaty Organization (NATO), in support of their West German allies, refused to recognize the German Democratic Republic and that government's passports. East German athletes, while still a part of a joint German team, insisted on traveling with their government's passports and on wearing "DDR" (the German abbreviation of their government's name) on their uniforms together with the state symbol of the compass, the hammer, and a sheaf of corn. The West German government objected to this practice, and it remained to be seen how long the IOC would be able to keep the two German teams under one banner.

The problem of the recognition of GDR passports and thereby implicitly of the GDR itself fell into the IOC's lap with the holding of the 1960 Winter Olympics in Squaw Valley, California. For several years, the IOC had been warning the Americans they would have to accept all duly accredited competitors from the communist states of Eastern Europe or face the prospect of the Games' being taken away from Squaw Valley. The United States government yielded, but only with grave misgivings. When the time of the Games arrived, the American government then refused to admit 10 East German officials and five journalists. The IOC accepted the ban on the officials, since the total number in the East German party had exceeded a prearranged quota, but it protested the ban on the journalists. In response, the United States State Department complained that an East German had used his accreditation to the United Nations in New York to imply the United States had been forced to recognize his government (Espy 1981). The controversy promised only to grow.

Although Richard Pound (1994), a prominent member of the IOC, later called the Winter and Summer Games of 1960 the "last games of innocence," they in fact displayed ample signs of deeper problems and international rivalry. The Winter Games in Squaw Valley marked the first time the United States had hosted the Games since Los Angeles in 1932, and although the Americans only won three gold, four silver, and three bronze medals in all—as contrasted to the Soviets' seven, five, and nine—they took great pride in their hockey team's victory over the Soviets. In Rome the Nationalist Chinese, who were marching under the banner of Taiwan, caused a small sensation at the Opening Ceremonies by briefly flashing a sign "Under Protest." A Danish bicyclist, Knud Jensen, died, apparently of an overdose of a drug administered to intensify his blood circulation. Shocked by this evidence that athletes were using performance-enhancing drugs, the IOC began discussions that eventually led to the formation of the Medical Commission to test athletes for drug use. At the 1960 Games there were also the usual complaints about the judging and officiating, but observers still called both sets of Games successful.

The Rome Games also offered significant commentary on the changing standards of the IOC itself. All visitors stood in awe of the Eternal City with its marble relics of Mussolini's fascist regime. The Rome Organizing Committee, moreover, had raised a considerable amount of money through a lottery based on the Italian professional soccer league's play. In 1948, Brundage had expressed misgivings about using Wembley Stadium in London for the Olympic Games because the stadium was used regularly for professional soccer; now the Olympic Games were enjoying the fruits of a fascist dictatorship, professional sports, and gambling.

Another significant innovation in the Rome Games concerned the decision of the Organizing Committee to rearrange the traditional calendar

---

The Death of Knud Jensen:

The 100-km road race for cyclists was held on an extremely hot day. Three Danish cyclists suffered heat stroke, and one of them, Knud Enemark Jensen, died. In the subsequent investigation, it was determined that all three had taken nicotinyl alcohol by injection before the race with the expectation that it would cause vasodilatation in the leg muscles. Taking this substance may have contributed to the severity of the heat stroke, although lack of acclimatization was probably a more important factor. One result of this unfortunate occurrence has been an increased concern regarding the use of drugs by athletes.

Ryan (1968).

---

of competition. Track and field events, which always drew many spectators, usually followed immediately after the opening ceremonies. The Rome organizers, however, feared that once the track and field events had ended, the audiences would shrink as people left the heat of the city for the countryside. Therefore, in order to sell more tickets, the organizers rescheduled the track and field events for the latter part of the two weeks of competition. While Brundage had insisted the Games were held for the benefit of the participants rather than the spectators, the IOC and the Organizing Committee obviously had interest in maximizing income from gate receipts.

The major new development of the Olympic Games in 1960 lay in the field of communications, and American television entered into the Olympic picture for the first time. In 1928, Amsterdam officials had blocked radio broadcasts of results, declaring this would be unfair to the journalists who had come to the Games (Van Rossein n.d.). In 1936, the Germans had experimented with local television transmission of the competition. In 1948, the BBC paid £1,500 for the rights to televise the Games, and it used nine cameras to send pictures out in a radius of about 50 miles. The Helsinki Games of 1952 were out of the range of western television of the day, and at Melbourne in 1956 there was no television because of a dispute over rights and payments. (The movie newsreel services refused to film every final as the IOC demanded; the IOC feared that giving American television officials the right to air three minutes each day would undermine the IOC's own desire to produce a documentary film. [Melbourne OCOG 1958].) In 1960, CBS televised both the Winter and the Summer Games, paying the Squaw Valley Organizing Committee $50,000 and the Rome Organizing Committee $660,000 for the right to set up its cameras (Wenn 1994).

American television executives still viewed the Games as news rather than entertainment; indeed, CBS's anchorman was Walter Cronkite, a veteran newsman. CBS broadcast only 15 hours from Squaw Valley, 2 of them in prime time, and 20 hours from Rome, 5 of them in prime time, using tape delays. (The British sent home about 40 hours of live telecasts from Rome.) In all, this constituted only a modest beginning for the dynamic and profitable relationship between American television and the Olympic Games.

Brundage himself seemed at first oblivious to the possibilities inherent in the Olympics' new link with television. Instead, he continued expressing concern about the insidious influence of commercialism, especially into the Winter Games. Meeting in Rome on the occasion of the Olympics, the IOC, at Brundage's initiative, actually considered dropping the Winter Games. When it finally decided to let them continue, Brundage lectured the NOCs and the IFs, explaining that among the concerns that motivated the IOC's discussion was the "feeling that in some winter sports the Olympic Games for many participants were merely filling the undignified position of a steppingstone to a professional career." The international amateur winter sports federations, he warned, had better take care that their sports "be better controlled, especially from the amateur point of view, if the Games are to continue" (Brundage Archive).

Once the Rome Games were over, the Soviets renewed their drive for the restructuring of the IOC. In March 1961, they insisted it was now time for the IOC to consider their program. Declaring that their "constructive proposals" of 1959 had won the endorsement of "many International Federations" and "many National Olympic Committees," they declared the new states of the world, having realized "magnificent victories in the struggle for freedom from colonial oppression" now demanded their rightful place in the "world Olympic movement, a place that they did not have in the past." The IOC should recognize that its format had outlived its time and should consider the Soviet proposals for its reorganization. It should also cease its efforts to restrict the size of the Games and its arbitrary treatment of applications from newly established states (Brundage Archive).

Brundage stood firm against this new offensive. After the IOC had formally rejected the Soviet proposals, he explained at a press conference, "If the Russians had got their way, it would have meant the end of the International Olympic Movement—and I told them so." In June 1962, when the IOC met in Moscow, the Soviet delegates offered a modified set of proposals, aimed at establishing the accountability of the IOC to the NOCs and the IFs. The IOC rejected most of the proposals, but while it turned down a move to expand the Executive Board, it accepted the principle of observing a "just geographical representation" on the board (Brundage Archive).

In opposing the Soviet proposals, Brundage enjoyed strong support in the western press. Western journalists considered Soviet proposals to expand the Games as representing a drive for still more points in the "unofficial" team competition, and they opposed any reorganization of the IOC. "Only two world-wide organizations have survived the wars of the 20th century," exclaimed the London *Daily Mail* of July 31, 1961, "the International Red Cross and the International Olympic Committee. Today a Red shadow falls across the Olympic games as the sun of Soviet mass sport rises in the sky." The Soviet proposal to include all NOC Presidents, it continued, "would be to invite from behind the Iron Curtain a series of political appointees, puppet presidents mouthing party dogma, toeing the propaganda line, dedicated above all else to the prizing of political gain from Olympic success." In the light of the criticisms he had received for his "China policy," these comments must have had a bittersweet taste for Brundage.

By the early 1960s, Brundage's grandiose visions of restructuring the Olympic Games along the lines of what Coubertin, the Games' "Worthy Founder," might have wanted had obviously disintegrated. He placed amateurism, which, ironically, had never been a part of the ancient Games, at the foundation of his vision, but he could not conquer what he called the "materialism" of the modern world. He argued that team sports had not been a part of the ancient Games and therefore should be dropped and that women had also not competed in the ancient Games and therefore perhaps their events should be eliminated or at least reduced; both of these ideas found little support in the IOC. As his hopes of restructuring and streamlining the Games faded, he blamed the press for seizing on every scandal and problem, and he hoped against hope that the Olympic Movement could yet bring the world back to its senses.

Chapter 9

The Issue of Political Discrimination

Many American black athletes had considered boycotting the Mexico City Games (1968). Some athletes who then competed looked for ways to demonstrate their feelings. Here, the members of the 4 × 100 men's sprint relay team accept their gold medals.

In the course of the XVIIth and XVIIIth Olympiads between 1960 and 1968, the IOC struggled to maintain and extend its sway over international sport in a new world in which sport competition had assumed heightened diplomatic significance and sport itself became even more clearly an instrument of foreign policy. Professing its belief in the usefulness of international sport competition as an educational tool for realizing hopes of international peace, the Committee spoke of welcoming all nations, regardless of social system. But antagonisms between states and peoples intruded as governments chose not to compete against the athletes of this or that other state. A corollary question developed: What justification could there be to refuse to compete, object to others' competing, or, for that matter, to insist on holding competition despite protests? The IOC faced these new problems and challenges.

The decade started with Soviet complaints about "political discrimination" against communist states. Building on the controversy created by the United States' restrictions on East Germans at the Squaw Valley Games, the Soviet Union and other East European states demanded the IOC condemn the refusal of NATO powers to grant GDR athletes free access to international sporting events. Yugoslavia complained the Philippines had refused its basketball team visas to participate in a tournament in Manila, and FIBA, with the support of the IOC, moved the tournament. Meanwhile, the western powers complained of discrimination against Israel and Nationalist China on the part of other Middle Eastern and Asian countries. As controversy also grew over the participation of South Africa in the Games, the IOC struggled to find a consistent path through these troubles.

In August 1961, the German question intensified after communist authorities suddenly erected a wall to divide East and West Berlin. Tensions had already been rising: In March, the West Germans had refused to play the GDR team at the world hockey championships in Geneva for fear of losing and thereby being forced to pay their respects to the East German flag and anthem. The West Germans had barely escaped sanctions from the IF, but when the wall went up, FRG sport officials immediately broke off relations with GDR sport organizations. The FRG's NATO allies followed suit, and France and the United States denied visas to East German athletes wanting to compete in world championships in hockey and skiing. The IOC and various IFs promptly called the NATO countries to account for their discrimination against the GDR, and NATO members responded they would admit East German athletes, who, in accordance with past agreements, were a part of a joint team with the West Germans. When the IOC pressed for unconditional acceptance of East German competitors, United States officials declared they opposed any steps that implied recognition of the East German regime.

From Brundage's Speech to the IOC Meeting in Munich, May 1959:

One of the basic principles of the Olympic Movement is that there shall be no discrimination against any country or person because of race, religion or politics. Were this fundamental principle not followed scrupulously the Olympic Movement would surely founder. . . .

In 1936, there was an organized and well-financed attack on the Games of the XIth Olympiad, because certain individuals and groups did not approve of the German Government at that time. . . .

Following the IInd World War there was another battle, when many opposed the recognition of certain Olympic Committees because of the political complexion of their countries. . . . It is never governments but only sport organizations which are recognized.

In 1956, just before the Games of the XVIth Olympiad, there was another intrusion of politics when, following the events at Suez and in Budapest in the fall of that year, certain countries wavered about participating against teams from other countries whose actions they deplored. . . .

Recently we have once more had evidence of political activity. Some misguided persons seem to think that Olympic sport can be made a political tool. This is as erroneous as anything can be. The minute political activities are permitted in Olympic affairs the Games are finished. . . .

Modern journalism, seeking sensation, has taken over the Games, overemphasized the competitive sport features, overstressed record breaking and national rivalries, and in general ignored the noble and idealistic real objectives of the Olympic Movement. . . . The marvel is, considering political conditions, and the materialism of our times, that there are any Olympic Games at all.

Brundage Archive, University of Illinois.

The East Germans, in turn, intensified their demands for separate recognition, and although the IOC insisted on maintaining the structure of a merged German team for the 1964 Olympics in Tokyo, the IAAF agreed to admitting separate German teams for its 1966 European championships. The IOC finally followed suit, approving separate teams for the 1968 Games in Grenoble and Mexico City. In August 1968, the IOC recognized the East German NOC. The GDR, with the backing of the Soviet Union, had succeeded in exploiting athletic competition as an entry wedge into Western European society.

GDR officials understood very well what they were doing. In previous years, Brundage had been very critical of the East Germans. After all, in 1951, they had backed out of an agreement he thought he had arranged. In a letter to Andrianov in 1958, he had complained, "I must tell you that we have had much trouble with East Germany because of the almost continuous efforts to use sport for political purposes" (Brundage Archive). The East Germans, however, harbored no grudges. In 1968, Heinz Schöbel, an East German publisher who had become a member of the IOC two years earlier, issued a volume entitled *The Four Dimensions of Avery Brundage*, in which he wrote, "Brundage's Olympic activities are founded on the firm conviction that further peaceful development of the nations must be based on high ethical values." Brundage surely appreciated the East Germans' praise.

Brundage had no such amenable partners in his efforts to deal with political discrimination in Asia, where President Sukarno of Indonesia was establishing his position as a leader of the "Newly Emerging Forces" of the world. In 1958, the Asian Games Federation had chosen Indonesia as the site of the Fourth Asian Games, scheduled for the fall of 1962. The Soviet Union stepped in with financial and planning help to construct a stadium with 100,000 seats and a natatorium with 10,000 seats as well as other facilities. Sukarno himself looked on the Games as a means to strengthen his own position among the Newly Emerging Forces of Asia, Africa, and Latin America that were "struggling against capitalism and trying to create a new world order" (Pauker 1964).

In appealing to Communist China and the Arab states, the Indonesians planned to exclude Nationalist Chinese and Israeli athletes from the Games, but knowing this would cause trouble with the IOC, the Organizing Committee delayed sending out formal invitations for quite some time. Insisting they had no intention of excluding anyone, they eventually sent blank pieces of cardboard, instead of identity cards, to the Taiwanese and Israelis. When the recipients complained, the Indonesians promised to investigate, but time passed without any explanation.

With the athletes already arriving in Jakarta in August 1962, the Taiwanese called for sanctions against the Games, but when a Nationalist Chinese representative, Gun-Sun Ho, came to Jakarta without a visa, he received warnings his life was in danger, and he beat a hasty retreat. The Israelis tried to telephone, but the calls were interrupted. "Bad communications," the Indonesians mumbled. An Indian member of the IOC, G.D. Sondhi, attempted to have the Asian Games Federation declare these to be the Jakarta Games, rather than the Fourth Asian Games, but the Indonesian organizers ignored him. The delegations that participated in the Games exhibited little concern about the absence of the Israelis and the Nationalist Chinese, and Sukarno could claim a significant propaganda victory.

Denouncing the "scandalous occurrence at last year's Fourth Asian Games in Jakarta," the Board then suspended the Indonesian National Olympic Committee (Brundage Archive). The Indonesians would be reinstated only after they had guaranteed there would be no recurrence of political discrimination against other members of the Olympic family. The Board's decision, Brundage told the press, was final and did not require the approval of the full Committee.

The IOC Response

Sondhi complained to the IOC's Executive Board, accusing the Indonesians of having violated the Olympic *Charter*. Brundage and the other two Executive Board members present, still struggling with Soviet complaints about discrimination against the East Germans, listened to their Indian colleague sympathetically and then resolved the issue as follows:

1. The IOC and the IFs are completely opposed to any interference in sport on political, racial or religious grounds, and particularly any which prevents the unhindered passage of competitors and officials between their member countries.
2. The IOC already includes this rule in connection with the Olympic Games and will continue vigorously to enforce it, including, if necessary, alteration of their venue or their cancellation. . . . The IOC will not award the Olympic Games to any City nor grant its patronage to any regional Games unless free access is guaranteed.
3. Invitations shall be sent to all the countries within the area of the Games whose national federations are affiliated to the international federations controlling the sports which form the program of the Games in question.

Brundage Archive, University of Illinois.

The support of Israel implicit in the Executive Board's action marked a new step for the IOC. In 1948, the IOC had done nothing to help the Israelis attend the London Games, and when regional Mediterranean Games began in 1951, it had refused to force the Arab states to invite the Israelis. In 1955, Brundage had declared the IOC had no authority to regulate regional games, and in 1959, when pressed by the British to support the Israelis, he pointed out the British had themselves refused to invite the Germans to London in 1948. Nevertheless, in the mid-50s Brundage already foresaw the necessity of some sort of action. Once the IOC had grappled with the Soviet complaints concerning treatment of the East Germans, Brundage accepted the argument that the IOC must be ready to intervene in the organization of regional games.

Andrianov protested against the suspension of Indonesia, insisting such a decision needed the approval of the full IOC. The Soviet Union, he declared, saw no similarity in the cases of Israel and East Germany, and while he approved of the resolution against political discrimination, he objected strongly to the action against Indonesia. The Board, he argued, had not heard testimony from the Indonesian NOC. This contrasted sharply with the "definite patience" shown toward the NATO states "which pursue open political discrimination of sportsmen from the GDR." The

Andrianov's Letter to Brundage, April 10, 1963:

As it was to be expected the decision of the Executive Board gave rise to a justified wave of indignation among national Olympic Committees in a number of Asian and Arab countries. The situation has become more serious after the decision of the Indonesian Olympic Committee to withdraw from the IOC. One should not ignore the probability of Arab countries withdrawing from participation in the 1964 Olympic Games. All this cannot help causing a tense atmosphere in the international Olympic movement on the eve of the Olympic Games, the reasons for which this time being not political interference from outside but a hasty decision of the Executive Board itself.

Brundage Archive, University of Illinois.

IOC's action against Indonesia, he insisted, was "contrary to the spirit of international cooperation, mutual understanding and friendship of sportsmen all over the world" (Brundage Archive).

In response Brundage argued that the Indonesians had "continued to make public statements of defiance that are circulated throughout the world." Therefore the Board had no choice but to act: ". . . The failure of the International Olympic Committee to take action would have seriously weakened the Olympic Movement in many parts of the world." It was too bad, he added, "that the Russian sportsmen who were responsible for the fine facilities provided for the Games [in Jakarta] did not teach the Indonesians some of the basic principles of international Olympic sport." The action, he pointed out in conclusion, had been suspension, not expulsion, from the Olympic family (Brundage Archive).

The Indonesians paid no attention to the distinction between suspension and expulsion, and Sukarno carried his challenge to the IOC further, announcing the establishment of "GANEFO, the Games of the New Emerging Forces—Asia, Africa, Latin America, and the socialist countries." Declaring the IOC had deviated from Coubertin's original conception of the Games, he called for "Olympic Games between the nations of the New Emerging Forces! Games of the Asian Peoples, Games of the African Peoples, Games of Latin American Peoples and Games of Socialist Countries Peoples! Games of all New Emerging Forces—against the Old Established Order!" Accordingly, Indonesian officials scheduled the first Games of the Newly Emerging Forces, GANEFO I, for November 1963 (Pauker 1964).

The IOC had to consider Sukarno's challenge very seriously because the 1964 Summer Games were scheduled for Tokyo, this marking the first venture of the Committee, at least since the ill-fated 1940 Games, to reach out to the Asian sport world. In his complaint about Indonesia's suspen-

Sukarno's Criticism of the IOC:

I remember very well the ideas put forward by, for example, the founder of the International Olympics, Coubertin, Baron de Coubertin.... Baron de Coubertin said that sports are just a means, means to produce men, means to restore the national community, means to build the nation, means to create international understanding and goodwill....

Then the International Olympics have been established and what do we see? We see that this, this thing put forward by de Coubertin has not been achieved! No! That even the International Olympic Games sometimes are against this. In their practice they are betraying this....

We gladly joined the International Olympic Committee, because we thought of the ideals put forward by Baron de Coubertin. But what did you experience in the International Olympic Games? Their behaviour has shown that they are just an imperialistic tool and include politics! We have had some very painful experience with the Asian Games! ...

The International Olympic Games have proved to be openly an imperialistic tool. They said to have sports without politics in the Olympic Games; to have them only among nations who are not communistic, who are not against colonialism; and even the International Olympic Committee have excluded Indonesia from the International Olympic Games ...

LET US NOW ESTABLISH THE GA-NE-FO: THE GAMES OF THE NEW EMERGING FORCES!

Department of Information of the Republic of Indonesia 1963, pp. 10-13.

---

sion, Andrianov warned of the danger of a mass boycott of the Tokyo Games, and a *New York Times* correspondent wrote, GANEFO "could come to symbolize in sports the resentment of the have-not nations against the haves. As such, it could be a significant and dismaying development from the Western viewpoint." The Communist Chinese, who were still boycotting the IOC, played a key role in supporting the alternative games, covering, by various estimates, 35 to 50 percent of GANEFO's foreign exchange costs. If GANEFO I received strong support in Asia and Africa, the IOC would have to surrender its dream of reaching out to the entire world.

In October 1963, the IOC struck back, warning athletes who participated in GANEFO could be banned from Olympic competition. When asked to explain its authority for such a step, an IOC spokesman pointed out that IFs would suspend athletes who took part in unsanctioned competition. Since the IAAF and FINA (the swimming federation) did not recognize Communist China, athletes competing in Jakarta in those sports would run the risk of being suspended for other international competition.

In November 1963, GANEFO I nevertheless drew some 3,000 athletes from 48 countries. The Chinese, who sent their best, claimed the team championship, winning 68 gold medals, 58 silver, and 45 bronze. The Soviets, who sent athletes who would not qualify for Tokyo, finished second, with 27-21-9 (Pauker 1964). For the Soviets, this result emphasized their awkward situation. In the light of their developing dispute with the People's Republic of China, they could not be satisfied with finishing second; but yet, in order to maintain their stance as the champion of the Newly Emerging Forces, they had no choice but to participate. They would yet have to decide how they could encourage Sukarno without compromising their position within the IOC. The Chinese, in contrast, trumpeted their support of this challenge to the "haves" of the world.

The Indonesians were pleased with the results of their work. Indonesian Foreign Minister Subandrio declared, "Sport cannot be separated from politics, and Indonesia uses sports as a political tool to foster solidarity and understanding between nations." The Indonesian government announced plans to hold GANEFO II in Cairo in 1967. Sukarno took the title "Founder and Honorary President of the GANEFO"; the Indonesian Minister of Sports, Maladi, was the President of GANEFO's Executive Board; and Jakarta was the site of GANEFO's permanent headquarters. The organization's motto was "Onward, no retreat" (GANEFO 1965).

The IOC reacted cautiously to the GANEFO's apparent success. Wanting to protect the Tokyo Games, it offered to forgive the Indonesian NOC and reinstate it if it would simply apply for readmission. The Indonesians complied, but they showed no sign of repentance. When FINA and IAAF refused to permit Indonesian and North Korean swimmers and track and field competitors who had competed in Jakarta to participate in any of their meets, Sukarno angrily withdrew from the Tokyo Games, and he forbade Indonesian newspapers to report anything about them.

The only Asian government that followed Indonesia's lead was North Korea, but from the point of view of the IOC, the Korean question presented a separate problem altogether. The Soviets had been demanding the North Koreans' admission to the Olympic family for some years; in 1962, the IOC granted provisional recognition on the condition there be a joint North and South Korean team. When the South Koreans proved intractable in negotiating the arrangements, the IOC recognized the North Koreans as an independent NOC. Tokyo, therefore, represented North Korea's first chance to participate in the Games, but the North Koreans joined the Indonesians in boycotting the Games.

Fearing other Asian and even African countries might follow the lead of the Indonesians, the IOC acted very cautiously throughout 1963 and 1964 in other matters about which the countries of the Third World felt strongly, and particularly in the question of South Africa's participation in the Olympic Games. The IOC had heretofore generally refrained from considering a country's domestic policies as a qualification for membership in the Olympic family, but African and East European pressures forced it to take up this particular problem. At its meeting in October 1963, at which it threw down the gauntlet to GANEFO, the IOC had also planned to discuss the South African question: whether the system of apartheid warranted the exclusion of the South Africans from the Games. Unfortunately, that meeting was scheduled for Nairobi, and the Kenyan government refused to grant a visa to the South African representative who was to present his country's case. Brundage hastily moved the meeting to Baden-Baden, Germany, and, wanting to minimize conflict with his African colleagues, he ruled out any discussion of the reason for this sudden change of venue.

In speaking to the IOC, the representative of the South African NOC (SANOC) gave the group no satisfaction on the question of whether blacks would be permitted to participate on South Africa's Olympic team. Still hesitant to expel the South Africans, the IOC set a deadline of December 31, 1963 for some sort of positive action to end racial discrimination in South African sport. When SANOC failed to make any accommodating moves, the IOC withdrew its invitation to South Africa to participate in the Tokyo Games. The South African government defiantly responded, "The South African custom, which is traditional, finds expression in the policy that there should be no competition in sport between the races within our borders, and that the mixing of races in teams taking part in sports meetings within the Republic of South Africa and abroad should be avoided" (Brundage Archive). The IOC had neutralized this issue for the moment, but South Africa's participation in future Olympic Games remained unresolved.

In this atmosphere of controversy, the 1964 Winter Games in Innsbruck and the Summer Games in Tokyo both went on schedule. South Africa was excluded; Indonesia and North Korea boycotted; and the East and West Germans, under duress and with misgivings on both sides, competed for the last time as a combined team. Even so, the weather presented greater problems for the Games' organizers than the human political problems did: A lack of snow made the ski runs in Innsbruck extremely dangerous, and in Tokyo, a mild earthquake and heavy rains caused concern. Still, the athletes had a good time in both competitions (as they usually did), and the Japanese celebrated the Tokyo Games as an announcement of their country's emergence as a major political and economic force in the world.

Of particular note at Innsbruck was the absence of the daily point counts of teams that had dominated the competitions since Helsinki. At the urging of the IOC, western journalists had now more or less agreed to drop the point count and instead to concentrate on adding up the numbers of medals won. This was still an unofficial count as the IOC refused to adopt any official system of scoring by teams; and the Soviets, who kept their own point count, declared the westerners were simply trying to make the Soviet victories look less overwhelming. The Soviets emerged, however, as the leader at both Innsbruck and Tokyo by almost any system of reckoning team points.

In Brundage's mind, the Winter Games still remained suspect because of their commercial dimensions. After the conclusion of the competition in Innsbruck, Brundage personally forced a pair of West German figure skaters, Marika Kilius and Hans-Jurgen Baumler, to return their silver medals when he learned they had already signed a professional contract. A Canadian pair was then to receive the medals, but the male partner had himself now become a professional. Frustrated, Brundage complained, "This illustrates very well why sports which have been developed commercially should not be on the Olympic program" (Brundage Archive). He continued his campaign to eliminate the Winter Games, but he still could find very little support within the ranks of the IOC.

Brundage's continued efforts to reduce nationalist celebrations at the Games also drew criticism. In the name of the socialist camp, Andrianov objected to a change in the Olympic ritual whereby the athletes' oath spoke of competing "for the glory of sport and for the honor of their teams" rather than "for the honor of their countries." Firmly supporting the idea of "healthy patriotism," the Soviets objected strongly to any thought of eliminating national symbols at the Games. They insisted the athletes indeed competed as representatives of their countries and of the countries' economic and social systems. Olympic victories testified to the strength of the socialist system, they argued. Aleksei Romanov insisted, "Sport as a social phenomenon, cannot exist isolated from social-political life, independent of domestic and international circumstances" (1963). An explanatory note to Romanov's publication, which was a handbook for public speakers in the Soviet Union, directed "In the lecture it is obligatory to talk about the achievements of Soviet athletes at the Olympic Games of 1952, 1956, and 1960, and about how the athletes of the capitalist lands, especially the USA, are losing their positions." The Soviets wanted their victorious athletes identified with all the official trappings of the system they were representing.

In examining where things stood after the 1964 Games, the IOC still had to consider its problems with the Indonesians and with the South Africans, but it soon found relief on its Asian front: GANEFO self-destructed in 1966. Revolutionaries overthrew the Sukarno regime, and the new government in Jakarta hastened to make its peace with the western world, including the IOC. The organizers of GANEFO II discovered they had no money as the Chinese were no longer interested, and the whole structure of the games collapsed. The IOC faced no further challenge by rival organizations in this part of the world.

The South African question, however, only became more complicated. When SANOC announced that in principle it would accept the idea of a racially mixed Olympic team, Brundage thought perhaps that question was on the verge of being settled. The African states, however, intensified their campaign against South African participation in the Olympic Games. In 1966, 22 African states organized the Supreme Council for Sport in Africa (SCSA), generally meant to promote sports in Africa but more specifically directed as a lobby against South African participation in international sport. While African sport leaders proclaimed their determination to force the South Africans to "comply fully with the IOC rules," in fact they took their lead from their own governments, which sought victory, not compromise, in their struggle against the system of apartheid. The African states could also count on support in this struggle from the East European states.

In 1967, Brundage named an investigating commission, headed by Lord Killanin, to visit South Africa and consider the promises now being made by SANOC for equal treatment of black athletes. In his instructions to Killanin, Brundage harkened back to the battles of the past:

> We had an analogous situation in 1936 when most of the world condemned Nazism and many wanted to remove the Games from Berlin. So also, after the Second World War, many of those who were against Communism wanted to keep the Eastern countries out of the Games.
>
> We must not become involved in political issues nor permit the Olympic Games to be used as a tool or as a weapon for an extraneous task. Please accept my best wishes for an interesting, successful, and not too arduous commission (Killanin 1983).

Brundage hoped to find a way to keep South Africa in the Olympic family.

Killanin understood he was not to judge apartheid as such but to investigate what SANOC was doing to meet the IOC's demands. He could not, however, ignore the functioning of apartheid: The black member of the commission, Sir Ade Ademola of Nigeria, was asked not to use public men's rooms, and on another occasion Killanin and his colleague were informed they could not sit together on a public bench. In his report back to Brundage, Killanin sanguinely declared SANOC had tried to improve conditions but "it could not operate in open defiance of its government" (Killanin 1983).

Brundage and many other members of the IOC were ready to accept SANOC back into their company, but black Africans protested. Commentators aimed their harshest criticism at Ademola, who, they insisted, had not even challenged apartheid and had refused to endorse the South African Non-Racial Olympic Committee (SANROC) (Bose 1994; Booth 1998). The SCSA would brook no compromise; it wanted South Africa out of the Games. Thus, one after another, African states announced they would boycott the Games in Mexico City in protest against the IOC's readmission of South Africa.

The threatening storm grew rapidly, and the IOC had to act. The Mexico City Organizing Committee anxiously asked Brundage to have the IOC reconsider its readiness to invite the South Africans to the Games. When Brundage suggested the South Africans withdraw voluntarily, the head of SANOC reportedly replied that he would "rather be shot in Mexico City than lynched in Johannesburg." The South Africans understood, in the words of an editorial in *Die Volksblad*, that "every international sports success of South Africa is a blow against our sports and political enemies." The IOC Executive Board then agreed it would be "most unwise for a South African team to participate in the Games of the XIXth. Olympiad" (Brundage Archive). It recommended the invitation be withdrawn, and the IOC, on the eve of the Mexico City Games, complied, barring the South Africans from the festival but again still leaving the question of South Africa's participation in future Games open.

In the Olympic Year of 1968, trouble seemed to be besetting Brundage from all sides, and he vented his anger by intensifying his campaign against the Winter Games. While Americans sang the praises of Peggy Fleming's figure skating at Grenoble and the French hailed the victories of skier Jean-Claude Killy, Brundage complained about local arrangements—the weather was bad, the competition venues were too far from each other, and transportation was inadequate. He objected especially to the growing commercialization of skiing and other winter sports, targeting the advertising material on skiers' equipment. "In the opinion of many," he wrote in 1969, "the Xth Olympic Winter Games strayed so far from the objectives of the Olympic Movement that if they cannot be reformed they should be abolished." If he could not abolish the Winter Games, he was ready to settle for the abolition of skiing: "It seems that sliding down mountains is not the most important sport in the world, and it is doubtful that it should be on the Olympic program." Again, however, the IOC refused to follow his lead; on this front Brundage was fighting a losing battle.

In the time between the Winter and the Summer Games of 1968, Brundage also had to wrestle with problems arising from sources totally outside the Olympic Games. In international affairs, 1968 was the most turbulent year since 1956. Student revolts in both France and the United States, a heated American presidential election, a Soviet-led invasion of Czechoslovakia, a controversial American war in Vietnam—all had their impact on the deliberations of the IOC. The United States endured the agony of two major assassinations—Dr. Martin Luther King, Jr. and Robert Kennedy. Members of the IOC also worried about possible violence in Mexico City, but at the same time, they dared not raise their questions aloud for fear of offending their Mexican colleague.

The turmoil in the United States spilled into the Olympic arena when an American, Harry Edwards, called on black athletes to protest the

Brundage's "Reflections on the Xth Olympic Winter Games," Dated April 26, 1969, Circulated to Members of the IOC:

Numerous widely distributed articles in newspapers and magazines following the Games referred to the "Grenoble fiasco," the "Grenoble disaster" and said they were "marked by the three vices, nationalism, gigantism and commercialism. . . ."

In the opinion of many, the Xth Olympic Winter Games strayed so far from the objectives of the Olympic Movement, that if they cannot be reformed they should be abolished. . . .

As long as the Winter Games bear the designation "Olympic" they are part of the Olympic Movement. It is certain that the Olympic Movement was seriously damaged by the rank commercialization and the other violations of Olympic principles at Grenoble. . . .

Winter sports can never be universal as Olympic sports are supposed to be, and it is even doubtful that they are widely practiced in 25 countries as required by Olympic rules. Moreover, they are subject to weather conditions which frequently interfere with the competitions as they did at Grenoble.

In the sense that snow sports have been introduced to all the world, the Olympic Winter Games have been a huge success and the IOC deserves great credit, but it is a grave question whether, because of their size, they can be continued along Olympic lines and in conformity with the high principles of the Olympic Movement. . . .

Does a sport which has become so much a part of the entertainment business that winners of Olympic medals receive offers of several hundred thousand dollars belong on the Olympic program?

Brundage Archive, University of Illinois (emphasis in original).

general condition of blacks in the United States by refusing to compete under the American flag in the Olympic Games. "We are not Americans, we are black people," he declared (Daniels 1996). His Olympic Project for Human Rights, which dealt "specifically with mobilization to boycott the Olympic games" (Edwards 1969) won public endorsement of an Olympic boycott from a Los Angeles Black Youth Conference in November 1967, and American sport officials had to pay attention. Many black basketball players refused to try out for the Olympic team, and the AAU manipulated its selection processes in track and field so as to be sure of having athletes to represent it at the Games. In the end, some black athletes who favored boycott, including the sprinters Tommie Smith and John Carlos, agreed to go to Mexico City with the thought of making a pointed statement there in front of the world (Edwards 1969).

In August 1968, the Soviet Union sent troops of the Warsaw Pact into Czechoslovakia, interrupting a period of considerable political ferment in that land. (The Czechs had beaten the Soviet hockey team at Grenoble, beginning a series of bitter matches between the two

---

From the Resolution of the Black Youth Conference, Los Angeles, November 23, 1967:

Whereas: The United States has failed to use its power—governmental or economic—to effectively alleviate the problems of 22 million black people in this country. . . .

Resolved: Black men and women athletes at a Black Youth Conference held in Los Angeles on the 23rd of November, 1967, have unanimously voted to fully endorse and participate in a boycott of the Olympic Games in 1968. . . .

Black track and field athletes have unanimously voted to boycott anything even remotely connected with the NYAC [New York Athletic Club]. . . .

Black men and women athletes have voted unanimously to boycott any meet in which participants from two countries in particular might be in participation.

These countries are:

1. South Africa
2. Southern Rhodesia

Harry Edwards, *The Revolt of the Black Athlete* (New York: The Free Press, 1969), pp. 55-56.

---

national teams.) Immediately there were calls—supported by prominent Czech Olympians—to withdraw the Soviets' and the East Germans' invitations to the Games. Brundage ignored efforts to draw a parallel between this and the South African question, and he repeated his statement of 1956, "If participation in sport is to be stopped every time the politicians violate the laws of humanity, there will never be any international contests" (Brundage Archive). The Olympic Games, Brundage kept insisting, had their own rationale and provided their own justification.

On the very eve of the Games, trouble erupted in Mexico City itself as rioting broke out among students who protested the cost of the Games as well as a variety of social problems. The Mexican military intervened, and after the military had established its control of the area, the Games could proceed as scheduled. The official body count in what John Hoberman (1986) has called the "Tlatelolco massacre" was 49 dead; other accounts put the number at over 250. Thus, the Mexico City Games opened under a dark cloud of political and social protest.

Brundage's basic arguments in struggling to keep his world intact despite the carnage in the streets revealed the consistency in his thoughts through the years. When the demonstrations began, he called on the Mexican authorities to keep the violence off "Olympic territory." In the 1930s, Brundage had approved of Baillet-Latour's insistence that the Games enjoyed an extraterritorial quality wherever they might be. The "sacred Olympic territory" encompassed a special realm that had a meaning and significance completely independent of what might be happening around it. In years to come, many observers would see the political demonstrations both outside and inside of the stadium in Mexico City as a precursor for violence in future Games. Hoberman called it the "worst crime in Olympic history," but Brundage and his colleagues gave no sign of recognizing this problem.

The political divisions in the world were, however, too real and too deep for the IOC to cover over. The Committee repeatedly had to make decisions and choices. To keep the black African states as members of the Olympic family, it had to exclude South Africa. To keep American runners in Munich, it agreed to disinvite Rhodesia. In trying to force the Indonesians to accept Israeli and Chinese Nationalist athletes, it faced challenges from the Soviets and others. In Tokyo the Iraqis refused to march beside the Israelis as the alphabet dictated. And yet, through it all, Avery Brundage still believed international amateur athletic competition, ritualized in the Olympic Games, could bring the peoples of the world together in peace and harmony.

Chapter 10

Brundage's Troubled Last Term

© Archive Photos

The terrorist attack against Israeli athletes at the Munich Games (1972) shattered the last illusion anyone might have had about the role of the Olympic Games as a haven from world politics. Although many called for the competition in Munich to end, Brundage ordered the Games to continue.

In the 1960s, Avery Brundage's supporters insisted he had done much to keep the Games free of politics; his critics accused him of insensitivity, prejudice, and obstinacy. Although he faced more and more opposition within the IOC, he still felt a mission to defend "amateur" athletics. In Mexico City he ran for reelection to another four-year term as IOC President. He won only with difficulty, however, and he essentially promised he would retire in 1972. The expansion of the Olympic Movement, increase in the number of participating countries, and new issues that intruded into the IOC's considerations were all to make his last term as President extremely difficult and taxing. He could justifiably claim the Olympics had achieved a new grandeur and attention during his time in office, but he was obviously incapable of controlling the IOC's further development. His critics impatiently awaited his departure.

To the casual observer, the Olympic competition in Mexico City seemed to rise above human strife. Before the Games there had been concern about both the altitude and climate of the city, but Brundage, long a propagator of sport in Latin America, had strongly supported the Mexicans. The Americans won more medals than ever before, collecting 45 gold, 28 silver, and 34 bronze, as compared to the Soviets' harvest of 29, 32, and 30. The closing ceremonies became a great festival when athletes unexpectedly surged onto the field to celebrate. "The Olympic Stadium," wrote one observer, "was now no longer a stage but a family circle. . . . The grass of the Olympic Stadium became a dance meadow. The Olympic closing ceremony transformed itself into a folk festival, unorganized, spontaneous, with infectious cheer" (Umminger 1968). Brundage, who had no love for spontaneity in Olympic ceremonies, was captivated by the scene: "The spontaneous demonstration of international good will during the emotion-charged closing ceremony left hardly a dry eye in the stadium" (Brundage Archive).

The celebration on the floor of the stadium, however, would not dominate the memory of the Games; instead, the Games's lasting image was one of protest. John Carlos and Tommie Smith caused a sensation during the awards ceremony for their medals in the 200-meter sprint when they raised their fists and stared at the ground during the playing of the American national anthem. For them, this was their contribution to the American black protest movement. The Olympic hierarchy reacted angrily: the Marquis of Exeter, David Lord Burghley, who was awarding the medals, indignantly threatened to halt all victory ceremonies, but history remembers the picture of protest as a trademark of these Games.

The Games also witnessed new suspicions concerning the athletes, marked by the introduction of tests both for drug use and determining the sex of the participants. Drug use by the athletes had long constituted a hazy subject in the shadow of the Games, brought into the open only occasionally as after the death of the Danish cyclist in 1960. In 1967, the IOC had established the Medical Commission, which drew up a list of forbidden drugs and insisted athletes at the Games must agree to "any examination thought necessary." There were no athletes disqualified for using forbidden substances at the Grenoble or Mexico City Games, although a Swedish pentathlete lost his bronze medal because of alcohol in his system. The IOC, however, could only test for drugs it had the means to detect. Rumors of drugs not yet traceable abounded in the Olympic Village; the IOC's battle with chemicals was just beginning.

The test for gender determination arose as a result of both complaints and revelations. Social commentators later questioned why such tests were necessary, but the all-male IOC had no doubts. As Allan Ryan, a medical historian noted, "There has been concern for a number of years that among the more successful female competitors many would be found who exhibited male characteristics" (1968). In the 1960s, western observers frequently questioned the character of some East European women champions. The Olympic authorities instituted a chromosome test for all women competitors in Mexico City, and while no women were disqualified, several recent East European champions failed to show up for the competition.

The Mexico City Games also marked a major step in the union between the Olympic Games and American television. Up to this time, American television executives had been unsure whether to treat them as news or entertainment. In 1964, ABC had obtained the rights to the Winter Games in Innsbruck for $200,000, and NBC had broadcast the Tokyo Games for a fee of $1.5 million. Prime time on the East Coast of the United States (8 to 11 P.M.) continued to comprise television's top market, and, faced by differences in time zones, neither network could offer much live programming despite earth satellites. In short, network executives did not yet believe in the potential of the Games for profitable evening broadcasting in the American market.

ABC purchased the rights for both the Winter and Summer Games in 1968, paying $2.5 million to the Grenoble organizers and $4.5 million to the Mexico City organizers. With no problem concerning time zones, ABC broadcast 44 hours of coverage from Mexico City, 10 of them in prime time. The network claimed great success in its programming and insisted it had now established the "standard by which all future [Olympic Games] would be judged"; the producer, Roone Arledge, in the words of Bert Sugar, had "caught it all. . . . Everything from Tommie Smith and John Carlos raising their black-gloved fists and lowering their heads during the playing of the American National Anthem to a Czech gymnast turning away her head during the playing of the Soviet Anthem" (1978). The broadcasts, to be sure, earned a Nielsen rating of only 14.0, with a share of 25 percent of the television sets in use, but ABC executives looked forward to greater achievements in the future.

Brundage had some misgivings about this new wealth. In 1967, he noted that the first consequence of the flow of television money had been the expansion of the headquarters of the IOC in Lausanne. The budget for 1966 had been over $60,000, as compared to an average of about $10,000 per year in the 1950s; the budget for 1967 was almost $120,000, and it would surely continue to grow. "The minute we handle money," he warned, "even if we only distribute it, there will be trouble. . . . In other words, we are in business, with all the problems that follow." The IOC nevertheless welcomed the money, which in turn stimulated new demands by NOC representatives, who organized themselves as the Assembly of NOCs (first GANOC, then ANOC), and IF representatives, who formed the General Assembly of International Sports Federations (GAIF). Brundage resisted these demands, but his critics and opponents simply waited all the more expectantly for his retirement in 1972.

The Soviets, who supported the demands of the ANOC and the GAIF, had some other ideas of reform. In both sets of Games in 1968, Soviet women competitors were less successful than they had been in the past. By the Soviets' own count, at Grenoble the Soviet women cross-country

---

Circular by Avery Brundage, April 17, 1967:

Until 1960, the operating expense of the Committee averaged about $10,000 a year for the Lausanne office (the President's office in Chicago operated at no expense to the Committee). The only money the Committee had then was the insignificant dues paid by the members and some small contributions from organizing committees. In 1961 and 62 for the first time, substantial sums were received from Rome, Innsbruck and Tokyo, and our expenses began to increase rapidly, until last year they were 266,669.23 Swiss francs, or over $60,000.00, an illustration of one of Parkinson's laws. . . .

Now our treasurer (we never even had a treasurer until recently) has presented a budget for 1967 of 505,000 francs, or almost $120,000, advancing to 600,000 or over $140,000.00 in the next three years. . . .

The minute we handle money, even if we only distribute it, there will be trouble, as we have already discovered. It is Olympic money; since we accept it we have assumed responsibility for its ultimate use and we must watch and approve how it is spent. In other words, we are in business, with all the problems that follow. . . . The International Olympic Committee was never designed to be a business organization and I am not sure we want it to be one.

It is time for a searching examination of where we are and where we are going.

Brundage Archive, University of Illinois.

---

skiers and the women speed skaters produced 72 points less than they had at Innsbruck in 1964. In Mexico City, the Soviet women track and field athletes garnered only 30 points, as opposed to 74 in Rome and 60 in Tokyo; some western commentators attributed this shortfall to Soviet concerns about gender testing in Mexico. Soviet analysts chose to concentrate on American successes they attributed to an overemphasis on the swimming competition, in which the American women had outscored the Soviet women 163-16, as opposed to 86-15 in 1964, and the American men had outscored their Soviet counterparts 152-45, as opposed to a 99-15 margin four years earlier. Altogether, the American swimmers accounted for 44 percent of the Americans' points; this, wrote Aleksei Romanov, "distorted" the team scores and "perverted" the "picture of harmony of the development of Olympic sports in various countries" (Brundage Archive).

As a result, the Soviets pressed the IOC and FINA for a reduction of the Olympic swimming program. In January 1971, Andrianov questioned "why there should be four different ways to swim 100 meters," and he attacked the introduction of "the 'intermediate' 200 meters distance" in various strokes. Swimmers, he argued, should not be permitted to compete "in 4, 5, 6, or 7(!) events" (Brundage Archive). (The Soviets never challenged multiple entries in gymnastics, in which they were strong.) Andrianov called for reducing the number of events, the number of entries allowed each country in an event, and the number of events in which one individual could compete. The Soviet campaign succeeded: FINA eventually dropped one women's event and agreed to limit each country to only two entries in an event. The cutback in the swimming program, together with the later emergence of the GDR as a major power in women's swimming, ate heavily into American point and medal production in subsequent Olympic competition.

The Soviets, however, suffered a great disappointment in their campaign to host the 1976 Summer Olympic Games. When the IOC met in Amsterdam in May 1970 to make the award, the contenders for the Summer Games were Montreal, Los Angeles, and Moscow. The Soviets still carried the burden of their government's intervention in Czechoslovakia: In Mexico City, their athletes had to eat separately from the athletes of the rest of the world, and their athletic contacts had suffered badly in 1969 (see table 10.1). Soviet officials nevertheless seemed more insistent on hosting the Olympic Games; Andrianov insisted there were "no political, economic, or sporting reasons why Moscow should not be chosen." When Brundage, at the conclusion of the first ballot, announced Moscow had the most votes, the Soviet delegation delightedly reported home that they had won.

Their triumph was ephemeral. Brundage called for a second ballot as the winner needed a majority of the votes, not just a plurality. The Pan-American vote, which had first supported Los Angeles, shifted to

Table 10.1

Decline of Soviet International Sports Relations in the Aftermath of the Czech Crisis, 1968

	EXCHANGE OF SPORTS DELEGATIONS					
	1966	**1967**	**1968**	**1969**	**1970**	**1971**
Going abroad						
Delegations	741	806	707	533	382	477
Athletes	7,952	8,677	8,238	7,585	5,803	6,388
Received in the USSR						
Delegations	529	699	636	504	110	389
Athletes	5,070	5,652	5,919	7,108	1,959	4,606
Countries	66	71	61	64	57	54

A.O. Romanov, *Mezhdunarodnoe sportivnoe dvizhenie* (Moscow: Fizkul'tura i sport, 1973), p. 196.

Montreal, and the IOC chose the Canadian city to host the 1976 Games. In their disappointment, the Soviets pointed out the 1976 Winter Games would go to Denver, Colorado, and they were sure that they could smell collusion. "The secret second ballot," declared Sergei Pavlov, the head of the Soviet NOC, "was not inspired by interests of sport and of strengthening Olympic ideals." Soviet publications mumbled darkly about past pro-Nazi sympathies among members of the IOC. Then in February 1971, Pavlov went so far as to threaten a Soviet boycott of Montreal: "There is no doubt that the West is misusing sport for political and ideological purposes. There is good reason, therefore, to assume that the Soviet Union will not take part in the 1976 Olympic Games" (Brundage Archive). Eventually, however, Moscow chose another course: Mobilizing their campaign for the 1980 Games more carefully, they reconstructed their international sport contacts and lobbied vigorously for Brundage's support, even though the American would clearly not be participating in the IOC's next decision on awarding future Games.

Brundage's last Games in 1972 brought together all the problems he had been struggling with. In preparation for the Winter Games in Sapporo, he had waged a prolonged battle with the International Skiing Federation (FIS), attacking the role of manufacturers in underwriting international competition. (His critics argued he should look more closely at the scandalous efforts of Puma and Adidas to sign up athletes in his beloved track and field competition, but Brundage only had eyes for problems with the Winter Games.) He had earlier wanted to ban 10 skiers for having coached in a camp, but when six countries threatened to boycott the Games in protest, FIS intervened to find a compromise. Then the Austrian Karl Schranz openly admitted to journalists in Japan he had taken payments from a ski manufacturer, and, complaining about the IOC's "nineteenth century attitudes," he declared the IOC favored "rich competitors over poor ones" (Espy 1981).

Schranz, whom Brundage criticized for being "disrespectful of the Olympic movement," (Brundage Archive) had been on the payroll of an Austrian ski manufacturer for some years and was reportedly earning some $60,000 annually skiing. He was, in fact, no exception. The number of participants in the sport had increased some five times since the end of World War II, and this was big business. Indeed, ski manufacturers contributed heavily to various European ski federations. Brundage declared in Japan, "If we confine the skiers allowed to compete in the Olympics to those who can meet the eligibility requirements of the IOC, then all the prominent skiers of the world—both Alpine and Nordic—must be disqualified" (Brundage Archive). At Grenoble, Brundage had objected to the skiers' displaying brand names on their equipment; in Sapporo, he decided to make an example of Schranz. Brundage persuaded the IOC to expel him from the Olympic Village, calling the Austrian the "most blatant and verbose" offender among the skiers (Brundage Archive).

Controversy ensued: Austrian skiers threatened to withdraw from the Games, the Austrians made Schranz a national hero, and callers threatened the American embassy in Vienna. But Brundage held his ground, rebuffing Schranz's appeal for a hearing before the IOC with a terse "We don't deal with individuals" (Brundage Archive). In the end, Schranz, excluded from the Games, went home to a hero's welcome, and the skiers lined up with all the others who were impatiently awaiting Brundage's retirement.

Otherwise, the competition in Sapporo saw no serious incidents. The Americans won second place in hockey, while the Soviets took the gold for the third time in a row. (Brundage had reportedly threatened some sort of challenge to the amateur status of the Soviet hockey players, then he apparently thought better of it.) In the medals recapitulation at the end of the competition, the Soviets led with a total of 16, 8 of them gold, but a sign of the future lay in the victories of the East Germans. The GDR boasted 14 medals, 4 of them gold. The United States stood fifth in total medals, seventh in the unofficial point count.

When the IOC turned its attention to the upcoming competition in Munich, Brundage and his colleagues hoped they had put the South African question behind them. In December 1968, the United Nations General Assembly had called for the ending of all sport relations with the

Republic of South Africa, and one international sports federation after another had been breaking off all ties with the beleaguered state. The IOC had chosen not to act in 1969, but at its Amsterdam meeting of 1970, it hoped to resolve its African tangle once and for all when it withdrew recognition of SANOC. Even so, the vote was only 35 to 28, with three abstentions; a significant proportion of the IOC's membership still opposed forceful action. Even so, the IOC had unloaded its South African albatross.

Then to its dismay, the IOC discovered the SCSA and the Organization of African Unity (OAU), a council for coordinating the diplomacy of African states, were now focusing on Rhodesia. In the latter 1960s, Southern Rhodesia had declared its independence of British rule in the midst of dispute over its domestic racial policies. The Commonwealth refused to recognize this action, and the United Nations Security Council called upon member states not to recognize Rhodesian passports. In 1968, Brundage had tried to arrange for Rhodesian athletes to use Olympic identity cards in lieu of passports in coming to Mexico City, but the Mexican authorities would not permit the Rhodesians into the country. In preparation for Munich, the IOC renewed this proposal. Brundage was convinced there was no discrimination in Rhodesian sport on the scale of South African sport, and he did not want to exclude the Rhodesians from the Games: Rhodesia planned to field a racially mixed team; an IAAF investigation in 1971 had found athletic facilities in the country in order. At first, African Olympic officials approved of the IOC's efforts to find a compromise solution to the question, but at the insistence of OAU leaders, they then reversed themselves, calling for Rhodesia's outright exclusion from the Games. Certainly, the issue of Rhodesia's participation in the Munich Games dealt with the political, not the sport, situation in Rhodesia (Daniels 1996).

By arrangement, the Rhodesians arrived in Germany using Olympic identity cards instead of British passports, but their blazers carried the name "Rhodesia." A Rhodesian Olympic official reportedly declared, "We are ready to participate under any flag, be it the flag of the Boy Scouts or a Moscow flag. But everyone knows very well that we are Rhodesians and will always remain Rhodesians." Calling this statement "arrogant," opponents claimed the Rhodesians had violated the terms of their agreement with the IOC.

The athletes pouring into Germany for the Games soon entered the debate. In a remarkable mixture of politics, sport, and journalism, an ABC correspondent, Terry O'Neil (1989), covering the Games for his network, helped American track and field athletes draw up a formal resolution the American delegation then passed on to the IOC. When a Rhodesian team, seven of whose eight members were black, showed up at a practice meet

---

Protest of the US Track and Field Team Against the Presence of Rhodesia:

Many athletes and staff are personally concerned and disturbed about the social injustices caused as a result of the racial discrimination enforced and practiced through the political and governmental structure of S. Rhodesia. . . .

It must be pointed out therefore that the present position of the IOC on this question has placed the subject in the political atmosphere which is contrary to the basic ideals of the Olympic Movement which the IOC has so strongly pursued through its long history.

It is strongly felt that the previous decision to allow S. Rhodesia to participate in this Olympiad should be re-examined. Hopefully S. Rhodesia will also re-examine its position in light of recent developments and voluntarily withdraw. Otherwise the IOC should use its influence to have S. Rhodesia withdraw or reverse the earlier position which authorized their participation.

Through these actions S. Rhodesia or the IOC will free the Olympic athletes of the moral and political decision presently confronting them, and they will be able to join all other athletes in the free spirit of Olympic competition.

Brundage Archive, University of Illinois.

---

outside of Munich, all the African nationals present, together with 18 Americans, refused to compete.

By the narrow vote of 36-31, with three abstentions, the IOC backed down and disinvited the Rhodesians at the last minute, declaring their passports were not in order. Brundage, who called the pressure exerted on the Committee "political blackmail," bitterly opposed the decision. He later wrote to Ian Douglas Smith, the Rhodesian Prime Minister, "For the first time in 20 years, the Committee failed to follow my recommendation. If the African politicians, however, think they won a victory, they are mistaken. . . . The general public has announced emphatically that it will not tolerate political interference in amateur sport and the Olympic Games" (Brundage Archive). Obviously, Brundage and the Olympic Movement had reached a parting of ways; indeed, Brundage could not reconcile himself to the Games' new agenda.

As the Olympic world focused on Munich, the Soviet Union was expressing other concerns that failed to reach the public agenda. From the time the IOC, in 1966, had chosen Munich as the host for the 1972 Games, Soviets had been complaining that the city—"the site of numerous emigré and neo-Nazi organizations, revanchist clubs and societies, 'Liberty' and 'Free Europe' radio stations, financed by the CIA and conducting sabotage against the socialist states"—was unfit for the honor and even unsafe for East European athletes (Grigor'ev et al. 1974). The German government

Statement of the USSR Olympic Committee, Included in Andrianov's Letter to Brundage, March 2, 1972:

As the opening of the XXth Olympic Games in Munich is coming nearer, the international sports circles are more and more interested in their preparation, and in the situation in the organising country. The fear showed by the sporting world is quite normal and understandable: during the last few years, various reactionaries have been increasing their activities in the FRG, to revive hate and enmity between peoples of the world. The Radio stations "Liberty" and "Radio Free Europe" whose headquarters are in Munich, close to the Olympic Stadiums, are striving to spread discord between the participants of the Olympic Games of all countries and continents. . . .

We have heard that right now, projects are being planned with the aim of creating a "500 metres zone" around the Olympic areas in Munich and Kiel, within which limits, any action by political groups is forbidden. These proposals contribute a political subterfuge and offer favourable conditions for the activities of the scum of emigrants, of all kinds of reactionaries, and of mercenaries hired by the Neo-Nazi organizations. It is useless to prove that these "plans" rudely scoff at the Olympic traditions. . . .

The USSR Olympic Committee condemns the provocative activities of these different political groups and organisations in the FRG, which threaten the smooth holding of the Olympic Games. . . . We propose that the IOC Executive Board should study the problem of establishing the necessary conditions for the smooth running of the 1972 Olympic Summer Games in the FRG, according to the Olympic tradition of peace and friendship.

Brundage Archive, University of Illinois (original in English).

proclaimed "forbidden zones" around the Olympic sites where no political demonstrations would be tolerated, but the Soviets still considered the city hostile territory.

Adding to the tension in Munich was the old rivalry between the two Germanies. The West German government had made significant steps toward establishing a more cordial relationship with the GDR in the last several years, but West German officials still looked with some trepidation at the prospect of East German athletic triumphs in Munich. In fact, several years earlier the President of the International Olympic Academy, a West German, had suggested that at Munich the "playing of the national anthem and the raising of the national flag be dispensed with and instead the Olympic flag should be raised and a neutral anthem played." The East Europeans, who in any case insisted on maintaining all the national symbols in Olympic ceremonies, interpreted this as specifically a maneuver to avoid honoring East German victors in Munich. Thus, the national anthems and the national flags remained a part of the ceremonies.

Once the Games began, the Americans suffered one disaster after another. Their favorite wrestler, Chris Taylor, lost to a Russian, Aleksandr

Medved, in the first round of the heavyweight competition. The Americans protested the officiating, but although the Turkish referee was fired, the decision stood. The bad luck did not end there, however: The American pole vaulter Bob Seagren saw his pole outlawed at the last moment. Because a track coach could not read his timetable, two runners, Eddie Hart and Rey Robinson, missed their events. An American swimmer, Rick DeMont, lost his gold medal when tests discovered banned substances in his system. Overall, American Olympic officials seemed disorganized, and a heavy barrage of criticism focused on the organizational structure of the American delegation. There were successes, however, such as Mark Spitz's seven gold medals in swimming—the new FINA rules provided that this could not be repeated in later Olympics, however.

In the early morning of September 5, political violence intruded into the Games when a group of terrorists sneaked into the Olympic Village and broke into the quarters of Israeli wrestlers, taking them hostage. While ABC TV broadcast the drama to the world, the Games halted, and the terrorists demanded access to world press and television, transportation for themselves out of Germany, and the liberation of prisoners in Israel (Daniels 1996). After a day-long standoff, under cover of darkness, the

---

From a Statement Sent by the Captors of the Israeli Athletes to the German Authorities:

To be publicized!
America belongs to Indians from creation till forever.
Africa to colored peaple [sic].
Palestine to Arabs.
Australia to Australians.
Sons and dothers [sic] of God
Buddha who showed how to live
Mahommad who exampled how to live
Gandhi who chased english crooks
Hitler who cleaned Europe out of Jewish dirt and [illegible] accomplices
He will be back to finish his good work.
Jeanne of D'Arc who chased English crooks and witches by them burned as a witch she came back to [illegible]
Mao tse Tung who chased all crooks
Indira Gandhi who chased crooks ist [sic] beautiful and doing is [sic] good work.
Fidel Castro who cleaned his country out of Jewish and American bastards.
Geronimo Indian Freedom Fighter

Brundage Archive, University of Illinois (original, including grammatical and spelling errors, in English).

German authorities provided the terrorists with helicopter transportation to the airport, where, in a shoot-out, all the Israeli hostages and five of the terrorists were killed. Amid debate over the actions of the German authorities, the question arose whether the Olympic Games should continue.

The IOC had already elected Lord Killanin as its new President, but Brundage was due to retire only at the conclusion of the Games. Therefore, Brundage was still in office at the time of the terrorist attack, and he pointedly ignored his colleagues and even his successor. He attached himself to the German crisis staff, where his first concern—an echo of his demands of Mexican officials in 1968—was that the terrorists and their hostages should leave Olympic territory as quickly as possible. His intervention, however, was ineffectual; he played no significant role in the drama.

After the death of the athletes, Brundage, echoing his positions in 1936, 1956, and 1968, insisted the Games must nevertheless continue. On the evening of the 5th, he met with the IOC. Killanin, furious at having been ignored, had called the Committee into session, and, amid news some national delegations were withdrawing and individual athletes were fleeing the Olympic Village, he won the Committee's agreement to continue the Games. "The decision—to cancel or not—was a hard one to make," Killanin wrote later, "but I believe that Brundage was right to continue and that his stubborn determination saved the Olympic Movement one more time" (1983). To cancel the Games at this point, Killanin thought, would only cause further trouble: "It would be impossible to evacuate all the competitors, officials, and spectators rapidly from Munich and there would inevitably be demonstrations." Despite all justifications, the decision to continue the Games sat poorly with many observers, some of whom still resented the way in which the IOC had ignored the violence in Mexico City four years earlier.

The IOC scheduled a memorial service in the Olympic Stadium for the morning of the 6th, and there Brundage compounded the controversy already swirling around him by linking the killing of the Israelis with the threats of a black boycott over the Rhodesian issue (Brundage Archive):

> Sadly, in this imperfect world, the greater and the more important the Olympic Games become, the more they are open to commercial, political and now criminal pressure. The Games of the XX Olympiad have been subject to two savage attacks. We lost the Rhodesian battle against naked political blackmail. We have only the strength of a great ideal. I am sure that the public will agree that we cannot allow a handful of terrorists to destroy this nucleus of international cooperation and good will we have in the Olympic Movement. The Games must go on and we must continue our efforts to keep them clean, pure and honest and try to extend the sportsmanship of the athletic field into other areas.

Killanin later suggested, "It was not what he said that was objectionable in itself, but the occasion on which he said it" (Killanin 1983). The shock waves came rolling in immediately as the African states objected to Brundage's comments.

SCSA leaders in Munich protested, delivering a statement deploring the killings of the day before but also denouncing Brundage's "unjustified attack" on the decision to exclude Rhodesia, which "was taken by the majority of the members of the IOC within the framework of the Olympic *Charter*" (Brundage Archive). The protest castigated Brundage's references to "savage attack" and "naked political blackmail" and concluded, "In spite of the insult to us and to the members of the IOC, we reaffirm our faith in the Olympic movement, and appreciation for the efforts of the Organizing Committee of the Games of the XXth Olympiad." Like many others in the Olympic community, the Africans had now separated Brundage from their image of the Games; they too were looking forward to his retirement.

Despite the horror expressed by his colleagues in the IOC, Brundage insisted, "The reference to Rhodesia in my remarks this morning was deliberate," but finally he yielded. "As President of the International Olympic Committee we regret any misinterpretation of the remarks made during the solemn memorial service in the stadium yesterday," he stated

---

Press Release by the Supreme Council for Sport in Africa:

1. We, the National Olympic Committees of Africa condemn the tragic incident which occurred yesterday at the Olympic Village that threw the entire Olympic Movement into mourning and wish to express our profound condolence to the families of the victims.

2. We deeply deplore the unjustified attack made by Mr. Brundage, President of the IOC, in his statement at the solemn memorial service held this morning at the Olympic Stadium.

3. The decision to exclude Rhodesia from the Munich Olympic Games was taken by the majority of the members of the IOC within the framework of the Olympic Charter.

4. We strongly disapprove the President of the IOC's reference to the Rhodesian question which was tackled in a constitutional manner, but described by him as a "savage attack" and "naked political blackmail," and his linking of the issue with the tragic incident of yesterday. We regard this as an attempt to mar the peace and goodwill which the President of the Federal Republic of Germany appealed for.

5. In spite of the insult to us and to the members of the IOC, we reaffirm our faith in the Olympic Movement, and appreciation for the efforts of the Organizing Committee of the Games of the XXth Olympiad.

Munich, 6th September, 1972

Brundage Archive, University of Illinois (original in English).

---

publicly. "There was not the slightest intention of linking the Rhodesia question, which is purely a matter of sport, with an act of terrorism universally condemned" (Brundage Archive). And the Games went on.

The troubles of the Americans continued as before. Two black athletes, Vince Matthews and Wayne Collett, having placed first and second in the 400-meter run, echoed the black protests at Mexico City by refusing to stand at attention during the awards ceremony. At Brundage's urging, the IOC Executive Board denounced their action as a "disgusting display" and ordered them out of the Olympic Village. The American team was torn by dissension and recriminations, and then, as if the product of a poor scriptwriter, the American basketball team lost to the Soviets in a disputed ending for the gold medal. Juxtaposing the loss in basketball to the unexpected success a Soviet hockey team was having at the same time in playing Canadian professionals in a special separate confrontation, some American commentators thought they were witnessing the "collapse" of western civilization.

When the Games ended, the Americans were distraught, the Soviets jubilant. The Soviets boasted a harvest of 50 gold medals—symbolic, they declared, of their celebration of the 50th anniversary of the formation of the USSR in 1922. Whether one calculated the results in points or medals, the Soviet Union stood far ahead of the United States in terms of team achievements at Munich, and Soviet officials believed they had fully recovered from whatever problems they had faced in Mexico City.

After Munich, Brundage departed the Games, which had grown beyond his comprehension and his capacity to adjust. The NOCs and the IFs were revolting against his arbitrary administration; violence had invaded his holy mountain and was giving every indication of returning; despite all his efforts to reach out to the world through athletics, he stood accused of bigotry and both racial and class prejudice, not to mention the denunciations proclaiming him politically naive. After Brundage's clash with Karl Schranz in Sapporo, Red Smith wrote of him, "Avery Brundage is both the president and symbol of the IOC. He is a rich and righteous anachronism, at eighty-four a vestigial remnant of an economy that supported a leisure class that could compete in athletics for fun alone. His wrath is the more terrible because it is so sincere and unenlightened" (1983). For Brundage, the killing of the Israeli athletes in Munich had delivered a final, crushing blow. In the words of John Lucas, "His beloved Olympics had been used for pillage, political blackmail, and murder—a travesty of all the Brundage utterances of a half-century" (1980). Few mourned his departure from the Olympic scene, and the International Olympic Committee turned to his successor, who, its members hoped, would be better suited to handle the new issues on its agenda.

Part III

"Opening" the Games

Lord Killanin, the President of the IOC, speaks to the press just before opening the Montreal Games (1976). A number of African teams boycotted these Games, and it would be another twelve years before the Summer Games would be again free of major boycotts.

Brundage's successor as President of the IOC, Michael Morris, Lord Killanin, an English-Irish nobleman born in 1914, had been a member of the IOC since 1952. In 1966, he became the Committee's Chief of Protocol. In 1967, he joined the Executive Board. In 1968, he became Vice President, and in 1969 he became Chief of the Press Section. Considered a pragmatist, much in contrast to Brundage's idealism, Killanin offered a completely new style of management, professing to want to hear everyone out, but still maintaining ultimate control of the Games. He convened the first Olympic Congress in over 40 years and made his peace with the ambitious leaders of the NOCs and IFs. He also successfully defended the Games against an effort by ambitious UNESCO leaders to take them over. Most importantly for the character of the competition, he supervised the liberalization of eligibility rules, preparing the way for his successor, Juan Antonio Samaranch, to "open" the Games to professionals.

This was, however, an age of boycotts. The threat of boycott was itself not new: The Berlin Games of 1936 had faced it; Avery Brundage threatened an American boycott in St. Moritz in 1948; a number of countries threatened boycott in 1956; African countries had threatened to boycott the Games in Mexico City in 1968; and black athletes threatened to boycott both Mexico City in 1968 and Munich in 1972. The major difference in the next three Games—1976, 1980, and 1984—was that countries followed through on their threats: Black African states withdrew from the 1976 Games in Montreal; the United States and a number of other states kept their athletes from Moscow in 1980; and the Soviet Union and its allies refused to go to Los Angeles in 1984. The future of the Games often appeared to be in doubt, but the athletes and dignitaries who attended the Games that were under attack nevertheless enjoyed their moments in the Olympic sun. The boycotters insisted the competition was inferior because they had stayed away, but while the boycotts allowed many athletes to win medals who might otherwise not have had a chance, the winners spent little time regretting the absence of those who had not come. Eventually all sides began to reconsider the usefulness of boycotting competitions that went ahead without them.

During Killanin's term of office, the IOC also faced a unique series of problems in its dealings with local Organizing Committees. Denver backed out on its bid to host the 1976 Winter Games, and the costs of the Montreal Games outstripped income. Only one city, Los Angeles, bid for the 1984 Summer Games, and Killanin thought the Los Angeles organizers' intention of running a low-cost Games foretold disaster. So when the Lake Placid Winter Games of 1980 experienced a plethora of problems in their local arrangements, Killanin had little good to say about any Americans. He much preferred the style of the Soviet authorities who generously invested state funds in the Moscow Games of 1980. In spite of these problems, however, Killanin (1983) was proud to report that under his stewardship, 1972 to 1980, the IOC's assets had grown from $2 million to over $45 million.

Lord Killanin retired as President of the IOC in 1980 for reasons of health, and his successor, Juan Antonio Samaranch, a Spaniard, completed the process of bringing the Olympic Games into alignment with the modern sport world. A one-time Sports Minister in the Franco government in Spain, Samaranch, who joined the IOC in 1966, served as Spanish ambassador to Moscow for the four years preceding the Moscow Games of 1980. As President of the IOC, he had to deal with the Soviet boycott of Los Angeles in 1984, with the challenge of the Goodwill Games of 1986, and the political booby traps surrounding the Seoul Games of 1988, yet under his leadership, the Games and the IOC have enjoyed unprecedented prestige and wealth.

Probably the two greatest developments in the operation of the Games Samaranch has overseen have been the growing role of women in the IOC itself and opening the Games to "professionals." As mentioned, Samaranch named the first two women to the IOC in 1981. In 1997 when he won reelection as President of the Committee into the 21st century, popular speculation suggested that a woman might be his eventual successor.

The introduction of professionals had mixed results. Track and field performers tended to compete longer now that they had legal, assured incomes. The domination of the basketball competition by American professionals, dubbed "Dream Teams," caused many American observers to fret about issues of fairness. The admission of professional soccer players seemed to have little impact since FIFA insisted upon imposing age limitations on Olympic soccer, thereby maintaining the World Cup as its premier competition. Major League Baseball has yet to come to terms with Samaranch's desire to have its players compete in the Olympics. In contrast, the decision of the National Hockey League to suspend its season for a few weeks in 1998 so its players could represent their home countries in the Olympics appeared successful.

Baron de Coubertin could hardly have had an inkling of the financial rewards the IOC would realize in the latter part of the 20th century. Television has introduced the word "billions" into Olympic vocabulary. Shoe and equipment companies have now joined ski manufacturers in the struggle to clothe athletes and appeal to buyers. The IOC itself has established a marketing structure to secure its own direct funnels for cash. Olympic officials insist they are not compromising with commercialism or show business, but they fully recognize they have to sell their product to the public cash cow that supports their work.

The Seoul Games of 1988 marked the last time a Soviet team would compete. By the time of the 1992 Games, the Soviet Union had collapsed, and 15 new republics had sprung from its rubble. The German Democratic Republic, moreover, disappeared altogether, swallowed up by the Federal Republic of Germany. The Soviet Union had played a major role in international sport, and in the late 1980s, even in the death throes of their state apparatus, Soviet officials could still mobilize support from the IOC and especially from FIFA, the international soccer federation, against their internal opponents. This would suggest a great deal about the ways in which established sport programs can support political authorities regardless of ideology. The Games themselves, however, went on.

In any case, the collapse of the Soviet Union meant the end of the Cold War with all its ramifications for Olympic politics, but this did not mark the end of Olympic politics. Nor did it mean the end of national rivalries in the Games any more than the end of the Cold War meant the end of national conflicts in Eastern Europe. The massive sport confrontations of the Cold War era would now seem to have dissolved into a number of lesser clashes spread across a variety of sports. Athletes who once represented the Soviet Union now represent Russian ice hockey, Lithuanian basketball, or Kazakhstani skating. For the moment, confrontations occur in specific sports rather than across the entire intersport spectrum. Yet, when American wrestlers competed in Iran in 1998, observers wondered whether they were hearing echoes of Chinese "Ping-Pong" diplomacy.

The major national rivalry on the horizon seems to involve the relationships between the United States and China. After a generation of ignoring the Olympic Games, the People's Republic of China rejoined the Games in the 1970s, and by the 1990s, it was offering formidable athletic competition to the rest of the world. On the basis of the experiences of the second half of the 20th century, one can expect strong sport performances from a system in which a powerful, centralized government supports an athletic program that can draw on a population of over one billion people. The question might simply be "Will China focus on the Olympic program as the Soviets did or will it concentrate on select sports?"

Chapter 11

Seeking the Lee

Olga Korbut, a Soviet gymnast, helped publicize women's gymnastics at the Munich Games (1972) and was the media darling of the Montreal Games (1976).

Michael Morris Lord Killanin, Avery Brundage's successor as President of the IOC, directed the Games through eight stormy years. When he took office, the NOCs and IFs were rebelling against Brundage's autocratic rule; the influx of television money was evoking plans for spending it; the Soviets were still pouting about Moscow's rejection as the site for the 1976 Games; and Olympic officials were generally shaken by the bloodshed in Munich. Although the IOC entertained no regrets for having continued the Games in Munich after the deaths of the Israelis, a few voices, recalling the death toll in Mexico City, were questioning whether the Games were in fact worth the dangers that now seemed to accompany them. Brundage, in his parting words, warned that Montreal would be unable to meet its commitments. It was Killanin's task to search for calmer waters in which to survive the Games' immediate troubles as well as reestablish their mystique as a meeting of the world's youth.

Killanin felt Brundage's manner and mannerisms had needlessly caused problems, and he brought a new style of leadership into the Presidency. As President, he would never take the precipitate, compulsive actions Brundage had, and he was far more ready to hold general meetings and work with subcommittees. Nevertheless, he was, in John Lucas's words, "every bit as adamant as was Brundage regarding the need to continue the nondemocratic, self-selecting characteristics of the IOC, and to strengthen rather than diminish the power of its presidency" (1980).

The new President ran into his first major crisis with the failure of Denver, Colorado, to meet its promises for holding the 1976 Winter Games. "I shall always remember the confidence and panache with which the Denver delegation made the original bid for the Games," Killanin (1983) later recalled bitterly. In November 1972, because of local environmentalist opposition to the Games, the question went to a referendum of the voters in the state, and the Colorado electorate declared they would not support the Games. Denver organizers had to give up. While Killanin insisted the people had rejected their own politicians rather than the Olympic Games, the IOC had to find another site with barely three years left to prepare. It chose Innsbruck, perhaps to some degree as a payment of conscience for what Brundage had done to Karl Schranz in Sapporo only a year earlier.

This first crisis resolved, Killanin set about reforming the Olympic structure. The NOCs and the IFs had been demanding a joint meeting of the various branches of the Olympic structure for some time, but Brundage had kept putting it off, preferring to deal with other Olympic institutions on an individual basis. In the fall of 1973, an Olympic Congress, called the Xth, brought the IOC together with representatives of the NOCs and IFs in Varna, Bulgaria. The Soviet Union had been particularly active in pushing for such a meeting. Soviet commentators spoke darkly of "reactionary elements" in the IOC who had willfully blocked efforts aimed at "democratizing" the Olympic Movement, and they argued the VIth Congress, which had met in Paris in 1914, had established the Congress as the "legislative organ of the IOC," and the VIIth, which had met in Lausanne in 1921, had achieved the stature of "supreme organ of the IOC" (Romanov 1973). In the face of such views, Killanin had to tread carefully.

Preparing for a confrontation, Killanin created a Tripartite Commission, made up of representatives of the NOCs, the IFs, and the IOC. Brundage had proposed such a group in 1968 to consider major problems of the Olympic Movement, but at that time both the NOCs and the IFs were still building their separate constituencies and were not ready for such coordination. Now the time had apparently arrived. Killanin designed the Commission to stand below the IOC, thereby reducing the ANOC and the GAIF to yet another level lower in the bureaucratic flowchart of Olympic institutions. He took the post of Chairman of the Commission for himself. When he permitted the Commission to continue to exist after the Congress had disbanded, some of his colleagues feared it could threaten the authority of the IOC, but, in fact, Killanin kept tight control over the reins of power.

In another move while preparing for the IOC's confrontation with the NOCs and the IFs, the IOC launched a new program called Olympic Solidarity. This provided aid for developing sport programs in the Third World, both in helping athletes and coaches to visit major sport centers throughout the world and sending experienced coaches in various sports to the countries that wanted them. An analogous program had failed in the early 1960s for lack of money, but now, backed by television revenues, the IOC had the funds to make it work. In turn, the NOCs of the Third World, the members of the Olympic family most in need of outside financial assistance, found many of their needs satisfied without needing to pursue further institutional change in the Olympic structure.

The Olympic Congress, which had power to recommend but not to legislate, paid special attention to two major questions: It called for greater participation of women in the Olympic Movement and liberalized the rules for eligibility in the Games, dropping the historic references to "amateurism." Both sets of issues enhanced the responsibilities and programs of the IFs, and neither could have been resolved under Brundage's rule. The one women's team sport Brundage had brought into the Games was women's volleyball, and that was because he had been very impressed by the dedication and determination of the Japanese women playing the sport. Women's basketball, which began in 1976, had to wait both because of Brundage's aversion to admitting new team sports and also FIBA's concern that the available court space in the Olympics barely sufficed for the men.

Women's field hockey, which joined the Games in Moscow in 1980, had long faced exclusion because their officials had refused to merge their organization (IFWHA), which had existed since 1927, into the men's federation (FIH). Now they reached a compromise, and the two federations merged in 1983.

The Congress also recommended that more women participate in Olympic institutions and in the IOC, but the IOC was slow to follow this recommendation. Killanin (1983) later explained he had had some women in mind as candidates, but they were from lands already fully represented in the IOC by males. At least one current member of the Committee, he declared, had actually withdrawn his offer to retire when he learned a woman would replace him. Whatever his reasons, Killanin named no woman to the IOC during his term in office.

On questions of "amateurism" and "eligibility," the IFs had long argued they should have the power to determine the eligibility of competitors in their sports, but Brundage had insisted the IOC should control questions of amateurism and eligibility. Killanin hoped to settle the question through compromise. As he recounted in his memoirs "When elected president, I was asked by the press whether the Olympic Games would ever be 'open,' i.e., for professionals and amateurs. Unfortunately, I replied harshly, 'Never'; from then onwards I have never used the word 'never'" (1983). At Killanin's urging, the Olympic Congress approved the principle of broken-time payments, but the athletes still had to meet both the requirements posed by their respective federations as well as the by-laws of the IOC.

The new rule on eligibility pointedly dropped the use of the term "amateur," and the IOC's by-law specified a competitor may be a physical education or sport teacher who gives elementary instruction and he or she may accept assistance through an NOC or a national federation for food and lodging, transportation, pocket money, insurance, equipment, and medical treatment. At the same time, he or she could not be a professional in any sport, allow his or her name to be used for advertising, carry advertising "other than trademarks on technical equipment or clothing," or have been a coach. The federations would have liked the IOC to have no by-laws at all on eligibility, but the IOC was not yet ready to go that far.

In all, the Xth Olympic Congress endorsed Killanin's leadership, and the spirit of the meeting also gave great promise for the future. With the tensions of the Brundage era eliminated, the members of the IOC hoped they could also put the nightmare of Munich behind them. The Soviets enthusiastically welcomed the changes proposed by the Congress because now their own practices were beyond any western reproach. In 1974, the IOC formally adopted the Congress's proposal, and in so doing, it reaffirmed its own status as an institution superior to the Congress, with the power to accept or reject the Congress's recommendations.

The spirit of Varna carried over into the IOC's annual session in 1974, at which it accepted the Congress's recommendations and made its selection of sites for the 1980 Games. It granted one wish to each of the two superpowers: Lake Placid received the Winter Games and Moscow the Summer Games. Los Angeles had also applied for the Summer Games, but the Soviets, now recovered from their post-Prague ostracism, won as had been expected. To avoid the confusion of 1970, Killanin announced the decision in Moscow's favor was unanimous.

Despite the orderliness of the IOC's affairs, however, observers greeted the Winter Games of 1976, held in Innsbruck, with a certain trepidation. These would be the first Olympic Games held since the bloodshed in Munich, and the Austrians provided elaborate security. Indeed, the police in Innsbruck outnumbered the athletes by two to one. The Soviets won their fourth straight hockey championship. The American hockey team failed to win a medal, but the players received special attention for having engaged in a barroom brawl that resulted in the arrest of two of them. Some IOC members noted this latest misadventure of their American cousins and, remembering their anger over Denver's decision to withdraw, wondered whether they had acted properly in choosing Lake Placid for 1980. The Soviets won 13 gold medals and again claimed the unofficial team championship, while the East Germans demonstrated the strength of their program by finishing second. The festival passed without any serious political controversy, and IOC members breathed more easily.

Then the Summer Games in Montreal brought new controversy and problems. Montreal's mayor, Jean Drapeau, now in office for some 20 years, wanted the world's attention upon his city, and he pointed to Expo '67, the World's Fair held in Montreal a few years earlier, as proof of the city's potential for handling an international extravaganza. Although the fair had run a deficit of $200 million, which Canadian federal and provincial authorities had picked up, Drapeau argued that since money was still coming in from an amusement park built for the fair, the books on Expo '67 were not yet closed (Ludwig 1976). The IOC accepted Drapeau's declarations at face value. Killanin explained that the choice of Montreal represented an effort to show that hosting the Olympic Games should not be a costly enterprise beyond the means of some of the world's smaller great cities.

Drapeau promised this would be an inexpensive and self-financing celebration, and, in contrast to the ongoing efforts of western Canadians to host the Winter Olympics, he requested no special aid from the federal government of Canada. This left him with a free hand in making arrangements, and he dismissed questions about his budget with the vague estimate, "About 300 million, but don't ask me to break that down." He was widely quoted as having asserted, "The Montreal Olympics can no more have a deficit than a man can have a baby" (Ludwig 1976).

Preparations for the Montreal Games became more confused and controversial as the Games grew closer. Unable to raise enough money from the provincial government, Drapeau turned to private business, looking for corporate sponsors. At the same time, he persuaded the Canadian Prime Minister, Pierre Elliot Trudeau, to provide security, mint a commemorative coin, help pay for a broadcasting center, and sponsor an Olympic lottery. The Organizing Committee angered many Canadians by hiring a Parisian, not a Canadian architect, and then it opened bidding only to select companies. As Drapeau explained to a journalist, "A closed group was invited by telephone to file a bid with an estimate" (Ludwig 1976).

Financial problems grew apace. Construction, already extravagant, ran afoul of labor problems and galloping inflation. Stories abounded of workers' striking so as to extort more money and then still not working so as to enjoy large overtime payments. Soviet historians put the blame on the contractors and financiers, who, they say, exploited the Games (Stepovoi 1984). While costs mounted, sources of anticipated income dried up: European television rights brought less than one-third the revenue expected; the Olympic coin netted only half its anticipated take; security costs soared in the aftermath of the Munich killings. Drapeau blamed the financial problems on inflation, especially the soaring costs of oil and steel, but critics insisted the whole management procedure was wasteful. Estimates on the total deficit in staging the Games ran to well over $1 billion with various construction projects still unfinished.

Then came the Games' political problems, involving first of all China. The mid-1970s saw the reentry of the Chinese People's Republic into international sport competition, heralded by "Ping-Pong diplomacy," whereby a visit of American table tennis players to mainland China signaled that more significant political and economic relations might follow. To reenter the international sport world, the Chinese moved first into those federations in which the Nationalist Chinese (the Taiwanese) did not compete. In an established, well-organized sport like swimming, the PRC ran into problems: When the United States State Department proposed a visit to China by a group of American swimmers, FINA threatened to suspend anyone who took part because the PRC was not a part of FINA. Asked to make an exception, FINA refused, explaining that it had invited China to rejoin FINA, but Beijing continued to demand that Taiwan resign from the federation. A group of American swimmers went anyway, apparently having decided their days of international competition had ended. Still, the Chinese return to international sport competition obviously faced a variety of hurdles.

By 1975, the PRC had reorganized its National Olympic Committee, and it applied to the IOC for readmission to the Olympic family. Again the question rose whether to recognize two Chinas or to expel Taiwan. The "momentum," as sport analysts like to say, now lay with the People's Republic. Killanin planned to make a fact-finding visit to China, but he could not fit it into his schedule before the Montreal Games. So as the athletes began to arrive in Canada for the competition, the Chinese question still hung in the air.

The Canadian government had followed a one-China policy since 1972, recognizing only the People's Republic, and in 1976 it was in the middle of a big grain deal with the PRC. When Beijing asked the Canadians to bar the Taiwanese from the Games, Canadian Prime Minister Trudeau accommodated them, ordering the Taiwanese not be admitted to the country. The IOC objected and the IAAF protested, but the Canadian government, to the dismay of its own Olympic Committee, stood firm. Although the Count Jean de Beaumont, a long-time French representative in the IOC, suggested the Games be canceled or at least moved from Montreal, Killanin chose to negotiate. Finally Trudeau and Killanin reached a compromise that would permit the Nationalist Chinese to compete using their own flag but under the name Taiwan.

The United States government objected to the Canadian government's action, and talk arose of boycotting the Games, even though the athletes were already settling in place in Montreal. *The New York Times* declared that the Olympic Games were "not worth holding." The Nationalist

---

Killanin on the China Crisis in Montreal:

[In 1975] no concern was expressed to the IOC. Had this been done and in view of the construction situation in Montreal, the question of the withdrawal of the Games would have arisen.

In February at Innsbruck when the Republic of China (Taiwan) was competing in the Winter Games, this status quo was reiterated and again no indication was given by the Canadian authorities.

On 11th April 1976, the Canadian Ministry of Immigration confirmed to the Organising Committee identity cards as travel documents without any exception in regard to the Republic of China (Taiwan). . . .

The first intimation of the refusal of entry to the Republic of China was confirmed in a letter to me dated 28th May 1976 from Mr. Mitchell Sharp, Acting Secretary of State for External Affairs. . . .

In regard to "normal regulations" referred to by Mr. MacEachen, the Canadian Olympic Association and the Mayor of Montreal, Jean Drapeau, confirm that they did not assume this to be a political reservation and had this been so they would not have made the bid for the 1976 Games.

Lord Killanin, "Clarification by the IOC," *Olympic Review*, 1976, p. 460.

Chinese announced that they would not compete under these conditions, and American Secretary of State Henry Kissinger registered his disapproval of the Canadian government's action by demonstratively refusing to attend the Games. Even so, the American team remained in Montreal and competed, while the Nationalist Chinese stayed away. The controversy ended with Killanin's mumbling that if the IOC had known the Canadians' position six months earlier it would have taken the Games away from Montreal; in the future, he declared, the IOC should be ready to move the Games at any time up to their opening.

The problem of racial discrimination in South Africa also reappeared on the IOC's agenda in preparation for the Montreal Games. The IOC, to be sure, thought it had rid itself of this headache: The campaigns against Rhodesia and South Africa had succeeded in driving both states out of the Games, and a series of international sports federations had also excluded them from competition. Now, however, the SCSA, the Supreme Council for Sport in Africa, attacked on another front, in a sport with which the IOC had no connection—rugby. South Africans used rugby competition as their own diplomatic weapon, seeking matches wherever they could, and now a visit to South Africa by a New Zealand rugby team, the "All-Blacks," aroused new protests (Guelke 1986). Although rugby was not an Olympic sport, the SCSA decided to make an issue of this tour, demanding the expulsion of New Zealand from the Olympic Games. The OAU, the Organization of African Unity, called for a boycott of the Games if the New Zealanders were allowed to participate. The IOC refused to yield, saying it had no jurisdiction over the actions of rugby players. In protest, a number of African

---

Mohamed Mzali, Vice President of the IOC and President of the Tunisian NOC, on the African Boycott of Montreal:

Up to their arrival in Montreal most of the African sports leaders, Olympic or otherwise, had no idea about the question. We were simply informed of the fact that a New Zealand rugby team was touring South Africa.

Three days before the opening of the Games, there was no concerted effort, strategy or agreement on any attitude to take. 48 hours before the opening 13 African countries sent President Killanin a letter in which they demanded no more, no less than the exclusion of New Zealand from the Olympic Games if it did not withdraw its rugby team from South Africa. . . .

The withdrawal of the Tunisian delegation had become as it were compulsory from the moment that the vast majority of African and Arab-Muslim countries withdrew.

Mohamed Mzali: "I am sorry about the boycott of the Montreal Olympic Games." *Olympic Review,* 1976, p. 463.

---

governments thereupon ordered their athletes out of Montreal, undermining the quality of competition in several running events.

The African boycott forced the IOC to rule once again that it dealt with athletes only through the respective NOCs. An African sprinter, James Gilkes of Guyana, requested permission to stay and compete as an individual under the Olympic flag, and the IOC refused, insisting athletes could compete in the Games only when they had been certified by the appropriate NOCs. If the NOCs did not participate in the Games, no athletes from that country could compete. This practice constituted the reverse side of the policy of excluding individual South Africans; for example, because he would not renounce his citizenship, the world class swimmer Jonty Skinner could not compete at Montreal.

Soviet authorities, one should note, took a cautious stance in supporting the position of the Africans in Montreal. Naturally they expressed sympathy for the Africans' motives, but since Moscow had already been chosen as the site of the 1980 Games, Soviet officials now suggested that boycotts were perhaps not the best tactic for the occasion. They argued that successful athletic performances could strike more telling blows at racism than boycotts could (Novikov 1983), but of course they did not carry this argument to the point of saying one should compete with the South Africans in order to demonstrate the talents of other races.

Once the athletes could begin actual competition in Montreal, they produced a new crop of scandals. In fencing competition, a Soviet, Boris Onishchenko, who had won a medal in the pentathlon at Munich, lunged at his opponent and obviously missed—yet the touch light flashed. His English opponent protested, and the ensuing investigation revealed the Soviet fencer's épée had been illegally wired. Soviet officials declared they knew nothing of this misdeed, but Onishchenko was disqualified. Drug testing led to the disqualification of three medal winners in weight lifting, two Bulgarians and a Pole. A Soviet diver, Sergei Nemtsanov, who had had a disappointing performance, disappeared. The Soviets claimed he had been kidnapped, and they threatened to withdraw from the Games if he was not returned. When Ukrainian emigrés attempted to mount an anti-Soviet demonstration outside the Olympic Village, Canadian police quickly drove them off. The diver, who had received a residence permit in Canada, returned to the Soviet Union after the Games: He claimed to have been drugged, but western sources suggested he had sought consolation with an American woman whom he had met.

Another Soviet athlete chose not to make a demonstration he had been considering. Remembering the demonstrations of American black athletes on the winner's platform, Arvydas Juozaitis, a Lithuanian who won the bronze medal in the breaststroke, debated with himself whether to stand on the winner's platform wearing a jacket that had "Lietuva" (Lithuania)

The personal and national stakes at the Olympic Games have sometimes fostered unsportsmanlike conduct. Here an official at the Montreal Games (1976) examines the foil of a Soviet pentathlete, Boris Onishchenko, before disqualifying him for doctoring his weapon.

on the back. In the end he chose not to because of the obvious repercussions that would fall on his family back home. Instead he quietly accepted his medal, returned home, and eventually, more than a decade later, became a prominent figure in the process of Lithuania's separation from the Soviet Union.

By Soviet calculations, the USSR scored the most team points, 792.5, while East Germany took second place with 638 points, and the United States finished only third with 603.75. "The athletes of the socialist countries" had won 344 of the 613 medals awarded at the Games. According to the Soviet sports historian V. V. Stolbov, "The athletes of the USA had not experienced such a defeat in the whole 80 year history of the Olympics. This defeat was all the more palpable because the Olympic Games had taken place on the American continent in the year of the bicentennial of the USA" (1983). Declaring the "ruling circles of the USA had looked forward to victory in Montreal as a powerful means for expressing the politics and ideology of bourgeois society," Stolbov called the East Europeans' harvest of medals the "result of the successful construction of socialism, the progress of socialist sport" (see table 11.1).

Western journalists for some years had been totaling medals to come up with team standings, however, and they calculated the United States had finished second with 34 gold, 35 silver, and 25 bronze, to the GDR's 40, 25, and 25. A few enthusiasts, like the Canadian journalist Doug Gilbert, insisted gold medals should be all that mattered, and therefore the East Germans had defeated the United States in medal count. Giving equal weight to gold, silver, and bronze medals, he argued, constituted a "new scoring system as yet unknown to any prior Games or wire service" (1980). But however one calculated team points, East Germany was a rapidly growing sport power.

The East Germans had carefully structured their efforts toward winning points in women's competition. As one of their officials explained, "While

Table 11.1

USSR/US/GDR Competition, 1964–1976

	Points (7-5-4-3-2-1)	Gold medals	Silver medals	Bronze medals
1964				
USSR	607.8	30	31	35
US	581.8	36	26	28
GDR	–	–	–	–
1968				
USSR	590.8	29	32	30
US	713.3	45	28	34
GDR	238	9	9	7
1972				
USSR	664.5	50	27	22
US	638.5	33	31	30
GDR	472	20	23	23
1976				
USSR	792.5	49	41	35
US	603.8	34	35	25
GDR	638	40	25	25

Khavin 1979, 138-39.

other nations can produce men's teams as good if not better than ours, they lose to us overall because they are not tapping the potential of their women" (Gilbert 1980). The East Germans, moreover, concentrated on individual events, which would reap more medals (table 11.2). They won the gold medal in soccer, to be sure, but, however important, this earned the national team only one gold medal for seven points. The GDR had no ice hockey team in Innsbruck and no men's or women's basketball teams and no men's volleyball team in Montreal. In Montreal, the East German women won 348 points, or 54 percent of the East German total. Soviet women, in contrast, earned 227 points, 28 percent of their team's total, and the United States women garnered 117, only 19 percent of the American total, and over half of these in swimming and diving. At times, even the Soviets expressed dissatisfaction with the way their German colleagues were concentrating their resources on medal-rich sports.

On the American side, the performance of the athletes from the United States was disappointing—despite swimming victories by Jim Montgomery and John Nabors and the basketball team's recapturing the gold medal. In combination with the memories of the troubles in Munich, this disappointment gave further impetus for Federal intervention into the structure of American sports. Rivalries between the AAU and the NCAA,

Table 11.2

Points in Selected Sports

	1964		1968		1972		1976	
	Men	Women	Men	Women	Men	Women	Men	Women
Gymnastics								
USSR	59	58.5	52	54	43.5	69	57.5	52.5
US	0	0	0	3.5	0	3	4	1
GDR	–	–	7	23	15	48	13.5	20.5
Track and field								
USSR	64	60	60	30	84.5	36	54	55
US	144.5	27	162	40	133	21	125	22
GDR	–	–	31	39	50	54	128	55
Swimming								
USSR	15	15	45	16	20	12	25	35
US	99	86	152	163	166	131	159	55
GDR	–	–	22	38	29	41	16	129

Khavin (1979).

which controlled college athletics, had frequently hampered the formation of American teams for international competition, and a Presidential Commission recommended the dissolution of the AAU. Instead, national sports federations would emerge, and the USOC, which would direct international sport competition, would consist of representatives of the federations. In an action that would have shocked Coubertin or Brundage, the United States Congress in 1978 accordingly passed legislation that completely reorganized American sport and the United States Olympic Committee.

The intervention of the American government into the sport structure followed, to a certain extent, television's success in televising the Olympic Games. Simply put, as the Games' popularity grew, the American public wanted its representatives to perform better. Television's success, to be sure, had been slow. In 1972, NBC had the rights to the Winter Games in Sapporo, but as Bert Sugar put it, NBC won the battle and lost the war. Since the network had to use Japanese camera work and add its own subtitles, the result was an "artistic disaster and a commercial debacle" (Sugar 1978). ABC's ratings for the Summer Games in Munich had profited by the attention given the terrorist attack on the Israelis, however, and the network's 41 hours of prime-time broadcasting received a Nielsen rating of 24.4, claiming 44 percent of the American television sets in use.

ABC won the rights to the Montreal Games by taking advantage of the peculiar practices of the Montreal Organizing Committee, negotiating a deal with the delegation that attended the Munich Games. The network paid Montreal organizers $25 million and the Austrians $10 million for the Innsbruck rights. The 1976 Winter Games claimed a Nielsen rating of only 21.7 and a market share of 23 percent, but the Summer Games, broadcast live in prime time, received a rating of 24.8 and a market share of 48—almost half of the television sets in use in the United States. In the opinion of ABC executives, "The 1976 Games were a terrific launching pad for programming in the fall." Indeed, the Games were subsequently credited with greatly improving ABC's competitive ranking in the television season of 1976-1977.

The IOC, upset by ABC's cozy deal with the Montreal Organizing Committee, insisted on supervising future negotiations for broadcast rights, and at the same time, Olympic organizers calculated growing television revenues into their budgetary plans. In his day, Brundage had criticized professional sport as "entertainment" rather than "true" sport; the IOC, now seeking its own share of the money from the competitive American television market, was finding itself more and more concerned with exploiting the Games as entertainment for an American audience.

When the Olympic flame was extinguished in Montreal, Olympic officials tried to ignore the financial debacle left behind in Montreal, claiming the loss came in capital expenditures and the operation of the Games themselves had shown a profit. "There is no doubt at all that exaggerated costs were reported after the Games in Montreal," declared Killanin. "In point of fact, Montreal made a cash profit of 116.6 million Canadian dollars, but they did make massive capital expenditures. We do not ask that this should be done, although if there is capital expenditure which can be of long-term benefit to the city it is on the plus side for posterity" (Killanin 1983). Richard Pound (1994), an IOC member from Canada, has insisted that, in fact, Montreal saved the Olympic Games. Despite this determinedly sanguine attitude, however, Killanin had to recognize Montreal's financial problems had "tarnished the reputation of the Olympic Movement and undoubtedly frightened potential hosts, who believed that it was no longer possible to stage the Games at a reasonable cost" (1983).

On a more positive note, Olympic officials rejoiced because the 1976 Games had seen no recurrence of the ghastly events of Munich. In his first term as President, Lord Killanin had apparently found his calmer waters. Of course, political problems persisted, but neither Innsbruck nor Montreal saw political violence. The only untoward incident occurred in the closing ceremonies at Montreal when a streaker came onto the field, apparently without an identity card.

Chapter **12**

Boycott!

In protest against the Soviet invasion of Afghanistan, many western states, including the United States, boycotted the Moscow Games. Some western athletes participated in the Games under the Olympic flag rather than under their own national flags.

With Montreal behind him, Lord Killanin faced new problems in preparing for the 1980 Winter Games in Lake Placid and the Summer Games in Moscow. For the two superpowers to host the Games in the same year was unprecedented, and a keen rivalry loomed. Soviet spokesmen hailed the decision to give Moscow the Games as a victory for socialism. As one commentator wrote, "The contribution of the Soviet sports organization to the Olympic Movement is great, and this had its effect on the IOC in the selection of the city for the 1980 Games" (Stolbov 1983). The Moscow Games would constitute a grand celebration of international peace and friendship under the sponsorship of the world's first socialist state: "The Soviet people, the Communist Party, and the Government of the USSR view the Olympic Games as an outstanding event in international sporting life, reflecting the striving of peoples for peace, detente, cooperation, and mutual understanding."

From the moment of the announcement of Moscow's selection, however, hostile voices called for boycotting the 1980 Games. Even before Moscow's selection, there had been protests against the thought of holding the Games in the Soviet capital, including complaints about anti-Jewish and anti-Israeli demonstrations at the World University Games, held in Moscow in 1973. Boycotts, and the threat of boycotts, now held a well-established place in the arsenal of sport diplomacy, as observers attributed moral significance to competition in specific arenas and stadiums. The Soviets themselves had boycotted other athletic competitions for openly political reasons. In 1976, the United Nations established a special committee to pursue the campaign against apartheid in sport and tighten the boycott against South Africa. As the head of the Soviet Sport Committee explained the Soviets' decision to boycott the 1978 World Cup tournament in Chile, "When Soviet football players refuse to play a match [in Chile], this is also of course politics" (Popov and Srebnitsky 1979). Therefore, he continued, "Whenever someone says that sports lies outside the framework of political relations, we feel their remark is not a serious one."

The IOC objected to such political statements, and at the same time it had to struggle to maintain its own control of the Games. In 1977, the IOC declared that in the future, Olympic Committees that withdrew from the Games for unexplainable reasons would be subjected to a five-year suspension, and it censured 23 African states for having withdrawn from the Montreal Games. At the same time, it rejected moves by UNESCO, the United Nations Economic, Social, and Cultural Organization, to establish its authority over the Games. Killanin told UN officials the IOC welcomed aid from governments, but "We do ask that sport should not be a shuttlecock of national politics and that all NOCs must have freedom of action, not to be dictated to by political considerations or control, which would endanger the freedom of the individual or sport" (1983). He expressed "pleasure that UNESCO has now taken the initiative in assisting in developing sport," but his Tripartite Commission obligingly warned "against certain aspects of interference that risk diverting sport from its true purpose."

The Moscow Organizing Committee, "Olimpiada-80," directed special effort toward avoiding a Third World boycott of its presentation, but persuading the Africans to change their tactics required considerable care and perseverance. When the head of the SCSA warned the Africans might yet feel compelled to boycott the Moscow Games, Ignatii Novikov, the President of the Moscow Organizing Committee, protested that Olimpiada-80 should not be held responsible for the actions of the "rugbyists or, let us say, the masters of cricket from New Zealand or the United States of America" (1983). It would be far more useful, he suggested, to use the Games as a "tribune" than to stay away from the Games altogether. In 1978, when Novikov took his case directly to the General Assembly of the SCSA, he found strong sentiment for boycott, but also a feeling that perhaps the boycott in Montreal had not served its purpose. The SCSA established a special commission to consider the question, and the Muscovites had strong hopes for success.

The South Africans, however, still had their own cards to play, and they arranged rugby tours in the fall of 1979 in England and France, arguing politics should not be permitted to intrude into sport relations. When the African states protested, the French government avoided a crisis by refusing to grant visas to the South Africans, but the British government declared it could not block the visas. British Prime Minister Margaret Thatcher called this a private matter of the athletes involved, and the British let the rugby competition go ahead as scheduled.

The Soviets' first reaction was to threaten to exclude any country that supported sport exchanges with the South Africans: "We prefer to sacrifice one country rather than ten." The IOC, however, refused to deal with rugby, which was not an Olympic sport, and therefore it would do nothing. The Soviets denounced Thatcher's "political adventure," but in the aftermath of Canada's policy regarding China in 1976, they dared not take unilateral steps toward the British. They had already caused an embarrassing furor in 1978, when they had questioned whether athletes from West Berlin should be permitted to compete on the West German team. The West Germans objected strenuously, and Soviet authorities subsequently insisted this had simply been a misunderstanding. Certainly, Moscow wanted to make no further untoward moves against any important sectors in the IOC.

Novikov hurried back to Africa to plead his case at a plenary session of the SCSA. As he explained in his memoirs, "All our work in the lands of Africa was a dialog of mutual interest" (1983). The Soviets were sending coaches and equipment to various African states, and Novikov lobbied heavily with Killanin and Monique Berlioux, the IOC's chief administrative officer, for a relaxation of the IOC's conditions for the admission of new NOCs into the Olympic family. (Thirteen new countries eventually gained recognition before the Moscow Games.) In December 1979, the SCSA finally decided to attend the Moscow Games while continuing its fight against apartheid on other fronts.

Immediately upon the heels of this victory, new problems arose when Soviet troops moved into Afghanistan at the end of December 1979. The Soviets insisted they had been invited in to protect the Afghans from the Chinese and the Americans, but protest swept through the world, culminating in a resolution of the United Nations General Assembly, accepted by an overwhelming vote of 104-18, with 18 abstentions, condemning the Soviet invasion. Killanin indicated in his memoirs that "his initial reaction [to the news of the invasion] was not one of alarm" (1983), but the American government soon launched a campaign aimed directly at undermining Moscow's hosting the 1980 Olympic Games.

Soviet commentators and historians insisted the Afghan situation was not the real cause of the American move against the Moscow Games. According to Novikov, the selection of Moscow to host the Games "became a signal for attack to which rallied not only open anti-Soviets but also all opponents of Olympism, all who openly or secretly struggle against peace and international cooperation" (1983). The Soviet sport historian V.V. Stolbov wrote "enemies of the Olympic movement, opponents of detente, and enemies of socialism and communism . . . attempted to disrupt the Olympic Games in Moscow and to split the Olympic Movement" (1983). The situation in Afghanistan, the Soviets argued, was only an occasion for the American administration's purposes, not the cause of its actions.

For President Jimmy Carter's administration, facing reelection in 1980, the Soviet move into Afghanistan virtually screamed for a strong response. Iranian radicals were holding American diplomatic personnel hostage in Iran, and the American media were daily emphasizing Washington's inability to mount a meaningful response. The idea of striking at the Olympics arose immediately when news came of the invasion. NATO officials discussed it on December 30, 1979, but put it aside for the time being. Within the Carter administration, the idea apparently came first from the Vice President, Walter Mondale. Word came that the Soviet dissident Andrei Sakharov supported a boycott as a protest against the invasion of Afghanistan, and the President's National Security Adviser, Zbigniew Brzezinski, predicted the Moscow Games would be a "major propaganda festival" advancing the Soviet cause. Thus, over the objections of Secretary of State Cyrus Vance, the President announced that unless the

Soviets withdrew their forces from Afghanistan within the next month, the United States would demand the Olympic Games be moved from Moscow to an alternative site or multiple sites or else be postponed or canceled. Failing any of those alternatives, he proposed boycotting the Moscow Games.

Calling for unity against the Soviet action in Afghanistan, the United States government then sent messages to over 100 heads of state, urging them to support shifting the Games from Moscow. A conference of Islamic states, meeting at the end of the month, condemned the invasion of Afghanistan and supported a boycott of the Games if the Soviets refused to evacuate the country. France openly opposed even the thought of a boycott, but West Germany, the People's Republic of China, and Japan indicated they would consider cooperating.

Promoting and implementing the policy at home proved to be complicated, however. According to Brzezinski, the White House believed "domestic pressure" in favor of an Olympic boycott was steadily mounting, and it counted on strong public support for its policy (1983). Congress quickly approved the policy, but the administration met opposition when it turned to the USOC and the IOC. The USOC's Executive Board supported the formula of "transfer, postponement, or cancellation," but it postponed discussion of boycott, which it clearly opposed. The USOC agreed to carry the White House's formula as a recommendation to the next meeting of the IOC, to be held on the eve of the Winter Games in Lake Placid, but in the meantime, it continued its plans to send athletes to Moscow.

Lord Killanin objected strongly to what he considered the White Houses's "arrogance" and "high-handed approach" (1983). It would be "both legally and technically impossible" to take the Games from Moscow, he insisted, and he considered the American administration completely ignorant about the politics and structure of the modern Olympics. He put some hope in reports of resistance within the USOC, but he knew he could not count on this group, now barely two years old after having been organized by act of Congress in 1978. Thus, the IOC would have to take its stand in Lake Placid.

President Carter chose not to attend the Games in Lake Placid, instead sending Vice President Mondale and Secretary of State Vance to bid the IOC welcome and then to lecture them on the ideals of the Games. (The IOC considered it the obligation of the chief of state of the host country to open the Games.) Speaking of the Soviet Union only as the "nation selected as host," Vance argued it would be a violation of "fundamental Olympic principles" to conduct or attend the Games in Moscow, especially, he added, since the Soviet government was speaking of the IOC's decision to hold the Games in Moscow as a recognition of the "correctness" of Soviet foreign policy.

Secretary of State Vance's Statement to the IOC in Lake Placid, February 9, 1980:

Let us be clear about the fundamental issue we face. This is not a question of whether a national team should be barred from competing on political grounds. We welcome every team this committee has invited to these winter games.

The question we now confront is entirely different. It is whether the games should be held in a country which is itself committing a serious breach of international peace. . . .

To hold the Olympics in any nation that is warring on another is to lend the Olympic mantle to that nation's actions.

We already see the nation selected as host of the summer games describing its selection as recognition of "the correctness of [its] foreign political course" and its enormous services . . . in the struggle for peace. . . ."

The preferable course would be to transfer the games from Moscow to another site or multiple sites this summer. Clearly there are practical difficulties, but they could be overcome. There is also precedent for cancelling the Games. Or it would be possible, with a simple change of rules, to postpone the games for a year or more. . . .

[W]e support the establishment of permanent homes for the Summer and Winter Olympics.

Department of State Bulletin, March 1980, p. 50.

The IOC stood firm. Having seen the text of Vance's speech in advance, Killanin urged the Soviet members of the IOC to stay away from the meeting, and the IOC coldly heard out the USOC's request that the Games be transferred, postponed, or canceled. It then reaffirmed its intention to hold the Games of the XXIInd Olympiad in Moscow in the summer, insisting the Games had been awarded to the city of Moscow and not to the government of the Soviet Union. Urging the NOCs of the world to participate, Lord Killanin expressed the hope of compromise before the deadline for filing entries on May 24, but there seemed little prospect for agreement.

The American government's challenge to the Moscow Games was not the only political problem facing Olympic officials in Lake Placid; there was also a new twist to the Chinese question. In 1979, the IOC had tried to resolve this persistent problem by ruling the PRC had the right to the name "Chinese Olympic Committee," while the Nationalists would be designated "Chinese Taipeh Olympic Committee." The Nationalists objected, and, after Taiwanese officials had failed to overturn the decision in a Swiss court, one Taiwanese athlete appealed to a New York court, demanding the right for himself and his teammates to use the name "Republic of China." The judge ruled in his favor, but on an appeal another judge dismissed the case. Ironically, the United States government now helped defend the Lake Placid Organizing Committee against the athlete's suit. In answer, 18 Nationalist Chinese athletes and 10 officials went home in protest, refusing to participate in the Winter Games.

Not surprisingly, the Lake Placid Games ended with bitter feelings. Lord Killanin tersely commented that the New York town "unhappily did not make many contributions to Olympic advancement." He called the giving of the Games to such a small town a "quaint idea that is impractical." He declared of the Organizing Committee's work, "They were clearly close to bankruptcy; furthermore, there was not enough transport, and from the word 'go,' it did not seem to work properly" (1983). Soviet representatives left complaining about their housing and Ukrainian anti-Soviet demonstrators. "I have never seen a worse Olympics," wrote one (Zaseda 1981).

For Americans the memories of the Games, to be sure, would be quite different. The unexpected victory of the United States hockey team—former President Jimmy Carter's memoirs note his exultation at this triumph—and the speed skating victories of Eric Heiden, who won five

The American goalkeeper, Jim Craig, celebrates the American victory after the American ice hockey team defeated the heavily favored Soviet team in the semifinal game at the Lake Placid Games (1980).

gold medals, overshadowed everything else. The hockey victory, the second time the Americans had defeated the Soviets for the Olympic gold medal, had a particularly exhilarating effect on a people worried about their diplomats in Teheran and inflation at home. Even the reported $8.5 million deficit the LPOOC had reportedly incurred and the fact the Americans finished only third in the medal count (behind the Soviet Union and the GDR) did not dampen American spirits to any degree.

Secretary Vance, however, had struck at a sore point in the Olympic mystique when he quoted a Soviet publication as saying that the IOC's selection of Moscow as the site for the Games represented an endorsement of Soviet foreign policy. The quotation, which came from a handbook for party activists, embarrassed Killanin, who then felt it necessary to take up the matter with Soviet officials. According to Killanin's memoirs, Soviet President Leonid Brezhnev at first saw nothing wrong with the statement, but then Novikov intervened to assert the handbook was only a minor publication of little significance (1983). The publication, Novikov declared, "had nothing to do with the Organizing Committee, the Sport Committee of the USSR, or our Olympic Committee." Novikov's memoirs (1983) of the exchange pictured Killanin as confused and embarrassed in even raising this issue. At any rate, Killanin was only too happy to drop the issue once he had received some sort of explanation.

The Americans, moreover, had struck another sore point when President Carter, in his efforts to wrest the Games from Moscow, had endorsed the thought of holding the Olympic Games in one permanent site. *The New York Times* endorsed the idea in at least six editorials during 1980, and the suggestion evoked new enthusiasm from the Greeks, who had repeatedly expressed the hope the international sport world would accept Greece as its physical as well as spiritual home. The IOC had to consider the matter, but as it had since the days of Coubertin, it eventually resolved that the Olympic Movement would still be better served by moving from city to city in different parts of the world every four years, at least as long as there were still cities bidding to become hosts.

The question of a permanent home, however, was only what Killanin justly called a "diversion," and on February 20 President Carter's deadline for the withdrawal of Soviet troops from Afghanistan passed. Declaring neither he nor the American people would support the sending of American athletes to Moscow, Carter announced his "irreversible" decision that the Americans should boycott the Moscow Games. He used his presidential powers to block business involvement in the Moscow Games—including NBC's televising of the Games, the United States Postal Service's sale of commemorative stamps and postcards, as well as export of "any goods or technology" related to the Moscow Games. He also pressed the USOC to support a boycott, threatening financial and legal

White House Statement on Transactions Prohibited for the 1980 Olympic Games, March 28, 1980:

With respect to the Moscow Summer Olympics, the President has announced that neither he nor the American people would support the participation in the Olympics by the US Olympic Team, and he has urged US businesses not to participate in or contribute to the holding of the Summer Games in Moscow.

The President... has today directed the Secretary of Commerce to take the following actions:

1. To deny all pending validated license application for goods and technology to be used in support of or in connection with the Summer Olympic Games in Moscow;
2. To revoke all outstanding licenses for Olympic-related exports that have not already been shipped;
3. To impose validated license controls on all exports now not requiring validated licenses to be used in support of or in association with the Summer Olympic Games in Moscow. No such licenses shall be granted;
4. To prohibit other transactions and payments associated with all Olympic-related exports. Among other transactions, the order will bar NBC from making any further payments of exports under its contracts relating to the US television rights for the Olympic Games.

Department of State Bulletin, April 1980, p. 3.

---

reprisals if it did not comply. In April, the USOC yielded, formally resolving not to go to Moscow.

The American decision cost NBC dearly. After ABC's success in televising the Montreal Games, the networks had competed intensely for the rights to the Moscow Games. The Moscow organizers set their asking price at $210 million and made clear they expected more than merely money. ABC, CBS, and NBC made special efforts to ingratiate themselves with the Muscovites, who twice reopened the bidding after it seemed a deal had been struck. NBC finally seemed to have won with a bid of over $80 million, but even then the IOC felt the Soviets were getting "as much as they can." NBC added another $3 million to the pot, and on February 1, 1977, the contract was signed. When NBC had to cancel its coverage of the Moscow Games, it had reportedly paid some $70 million to the Soviets, and while it recovered 90 percent of this through an insurance policy with Lloyd's of London, it lost significant advertising income, and of course it lost the prestige and whatever programming advantages that may have been had as a result of being the network of the Olympics.

Lord Killanin called the USOC's withdrawal a "breach of the Olympic *Charter*," (Killanin 1983) and he struggled industriously against the White House's campaign to bring foreign governments into line with its policy.

He was somewhat embarrassed when it became known he was part of the group at Lloyd's of London that had insured NBC against loss in its contract with the Soviets, but he insisted this did not affect his views in the matter (1983). In order to defuse the political issues surrounding the Games, the IOC declared teams would have the option of using the Olympic flag and the Olympic hymn instead of their national symbols and athletes could stay away from the opening and closing ceremonies if they so wished.

In an effort to save "Olympic ideals," Killanin visited President Carter and President Brezhnev in May. He took hope in Brezhnev's promise to "do his very best so that the atmosphere might improve," but he found no common ground with the American President. It was a pity, Killanin told Carter, that the American "constitution could not be changed so that the primary and presidential elections did not coincide with the Olympic Games, as will happen again in Los Angeles in 1984" (1983). The President did not respond to this bold proposal for reforming the American government. On May 19, Killanin announced he would not run for reelection as IOC President, indicating the boycott controversy had been the decisive element in his decision to retire.

In contrast to their earlier pronouncements on the relationships between politics and sport, the Soviets now spoke of the need to keep politics out of sport as they worked with the IOC in defense of the Games. (In 1979, Soviet officials had called for Communist China's expulsion from the Olympics because of the Chinese invasion of Vietnam.) The Soviet government had invested a great deal in preparing for the event; foreign estimates ran to over two billion rubles (according to the official rate of exchange, over three billion dollars). The city of Moscow had undergone extensive facelifting and new construction. Plans for the Games included such details as stocking the stores with attractive merchandise for the tourists, speeding up the escalators in the subway stations so as to handle

---

White House Statement, May 16, 1980

The President met today with Lord Killanin . . . and Mme. Monique Berlioux . . . at their request. The President reaffirmed that the position of the United States in opposition to sending a team to the 22d Olympic Games in Moscow results solely from the Soviet invasion of Afghanistan and our belief that it was not appropriate to attend the games in a host nation that was invading its neighbor.

The President made clear that this position does not detract in any way from our support of the international Olympic movement, and that we will welcome athletes from any eligible Olympic nation at the 23d Olympic games in Los Angeles in 1984.

Department of State Bulletin, June 1980, p. 30.

---

more traffic, and advising dissidents to leave the city for the summer so as to avoid contact with foreign media. In the latter part of June, Moscow became a closed city, and Soviets from other parts of the country could enter only with special permits. The Games, the Soviets asserted, would be a "festival of peace and friendship."

In the end, 87 countries agreed to attend the Games in Moscow, and 81 actually came; 36 officially refused the IOC's invitation. Twenty countries did not respond at all, and the IOC had already suspended four more because of problems such as failure to pay dues. The American government failed in its goal of winning 80 abstentions. In March, representatives of 16 European NOCs, meeting in Brussels, had declared their opposition to boycott, and some delegates spoke of sending athletes to Moscow even if their respective governments supported the American boycott. Puerto Rican officials declared their athletes would participate in the Games (Puerto Rico had had its own Olympic Committee since 1948). African leaders, having just agreed to set aside their objections to British-South African rugby matches, considered President Carter's choice of Muhammad Ali as a special envoy to persuade them to boycott Moscow to be condescending and insulting. Some NOCs decided to go over the express objections of their governments. The most significant powers joining the American boycott were West Germany, Japan, and the People's Republic of China.

In Moscow's opening ceremonies, 16 national teams chose to march under the Olympic flag rather than their own, and, as Killanin noted, "It was agreed that each NOC could use its own name rather than its country's

---

The Hopes of the White House: Department of State Analysis, May 24, 1980:

The Department of State today issued the following analysis of the success achieved by the boycott of the Moscow Games.

Of the national Olympic committees outside the Soviet bloc which have made their decisions, one-half (58 out of 116) have decided not to send teams to Moscow. The decisions of 17 additional committees are not yet known.

A number of the committees which decided to send teams to Moscow had been urged by their governments that it would be inappropriate to do so because of the continuing Soviet invasion of Afghanistan. . . .

Those national teams and sports federations not participating in Moscow won 73% (58 out of 80) of all the gold medals won at Montreal in 1976 by athletes from nations outside the Soviet bloc. For all medals—gold, silver, and bronze—the comparable percentage is 71%.

Those national teams and sports federations not participating at Moscow accounted for approximately 50% of the athletes from nations outside the Soviet bloc who participated in the 1976 games at Montreal.

Department of State Bulletin, June 1980, p. 30.

---

name." While "this use of the Olympic flag might have been construed as a political demonstration," he argued, "it was within the revised charter and part of an effort to denationalise the Games" (1983). On July 24, for the first time in the history of the Games, a medals ceremony took place without any national flags or hymns as the three medal winners in the 4,000-meter individual pursuit cycling event—a Swiss, a Frenchman, and a Dane—were honored under Olympic banners.

As the Games progressed, foreign correspondents sought out signs of tension while Moscow demanded pictures of harmony. British television cameras showed the British athletes under the Olympic flag rather than under the Union Jack; Soviet television panned away from such scenes, instead seeking out British flags in the stands to testify to the failure of the boycott. In response to the negative reports of some foreign correspondents, the Organizing Committee's press spokesman singled out the London *Daily Mail* and warned the authorities would investigate the "insulting attacks on the host country" (Booker 1981). The Mexican government, he noted, had deported two journalists in 1968. Soviet censors barred the transmission of a West German television film, and four journalists were detained for trying to photograph a demonstration in Red Square on behalf of jailed homosexuals.

Many westerners complained about the security measures, speaking darkly of the city's being controlled by thousands of special KGB agents. The Soviets justified all their actions as necessary for the safety of the athletes, and when correspondents questioned why victorious runners could not take their traditional victory laps, the Soviet press spokesman explained the Olympic *Charter* included no provision for victory laps and that in any case such behavior could "excite the public unnecessarily" (Booker 1981). Westerners also criticized the VIP treatment offered to Yasir Arafat, the leader of the Palestine Liberation Organization, as an unwelcome reminder of the killing of the Israeli athletes in Munich in 1972.

In the final tally of medals (table 12.1), the Soviet Union took 80 gold, 69 silver, and 46 bronze, for a total of 195, garnering—according to their system—1,219 points. The East Germans finished second, with 47 gold medals, 37 silver, and 42 bronze, for a total of 829 points. Between them, the USSR and the GDR had more medals than all the rest of the participating countries combined.

Soviet accounts of the Games sound like sheer rapture, speaking of the beauty of the competition and praising the "Olympic fairy tale—the Moscow Olympiad." Although western skeptics questioned the quality of the testing, commentators called the fact that no athletes had trouble with the drug testing a tribute to the spirit of the Games: "The Moscow Olympiad is one of the purest in Olympic history" (Kolodnyi 1981).

Table 12.1

Medal Count in Moscow

	Gold	Silver	Bronze	Total
USSR	80	69	46	195
GDR	47	37	42	126
Bulgaria	8	16	17	41
Hungary	7	10	15	32
Poland	3	14	15	32
Romania	6	6	13	25
Great Britain	5	7	9	21
Cuba	8	7	5	20
Italy	8	3	4	15
France	6	5	3	14

Seventy-four Olympic and 36 world records fell in the competition. The Soviets insisted that the Games had crushed the US efforts to disrupt them.

Lord Killanin decried the faultfinding of western correspondents and observers, but in his memoirs he declared, "The Games themselves were joyless. Too often we were thinking of the missing people, wondering and weighing up what might have happened" (1983). He rejoiced that the Games had survived their challenge, but he was concerned about the future. At the closing ceremonies, which, in fact, marked the end of his term as President of the IOC, he declared, "I implore the sportsmen of the world to unite in peace before the holocaust descends. . . . The Olympic Games are for the benefit of our children." In a press conference, he accused the American administration of being ignorant about international sport, and he sarcastically suggested that if American football and baseball were Olympic sports, "perhaps we wouldn't have had the boycott" (Killanin 1983).

Those same closing ceremonies, however, reflected the problems still facing the IOC. In the traditional ceremony of raising the flag of the next country to host the Summer Games, the IOC could not use the American flag. (Despite this tradition, of course, the IOC insisted it awarded the Games to a city and not to a country.) The Carter administration had prohibited its display at these Games, and at Monique Berlioux's suggestion, Olympic officials appealed for a Los Angeles city flag. Los Angeles

Mayor Tom Bradley hastily accommodated them, and the flag of the city of Los Angeles waved in Moscow's Lenin Stadium.

The report on the Games by the British Olympic Committee, which had defied its government's disapproval, insisted their experience in Moscow had been a positive one (1981). David Hunn complained about Soviet security, but he also criticized what he called "ministerial bootlicking" on the part of newspaper editors in modifying reports from Moscow to make them seem more negative. Ian Woolridge offered a broader judgment: "Historians will see it as the ultimate showdown in the long running skirmish between sportsmen and politicians, and they will have little difficulty in assessing who won. Sport won by a mile." In his own book a decade later, IOC Vice President Richard Pound argued that the Olympic Games came out of the Moscow experience stronger than ever (1994).

From the point of view of the American government, the boycott had some success, despite Monique Berlioux's assertion that the "absurd attempts at boycott . . . ended, despite their malicious nature, in a resounding failure" (1981). Soviet officials spoke of having entertained 340,000 Soviet and foreign tourists, but the boycott undoubtedly reduced the number of foreign tourists. In contrast, western sources spoke of 100,000 foreign tourists instead of the 300,000 the Soviets had expected. Correspondingly, the flow of hard currency to cover the costs of the Games must have been less than the Soviets had hoped for. Long after his departure from the presidential office, Jimmy Carter insisted the boycott had constituted the sharpest possible measure to bring home to the Soviet leaders the gravity of the situation in Afghanistan (1982).

Both Carter and his adviser Brzezinski had considered the Moscow Olympics to be a Russian show, and for them the Olympic Games themselves were only a secondary concern. While declaring their intentions of upholding fundamental "Olympic principles," they were determined, in Brzezinski's words, to make the "Moscow Olympics an empty event from an athletic as well as a propaganda point of view" (1983). In this regard, the Americans paid a heavy price both in their relations with the IOC and in the respect of their own athletes. Killanin and others deeply resented the failure of the Carter administration to recognize the investment of others in the Games wherever their locale. Even many American athletes who considered the boycott a legitimate action soon concluded their sacrifice for this policy had gone unappreciated and unnoticed.

As first considered in January 1980, in the heat of popular opposition to the Soviet invasion of Afghanistan, the thought of the boycott had enjoyed considerable support both in the United States and abroad. "It is unthinkable," wrote the popular sport columnist Red Smith, "that in the present circumstances we could go and play in Ivan's yard" (1983). The passions cooled quickly, however, and the government found itself bound to a policy Carter himself later called "necessary" but "politically damaging" (Carter 1982). The boycott's gains could not be measured, and its failures were obvious—the thought of organizing alternative games, for example, had no following. Intense debate ensued over the consequences of the boycott for the Olympics in general and for the American preparations for the 1984 Games in Los Angeles in particular. To date most commentators have considered the action futile; one of the few to continue to support it has been Howard Cosell, who wrote, "I ended up supporting the boycott wholeheartedly and repeatedly said so on the air. It was the right thing to do. . . . I'll always admire President Carter for having the guts to spoil their party" (1985).

Chapter 13

. . . and Again!

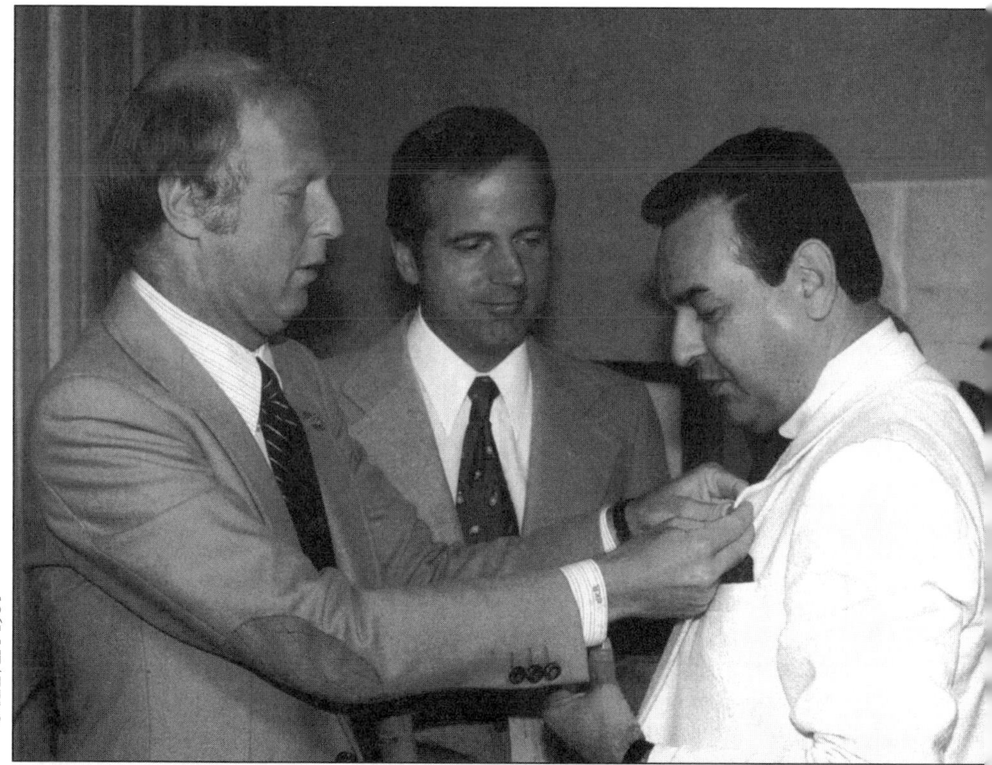

The Los Angeles Olympic Organizing Committee, led by Peter Ueberroth (center), created a new model for financing the Olympics. By relying on corporate sponsorships, the Los Angeles Games (1984) made a substantial profit, a stark contrast to the huge loss incurred by the Montreal Games only eight years earlier. Here Ueberroth joins in congratulating the president of Cervantes Neckwear (right), the first corporate licensee.

The extinguishing of the Olympic flame in Moscow put Los Angeles on the spot. The Soviets were calling for sanctions against the Americans, including taking the 1984 Games away from Los Angeles. Recalling his reception by Olympic officials at Lake Placid, Peter Ueberroth, the President of the Los Angeles Olympic Organizing Committee (LAOOC) later declared, "We were treated like pariahs"; and when he traveled to Moscow to report to the IOC, he found the atmosphere openly hostile. "You," said Reginald Alexander of Kenya, "represent the ugly face of capitalism and its attempt to take over the Olympic Movement and commercialize the Olympic Games" (Ueberroth et al. 1985). Ueberroth nevertheless had Lord Killanin's assurance the Games would remain in Los Angeles, so he simply aimed at weathering the storm.

Killanin, however, had anything but warm feelings for the Americans. "The American-Olympic connection," he sighed in his memoirs, "in my time has not been a very happy one" (1983). The IOC, Killanin warned, "may still come to rue" its arrangements with the LAOOC. But Killanin had now abandoned his position as President of the IOC. His supporters insisted he could surely have won reelection had he wanted to continue. "No one," declared Monique Berlioux in a book edited by His Lordship himself, "would have committed the folly of presenting himself as a candidate against a man who, with only the Olympic ideals as his strength, had just held at bay Herculean power" (1984). Unlike the Greek gods with whom he was here compared, however, Killanin, aware of his own mortality, chose to lay down his authority voluntarily, and his retirement at the Moscow Games probably helped the cause of the Los Angelenos.

The IOC turned to Juan Antonio Samaranch, who now resigned his post as Spanish ambassador to Moscow, to be Killanin's successor. A member of the IOC since 1966 and Chief of Protocol for the Committee for many years, Samaranch joined the Committee's Executive Board in 1970, and he served as Vice President from 1974 to 1978. As President, Samaranch was to prove to be a more flexible, determined, and forceful presence than Killanin had been.

The IOC's agreement with Los Angeles for the 1984 Games was controversial from the start. When Los Angeles was applying to host the 1984 Games in 1978, its third successive application to play host, it appeared at several points to have again failed. Both sides in these negotiations were facing unprecedented problems. After Montreal's financial debacle, the IOC demanded henceforth the city government and the appropriate NOC assume all financial liability. The Montreal experience, however, had also frightened away potential applicants, and when Teheran dropped out of the running, Los Angeles's bid for the 1984 Games stood alone. The state of California was itself now involved in a furor over taxation, which culminated in the establishment of a limit on property tax increases.

IOC members objected to the Los Angelenos' thrift. "Philanthropy and principles come to California after you have made a buck," declared John Rodda, a collaborator of Lord Killanin's, "and that is not the genteel way the International Olympic Committee moves" (Galford 1996). Los Angeles mayor Tom Bradley spoke of a "Spartan" Olympics, and Killanin questioned whether "Spartan" meant "economical" or "uncomfortable" (Killanin 1983). The IOC, Killanin declared, must make its own determination on how the Games should be run. "In other words," *The Los Angeles Times* scornfully responded, "Killanin's position was that the IOC would make the decisions, and the citizens of Los Angeles would pay the bills." Eventually the IOC gave in: "The IOC always compromises," Monique Berlioux explained. On August 31, 1978, the IOC Executive Board finally approved a contract, and the parties made final arrangements in October 1978. The LAOOC, now sharing responsibility with the USOC, could begin its work, aiming to show that private enterprise could run the Olympic Games at a profit.

Olympic organizers chose Peter Ueberroth, a successful businessman, to serve as President of the LAOOC. (He, curiously enough, had come into the world on the very day that Coubertin departed it, September 2, 1937.) "Ours," said Ueberroth, "will be the most financially successful Games ever." He estimated he could run the Games at a cost of $500 million and realize a surplus—the organizers did not like to use the word "profit"—of $20 to $50 million. He sold the television rights for the Games to ABC for $225 million, and he extracted another $500,000 for the radio rights. He declared he would charge journalists for everything from telephones to chairs, even including walls. Calculating that previous Olympic hosts had run into trouble by paying for construction projects, he persuaded private enterprise to build a swimming pool and a velodrome. USC and UCLA permitted their dormitories to be used as an Olympic Village. In choosing a few select but high-paying corporations as sponsors, he claimed to be turning down four for each one he picked while raising more money from sponsors than ever before. At the same time, he insisted the selected sponsors keep their advertising within tolerable limits, that they not take possession of the Games. He forbade Anheuser-Busch, for example, to set up a tall Budweiser advertisement in the immediate neighborhood of the Los Angeles Coliseum.

Keeping costs down represented the other side of Ueberroth's program (Reich 1986). He imposed severe budget restraints, made heavy use of volunteer labor, negotiated carefully with local authorities for public services, including security, and he held a tight line against the demands of the IOC and of the IFs. Moscow, he believed, had been more than generous in responding to the demands of various federations for their facilities, and he declared, "Comparing the Moscow Games to the forthcoming LA Games would be a propaganda game the LAOOC couldn't win." *Sports Illustrated* called him a "Miser with a Midas Touch." With time he won increasingly positive press, although journalists frequently complained about his inaccessibility.

When the Olympic family gathered in the fall of 1981 for the XIth Olympic Congress in Baden-Baden, however, the Americans were still on trial. Samaranch hailed the meeting as a sort of reunification after the troubles of 1980, but the Americans still had to prove themselves. "Baden-Baden is our world debut," Ueberroth told his staff; the Americans were still the "illegitimate children of the movement" (Ueberroth et al. 1985). Olympic officials rather pointedly ignored the organizers of the Lake Placid Games as it heaped awards for service to the Olympic Movement upon the organizers of the Moscow Games.

After some discussion of the possibility of "open games," that is, games open to all comers without any questions concerning professional status, the Olympic Congress decided to allow the various sports federations to set their own rules for eligibility in consultation with the IOC. The Soviets at first hailed this move as a defeat for western hopes of opening the Games to professionals, but they soon began complaining this decision had gone too far. They had strongly supported the approval of broken-time payments in 1973, calling the old rules "absurd," but they soon objected to the money that western athletes, particularly in track and field, began to collect. Sports federations in which East Europeans were especially

---

Circular Letter From Brundage to IOC Members, March 20, 1961:

[T]he Olympic Movement in these materialistic days in which we live carries the seeds of its own destruction. . . .

Just what are the objectives of the Olympic Movement? One can be certain they are not merely to win medals and to break records. The Baron de Coubertin when he revived the Olympic Games had quite different things in mind. He was aware of the ancient Greek ideal of a sound mind in a strong and active body, and he wished to stimulate interest in physical fitness and to bring to the attention of all the world, the necessity of physical training for the full development of man's potentialities and for a well rounded existence. . . .

One can be sure that he did not revive the Games as a commercial enterprise for profit, nor to entertain the public. He would have been horrified, after what he said about gladiators of the circus, to find the Games converted into a steppingstone to a career as a paid athletic performer. To have them used as a measure of the superiority of one political system over another was inconceivable. He would rather not have revived the Games than to see them perverted to such ends.

Brundage Archive, University of Illinois.

---

strong continued to impose much stricter rules for eligibility than did the IAAF. In any case, the IOC's position on athletes' rewards had already moved sharply from Avery Brundage's ideals.

In all, Samaranch praised the Congress for having proved wrong the prophets of doom who had insisted the Olympic Games were on the verge of collapsing. Meeting simultaneously, the IOC, moreover, now expanded its ranks to admit women for the first time; the "most exclusive club in the world" now accepted two, Flor Isava of Venezuela and Pirjo Haggman of Finland. In selecting sites for the 1988 Games, the Committee chose Calgary for the winter festival, and rather unexpectedly it awarded the Summer Games to Seoul, Korea, in preference to Nagoya, Japan.

Even after the Baden-Baden Congress, the LAOOC, licking its wounds, felt it was being measured by a special standard; certainly, the organizers of the 1984 Winter Games in Sarajevo faced no comparable criticisms. The Yugoslavs had trouble planning to combat traffic problems and smog, and the IOC was pressuring them to lower the daily charge for athletes in the Olympic Village. The Yugoslavs sold advertising space on the Olympic torches to be used in the torch relay, whereas the Americans did not. Even so, IOC officials focused their sharpest comments on the Americans, and the Soviets especially kept a drumbeat of criticism of Los Angeles going in the IOC, while they heaped praise on the Yugoslavs.

To Ueberroth's delight and relief, the attitude of Soviet officials underwent a rather significant change at the end of 1982, probably due to the death of Leonid Brezhnev and the accession of Yuri Andropov to power. Sergei Pavlov, the head of the Soviet NOC, suddenly resigned to become the Soviet ambassador to Mongolia, although he had just been reelected the previous February, and Marat Gramov stepped into Pavlov's place as Chairman of the Soviet NOC and of the USSR Sport Committee. As far as Ueberroth et al. (1985) could tell, the nature of the Soviet complaints did not actually change, but Gramov took a much more businesslike approach to the issues than Pavlov had. Thus, in the spring and summer of 1983, the prospects for the Los Angeles Games looked good.

Then in September 1983, Soviet jet fighters shot down a Korean Air Lines jet that had been crossing Soviet territory on its way to Seoul; all 269 passengers died. As Americans again erupted in a storm of outrage, the Soviets quickly canceled visits to the United States scheduled for athletic teams, and they recalled Soviet students who had just arrived in the United States on an official cultural exchange. The incident promised to have far-reaching repercussions not only for the Los Angeles Olympics but also the 1988 Games scheduled for Seoul.

The LAOOC now discovered that government agencies who had previously refused to take any responsibility for the Olympic Games wanted to dictate conditions to the Games' organizers. The California state legislature called for the exclusion of the Soviets as punishment for having shot down the Korean airplane, and a group calling itself "Ban the Soviets Coalition" began circulating a petition to the same effect (Senn 1985). With time, however, the furor died down, and Ueberroth took hope when the Soviets decided to send athletes for exhibitions in America. At the same time, Gramov announced he would visit Los Angeles in December.

Once in the United States, Gramov gave every indication his country intended to participate in the Games. At this time, he told newsmen, he saw nothing that would prevent the Soviets' coming, but his country would make its decision only in May 1984. While in Los Angeles, Gramov obtained the LAOOC's agreement to a series of special conditions, including the right for the Soviet airline Aeroflot to make 25 flights into Los Angeles and the right for a Soviet ship to dock in Long Beach Harbor. The United States State Department would have to approve the agreement yet, but matters looked promising. In February 1984, when the IOC gathered in Sarajevo in preparation for the Winter Games, Konstantin Andrianov, who still represented the Soviet Union on the IOC, expressed only satisfaction with the preparations in Los Angeles.

A more pressing issue facing the IOC as the Olympic family assembled for the Winter Games in Sarajevo concerned the eligibility of hockey players. FIFA had already declared that only soccer players who had participated in the World Cup tournament were ineligible for the Olympic Games, and the rules of eligibility for hockey were now unclear. The IOC thereupon ruled the only professional hockey players in the world were the ones under contract in the National Hockey League, and it permitted players who had contracts in the now defunct World Hockey League to participate in the Games. The ruling satisfied no one, but many observers considered it a significant step in the direction of open Games—open to professionals.

While the competition itself in Sarajevo went well, Olympic officials were disappointed by the poor ratings ABC's telecasts of the Games received with the American viewing audience. The broadcasts' overall Nielsen rating was 18.3, considerably below the ratings of Innsbruck in 1976 and Lake Placid in 1980. Experts attributed the low rating to a variety of problems, ranging from the disappointing showing of the American hockey team to snow delays on the skiing slopes, but the major problem seemed to lie in the necessity of using tape delays in telecasting because of the time difference between Sarajevo and New York. The delays at one point resulted in NBC's broadcasting pictures that ABC had not yet shown; in a pique, ABC forbade NBC from showing any more film footage until two days after a given event.

The Nielsen ratings made a particularly bad impression because right before the Sarajevo Games, the Calgary Organizing Committee had sold the television rights to the 1988 Winter Games to ABC for a stunning figure of $309 million. The Koreans immediately dreamed of a one billion dollar price tag for the Seoul Olympics in 1988, but Sarajevo's Nielsen ratings quickly dispelled that notion—American networks would surely pay no such amount now. Calgary at least had only a minimal time difference from the all-important American East Coast market, while Seoul had a time difference of 13 to 14 hours. The IOC therefore decided to postpone the awarding of the television contract for the 1988 Summer Games until a more favorable time.

In the competition at Sarajevo, the Soviets won the most medals, garnering 25, but the East Germans took home the most gold and silver medals, 9 of each. Probably the most colorful figure at the Games was the West German hockey coach, Xaver Unsinn, who upon arrival complained Yugoslav officials were discriminating against his team. Calling himself a "lone wolf," he therefore kept his players out of the opening ceremonies, and when facing a crucial match with the Soviet Union, he shocked everyone by suggesting perhaps the German players should all join the Communist Party so as to improve their chances of gaining at least a tie. Making the coach's name into a pun, the German newspaper *Die Welt* exclaimed, "Unsinn, dein Name ist Xaver" (Nonsense, your name is Xaver), and the *Hamburger Abendblatt* called him unfit to be coach of the German team. Otherwise, the Winter Games saw no serious political tension.

As attention now shifted toward the Summer Games in Los Angeles, the LAOOC ran into controversy from a new and unexpected quarter: the Greeks. At the beginning of February, the Greek Ministry of Culture objected to the LAOOC's program of selling laps in the Olympic torch relay in exchange for contributions to youth groups. This, the Greeks declared, violated the purity of the flame, and therefore they would not allow the IOC to take the sacred fire from Olympia. Samaranch rallied to the support of the LAOOC, but the Greeks yielded only to the point of allowing the IOC to strike the flame in Olympia at the beginning of May. They still refused to help in transporting it to the United States (Ueberroth et al. 1985).

By March, however, a much larger problem had erupted in the form of a new spate of complaints from the Soviet Union. Yuri Andropov, Brezhnev's successor as head of the Soviet Communist Party, died on February 9 during the Sarajevo Games, and the new Soviet leader, Konstantin Chernenko, appeared to many to be a throwback to the days of the Brezhnev era. Ueberroth expressed concern that Chernenko, as a close colleague of Brezhnev's, might still harbor resentment about the American boycott in 1980, but Soviet policy was in fact determined by more complicated factors.

The American government itself threw a wrench into the LAOOC's careful negotiations with the Soviets when it refused a visa to the man the Soviets had designated as their Olympic attaché in Los Angeles. Rumor had it he was a KGB agent, possibly assigned to guard against defections among Soviet athletes. Ueberroth criticized the State Department's decision, but the Soviets remained ominously silent. The State Department's approval of the agreement to allow Soviet planes into Los Angeles and a Soviet ship into Long Beach Harbor did nothing to cool the situation.

At the end of March, the Soviets began to emit stronger negative signals. The Soviet press had long complained about smog, traffic, and crime in Los Angeles, but now it added a new dimension to its reporting, speaking of specific threats to the safety of Soviet athletes. When Pavlov was still the Soviet NOC chairman, he had complained to Ueberroth about threats from emigrés in the Los Angeles area, particularly Lithuanians, but more

---

From the Warning Issued by the Soviet NOC, April 9, 1984:

On the eve of the elections, the US administration is trying to use the Olympic Games to further its own selfish political aims.

In the USA a broad campaign has been developed against the USSR's participation in the Olympics. Various reactionary political, emigré, and religious groups are uniting on an anti-Olympic platform. In particular, a "Ban the Soviets" coalition has been created with the support of the official services of the USA. Athletes and officials of the USSR and other socialist countries have become the targets of open threats of physical violence and provocative acts. There are even slanderous assertions that the Soviet delegation's participation in the Olympics could somehow threaten the safety of the USA. . . .

The American press reports that political demonstrations and meetings are being planned for the period of the Games and that posters and slogans hostile to the Soviet lands are being hung out. The danger increases that the civil rights of the athletes can be hurt and their dignity insulted. . . .

Under these circumstances, the agreement concluded last December between the USSR NOC and the LAOOC is being crudely violated on the American side. . . .

World public opinion has already been concerned about the unrestricted commercialization of the Games in Los Angeles. . . .

The violations of the Olympic Charter, the anti-Soviet campaign waged by reactionary circles of the USA with the connivance of US authorities, all create an abnormal situation. In this connection the USSR NOC appeals to the IOC and to its president, J. A. Samaranch immediately to consider the existing situation in Los Angeles at an extraordinary session of the Executive Committee of the International Olympic Committee and to demand from the American side strict observance of the Olympic Charter and effective measures to guarantee the necessary safety of participants and guests of the Olympics.

Sovetskii sport, April 10, 1984. Translated from Russian.

---

recently, the Soviet press had not discussed the issue. The Soviets now chose to emphasize the activity of the Ban the Soviets Coalition, which had decided to dedicate its efforts to helping Soviet athletes to defect (Senn 1985). Soviet authorities insisted western discussions of "defection" meant plots to kidnap and mislead Soviet young people.

The Soviet authorities dropped the first shoe on April 9, charging the Reagan administration was supporting a broad campaign against Soviet participation in the Olympic Games. The Ban the Soviets Coalition was said to be threatening violence against Soviet athletes. Summarizing their complaints about costs, the natural environment, and the political atmosphere in Los Angeles, the Soviet NOC called upon the IOC to make sure the United States abided by the terms of the Olympic *Charter*. The Ban the Soviets Coalition basked happily in its newfound attention, while the USOC and the LAOOC insisted the coalition was of no significance. The American and European press, however, publicized every possible provocation the Soviets might meet with at the Games. Samaranch tried to calm matters by bringing Gramov and Ueberroth together in Lausanne on April 24. In direct talks between Soviet and American officials a few days later, the United States State Department refused to give the Soviets any guarantees concerning the return of possible defectors.

On May 3, the Politburo of the Soviet Communist Party decided not to send a team to Los Angeles, and during the evening of May 8th, the Soviet NOC announced it would not participate in the Games because of the dangers that threatened the safety of its athletes. They did not want their action to be interpreted as being aimed against the Games, however. In fact, Gramov disingenuously insisted the word "boycott" did not exist in the Soviet vocabulary. The Soviets declared that for reasons of safety, they simply refused to go to Los Angeles. The Soviets blamed the United States government for this situation, saying the Americans had "crudely" violated the terms of the Olympic *Charter*.

The fundamental reasons for the Soviet action remain rather obscure; it was clearly not just a reflexive response to the American boycott of the Moscow Games. The Soviets complained about the threat of physical violence, but none of their athletic teams competing in the United States had ever faced any danger. They complained about the American government's having required visas rather than simply accepting Olympic identity cards, but the Soviets in any case were to submit a list of participants in advance, with the understanding the Americans might yet object to some. Their complaints about the Ban the Soviets Coalition probably reflected some concern about the behavior of their athletes—ironically, athletes from other countries who came to Los Angeles, including the Communist Chinese, all seemed to enjoy contacts with their cousins in America.

From the Declaration of the Soviet NOC, May 8, 1984:

As is known, from the first days of preparing for the present Olympics the American administration has followed a course of exploiting the Games for its own political goals. A chauvinistic mentality has been aroused, an anti-Soviet hysteria has been stimulated. . . .

Political demonstrations hostile to the USSR are being prepared; undisguised threats of physical violence have been made against Soviet athletes and officials. . . . In justification of this campaign the US authorities and the Olympic organizers made continuous reference to various sorts of laws. . . .

Under these conditions the USSR National Olympic Committee is forced to declare that it is impossible for Soviet athletes to participate in the Games of the XXIIIrd Olympiad in Los Angeles. To act otherwise would be equal to approving the anti-Olympic actions of the American authorities and of the organizers of the Games.

The USSR National Olympic Committee and the sports organizations of our country will continue in the future to support efforts . . . to strengthen the international Olympic movement and to preserve its purity and unity.

Pravda, May 9, 1984.

Ultimately, the Soviet decision probably sprang from traditional Great Power politics. Since the Americans were embarked on another presidential election, the Soviets may have debated whether they could hamper Ronald Reagan's campaign for reelection more by going to Los Angeles or by staying away and then decided they could best show their feelings by staying home. "Being a Great Power," declared *Sovetskii sport* of May 20, "the Soviet Union will not send its athletes to compete under conditions where they can be made targets and can be used as an instrument of an opponent's propaganda."

The Soviet boycott, or "non-participation," aimed at disrupting the work of the LAOOC, and the first reactions to the Soviet NOC's announcement made Soviet leaders think that they had been very successful. The American press argued whether the Games had been "devalued"; *The New York Times* declared the Soviet boycott would harm the Los Angeles Games more than the American boycott had harmed the Moscow Games; and officials at ABC expressed fears of a ratings catastrophe in return for their heavy investment. The Soviets welcomed all such signs their withdrawal had weakened the appeal of the Los Angeles celebration: "Interest in the 1984 Games is falling," announced *Sovetskii sport.*

In the end, however, the Soviet boycott fell short of its goals, as only the Soviet Union's socialist allies supported it. The Soviet success in persuading the African states to come to Moscow may actually have undermined possible support for their own boycott action in 1984; a number of African states quickly disassociated themselves from the Soviet

President Ronald Reagan's Response to the Soviet Charges (Press Conference, May 22, 1984):

Q. Senator Byrd says that our relations with the Soviet Union have reached the lowest point in 20 years. Did you misjudge the Russians? Are your hardline policies responsible for the boycott of the Olympics, the breakoff of the arms negotiations, stepped-up offensive in Afghanistan, more missiles off our coast?

A. I don't think I'm responsible for any of those things. . . .

And as for the Olympics, the only thing as a government that we did in the Olympics was insure them and meet virtually every request that they made with regard to their people there up to allowing their cruise ship to anchor, and we were going to spend about a half-a-million dollars on protection for that ship.

Department of State Bulletin, July 1984.

action just as they had the American efforts in 1980. In all, 139 NOCs announced they would come to Los Angeles (table 13.1), and the LAOOC was particularly delighted by the news the Communist Chinese and the Romanians would come. (This would mark the first time Nationalist and Communist Chinese would compete in the same Olympic Games.) The Soviet boycott, moreover, probably influenced FIFA's decision at the end of May to award the 1990 World Cup tournament to Italy rather than to the Soviet Union. (The Soviet press angrily blamed Coca-Cola and television interests for that decision.) As Ueberroth indelicately described the Soviet efforts to win support for their position, "In the sense of world opinion among sports people, they have failed miserably, and they've been given a kick in the backside."

In the early summer of 1984, the Soviet boycott nevertheless seemed to have cast a dark pall over the Games. As the last weeks before the Los Angeles Olympics wound down, the American press seemed full of

Table 13.1

Growth of the Summer Games in the Modern Era

		Sports	Countries	Participants
1976	Montreal	21	88	6,085
1980	Moscow	21	81	5,326
1984	Los Angeles	21	139	7,078
1988	Seoul	23	159	8,465

doubts. Questions of security vexed everyone; many people spoke of being afraid to attend the opening or closing ceremonies. *The New York Times* warned, "Women posing as prostitutes are luring hotel guests to their rooms, where they use knockout drops to put their victims to sleep while they rob them." And everyone knew Los Angeles always faced the threat of gridlock, a total standstill on the Southern California freeways that intimidates newcomers even when traffic is flowing. The Games, the press reported, would have a security force that included 18,000 to 20,000 persons, 140 helicopters, 14 dogs, and 500,000 rounds of ammunition. A writer for *The Chicago Tribune* suggested that LAOOC really meant "Lost And Out Of Control."

Events totally out of the LAOOC's control also cast their shadow. Offering testimony to the power of the American press to create its own international incidents, Bolivian sport officials asserted *The Washington Post* had insulted them. Officials in Korea and several African states received hate letters allegedly sent by the American Ku Klux Klan, warning them not to show up in Los Angeles. These were subsequently attributed to Soviet sources. Considerable controversy surrounded the British decision to allow Zola Budd, a teenage runner from South Africa, to join the British Olympic team at the Games. Upper Volta declared it would boycott the Games in protest against British links to South Africa, thereby becoming the third African state and the 19th state overall to announce its refusal to go to Los Angeles. The United States State Department refused visas to three Libyan journalists; rumor had it one of them was a suspected terrorist.

Ueberroth tried to counter these stories by pointing to the success of the torch run, but only slowly did the press recognize that indeed some sort of special spirit was arising. The flame had been lit amid controversy in Greece on May 3rd, and it began its journey across the United States on the 8th, only a few hours before the Soviet decision not to come to Los Angeles became known. Because of the furor surrounding the Soviet action, the flame traveled at first in comparative obscurity. As crowds began to gather to watch its passing, however, the torch became a rallying symbol for the Games, arousing considerable excitement and enthusiasm.

Nevertheless, even at the opening ceremonies on July 27, 1984, Ueberroth could still not be sure things would go smoothly. The news of a mass killing near the Mexican border and a berserk driver in Westwood put everyone on edge, and in the final moments before the ceremonies were to begin, Uebberoth (Uebberoth et al. 1985) received a frightening report: "There may be a bomb in the peristyle end [of the Coliseum] and we may not be able to light the torch. The LAPD bomb squad is on the scene." The scare was a false alarm, but these dark forebodings only gradually diminished in the face of a deeply ingrained feeling of disbelief things could actually be proceeding so well. Midway into the Games, when newsmen asked Monique Berlioux whether she had any complaints, she responded cautiously, "Nothing so far, but . . . we shall wait and see." The feared traffic jams, however, did not materialize, and, for the most part, neither did the smog. No terrorist acts occurred to challenge the security forces who watched the outdoor events from neighboring rooftops and other vantage points.

Overall, the Games were a great success, although they of course had their share of controversy, ranging from concern about terrorism, through traditional drug problems and arguments about judging, to the usual assortment of complaints about life in the United States and American television's coverage of the Games. The fear of terrorism lingered until the last athletes had departed. Meanwhile, the Americans complained about a Romanian judge in gymnastics; the Koreans complained that boxing judges were favoring the Americans. A Swedish wrestler and a Greek woman who threw the javelin were disqualified as a result of testing positive for banned drugs. An American doctor, however, announced he had been prescribing steroids to athletes who were evading detection: "I would like to brag about how many gold and silver medals my patients have won in the last week, but I can't," he told the press. Of course, in the absence of the Soviets and East Germans, the Americans won by far the most medals, and the American television audience gave ABC a delightful 23.5 rating with a 45 percent share of the television sets in use. Whereas ABC, immediately after the Soviet announcement, had been threatening to ask for some of its money back, its executives now declared themselves satisfied.

At one point, to be sure, major controversy threatened to erupt over the television coverage. Foreign teams and officials in Los Angeles objected to ABC's glorification of the American victors, and Samaranch asked Ueberroth for an explanation. The athletes were actually seeing the American coverage rather than the coverage that appeared in their own countries, in which commentaries would have been more to their tastes. "We'd made a mistake by not providing the international feed into the villages," Ueberroth explained, and an ABC official added, "The foreign athletes didn't understand that the rest of the world was seeing a different feed than the one we provide to American viewers."

Samaranch expressed satisfaction with these explanations, but criticisms of the coverage offered by Americans continued. The President of FIFA asked the IOC to "intervene immediately" in order to force ABC to televise more soccer competition. Foreign correspondents, and some Americans too, complained the flag waving and repetition of the American national anthem for gold medal winners was creating an atmosphere of chauvinism. ABC officials protested they were reporting what was happening, while ABC cameramen continued to urge spectators to wave their flags for pictures. (As a spectator at a swimming competition, I found my view being blocked by a giant French flag!)

Those who had absented themselves from the Games also wanted to be heard. Before the Games began, *Sovetskii sport* questioned whether, in view of the rampant criminal use of guns in Los Angeles, the starters' pistol shots would even be audible. These "most disorganized" of all Olympic Games, the Soviets insisted, were "a farce": Judges were openly favoring American competitors, and television coverage, which had evoked a "sharp" protest from Samaranch, was formulated in the Hollywood tradition of "our good guys" against "those bad guys." The United States government, charged one Soviet newspaper, had in fact gone to extra lengths to make Soviet participation impossible so the Americans could then dominate the Games. When challenged about the reports they were sending to Moscow, Soviet correspondents in Los Angeles insisted their dispatches were "not distorted." The correspondents explained they were "objecting to the cynical exploitation of the Olympics" by the American government. In any case, without the participation of Soviet athletes, they declared, victories were of questionable value; if the Soviets had come to the Games, added one of them, "We'd get a majority of the medals."

The Los Angeles Games passed into Olympic history as the first "capitalist" Games, and many commentators bemoaned the open presence of giant sponsors (Tomlinson and Whannel 1984). Some Olympic officials insisted the Americans were to blame for the Soviet boycott (Pound 1994). Even the fact the LAOOC's budget, after settling its bills, had a surplus caused controversy. Still, Peter Ueberroth's management of the Games created a model, stimulating new practices the IOC and succeeding Organizing Committees would use and follow. The success, however, could not completely dissolve the storm clouds hanging over the Games. The Olympic flag now traveled from Los Angeles to Seoul, and the next Summer Games had the potential to be even more controversial.

Chapter **14**

Reconstructing the Olympic Edifice

After the American boycott of 1980 and the Soviet boycott of 1984, American television magnate Ted Turner challenged the Olympic Games by bringing American and Soviet athletes together in a new multi-sports competition, known as the Goodwill Games.

Once the Los Angeles Games were behind him, Samaranch faced a rebuilding job that in many ways dwarfed the problems of reviving the Olympics after World War I and II: he had to bring the superpowers back in the arena together. Coubertin in 1919 and Brundage and Edstrøm in 1945 could ignore losers and concentrate on making peace with the victors first. Samaranch, in contrast, had to deal with both sides of a deeply divided Olympic family. To be sure, the Soviet absence from Los Angeles had not caused such a deep rift in the Olympic family as the American boycott of 1980 had; indeed, while less successful in persuading others to follow, the Soviets had also emphasized their concern for the continuation of the Olympic Games. Still, Samaranch feared that if the Soviet Union should boycott the Seoul Games in 1988, it could mean the end of the Olympic Games.

In the years between the Los Angeles Games and the scheduled Seoul Games, Samaranch's task had prodigious dimensions; he literally had to restructure the Games. He had to persuade the Soviet Union and its allies not to boycott Seoul; he had to work to develop new sources for financing for the Games; and he even faced a new, unexpected challenge from American television. At the same time, he supervised the broadening of eligibility to bring more professional athletes into the Games, the best in every sport as he saw it.

In short, the glow of success left by the Los Angeles Games could not eradicate the concerns for the Seoul Games. Indeed, many commentators foresaw only trouble. The shooting down of the Korean airplane in 1983 still cast a dark shadow over the probability of the Soviets' coming to Seoul as well as over the safety of those who wanted to travel to the Games. On May 29, 1984, an editorial in *The New York Times* suggested shifting the 1988 Games to another city. A writer for *The Los Angeles Times* declared, "By awarding [Seoul] the 1988 Games, the International Olympic Committee appeared to have a death wish." Throughout the summer, the American press indulged in gloomy predictions. *Newsweek* magazine asked rhetorically, "Are the Olympics Dead?" No one could be sure what would happen after Los Angeles.

How could the IOC avoid another boycott? There had been talk of possible sanctions against countries that boycotted the Games—"Maybe if a country is not taking part in the Games for political reasons," Samaranch told newsmen, "they will not have the opportunity to take part in the next Games"—but by November, when ANOC representatives gathered in Mexico City, no more such discussion took place. In December, however, the IOC agreed to exclude officials from countries not sending athletes to a given set of Games, as Ueberroth had complained about East European officials working at the Los Angeles Games. Samaranch determinedly expressed his confidence that the IOC

The Prospects for the Olympic Games:

Another boycott in 1988, when the Games are scheduled for South Korea, would surely risk the survival of the modern Olympics. . . .

Much as the South Koreans would be disappointed to lose the Games and spotlight in 1988, they'd make a greater mark by proposing that the IOC pick a permanent, neutral site. And since no site could be absolutely boycott-proof, the committee should also establish and enforce penalties. . . .

In ancient Greece, where this all began, athletes were subsidized. The amateurs-only rule for the modern Olympics was not born of idealism. It was meant to limit the Games to moneyed gentlemen. . . . It's time for the committee to declare all sports open to everyone.

National politics and the sham of amateurism have long since killed the original Olympic spirit. But the Los Angeles Games showed how much enthusiasm there exists for keeping the Games alive. Only strong leadership by the International Olympic Committee can realize that ambition.

Editorial, *The New York Times*, Aug. 26, 1984.

could "organize an Olympic games in which all the countries are present."

The Soviets had followed their boycott of Los Angeles with a major competition of their own, the "Friendship Games," as a consolation for athletes from the socialist countries (tables 14.1 and 14.2). Cuba hosted volleyball, water polo, and boxing, while Czechoslovakia staged the competition in gymnastics, women's track and field, and women's basketball. Moscow hosted competition in eight sports, including swimming and men's track and field, culminating in the men's basketball championship right before the closing ceremonies at the end of August. "In the name of peace, in the honor of sport," said one Soviet newspaper of the competition. As was to be expected, the Soviet Union and East Germany dominated the medal count.

Soviet authorities also pictured the Friendship Games as being "cleaner" than the Los Angeles show, proudly announcing no athletes had been disqualified in the Friendship Games, claiming this as a sign, as in the Moscow Olympics, of purity of motive in the Games. To the embarrassment of the Soviet officials, however, a few months later, the IAAF disqualified the Soviet woman who had won the 3,000-meter race in the Friendship Games when she refused to submit to a drug test in Paris. In the summer of 1985, three other East European athletes were disqualified as a result of drug testing in meets in the West. The Soviet press expressed indignation at the violation of drug rules by a Bulgarian, but it chose never to discuss the Soviet runner, who now retired from competition.

Even as they celebrated the Friendship Games, the Soviets were careful not to challenge the IOC. At the closing ceremonies, Gramov, as Chairman

Table 14.1

Comparison of Swimming Results at the Los Angeles Olympics and Friendship Games

	WOMEN'S				MEN'S			
	LA	**FG**	**LA**	**FG**	**LA**	**FG**	**LA**	**FG**
100 M Backstroke	1.02.55	1.00.99	–	x	55.79	55.67	–	x
200 M Backstroke	2.12.38	2.12.56	x	–	2.00.23	1.58.41	–	x
100 M Breaststroke	1.09.88	1.08.29	–	x	1.01.65	1.03.72	x	–
200 M Breaststroke	2.30.38	2.29.13	–	x	2.13.34	2.15.70	x	–
100 M Butterfly	59.26	59.41	x	–	53.08	54.26	x	–
200 M Butterfly	2.06.90	2.09.96	x	–	1.57.04	1.58.83	x	–
100 M Freestyle	55.92	55.75	–	x	49.80	50.26	x	–
200 M Freestyle	1.59.23	1.59.48	x	–	1.47.44	1.49.83	x	–
400 M Freestyle	4.07.10	4.07.66	x	–	3.51.23	3.49.27	–	x
800 M Freestyle	8.24.95	8.29.35	x	–				
1500 M Freestyle					15.05.20	15.03.51	–	x
200 M Ind. Medley	2.12.64	2.11.79	–	x	2.01.42	2.02.51	x	–
400 M Ind. Medley	4.39.24	4.43.78	x	–	4.17.41	4.18.29	x	–
4 × 100 M medley	4.08.34	4.03.69	–	x	3.39.30	3.42.15	x	–
4 × 100 M Freestyle	3.43.43	3.42.41	–	x	3.19.03	3.20.19	x	–
4 × 200 M Freestyle					7.15.69	7.20.78	x	–

Note. LA = Los Angeles Olympics, FG = Friendship Games, x = winner by comparison.
USA Today, August 28, 1984.

of the Organizing Committee, called the Friendship Games "one of the greatest sporting events of the season." Two other speakers thanked the "Communist Party and the Soviet government for their continued concern for the development of physical culture in the country," declaring that Soviet youth "honor their socialist Motherland with new remarkable successes." At the same time, the Soviets emphasized their own intentions to remain in the Olympic family: Gramov told a press conference the Soviet Union would continue to "support the strengthening of the unity of the Olympic Movement."

Table 14.2

Comparison of Track and Field Results at the Los Angeles Olympics and Friendship Games

	WOMEN'S				MEN'S			
	LA	**FG**	**LA**	**FG**	**LA**	**FG**	**LA**	**FG**
100 M	10.97	10.95	–	x	9.99	10.17	x	–
200 M	21.81	22.15	x	–	19.80	20.34	x	–
400 M	48.83	48.16	–	x	44.27	44.78	x	–
800 M	1.57.60	1.57.31	–	x	1.43.00	1.35.68	–	x
1500 M	4.03.25	3.56.83	–	x	3.32.53	3.36.65	x	–
3000 M	8.35.96	8.33.01	–	x				
5000 M					13.05.59	13.28.35	x	–
10,000 M					27.47.54	27.55.16	x	–
3000 M Steeplechase					8.11.80	8.27.15	x	–
Marathon	2.24.52	2.33.54	x	–	2.09.21	2.10.32	x	–
100 M Hurdles	12.84	12.53	–	x				
110 M Hurdles					13.20	13.52	x	–
400 M Hurdles	54.61	53.67	–	x	47.75	48.63	x	–
400 M Relay	41.65	42.62	x	–	37.83	38.32	x	–
1600 M Relay	3.18.29	3.19.12	x	–	2.57.91	3.00.11	x	–
30 KM Walk					1.23.13	1.21.57	x	–
50 KM Walk					3.46.26	3.43.06	–	x
Long Jump	22-10	23-5½	–	x	28-0¼	27-6	x	–
Triple Jump					56-7½	57-3½	–	x
Pole Vault					18-10½	19-0¼	–	x
Shot Put	69-2¼	72-0¼	–	x	69-9	71-0	–	x
Discus	214-5	240-8	–	x	218-6	218-10	–	x
High Jump	6-7½	6-5	x	–	7-8½	7-4½	x	–
Javelin	228-2	240-6	–	x	284-8	309-10	–	x
Hammer					256-2	261-6	–	x
Heptathlon	6390 pts	6477 pts	–	x				
Decathlon					8797 pts	8523 pts	x	–

Note. LA = Los Angeles Olympics, FG = Friendship Games, x = winner by comparison.

USA Today, August 28, 1984.

When the IOC met in June 1985 to consider the lessons of the past year, its members were not altogether happy about the news that the Los Angeles Games had enjoyed a considerable financial surplus in which they were not sharing. Whereas Ueberroth had at first estimated only a modest surplus, the final figure came to a surprising $225 million, which the LAOOC was to share with the United States Olympic Committee and youth sport programs in Southern California. IOC officials were aghast, and Samaranch reportedly considered filing suit against the LAOOC to get some of that money for the IOC. When the United States Olympic Committee blocked a proposal to refund the money that foreign teams had paid for housing (arguing that governments, rather than athletes, would get the money), the IOC's concerns for assuring itself a greater share of future revenues intensified.

Despite, or perhaps even because of, the fears for the 1988 Games, the IOC now resolved to establish its own sources of income. To this end, it entered into a contract with a multinational marketing firm, International Sports, Culture and Leisure Marketing (ISL) of Luzern, Switzerland (Hill 1996). Monique Berlioux reportedly opposed the arrangement, and some observers speculated this was a factor in her forced retirement at this IOC gathering. In response to complaints about "commercialization" of the Games after Los Angeles, Samaranch declared, "Sport without money is impossible today. . . . The Olympics is of course a business, but it has not become a product one can consume" (*Korea Herald*, May 24, 1986). Yet the agreement marked the triumphal ascendancy of Horst Dassler, the head of the Adidas equipment firm, who owned 51 percent of ISL and already had the marketing rights for FIFA; a Japanese marketing firm, Dentsu, owned the other 49 percent of the company. (As firms, ISL and Adidas were independent of each other.) Dassler quickly won the acceptance of the program by all the NOCs and soon completed his own ring by obtaining the marketing rights for the IAAF. After Dassler's death in 1987, ISL remained strong, adding FIBA to its list of clients in 1989 (Simson and Jennings 1992). In partnership with the IOC, ISL has played a major role in the growing prosperity of the Games.

Copying Ueberroth's success in recruiting fewer sponsors who would donate more, the IOC established TOP (The Olympic Program), which was to find multinational concerns that would give money to obtain what Anheuser-Busch, a a Centennial Games sponsor for the Atlanta Games of 1996, would call "promotional category exclusivity" for their products (Hill 1996). TOP I, created for the Calgary and Seoul Games, attracted nine participants who paid a total of $95 million to the IOC for the privilege of using the Olympic symbol in their advertising. In the competitive business world, other firms soon tried to find other accesses to the symbol, sponsoring national teams or even teams in specific sports, a practice called "ambush advertising," or "ambush marketing," but the IOC would do its utmost to protect the value of the sponsors' investments.

These commercial innovations came at a time when American television was showing signs of reconsidering the economics of televising the Olympics. The Seoul Olympic Organizing Committee, which had once dreamed of one billion dollars, learned ABC's success in its broadcasts from Los Angeles could not offset the disappointment with the troubled ratings for the broadcasts from Sarajevo, because the time difference in broadcasting from Seoul for the American East Coast market would be even worse than it had been in Sarajevo.

To sweeten the product, the Koreans and the IOC pressured key sports federations to stage their final events in the morning, so they could be broadcast live in the evening in New York, but several important federations, including the IAAF and FINA, balked, wanting at least more money from the pot for themselves. In the first round of negotiations, NBC put in the highest bid at $325 million. In the words of a *Sports Illustrated* correspondent, the Koreans were "stunned and demoralized by the initial offers." In the fall of 1985, NBC won the rights for the Seoul Games with a complicated bid that guaranteed $300 million and promised to share profits up to a maximum of $500 million. In 1987, the Seoul organizers reached an agreement with Japanese broadcasters for $52 million when they had been hoping for $100 million. The Koreans had counted on at least $500 million to meet upcoming bills and now had to cut costs and calculate how to raise money elsewhere.

In this period of uncertainty and change for the Olympic Games, the American television mogul, Ted Turner of Turner Broadcasting (TBS), issued his challenge to the Games, attempting to exploit the situation for his own profit. A yachtsman, sport fan, competitive businessman, and an idealist, Turner declared himself to be upset by the Great Power Olympic boycotts of 1980 and 1984, together with the threats being posed for 1988, and he approached the Soviets directly with a proposal for organizing competition between American and Soviet athletes. On August 6, 1985, a transoceanic teleconference announced the First Goodwill Games would take place in Moscow in July 1986: TBS spoke first of its agreement with Gosteleradio, while Soviet authorities spoke of an agreement "between the Sport Committee of the USSR, Gosteleradio of the USSR, American sports federations, and the American television company TBS." As TBS spokesmen put it, these Games constituted a "means of taking the politics out of superpower sports," and Turner himself hoped this venture would help "turn back the clock" in relations between the superpowers, returning to some simpler time without the threat of nuclear holocaust.

The Goodwill Games obviously posed a threat to the Olympics: If the Olympic Games became paralyzed by boycotts, could the Goodwill

The Purpose of the Goodwill Games:

As a pioneering venture towards the universal goal of global peace, R. E. "Ted" Turner, Chairman of the board and President of Turner Broadcasting System, Inc., conceived and launched the Goodwill Games.

"I thought, how can we go back and undo the wrongs that occurred both ways (1980 and 1984 non-participations) and start all over again," Turner said after returning from a trip through the Soviet Union last Winter. . . .

"We can best achieve global peace by letting the peoples of the world get to know each other better and learn to work together toward common goals," Turner said. "Not only will the participants compete together in the spirit of good sportsmanship, but audiences worldwide will be able to see the harmony that can be fostered among nations. . . ."

"I hope this means our nations will meet on the athletic field and never on the battlefield," Henrikas Yushkiavitshus [Juškevičius], vice-chairman of Gosteleradio said at the news conference in Moscow. . . .

"Maybe with the spirit of cooperation that the Goodwill Games can foster, we'll really be turning back the clock to start all over again," Turner said.

"1986 Goodwill Games Backgrounder," Goodwill Games News Bureau, undated [1986].

Games, as a direct confrontation of the superpowers, supplant them in the hearts of fans, sponsors, and advertisers? Could the Goodwill Games capture the American television market? The Soviets had no such intention, and there would certainly be no territorial dispute between the Soviet State Sport Committee, *Goskomsport*, and the Soviet Olympic Committee. On the American side, however, the challenge was clear. From the start, Turner called the boycotts of 1980 and 1984 failures of the Olympic structure and promised his network would do a better job than ABC had in telecasting the Los Angeles Games. In a way, Turner's venture harkened back to alternative competition proposals of the past: James E. Sullivan's for organizing a "true Olympics," the Soviet sponsored "Workers' Olympics," and Sukarno's GANEFO Games. Turner's venture into international sport, however, had the advantage of the television facilities—the Turner cable system.

TBS executives first called the Goodwill Games simply a "commercial venture," and Rex Lardner, director of TBS Sports, declared that since they were a "privately arranged" event, they did not fall within the jurisdiction of the USOC. At the suggestion of the Soviets, TBS turned to Ollan Cassell, the executive director of TAC (The Athletics Congress, the national governing body for track and field in the United States). Cassell, who had headed the AAU before the United States Congress stripped its powers, sounded out the national governing bodies (NGBs) of major American sports federations, and, satisfied, TAC signed a contract with TBS, agreeing to coordinate the participation of the appropriate American sports federations.

When the Soviets suggested expanding the Games to include outstanding athletes from other countries, TBS, exulting in the thought that "the best meet the best" under its aegis, agreed. Turner announced that more than 5,000 athletes from every country but South Africa would participate in the Games. "We will get everybody in the world together," he told *USA Today*. "The last two Olympics have been shams. . . . The best athletes in this country are going in every event. I can't believe this will be a money-losing venture. I think our chances of losing money on it are zero, because this event is bigger than the Olympics." Robert Wussler, Executive Vice President of TBS and President of WTBS, called the Games the "biggest sporting event of the year." The Soviets, however, more aware than the Americans of the soccer World Cup in Mexico City, qualified the Games as the biggest multisport event of the year.

Despite TBS's sanguine expectations, the Goodwill Games ran into scheduling conflicts and therefore could not count on the unreserved enthusiasm of all the major sports federations. TAC officials strongly supported the Games, two days of which were designated Grand Prix events, offering financial rewards for the winners; volleyball and gymnastics welcomed the opportunity to fill their schedules in a quiet summer; women's basketball looked at the Games as a good warm-up for the World Championships to be held in the Soviet Union in August. When Turner discovered the dates of the Goodwill Games conflicted with the men's World Basketball Championships in Spain, he bought the television rights to the basketball tournament and announced that these broadcasts would be included in TBS's coverage of the Games in Moscow. With the World Swimming Championships scheduled for August in Spain, however, United States Swimming decided to send only its "second team" to Moscow. Obviously miffed, Wussler snorted, "If US swimmers get their butts handed to them in Moscow, it's not our fault."

In preparing for the competition in Moscow, American sports federations bypassed both the United States Olympic Committee and the respective international sports federations, dealing directly with their Soviet counterparts through TAC headquarters in Indianapolis. TAC officials had hoped for support from the USOC, but they were ready to go ahead without it. Many officials of other federations claimed to be delighted to be escaping the bureaucratic tentacles of the Olympic structure; TAC officials were ready to challenge the USOC.

In turn, the USOC responded negatively. Robert Helmick, head of the USOC and a member of the IOC, objected strongly to Turner's denigration of the Olympics, and other officials of the USOC expressed concern that the organization of the Goodwill Games could weaken the Committee's position as the body designated by the United States Congress to supervise American international athletic competition. (TAC officials responded that the USOC "cannot force any group against its will to respond to such harmonizing efforts.") The Committee eventually agreed to cooperate with the NGBs, although it would not "endorse or sanction" American participation in the Games.

In contrast, Soviet sport officials threw themselves into the project with enthusiasm. At first they seemed to view the Games as an example of the cooperation anticipated in a bilateral agreement between the United States and USSR Olympic Committees, signed in Indianapolis in September 1985, but soon the Games emerged as a festival in their own right. *Sovetskii sport* emphasized their political dimension, calling them an "important event of international significance which will serve the cause of strengthening peace and developing friendly ties between the youth of the planet" in the spirit of the Geneva talks between United States President Ronald Reagan and Soviet Communist Party Secretary Mikhail Gorbachev. Turner's idealism fell comfortably within the Soviets' goals: *Sovetskii sport* quoted Turner as warning, "The threat of rocket-nuclear war hangs over the world, and I, with my whole heart, support the efforts of the government of the USSR to eliminate it, just as the effort to free humanity from any kind of arms race." The chief problem in American-Soviet relations, Turner reportedly said, is "anticommunism in the United States." Soviet journalists at first treated Turner's statements somewhat reservedly, but eventually they came to believe in his good faith and to defend him vigorously against his American critics.

Soviet officials saw the Goodwill Games as a channel for reaching the American public. The American boycott of 1980 had blocked extensive reporting from Moscow, and the Friendship Games of 1984 and the Youth Festival of 1985 had drawn very little attention from American media. Now, Soviet spokesmen could address Americans directly. The Soviet press repeatedly described how the "Goodwill Ambassadors," sent by TBS throughout the United States and even to cities abroad, had dissolved hostile stereotypes of Russians, offsetting the impact of movies such as "Rambo" or the antics of pseudo-Russian professional wrestlers. These were, according to Iurii Ustimenko, a Soviet journalist in the United States, aimed at "inflaming an anti-Soviet psychosis" so as to "justify the continuation of nuclear explosions in the USA." (Note, however, that TBS carried the professional wrestling that featured phony Russian wrestlers.) The Goodwill Games would present a favorable image of the "Soviet way of life."

As the host of the Games, Soviet authorities controlled the invitations to be issued to athletes of the world. Although Turner had spoken of inviting everyone but South Africa, the Soviets pointedly refused to ask South Korean or Israeli athletes to the party, explaining their government had no relations with the governments of these two states. In contrast, the Soviets entertained a "party-governmental delegation" from North Korea as special guests at the opening ceremonies of the Games. When questioned about such things, Turner usually responded that international sport had their own logic. On Ted Koppel's *Nightline* on July 9, 1986, Robert Helmick challenged Turner's equating South Africa with Israel, but the TBS executive dismissed the subject by simply saying the Goodwill Games could not "solve all the world's problems." Turner insisted the American side would control the invitations to the Second Goodwill Games, to be held in Seattle in 1990.

The opening ceremonies of the Goodwill Games, staged in Moscow's Lenin Stadium on July 6, 1986, displayed a prominent political dimension. With the entire Communist Party Politburo in attendance, Mikhail Gorbachev personally greeted the assemblage, declaring, "The Soviet Union has done much to make 1986 [an International Year of Peace]. Our peace initiatives are calculated to prepare the way to turn the dangerous race to the abyss the other way—toward disarmament. We await a serious answer from those in whom responsibility has been vested and who must, finally, hear the voice of protest against the arms race, which is sounding louder and louder on all continents" (*Sovetskii sport*). The ceremonies then went on to present a somber ballet on the horrors of war, denouncing once again the Americans' dropping an atomic bomb on Hiroshima in 1945. TBS broadcasters declared Gorbachev's appearance had not been a part of the program; when the staff of WTBS subsequently showed highlights of the opening ceremonies, they ignored Gorbachev's speech altogether, featuring instead the performances of circus artists, cowboys, and an occasional dancing bear.

The political topic TBS commentators at the Goodwill Games chose to emphasize was the last-minute decision of the United States Defense Department to forbid members of the American armed forces to compete in the Goodwill Games, saying military personnel could not take part in "commercial or political" events. Nine boxers, two pentathletes, two rowers, and the goalie of the women's handball team had to drop out. More boxers quickly came from home, and the Soviets offered to lend a goalie to the decimated handball team. TBS, the press (both Soviet and American), and even the USOC pilloried the decision as representing an undesirable intrusion of government into sport. TBS, which never publicly discussed the Soviet refusal to invite South Korean boxers, carried daily features on the confusion among the American boxers. Washington's clumsiness in the matter, together with its failure to offer a convincing explanation—according to *The Washington Post*, many believed that disgruntled elements in the USOC had prompted the Defense Department's action—further highlighted the confusion in America about the role a government might play in international sport.

The characterization of the Goodwill Games as a commercial venture now had an ironic ring. TBS officials had called their venture commercial when they launched it, and Turner had boasted he could not lose money: In order to reach beyond his own cable network, Turner had created a syndicated Turner Network Television (TNT) that could include noncable broadcasting. "I'm absolutely certain in my own mind that between July 5th to the 20th next year, the networks are going to have the lowest ratings in their history," he declared. "The Goodwill Games are going to blow them away" (*The Washington Post*, December 17, 1985). However, the expected sponsorship failed to materialize. TBS promised advertisers a Nielsen rating of 5. The actual ratings hovered around 2, reaching a high of 2.8 for the Soviet-American men's volleyball game on Saturday night, July 19. They averaged 1.7, and the Games' prime-time rating was 2.1, representing an audience of about 1.9 million of the almost 86 million television homes in the United States. After the first Nielsen ratings came in, the network ceased selling its national advertising time—which was then only 65 percent taken. TBS eventually had to compensate its advertisers already under contract for the poor ratings. After the Games had ended, Turner Broadcasting officials admitted to having lost some $25 million. Turner, whom *Sports Illustrated* portrayed as taking pride in the amount of money he owed, declared his purpose in staging the Games had simply been the easing of East-West tensions.

While TBS officials blamed their troubles on their weak network of participating stations, shortcomings in the sophistication of American viewers, and possibly "viewer turnoff" because of anti-Soviet feelings, they were in effect admitting the failure of their original conception of the Games' appeal as a direct confrontation between Soviet and American athletes. As for claims the three major networks had given the Goodwill Games the silent treatment, refusing to treat them as a news event, note that TBS forbade American stations to use any film reporting on the Games until the next day, a tougher rule than networks broadcasting the Olympics usually followed. This prevented late night news shows from using clips that might in fact have built interest in the next day's broadcasting. Thus, TBS had contributed heavily to its own problems.

Despite the bleak financial picture, both American and Soviet organizers declared themselves satisfied with the results. Rex Lardner insisted, "Our expectations have been fully realized." Wussler called the Games a "terrific success." Turner declared them an "unqualified success." Speaking at the closing ceremonies, Turner argued the Goodwill Games "have proved that all the people of the world can cooperate in sport in a worthwhile manner irrespective of our different political and religious beliefs." A Soviet journalist exulted at the thought of "129 hours of air time, such was the reporting that TBS sent to America. An unprecedented flow of truthful information from the Soviet Union to the American continent!"

Despite such enthusiasm, however, the Goodwill Games failed in Ted Turner's announced goal of being "bigger than the Olympics." Some 3,000 athletes from 80 countries participated, and while the general level of the competition was very good, it was not outstanding. Soviet athletes won about 40 percent of the medals awarded; American athletes won about 25 percent. The organizers celebrated two major world records, appropriately enough one by an American, Jackie Joyner in the women's heptathlon, and one by a Soviet, Sergei Bubka in the pole vault. The poor television ratings suggested that Great Power confrontation alone was not a sure selling point for winning the American television audience, particularly when most of the broadcasting uses taped replays. The Second and Third Goodwill Games, in 1990 and 1994, constituted barely a blip on the sports screen. Certainly, international sport would not automatically produce wealth for any ambitious entrepreneur; the mystique of the Olympic Games remained unscathed.

When the IOC met in October 1986 to choose sites for the 1992 Games, it knew it had survived the challenge of the Goodwill Games. Stimulated by the Los Angeles experience, the field of competitors for the 1992 Games, despite all the political controversies, had been the largest in years, and the IOC considered seven applicants for the Winter Games and six for the Summer Games. French Prime Minister Jacques Chirac made an eloquent speech on behalf of Paris's candidacy; but Berlioux, who reportedly masterminded the French effort, remained in the background. Barcelona, however, had the support of Primo Nebiolo of IAAF and João Havelange of FIFA. The French left a tactical flaw in their program by applying for both the Winter and Summer Games, and Barcelona supporters rallied strongly to Albertville's candidacy for the winter competition. The IOC chose Barcelona for the Summer Games of 1992 and Albertville for the Winter Games.

As a result of the IOC's decisions, in 1992, Western Europe, once the proud center of the Olympic Games, would host the Winter Games for the first time since 1976 and the Summer Games for the first time since 1972. The IOC also decided to divide the Summer and Winter Games: The Summer Games would continue to take place, as Coubertin had established, in the first year of an Olympiad, but the Winter Games, beginning in 1994, would occur in the alternate even-numbered years. The separation left the Winter Games in a secondary position vis-a-vis the Summer Games, but the decision had both a commercial and a sport rationale, spreading the impact of the Games more evenly across the period of an Olympiad.

The second major problem on the IOC's agenda in 1985 and 1986 concerned the question of athletes' eligibility, or what some anachronistically still called "amateurism." Against the opposition of traditionalists, Samaranch and Willi Daume, the German member in charge of the IOC's Eligibility Commission, were moving toward admitting the "best athletes" in the world without consideration of their sources of income. They recognized that modern competition required athletes to consider their participation to be their profession.

At Samaranch's urging, the IOC lumbered along the path of opening competition to all comers. The IOC's maneuvers in the controversy in ice hockey before the Sarajevo Games had raised more questions than they had resolved. (According to *The Washington Post*, when Daume, in Sarajevo, stood up after explaining what had been done, his ski pants fell down.) In February 1985, the IOC's Executive Board approved a plan to establish an age limit of 23 for participants in ice hockey and soccer. Opposition immediately arose, led by the Soviet Union and its allies, and the IOC backed off, instead coming up with a plan for an "athlete's code," whereby the competitors simply agreed to observe their respective federations' conditions. Again the Soviet Union led a protest, but in October 1986, the IOC approved the admission of professionals in soccer and ice hockey. In June 1987, it approved the admission of tennis professionals into the 1988 Games.

Despite all these building efforts, however, uncertainty still hung over the plans for the Seoul Games and indeed over the future of the Olympic Games. Because of the continuing tensions between North and South Korea, Seoul represented every bit as much a symbol of Great Power rivalry as either Moscow or Los Angeles had. The South Koreans themselves were going ahead with grandiose construction projects, with the government providing some 47 percent of the Seoul organizers' budget. Following the example of Tokyo in 1964, the South Korean government looked on the Games as a demonstration of their country's new economic strength, but commentators kept suggesting the Games be moved. Early on, the President of the French NOC, Nelson Paillou, proposed that the 1988 Games be moved to Barcelona—some interpreted this as a tactic to enhance Paris's bid for the 1992 Games. In 1987, the Rev. Jesse Jackson, putting forth his own candidacy for the American presidency, also urged that the 1988 Games be moved. Of course, Soviet sport officials had particularly severe misgivings about going to Seoul. The memories of the shooting down of the Korean airliner promised sharper demonstrations in Seoul than the ones they had pictured for themselves in Los Angeles. In the fall of 1984, a Soviet volleyball coach warned, "Who can guarantee that these Games would not be made into political games?" and *Sovetskii sport* suggested that “it is not too late” for the IOC to change their mind. When IOC leaders made clear their determination to stand by Seoul, the Soviets, backed by the socialist camp and perhaps reflecting the decline of Konstantin Chernenko's strength and authority and the rise of Mikhail Gorbachev's influence, shifted their position and began demanding that North and South Korea be designated cohosts for the Games. Although there was no precedent—either in history or in the Olympic *Charter*—for such reconsideration of awarding the Games, Samaranch agreed to negotiate with both North and South Korean officials on the possibility of arranging for the two Korean states to share the 1988 Games.

Samaranch recognized the future of the Games lay in the balance, but by the very nature of his position, he had to be optimistic. The IOC seemed most concerned with the problem of assuring the greatest possible participation in the 1988 Games at Seoul—always hoping, of course, that North Korea and South Korea could find a mutually acceptable accommodation and that domestic political conditions in the Republic of Korea would not interfere. The Chinese were to host the Asian Games in 1990, and Cuba would host the Pan-American Games in 1991. Bulgaria had unsuccessfully offered Sofia as the host for the 1992 Winter Games and indicated it would resubmit the bid for the 1994 Games. In December 1986, the International Volleyball Federation declared it would suspend any team that qualified for the Seoul Games and then refused to participate; Bulgaria and the USSR had already qualified for the 1988 Games. In a probably calculated move, the IOC scheduled the voting for awarding the 1994 Winter Games for its 1988 meeting in Seoul rather than for its meeting at the Calgary Games, hoping it could look forward to successful, if not quiet, Games in Korea. Everything, however, depended on the results of Samaranch's talks with North and South Korea.

Chapter **15**

The Last Cold War Games

Even between allies, nationalist politics can explode in the Games. South Koreans had protested the judging in boxing in Los Angeles (1984), and here an American boxer displays his surprise and disappointment with South Korean judging at Seoul (1988).

Although no one knew it at the time, the Olympic Games of 1988 were the last to occur in the context of the Cold War between the world's superpowers. By the time of the Albertville and Barcelona Games in 1992, the Soviet Union would no longer exist. As of 1987 and 1988, however, the politics of the Games still seemed to revolve around the same basic ideological conflicts that had tormented the Games since the 1940s—the clash of the superpowers that had produced boycotts in 1980 and 1984. American athletes had not faced Soviet and East German athletes in Olympic competition since 1976. If the 1988 Games went ahead as planned, East Germany (GDR) promised to win more medals than ever. Meanwhile, the Soviet Union was embarked on an exciting path of reform that promised new triumphs in the sport arena. Yet by the time of the next Olympiad, neither the GDR nor the Soviet Union would even exist.

As the time of the Seoul Games of 1988 approached, the major concern of the IOC was still whether the XXIVth Games could take place as scheduled. Since 1985, Samaranch had been mediating negotiations between North and South Korea on the question of arranging joint hosting of the athletic competition. In so doing, he was of course ignoring the Olympic myth holding that the Games went to a city, not a state, but the preservation of the Games was his paramount concern. Whether he expected to forge an agreement may be an irrelevant question as opposed to considering that by keeping the talks going he would be postponing a final confrontation and thereby perhaps weakening the chances of a boycott. At the very least, his aim was probably to split North Korea from its supporters in the communist camp, particularly the Soviet Union and China.

Charging the South Koreans were pursuing political goals, North Korean propaganda insisted the South Koreans planned to use the Games to finalize the division of Korea into two parts. Chong Jun Gi, North Korean Vice Premier, accused Seoul of "stepping up war preparations against us on a large scale as never before under the pretext of the Olympics . . . . Hence, to hold the Olympiad in South Korea is not a mere sports problem but a serious political problem." *The Pyongyang Times,* an official North Korean newspaper, asserted the "present South Korean strongman," Chun Doo Hwan, wanted to become "honorary Olympic president" when his term in office was due to expire in March 1988. North Korean propaganda made considerable use of "anti-US, antigovernment" demonstrations at South Korean universities, and also warned the world that South Korea was rife with disease:

> Now the Chun Doo Hwan group intends to communicate this disgraceful disease to foreign sportsmen, sports fans and tourists by a massive prostitution tourism around the Asian Games this year and the 1988

> Olympics . . . . If the Olympic Games were held in South Korea, many sportsmen and tourists of the world would meet death, infected with AIDS. (*The Pyongyang Times*, May 31, 1986).

While its propaganda focused on South Korea's absolute "unworthiness" to host the Games, the North Korean regime insisted on becoming the cohost. According to a Chinese declaration published in *The Pyongyang Times*, the sharing of the Games between North and South, "reflecting the common desire of all the Korean people, would be favourable to the independent and peaceful reunification of Korea and the proposal would record a significant page in the modern Olympic history." *The Pyongyang Times*'s gloss on this statement added that holding the Games in South Korea would write a disgraceful page in the annals of the Olympics and result in dividing its movement.

The South Koreans rejected such arguments, declaring that their intention, in the words of Park Seh-jik, acting President of the Seoul Organizing Committee, was to help the Olympic family "transcend political walls that have scarred the Olympic movement." As for the North Korean demand to cohost the Games, Park argued "we have made concessions" but, "the North Korean idea of sharing the Olympic events fifty-fifty is totally unacceptable because it is contrary to the IOC spirit." South Korean officials repeatedly warned that North Korea, which was reportedly strengthening its military ties with the Soviet

---

Warning Issued by Chong Jun Gi, Vice Premier of the Administration Council of the Democratic People's Republic of Korea, April 22, 1986:

We advanced the proposal on cohosting the 24th Olympic Games to save the Olympic movement, ensure the smooth holding of the 1988 Olympic Games and, at the same time, create a favourable atmosphere for peace in Korea and her peaceful reunification. . . .

To our surprise, at this time the south Korean authorities are stepping up war preparations against us on a large scale as never before under the pretext of the Olympics. . . .

If our proposal for cohosting the Olympiad fails to see its realization and the Olympic Games are held in south Korea owing to the persistent and stubborn moves of the United States and the south Korean authorities, participation in the games will result in freezing the division of Korea, aggravating the north-south confrontation and encouraging the US imperialists' occupation of south Korea and the south Korean dictatorial regime.

Hence to hold the Olympiad in south Korea is not a mere sports problem but a serious political problem.

If the Olympiad is held in Seoul it will also result in leaving a disgraceful blot in the Olympics history and splitting the Olympic movement.

The Pyongyang Times, May 3, 1986.

Union, might well try to disrupt international sporting events then being held in South Korea.

On June 11, 1986, Samaranch revealed a compromise proposal, his "final offer," that left Seoul as the host of the Games but gave North Korea the chance to stage archery and table tennis competition while sharing some events in cycling and soccer. The South Koreans grudgingly agreed, but the North Koreans still insisted the Games should be divided equally between the two parts of the peninsula, while indicating they might settle for being awarded the competition in eight sports. The North Koreans also wanted a share of the television revenues. Park vehemently opposed any further concessions to Pyongyang. Samaranch told a press conference at the Goodwill Games in July 1986, "We have encountered a number of political problems in the past few years. They may not entirely disappear by the year 1988" (Pound 1994).

The South Koreans worked assiduously to demonstrate their readiness to host the Games. In the fall of 1986, they believed they had significantly strengthened their case by successfully hosting the 10th Asian Games, which a Korean journalist called a "perfect dress rehearsal" for the 1988 Games despite a bomb that killed five persons at Kimpo airport immediately before the opening of the Asian Games. Pointing to the number of tourists who had come for the Asian Games, South Korean government spokespersons denounced North Korean warnings about the costs of hosting the Olympic Games as "malicious and inflammatory." At the IOC's meeting in Lausanne in October 1986, Park guaranteed "athletes' freedom of movement and personal safety" at the 1988 Games, promising security guards would smile more than they had at the Asian Games. In turn, the South Koreans welcomed the election of Kim Un-Yong as a Korean member of the IOC, and 10 days later Kim became President of the General Assembly of International Sports Federations.

At that same IOC meeting in 1986, Samaranch set a deadline of September 17, 1987—the day invitations for the Games would go out—for the North Koreans to accept his offer of four sports. He continued to put up an optimistic front. In Moscow at the end of the month, he declared he was "quite sure that the Soviet Union will participate in the 1988 Olympic Games"; the Associated Press reporter covering the press conference noted, "Marat Gramov, head of the Soviet Olympic Committee . . . was seated at Samaranch's side but made no comment on the issue of Soviet participation." Samaranch painstakingly collected promises from East European leaders to support the Games in Seoul, and in November he reported at a press conference "I can tell you that I now have the assurance that all the Socialist countries will be present in Seoul" (Pound 1994).

Meanwhile, South Korea maintained its own strong diplomatic offensive. In January 1987, the South Korean Foreign Minister announced the "primary diplomatic goals of the nation this year will be to deter North Korean aggression and to improve relations with the Communist bloc to ensure that the 1988 Olympics will be successfully staged in Seoul." Before it embarked on its Olympic venture, South Korea had no diplomatic relations with the socialist bloc. As the state broadened its sport and other nonpolitical exchanges with both the Soviet Union and China, however, South Korea's general international position improved dramatically, and, correspondingly, the relative status of North Korea declined.

At the same time, North Korea pressed its case on a number of fronts. Government spokespersons talked of the need to "democratize" South Korea. While the Pyongyang press carried information for tourists who might want to attend the Games, the North Korean NOC objected, claiming the western press was deliberately misinterpreting what was happening: If Samaranch wanted the Games of the XXIVth Olympiad to be successful, he "should not stick to any biased view or pursue a specific purpose but pay primary attention" to bringing about a North and South agreement. "The realities show," declared a North Korean official, "that our proposal that the 24th Olympics be co-hosted by the north and south has become the most important issue at present in the efforts to ensure the 1988 Olympic Games with success." In February 1987, the North Koreans accepted Samaranch's proposals "in principle" and then demanded five or six more sports; otherwise, they threatened, they might boycott the Games. Samaranch responded quietly, "I think the offer is a very generous proposal, a historic one, and it is difficult to offer any more. We cannot offer any more" (Pound 1994).

IFs, not formally a part of the negotiations, also played a part. FIFA disqualified the North Koreans from Olympic competition after they had refused to participate in regional pre-Olympic rounds in both soccer and women's volleyball on the grounds that as cohosts of the 1988 Games they should receive an automatic berth. (Samaranch supported the ban.) Amid reports that China and other communist governments were urging Pyongyang to yield, the North Koreans formally demanded the right to host eight sports, including the entire soccer competition. Some IFs grumbled that their interests were being ignored, and South Korea repeated its opposition to any further concessions.

Then, in the spring of 1987, political convulsions shook South Korea. South Korean President Chun Doo Hwan, who had seized power in 1979, had promised to leave office no later than March 1988. In turn, he urged, Koreans should not argue politics until after the Olympic Games. His opponents charged the government was using the image of the Olympics to bolster its prestige at home and abroad. Kim Young-Sam, leader of the opposition Reunification Democratic Party, compared the Seoul Olympics to the Berlin Olympics, and Chun's supporters responded that "Kim is playing into the hands of North Korea." A new wave of student demonstrations arose, evoking concerns around the world as to the viability of Olympic plans. American firms devoted to the prediction of business conditions in various sites made dire statements about the prospects in Korea, although some western journalists, such as William O. Johnson of *Sports Illustrated*, argued that "there appears to be little public support" for the "Olympics-be-damned sentiment" of people like Kim Young-Sam (Johnson 1987). Suggestions arose of moving the 1988 Olympics to Berlin or Los Angeles, but there was probably a greater chance of the Games' being canceled rather than of their being moved.

In June 1987, the crisis peaked (Ricquart 1988). Chun designated Roh Tae Woo, the chairman of the ruling Democratic Justice Party, as his chosen successor. Street demonstrations erupted with renewed vigor, rallying religious and business people, the "middle class," to the support of the students. At the height of the demonstrations, several international soccer games had to be interrupted because tear gas used against demonstrators came onto the pitch. On June 29, Roh announced his support of a direct presidential election as well as a number of other concessions to the demonstrators. This action eased the crisis, Korean Olympic officials breathed easier, and a spokesman for the Ministry of Sports declared, "All the dark clouds over the future of the Seoul Olympics have been once and for all cleared" (Ricquart 1988). An election campaign ensued.

In July, Samaranch gave the North Koreans what he called an "unprecedented" and "historic" offer of a total of 10 events in four sports plus a preliminary round in the soccer competition. Pyongyang still demanded a minimum of six sports, with special consideration of soccer: "Most important of all for us is the football competition. We must have it

---

Statements by Robert Helmick, USOC President, to a Press Conference, Seoul, June 1987:

In talking with the Korean and American business community, embassy staffs and US officials here in Seoul, we have not been given any information that will lead us to believe we should be considering alternative places or do other things. . . .

In a recent briefing by US CIA director [William] Webster, we heard that there is no event greater to bring public attention than an Olympics. Therefore we should anticipate in any Olympics, anywhere in the world, there will be people who would use the venue to demonstrate their cause peacefully or without peaceful means. . . .

We don't want to participate in any athletic events where tear gas is popping off outside the stadium.

Korea Herald, June 19, 1987.

---

all, especially the finals. There is no alternative." Although Samaranch repeatedly declared he would keep the "door open until the last minute," he gave both sides until September 17 to answer. Then in the middle of September, Samaranch declared the package offered North Korea could be "slightly" increased. North Korea suggested postponing the mailing of invitations, but Samaranch refused, agreeing only to add a note mentioning "that we are dealing with North Korea on the possibility of holding some sports in Pyongyang" (Pound 1994). He also posed a new deadline: January 17, 1988, the day by which NOCs had to respond to the invitations. He subsequently traveled to the Soviet Union and urged a gathering of socialist sport ministers not to boycott the Games.

The presidential election in Seoul in December 1987 finally opened the way out of the morass. Roh Tae Woo emerged victorious, and the East European governments declared themselves satisfied with developments in South Korea. The Soviet Union took the lead: The authoritative Soviet newspaper *Pravda* declared the Korean opposition had defeated itself, and the Soviet agency TASS called Roh a "flexible politician, showing a desire for dialog with the opposition." With this, the threat of boycott began to dissolve. Hungary and East Germany announced they would come to the Games, and an official Soviet NOC delegation came to inspect the facilities. On January 11, the Soviet Union announced it would attend the Games in Seoul; on January 14, China announced it was coming.

Proposal by the DPRK [North Korea] Olympic Committee, August 11, 1987:

By drastically slashing its earlier demand, the DPRK Olympic Committee proposes that five full games and one partial game be hosted by the DPRK side. . . .

Explaining the proposal in detail, Vice chairman Chin said, "We fully agree to table tennis, archery and women's volleyball proposed by the IOC, request that full football games, instead of one group of preliminaries, be hosted by us, and road cycling be replaced by another event. . . .

As for the motive of the demand of hosting of the full football games, he said that Pyongyang proceeded from the "fair stand" that equilibrium should be maintained at least on a minimum level since all such popular events as track-and-field, swimming, boxing, basketball, football and volleyball are now shared to one side unfairly.

"This is why we proposed from the first days of the Lausanne joint meeting and still demand strongly that we host the full football matches," he said. . . .

Vice chairman Chin blames [the impasse to now] on the south Korean side, saying that it totally rejected the co-hosting proposal of the DPRK side, "not giving up in the least its stand to use the Olympic Games for its insidious political purpose."

The People's Korea, August 29, 1987. English uncorrected.

Although Cuba declared it would not come, 161 countries reported their acceptance of the invitation before the deadline on January 17, 1988. Of the six who did not accept, only Cuba and Ethiopia declared their support for North Korea. Nicaragua, the Seychelles, and Albania felt unable to come for other reasons. Agence France Presse declared, "Juan Antonio Samaranch appears to have won his improbable wager that Seoul could avoid yet another Olympic boycott." At its February meeting, the IOC again considered ways to punish NOCs who in the future boycotted Games for "political reasons." Among the sanctions the IOC could enforce would be to bar a boycotting nation from participating in the Olympic Solidarity program.

In February, 1988, Olympic competition finally returned to the arenas, slopes, and fields with the opening of the Winter Olympics in Calgary. While the Korean controversy had dominated the world press, Calgary had its share of problems in preparing for the Games. Operating in the shadow of the Montreal fiasco, Calgary organizers established a firmer financial base than their predecessors had, but they saw their costs rise. At the time of its bid, Calgary was prospering as a result of the oil boom, but within a few years its vacancy rate among city apartments exceeded 10 percent, putting into question planned housing projects. Environmental activists added their objections to some of the planned competition sites, and a band of Cree Indians laid claim to traditional hunting grounds. The Crees succeeded in reaching the United Nations Human Rights Committee, and the mayor of Calgary complained, "The city of Calgary is being held to ransom in this dispute. It has the potential to mar the games." European critics tended to put Calgary's problems into a series of Olympic misgivings about North America, including Denver, Montreal, and Lake Placid.

Nevertheless, the Calgary Games went ahead, and by Olympic standards, with relatively little political controversy. The weather, however, did not cooperate. Skiers had troubles with surfaces on the Nakiska courses. Nevertheless, with the exception of the Americans, most participants went home pleased with their Canadian experience.

USOC officials had nurtured modest hopes of success, but disputes among the athletes, lawsuits, and mishaps in competition led to undistinguished results. One speed skater, dropped from the team when another threatened a lawsuit, appealed to the USOC but declared he did not want to "be on the starting line because I hired a lawyer." "Skaters not talking but lawyers are," read a headline in *USA Today* of February 15. When the American hockey team failed to meet expectations, although they matched their seeding, finishing seventh, Samaranch joined the chorus when he declared the American hockey players lacked teamwork.

The angry commentary of the American journalists forced a reaction from the USOC. On February 25, USOC President Robert Helmick announced the formation of an Olympic Overview Commission, to be headed by New York Yankees' owner George Steinbrenner and charged with the task of examining the effectiveness of the USOC's work. Steinbrenner explained his own conception of the IOC's charge by declaring, "I can find no fault with the competitive spirit of our athletes. But we have to ask the question: Are we doing enough to prepare them for competition?" Medal standings, Steinbrenner went on, constituted "the bottom line." (Helmick denied that the appointment of the Steinbrenner commission had anything to do with the medal count.) In its issue of March 7, 1988, *Sports Illustrated* suggested the United States should simply reconcile itself to being a loser in the Winter Olympics. In all, the Americans returned home in a state of disarray that boded ill for the upcoming Summer Games in Seoul.

American television coverage of the Games also came in for criticism. ABC won praise for its technical work, but it lost money in broadcasting the Games, despite a price scale that charged $40 million for exclusivity in advertising beer and $90 million for a "financial services" monopoly. ABC achieved a Nielsen rating of 19.3, higher than Sarajevo but well below Lake Placid's ratings and 10 percent below its own guarantee to sponsors. ABC officials dismissed viewer complaints about commercials and missed goals in hockey as insignificant, but *Sports Illustrated*, among others, concluded that "McKay, Roone Arledge and their colleagues once defined Olympic television, but they may have stayed for one Olympics too many." Indeed, Calgary marked the end of the ABC dynasty in broadcasting the Olympic Games.

American frustrations, of course, were merely a trivial aside for most other observers who deemed the Calgary Games a great success. The three gold medals won by Dutch speed skater Yvonne van Gennep, the two gold medals won by Swedish speed skater Tomas Gustaffson, and the two gold medals won by Alberto Tomba, an Italian downhill skier, all offered relief from the domination by Soviet and East German athletes, who won a total of 29 and 24 medals, respectively. All parties concerned left Calgary with warm feelings about the local arrangements, which IOC President Samaranch characterized as "perfect."

The Calgary Games done, the IOC could return to worrying about the Seoul Games. In the spring, student riots in Seoul resumed, but on a lesser scale than before, and negotiations with North Korea continued almost to the very beginning of competition in Seoul. Another threat of boycott rose briefly when, in what had become a routine challenge, an international rugby team was scheduled to play in South Africa in the summer. The Secretary-General of the Supreme Council for Sport in Africa threatened that as many as 50 countries might boycott Seoul if the tour went ahead. The IOC stood firm; Michele Verdier, IOC spokesperson, declared on

March 28, "The Olympics have nothing to do with this. It only concerns rugby, which is not an Olympic sport and should have no consequences on the games." The threat passed quietly, and the Games could go ahead.

Still, the threat of terrorism lingered on through the very opening of the Seoul Games on September 17. Both China and the Soviet Union, however, sent athletes, and their governments assured the United States that North Korea would make no effort to disturb the Games. Pyongyang, however, did not represent the only possible source of disruption; there were many other potential sources. Some American athletes openly expressed concern about their personal safety. For example, a former Olympic sprinter, Roger Kingdom, declared, "Getting a gold medal is great, but it's not worth your life." Olympic officials essentially held their breaths: When the opening ceremonies had passed quietly, Samaranch declared, "On October 3, the day after the Games are over without incident, then we'll be able to celebrate."

The competition, featuring the first Olympic competition between the United States and the Soviet Union since 1976, proceeded in an orderly fashion. In the final medal count, the Soviet Union led with 132 medals, 55 gold, and East Germany had won 102, 37 gold; the United States had won 94 medals, 36 of them gold. Some observers now wanted to minimize the medal count, saying these figures were no longer important. Writing for *Sports Illustrated*, the journalist Frank Deford noted the United States "didn't finish one or two in the medal count, and nobody got hysterical" (1988). Deford's quote of a colleague at the same publication, E.M. Swift, nevertheless pointed out that the medal count "showed that the U.S. has slipped in relation to the two Eastern bloc giants of sport," and called on the USOC to improve American performances in the sports that offered a significant number of medals (1998).

The 100-meter dash, one of the premiere events of any Olympics, produced the showcase scandal at Seoul. After establishing his claim to being the world's fastest human with a world record time of 9.79 seconds, Ben Johnson, a Canadian sprinter, failed his obligatory drug test, and Olympic officials revoked his medal. At the Calgary Games, Samaranch had insisted the IOC would now target "doping," and IOC representatives insisted the "gap between discovery of new products and the means of detecting them is narrowing." The IAAF imposed a standard two-year suspension on Johnson, but rumors of the way in which athletes could elude testing procedures continued to abound.

Almost inevitably, the Americans met with peculiar setbacks and disappointments. The men's basketball team lost to the Soviets in the semifinal and finished as bronze medal winners. Reminiscent of problems involving sprinters in Munich, a boxer, Anthony Hembrick, failed to show up on time for his first match because his coaches had misunderstood his schedule; he was disqualified without ever stepping into the ring. The Americans complained bitterly about the scoring in the boxing events: In the words of *Sports Illustrated*, "The US boxers could beat anyone inside the ring; they were no match for the officials outside." Nevertheless, the overall judgment was that on the whole the Americans had performed about as expected.

The Soviets went home very pleased with their results over the whole Olympic year. At Seoul and Calgary they had won the gold medals in all three of the country's most popular sports—soccer, ice hockey, and men's basketball. To be sure, the Olympic soccer championship was something below a World Cup championship, the hockey championship might take second place to the Canada Cup tournament, and the basketball championship did not include American professionals, but the Olympic Games constituted the main perceived goals of the Soviet sport apparatus, and the Soviet Union proudly held all three of these championships.

The championships were all the more valued because the Soviet Union was undergoing a confusing process of reform. Mikhail Gorbachev's program of *perestroika* aimed at making the Soviet economy more efficient and productive, but for Soviet sport this meant some cataclysmic changes as the government made clear its intention to cut back on subsidies. In effect, sport clubs were expected to generate more revenue themselves in order to support their activities. This meant improving gate receipts, looking for sponsors, and seeking other channels for improving their cash flows. Could they struggle with the new concepts of "economic self-sufficiency" and "profits" and still maintain the quality of their athletes who had up to now relied heavily on state support?

Gorbachev himself obviously put great weight on the performance of the Soviet athletes. In the summer of 1988, he had summoned coaches and administrators to a meeting in Moscow, at which he warned them of dire consequences should drug testing at the Summer Games produce problems for the Soviet Union. The Soviets maintained a ship in the harbor at Seoul: Soviet commentators insisted it was a place of haven where the athletes could feel comfortable; western commentators believed the Soviet authorities were conducting their own drug tests there. Soviet athletes reportedly even feared to drink Coca-Cola, lest their caffeine intake should register in the testing. The official drug testing found nothing wrong with the Soviets, and Soviet weight lifters improved their medal harvest considerably when Bulgarian lifters ran afoul of the testing. In all, the Soviet Olympic triumphs seemed to represent a confirmation of Soviet reform efforts.

Once back in Moscow, Soviet authorities insisted *perestroika* had brought rich rewards to the country. Soviets had won 17.9 percent of all the medals awarded in Seoul and 22.8 percent of the gold medals; 120

Soviet athletes, about 22 percent of the team, had returned with gold medals (including medals in team sports). In both Canada and South Korea, Soviet spokesmen insisted, their athletes had "convincingly showed how great desire and real effort will assure the growth of the authority of their Motherland." The weight lifter Iurii Zakharevich declared that in breaking the world record in his event, "I was not performing for myself. I represented our people, our Motherland." Marat Gramov, head of the State Sport Committee, expressed his thanks to "our Communist Party, its Central Committee, and the government" for their wise policies, which had "raised the Soviet image in the eyes of the world."

From the point of view of the Americans, the most controversial and disturbing Soviet victory at Seoul came in basketball. Although many Americans would later see the basketball team's failure in Seoul as the direct cause of the creation of the basketball "Dream Teams" of the 1990s, the Soviet victory owed much to the efforts of the National Basketball Association (NBA) to extend itself into an international market. In dealing with the Soviets, Ted Turner took the lead, and in the summer of 1987, he invited a select group of Soviet players to come to the United States to train in NBA camps. In October, the Soviet team played the Milwaukee Bucks in the first McDonald's Open. In April 1988, the star center of the Soviet team, the Lithuanian Arvydas Sabonis, traveled to Portland to undergo rehabilitation for his repaired Achilles tendon. Then in the summer of 1988, the Atlanta Hawks, owned by Ted Turner, played three games in the Soviet Union against the Soviet national team.

John Thompson, the coach of the 1988 United States Olympic team, complained sharply about the help the NBA was giving to the Soviets, and the Hawks tried to disguise the nature of their trip to the USSR, insisting that the first game, to be held in Tbilisi, Georgia, was not against the Soviet national team but against the Georgian All-Stars. The Soviet team that took the floor in Tbilisi, however, was made up of the same players as the Soviet national team. After a second game in Vilnius, Lithuania, the tour concluded in Moscow, where the Soviet team won, thereby making the Atlanta Hawks the first and only NBA team ever to lose a game to a Soviet team. Atlanta officials declared this was an exhibition and of no consequence, but delighted Soviet officials pointed out that the NBA Commissioner David Stern was in the stands, together with a pride of other NBA officials, and that the Hawks were wearing their official uniforms.

When the Soviet coach Aleksandr Gomelsky put together his squad for Seoul, he included Sabonis, even though Sabonis's Portland doctors had recommended he not play in the Olympics. With extended playing time, however, Sabonis's play improved dramatically, and in the semifinal game, he was a major factor in defeating the Americans (table 15.1). As angry telephone calls rained in on the Trail Blazers' headquarters in Portland,

Table 15.1

The US-Soviet Olympic Basketball Confrontations

		US	USSR
1952 Helsinki	Preliminary	86	58
	Gold Medal	36	25
1956 Melbourne	Preliminary	85	55
	Gold Medal	89	55
1960 Rome	Final round	81	57
1964 Tokyo	Gold Medal	73	59
1972 Munich	Gold Medal	50	51
1988 Seoul	Semifinal	76	82

Gomelsky, in Seoul, publicly expressed his thanks to the NBA for having helped him to prepare his team for the Games. After he had returned to Moscow, Gomelsky declared that now the Soviets would set the tone for world basketball for the next four years. In fact, however, Soviet basketball collapsed, but the NBA moved into the Olympic Games.

Probably the most disappointed participant in the Seoul Games was NBC, the television network. While Seoul hotels complained of empty rooms because foreigners had not shown up in expected numbers, NBC complained of low Nielsen ratings at home. NBC had guaranteed ratings of 21.2 to sponsors, so when the final figure came in at 16.9, it had to compensate advertisers. While the network still expected to at least break even in the final accounting, this meant the Seoul organizers would get only their guaranteed $300 million. Some critics declared that staging the Games in late September had been a mistake, but the Seoul organizers had already made the Games earlier than originally planned so as to avoid conflict with the baseball World Series in the United States.

The television ratings, while in line with a general decline in network Nielsen ratings, evoked considerable soul searching as to how to plan for the Barcelona Games in four years. CBS had already won the rights to the Albertville Winter Games of 1992 in May, offering $243 million, and its unhappy rivals were predicting the network would lose money. Judging that Americans wanted to see the "red, white, and blue," *Sports Illustrated* predicted, "Look for a Hollywood-style, celebrate-America's-medals version of the Barcelona Games each night." The magazine also predicted the winner of the television contract for Barcelona would also "sell the rights to individual events to a cable service."

In summarizing the Seoul Games, commentators were of course delighted the festivities had passed without violence. Most called for a renewed struggle against the use of performance-enhancing drugs. They expressed pleasure that North Korea's efforts to organize a boycott had realized only minimal success. For the most part, however, they were not sure about their attitudes toward the greater participation of professional athletes in the Games or the financial rewards that various countries promised their medal winners. The athletes welcomed the new rewards, but traditionalists thought it affected the competition. Frank Deford wryly declared, "Entertainment has superseded excellence as the central purpose of the Olympics." Many mourned the passing of the "amateur" and considered these Games the start of a new era. With the last appearance of the Soviet Union, however, it was more the ending of an old era; by 1992, even the question of boycotts seemed to be less urgent.

Chapter 16

The Collapse of the Soviet Union

After a twenty year lapse, the Summer Olympic Games returned to Western Europe with the competition in Barcelona (1992). These were the first Summer Games after the collapse of the Soviet Union.

In 1988 and 1989, as Korean President Roh thanked and rewarded individuals around the world who had contributed to the success of the XXIVth Olympic Games, neither Olympic officials nor Soviet sport authorities had any idea Calgary and Seoul would mark the last appearance of the Soviet Union in the Games. Since the press had no opportunity to celebrate the Seoul Games as the "Last Cold War" Games, in 1992 they wanted to apply the term to Barcelona—"Last of the 'Cold War' Games Plenty Hot," wrote *USA Today*. But by 1992, the Soviet Union had already collapsed, and the athletes who represented the new order that was then called the "The Commonwealth of Independent States" (CIS) entered the Albertville and Barcelona Olympics as a "Unified Team." This undoubtedly represented the "big story" of the XXIVth Olympiad, the period between the Seoul Games and the Barcelona Games, with the disappearance of the German Democratic Republic and the disintegration of Yugoslavia into warring republics as the second and third lead stories. The IOC and various other international sports organizations struggled to cope with the unprecedented disintegration of these European states.

Even at the time of the Seoul Games, however, the Soviet sport world was experiencing the strains of radical change. *Perestroika*'s charge that elite sport must support itself led sport officials to look for new sources of income and struggle for *valiuta* (convertible currency such as dollars). At the same time, they faced growing shortages of material goods, a decline in support from former sponsors, and diminishing interest on the part of the paying public. Soviet soccer attendance in 1988 averaged 20,892, 21 percent lower than in 1987; in 1989 it fell to 18,032 and in 1990 to 13,795. Naturally, clubs developed cash flow problems. Local governments throughout the Soviet Union looked to raising revenue through a tax on land, and the tax burden on playing fields and stadiums threatened to make them uneconomical to operate, much less repair. In answer, sport officials sought income to the point of fielding a soccer team in Central Asia under the name "Pepsico," and Soviet national teams looked for foreign sponsors to cover their hard currency expenses.

In this atmosphere there was some debate about the regime's commitment to Olympic sport. Writing in *Ogonek,* Valentin Iumashev (1988) questioned the mystique of the Games, pointing out poor attendance at Olympic competition and challenging the method of determining an overall team score. Did a gymnast who might win eight medals represent greater achievement for a country's sport program than a soccer championship? On behalf of the sport establishment, N. Liubomirov, writing in *Sovetskii sport* on December 3, 1988, criticized Iumashev's ignorance of Olympic facts and traditions. Poor attendance in Seoul, he explained, was the fault of the Americans—the result of NBC's insistence on holding major competitions in the morning for the benefit of American East Coast television audiences. Only the United States, he insisted, had expressed unhealthy thoughts about winning the Olympic Games "at any price." Sport, he concluded, "is one of the few social spheres where our standards are on the international level and even higher, where we consistently occupy the leading positions in the world. And should we not write approvingly of it?"

That honored Soviet position, however, was beginning to disintegrate. In the late summer and fall of 1988, the three Baltic republics of Latvia, Lithuania, and Estonia, already excited by the potential of *perestroika* in other aspects of their lives, began to consider the possibilities of organizing separate Olympic Committees, arguing they each had had NOCs in the 1930s before their forcible annexation by the USSR in 1940. In November, the Latvians proclaimed the "reestablishment" of the Latvian National Olympic Committee. Moscow protested vehemently, but after some uncertainty, the Lithuanians took the same step in December, and the Estonians in January 1989 (Poviliunas 1995). The Baltic republics encouraged similar actions in other republics of the USSR.

Soviet basketball fortunes were the first to suffer. Lithuanians had a special grievance in regard to Gomelsky's drafting Sabonis for duty in Seoul, and at the same time, they regarded the victory over the Americans in Seoul as their own; indeed, at one point there had been four Lithuanians playing. Not surprisingly, then, they spoke of taking command of their own resources. After the Seoul Games, Gomelsky accepted a contract to work in Spain, and the Lithuanians refused to play for the Soviet national team. When the Soviet team played abroad in December 1988 and January 1989, it did poorly. The Soviet coach Iurii Selikhov complained the Lithuanians were undermining the quality of the national team; at the same time, he complained the foreign promoters were not paying his team the money befitting the "Olympic champions." Gomelsky's boast at Seoul that Soviet basketball was now the best in the world rang hollow.

In many ways, national ferment in sport anticipated the disintegration and collapse of the Soviet Union. Early in 1990, Georgian officials took the lead in exploding the Soviet sport world when they ordered the two Georgian soccer teams to withdraw from the Soviet Major League. The Lithuanians followed the Georgians' lead in March 1990. After the Lithuanian parliament had declared the independence of the Lithuanian state, sport officials withdrew the Lithuanian basketball and soccer teams from further competition in the Soviet Major Leagues. In response, Soviet authorities called on international sports organizations to discipline both the Lithuanians and Georgians. The IOC maintained a hands-off policy, but FIFA rallied vigorously in support of Moscow, outlawing both the Lithuanians and the Georgians. FIFA fined an East German team for even

From a Speech by Kazimieras Motieka, Vice President of the Lithuanian NOC, to an IOC Commission in Lausanne, July 8, 1991:

In Lausanne, almost a year ago, August 1990, the IOC accepted the proposal of Lithuanian representatives to form a commission to help resolve the problem of Lithuania's participation in the Barcelona Olympics of 1992 independently of the USSR team. Now almost a year has passed, but we have received no word about the commission's work or a resolution of the problem. On the contrary, in that time we received advice from IOC representatives to wait until the USSR makes a political decision concerning a reestablished Lithuania. In addition, some thoughts were passed on that if the Lithuanian NOC sought to have its athletes compete in the 1992 Olympics not as part of the Soviet team, this would prevent Lithuanian athletes from participating in the Olympic Games. The athletes of Independent Lithuania consider such advice and explanations as completely ignorant of what is happening in Lithuania or else unwilling to understand those events, or to consider it natural that freed of fifty years of imposed dependence on the USSR, Lithuanian athletes should not continue to participate in the Olympics under the state flag of the oppressing country. I would very much hope that such advice comes solely from not understanding the situation.

Arturas Poviliunas 1995, p. 124. Translated from Lithuanian.

practicing with the Lithuanians, and as a result, if the Lithuanians and Georgians wanted to play international soccer, they had to find a way to get their teams together on the same field. Despite such help, however, Moscow could not keep its empire together.

The three Baltic republics—Latvia, Lithuania, and Estonia—sought international recognition at the Second Goodwill Games, held in Seattle in the summer of 1990, demanding entry into these Games as separate teams. In 1986, in response to the exclusion of Israel and South Korea from the Goodwill Games in Moscow, Ted Turner had insisted that in 1990 the Americans would control the invitation process and invite anyone they wanted. In the fall of 1989, when asked how TBS viewed the effort of the Baltic republics to win a place in Seattle, a Goodwill Games official made very clear that because the Soviets did not want the Balts admitted, neither did TBS. Baltic emigrés and sympathizers in the American Northwest, however, defiantly carried the flags of the three republics in full view of the television cameras covering the competition.

The year of 1991 proved to be fatal for the Soviet Union as a state. Soviet authorities resorted to force in their efforts to hold on to the Baltic republics. After the failure of a conservative putsch in Moscow in August, Gorbachev recognized the independence of Estonia, Latvia, and Lithuania. Then, as states of the world hastened to grant recognition to the emerging states, the IOC welcomed them into the Olympic family. The Soviet state continued to disintegrate, and in December 1991, leaders of the Russian, Belarussian, and Ukrainian republics announced the formation of a new state, the Commonwealth of Independent States (CIS). On Christmas Day, 1991, Gorbachev left office and the Union of Soviet Socialist Republics ceased to exist. Boris Yeltsin, the President of the Russian Federation, became the leader of the CIS, and the Soviets' sport network, sometimes called "The Big Red Machine" (Brokhin 1977), faced collapse.

The cataclysmic political denouement in Moscow came barely a month before the beginning of the 1992 Winter Olympics in Albertville, France. Olympic officials met frantically with Russian officials to determine how athletes from the CIS could participate in the Games. There was, of course, no problem with the three Baltic republics, which had already won general recognition, but enormous questions concerned the representation of the other 12 republics that had made up the USSR. By now all had declared their state sovereignty: Should they enter the Games individually or as the Commonwealth of Independent States? What could be done about team sports? How could they finance their participation? Decisions had to be made quickly so this vast region would not be unrepresented in Albertville. Samaranch negotiated these questions directly with Russian President Yeltsin.

With the aid of foreign sponsors—Adidas, Smirnoff vodka, and Turner Broadcasting System—Russian officials collected enough money to send athletes to Albertville. Negotiations between Samaranch and the Russians produced the idea of a "Unified Team" ("equipe unifeé") made up of five republics of the CIS: Russia, Ukraine, Belarus, Kazakhstan, and Uzbekistan. The athletes would march under the Olympic flag and the Olympic hymn would honor victors, but the athletes would wear their own national colors on their sleeves. The Unified Team in Albertville officially consisted of 119 Russians, 10 Ukrainians, seven Kazakhs, three Belarussians, two Uzbeks, and Darius Kasparaitis, a Lithuanian who by the end of the year was playing for the NHL's New York Islanders, and who played for the Russian hockey team in Albertville.

Unfortunately CBS television's coverage of the Albertville Games missed much of the post-Soviet drama. Baltic emigrés in the United States, who had actively supported the cause of their homelands, objected loudly when CBS officials, apparently unaware of the role of the Baltic peoples in the collapse of the Soviet Union, chose to switch to commercials and eliminated the arrival of all three Baltic teams in the Parade of Nations. Infuriated emigrés bombarded CBS with telephone calls complaining about this failure to recognize the new states. The next day, in a clumsy apology, CBS replayed a clip of what it called the Lithuanian team, but the sign carried by the athletes said "Lettonie" (Latvia).

Some Russian athletes in Albertville openly regretted the collapse of their system and spoke wistfully to foreign journalists of the old days under the Soviet flag. Two Russian biathletes even sewed hammer and sickle patches on their uniforms. In a more practical vein, many Russian athletes brought vodka, caviar, and pins with them to sell for western currency.

The German athletes in Albertville had problems of a different sort. After the opening of the Berlin Wall in the fall of 1989, many observers, including William O. Johnson of *Sports Illustrated,* saw no challenge to the continued existence of the GDR, and they spoke glowingly of the freedom that talented East German athletes would now enjoy (Johnson and Verschoth 1989). The GDR, however, collapsed, and the East and West German sport programs merged in July 1990. Many German sport specialists lost their jobs (Blume 1990). East German athletes came under suspicion as the result of new stories of past drug use and of having spied for the East German political police, known as the *Stasi.* As the Germans gathered in Albertville, such rumors whirled through the Olympic Village, and observers reported serious problems with team morale. Like the Russians, the former East German athletes also regretted the loss of their economic and political privileges.

In addition to these political concerns, the Albertville games had more than their share of natural or normal problems. Noxious ammonia fumes necessitated issuing gas masks to local residents, and many of those residents were in any case complaining about the restrictions imposed on their normal movements so the athletes could have their festivities. In addition, the internal bickering of local officials posed serious problems. Even so, once underway, the Albertville Games witnessed no special problems.

Contrary to what one might expect, the Russians' troubles did not automatically mean American domination of international sport competition, especially in the Winter Games. The Unified Team won the hockey championship, and its players, while selling their Soviet uniforms to souvenir collectors, scrambled for NHL contracts. Germany won the most medals, 26, 10 of them gold; the Unified Team won 23, including 9 golds. The United States won 11 medals (5 golds), but journalists paid special attention to the fact that American women won 9 of their country's medal harvest. Reports from Albertville directed special complaints at the United States hockey players, whom one journalist euphemistically called "emotional" and "graceless."

In March, the IOC modified its arrangements for the participation of the Unified Team in the Summer Games. In Barcelona, the team would combine the representatives of the 12 former republics of the USSR that did not have their own recognized NOCs. For team sports, whether ceremonies or victories, they would use the Olympic flag and the Olympic hymn, but individual victors would be honored by their own national flag and hymn. There still seemed to be more that bound these athletes together rather than separated them.

On the eve of the Barcelona Games, the IOC still had to settle the problem of how the territories of the former Yugoslavia could be represented at the Games. Albertville had hosted teams from Yugoslavia as well as from the two breakaway republics of Croatia and Slovenia. Yugoslavia planned to send 120 athletes to Barcelona, but in the face of UN sanctions for Serbian actions against other republics that had declared their independence, Spain refused entry to the Yugoslavs. The IOC, however, permitted Yugoslavian athletes to compete in individual events. These athletes, moreover, could not show the flag in the opening or closing ceremonies. The Serbs debated whether they should accept these conditions, but the federations representing individual sports carried the day. Belgrade accepted a compromise that opened the way for the IOC to recognize Bosnia and Macedonia, thereby raising the number of participating countries to 171, a new record for the Olympic Games. Although western observers in Albertville had noticed no hostility between Yugoslavs and Croatians and Slovenians, feelings ran higher in Barcelona.

In the new post–Cold War world, the IOC had considerable room for maneuvering, but its spokespersons still insisted they were keeping politics out of sport. Speaking in Birmingham, England, on June 13, Samaranch insisted the IOC had to be ready to deal with all new problems in the world, although, rather denying his own role in the Korean crisis of the 1980s, he insisted the IOC was not making policy: "The recent upheavals occurring in the world are a cause of serious problems with which the Olympic Movement will have to cope. . . . We should never try to move ahead of [political developments]. . . . We never intervene directly in politics."

The Summer Games in Barcelona ran from July 25 to August 9. Of course, they could not begin without historians' calling up memories of the failed effort at organizing Counter-Olympics in 1936. In 1931, the IOC had chosen Berlin over Barcelona for the 1936 Games, and the groups favoring a boycott of the Berlin Games had chosen to stage a Popular Olympics in the Catalan city. The effort had failed, disrupted by the Spanish Civil War, and now in 1992 Samaranch was bringing the real Olympics to his city. The city and the Spanish government invested billions of dollars in the celebration.

The city of Barcelona and its region, Catalonia, also faced more contemporary problems. Critics had predicted the Games would suffer from housing problems, replete with exorbitant rates and traffic congestion, but officials insisted everything was in order. Basque separatists had long waged a bombing campaign against the Spanish authorities, and Olympic organizers feared the Basques might choose the Games as a target. Spanish security forces set up metal detectors and surveillance equipment to guard against disruption. (The Basques, however, had chosen not to indulge in random killing, and the Games went on without incident on their part.) Catalonia had its own distinctive traditions of opposing rule from Madrid: Spanish flags flew inside the stadium, but Catalan flags flew outside. In addition, faced by a new threat of boycott by African teams, the IOC, on the eve of the Games, asked a museum in Banoyles, Spain, to remove an exhibit of a preserved African man. The Banoyles city council refused to comply, but the controversy passed without greater note.

A more serious controversy arose in the track and field competition. The American sprinter Butch Reynolds, who had won the silver medal in the 400-meter sprint in Seoul, obtained a restraining order in an American court against the IAAF's decision to suspend him for having tested positive for drug use, and he declared his intention to qualify for the United States Olympic team. The American track and field organization, TAC, backed him, and the IAAF in turn threatened to ban athletes who competed against him. A tense struggle ensued, and the IAAF finally backed down to the point of recognizing the court's injunction. Subsequently, IAAF officials breathed more easily when Reynolds failed to qualify for the United States team.

On the positive side, the long-standing South African controversy showed signs of finally resolving itself, as South Africa, in the process of dismantling the apartheid system, was returning. Although some sources in South Africa, including Bishop Desmond Tutu, called for protests against South Africa's participation in the Games, eventually the African National Congress (ANC) decided to stand aside. Using a special flag (with no springbok on it) and the Olympic hymn, a mixed South African team came to Barcelona. South African leader Nelson Mandela told athletes in the Olympic Village their presence at the Games had a "significance which goes beyond the boundaries of sport." The IOC was also pleased to have Cuba, Ethiopia, and North Korea participate in these Games.

The basketball competition epitomized all the contradictions, problems, and spirit of the new Olympic world that had evolved from the liberalized eligibility rules, growth of sponsorship, and collapse of the Soviet Union. The Unified Team, claiming to be the heir of the old Soviet Union, might have been considered the defending champions, but the bronze medal game between Russia and Lithuania, which the Lithuanians won, looked like an intrasquad match of the former champions. As an example of the personal choices available, a Latvian player, Igor Miglinieks, had chosen to play for the Soviet team rather than for the team of the Latvian republic, and as a result he experienced a variety of problems at

At the Barcelona Games (1992), the Lithuanian team that defeated the Unified Team (most of the former Soviet Union) included four players who had played for the Soviet gold medal team in Seoul (1988). Here Lithuanian players are wearing T-shirts designed and donated by the rock group The Grateful Dead.

home, because many of his countrymen objected to his representing Russia. Certainly, the Olympic basketball world was drawing new frontiers.

The major story of the basketball tournament, however, featured the American "Dream Team," made up of professionals from the NBA, which won its games in Barcelona easily to much adulation (table 16.1). The Dream Team aroused controversy as well. Although USOC leaders wanted all American athletes to stay in the Olympic Village, the NBA professionals wanted no part of the place; they would have no peace from the attentions of the press and other athletes. Charles Barkley summed up the feelings of many when, during the team's initial training, he declared, "Can't we play doubleheaders, wrap this up in a week, and get out of Dodge? I want to get home to Alabama." John Stockton added his sentiments: "The Olympic spirit for me is to beat the other athletes of the world, not live with them." Instead the Dream Team stayed in a first class hotel, and the players did not eat in the Olympic commissary or mix with other Olympic athletes. The Dream Team even drew whistles from spectators when it walked out of the opening ceremonies early. When it came time to accept their gold medals, real controversy exploded. Reebok had paid to have the team wear its warm-up suits, but Michael Jordan and Charles Barkley refused.

The "shoe wars" had now grown to the "outfit" wars. In the 1950s, Adidas had dominated the international market after the German soccer team won the World Cup tournament of 1954 while shod in Adidas shoes. Nike began as a small American firm called "Blue Ribbon Sports" in partnership with the Japanese maker Asics, paying coaches to encourage their runners to use the product. The firm soon split from Asics, took the name "Nike," and in the 1980s became a major force in basketball shoes when it recruited Michael Jordan's endorsement and created the Air Jordan line (Strasser and Becklund 1991). By the end of the 1980s, Nike was moving into general athletic wear, but it could not use its trademark in Barcelona because a Spanish firm controlled this name. Nike officials insisted they had nothing to do with Jordan's objections to the Reebok outfits (Katz 1994); Jordan himself may well have simply been protecting his commercial rights to his own name and face. As a compromise, Jordan and Barkley wore Reebok outfits but with the American flag draped over their shoulders to conceal the logo.

The Lithuanians, who won the bronze medal by beating the Russians, had no such problem. When they accepted their awards, they had no

Table 16.1

The United States Basketball Dream Team's Record, 1992

	Country	Score	Country	Score
Preliminary round	US	116	Angola	48
Preliminary round	US	103	Croatia	70
Preliminary round	US	111	Germany	68
Preliminary round	US	127	Brazil	83
Preliminary round	US	122	Spain	81
Quarterfinal	US	115	Puerto Rico	77
Semifinal	US	127	Lithuania	76
Gold Medal game	US	117	Croatia	85

Chuck Daly, *America's Dream Team* (Atlanta: Turner Publishing, 1992).

special sponsor to satisfy. Instead they wore either of two types of T-shirts that had been prepared as fund-raisers. Šarunas Marčiulionis, now a member of the NBA Golden State Warriors, had himself produced one, reading "Property of Lithuania Basketball," and he had arranged with the American rock group The Grateful Dead to produce another, a tie-dyed creation that featured the Lithuanian national colors of yellow, green, and red. A representation of The Grateful Dead shirt eventually found a place in the NBA Hall of Fame.

After the Games, some Americans nurtured feelings of guilt because of the ease with which the Dream Team had swept away its opponents; many focused these feelings on a blow Charles Barkley delivered to the chest of an Angolan player in the Dream Team's first Olympic game. Even though FIBA boss Boris Stanković defended the Americans' participation, *The New York Times* called the Dream Team a "boorish pack of prima donnas." A variant form of these guilt feelings regretted that the Americans, so embarrassed by their loss to the Soviet Union in Seoul and even to Brazil in the Pan-American Games of 1987, had changed the Olympic rules to send in a bunch of bullies to reassert American domination of the sport.

In fact, the American basketball officials had been among the last holdouts in the world against the admission of professionals to Olympic basketball. FIBA, under Stanković's direction, had led the way, first dropping the word "Amateur" from its name and then, even before the Seoul Games, preparing the groundwork for permitting professionals into international basketball competition. ABAUSA, the Amateur Basketball Association of the USA, housed in Colorado Springs, would face a challenge to its Olympic role. Soviet and Yugoslav officials, in contrast, looked forward to having their charges play for big money in the NBA and then represent their countries. In April 1989, FIBA formally agreed, over the negative vote of the Americans, and by fall of 1989 there were two former Soviet Olympians, Marčiulionis and Aleksandr Volkov, playing in the NBA.

The entry of American professionals into the Olympic Games, accordingly, owed little to the Soviet triumph at Seoul. There were at least two factors involved: the desire of FIBA to find profitable dealings with the powerful American professionals and the newly burgeoning international popularity of the NBA, which sought players and markets throughout the world. Although the first American Dream Teams dominated whatever international competition they met, FIBA looked forward to the day when another country would defeat the American representatives, as the Soviets had done in the world championships in the 1960s and then at the Olympics in 1972 and 1988. In the meantime, as Rudy Martzke of *USA Today* put it, the Dream Team "produced a historic marketing triumph:

one sports body surfing atop another sports group's TV time." The Dream Team spearheaded the NBA's invasion of the Olympic Games.

Samaranch welcomed the NBA as a part of his efforts to "open" the Games to the very best athletes, whether "professional" or "amateur." FIFA continued to resist his efforts to make Olympic soccer competition the equal of the soccer World Cup, but he eventually succeeded in winning the North American National Hockey League's cooperation in bringing professionals to the Winter Games of 1998 in Nagano. He has not been so successful in winning the cooperation of Major League Baseball to date.

In its telecasting from Barcelona, NBC won kudos for its camera work as well as for Bob Costas's efforts as the anchor on over half the network's 161 hours of broadcasting. The network professed itself pleased by its Nielsen ratings, which averaged 16.1 in prime time during the second week, 11 percent above the promise to advertisers, and it claimed to have had more viewers than for the Seoul Games in 1988. (After the Albertville Games, CBS had reported it had broken even.) Nevertheless, NBC recognized its appeal to women viewers had slumped in the second week of broadcasting. "The Olympics ought to add more female-appeal sports," declared NBC Sports President Dick Ebersol (Margulies 1992); a columnist in *USA Today* (Martzke 1992) specifically called for more synchronized swimming and diving in the second week of telecasting. NBC, to be sure, lost about $100 million, mainly attributed to its venture in pay-per-view broadcasting, "triple-casting," in selected sports such as basketball, but NBC nevertheless met all its guarantees to sponsors. NBC wanted to maintain its position in the Games.

The closing of the Barcelona Games saw the posthumous, last hurrah of the Soviet sport system, which for 40 years had played an important role in the Olympic Games. In Barcelona (see table 16.2), the Unified Team won more medals than the United States did, 112-108, and more golds, 45-37. The reunited Germans finished third in the unofficial standings with 82 medals, 33 of them gold, but this amounted to fewer medals than the East Germans alone had won in Seoul. Some years earlier, a specialist on East European sport wrote, "Communist nations have displaced capitalist nations as sports leaders in the Olympic Games and several other world championships" (Riordan 1986). He went on to predict, "The future of world sport, particularly the Olympic movement, may well depend on whether the Western nations, whose sports systems are mostly fragmented and relatively autonomous of government control, whose profit-making commercial sport takes precedence over 'amateur' events, will be reconciled to their increasingly weakening position in world, especially Olympic, sport." Now a *Sports Illustrated* writer, Sally Jenkins (1992), countered, "The heavily subsidized sports machines of the old authoritarian regimes have largely vanished." There were, however, other signs for

Table 16.2

Russian and East European Medal Totals, 1988-1996

	Seoul (G-S-B=Total)	Barcelona (G-S-B=Total)	Atlanta (G-S-B=Total)
GDR	37-35-30 = 102		
Germany	11-14-15 = 40	33-21-28 = 82	20-18-27 = 65
Soviet Union	55-31-46 = 132		
Unified Team		45-38-29 = 112	
Russia	–	–	26-21-16 = 63
Ukraine	–	–	9-2-12 = 23
Belarus	–	–	1-6-8 = 15
Kazakhstan	–	–	3-4-4- = 11
Armenia	–	–	1-1-0 = 2
Uzbekistan	–	–	0-1-1 = 2
Moldova	–	–	0-1-1 = 2
Georgia	–	–	0-0-2 = 2
Estonia	–	–	–
Latvia	–	0-2-1 = 3	0-1-0 = 1
Lithuania	–	1-0-1 = 2	0-0-1 = 1

Note: G = gold, S = silver, B = bronze.

the future: The Chinese finished fourth in medal count in Barcelona with 16 gold, 22 silver, and 16 bronze.

For the Olympic leadership, immediate problems focused on controlling growth while improving the product offered to the public. With the breakup of the Soviet Union, Samaranch noted, in 1996 the number of participating teams could approach 200. The IOC, he warned, must struggle to keep the number of participants at about 10,000 while maintaining the elite quality of the athletic performances. "The Games are the most important competitions in the world," he declared, "but we do not want athletes coming here to vacation on the beaches of Barcelona." Samaranch's imagery raised a number of interesting questions. What would be the meaning of the criticism of the athlete as "tourist"? Coubertin had at least paid lip service to the idea that participation was more important than winning. Did athletes have any legal right to demand a place in the Games regardless of quotas? Did the IOC mean to discard the image of a "grand party" such as Peter Ueberroth had used in Los Angeles no matter the consequences? Together with the rest of the world, the Olympic Games were indeed entering a new post–Cold War world for better or worse.

Chapter **17**

The Capitalist Centennial Games

Juan Antonio Samaranch, shown here at left with Muhammad Ali at the Atlanta Games (1996), has presided over the IOC since 1980. He will probably retire after the Sydney Games (2000).

When the Olympic Games closed in Barcelona, the attention of the Olympic summer universe turned to the Centennial Olympic Games, to be held in Atlanta, Georgia. But before that the IOC had to preside over the first Winter Games celebrated according to the new schedule. The choice of Lillehammer, Norway, a community of 22,000 inhabitants, as the host of the XVIIth Winter Games in 1994 had been something of a surprise. Some observers, including Lord Killanin, had predicted that after their experience in Lake Placid the Games would probably never return to a small town. Marc Hodler, the head of the International Ski Federation and the Association of Winter Sports Federations, however, declared that choosing a site for the Winter Games had its own rationale: "The Winter Games are a forced marriage between ice and snow sports," and a "compromise had to be found as to distances to the host sites for snow events." Lillehammer had what the IOC then wanted.

Apart from scandal and controversy arising from the American camp, the Lillehammer Games passed in exemplary fashion. Sweden defeated Russia for the ice hockey championship, and no one objected to the proliferation of Norwegian flags around the sport venues. Some thought the theft of Edvard Munch's painting "The Scream" from a local museum constituted some sort of political statement, but at the Games themselves the major storm came from the American figure skating community, namely the fallout from an attacker's attempt to cripple the American skater Nancy Kerrigan while she was still in the United States training for the Games. Lillehammer organizers won kudos for their concerns for protecting the environment through all the preparations and construction necessary for the Games. They subsequently met unexpected problems in the form of deficits in keeping Olympic venues in operation after the Games, but the Lillehammer experience became a touchstone for judging future Winter Games.

In contrast, the Atlanta Games promised more controversy. These were the brainchild of an Atlanta real estate attorney, Billy Payne, who had decided in 1987 that his city could host the Olympic festival of 1996. (He later admitted that at the time he did not know when the next Olympic Games would be held or how one should apply to host them.) With the support of Atlanta's mayor, Andrew Young, who had been United States Ambassador to the United Nations in the Carter years, Payne's Atlanta Organizing Committee (AOC) drew up its program. In April 1988, the Executive Board of the USOC selected Atlanta as its candidate to host the 1996 Games. The IOC then had to decide between Atlanta, Athens, Belgrade, Manchester, Melbourne, and Toronto (table 17.1). In all, 71 of the IOC's 91 members visited Atlanta and enjoyed local hospitality; Samaranch reportedly characterized his hotel as one of the best he had ever stayed in. Like Los Angeles, Atlanta proposed to finance the Games

Table 17.1

Voting for the Site of the 1996 Games
Tokyo, Japan, September 18, 1990

86 ballots cast in each round:

Athens	22	23	26	30	35
Atlanta	19	20	26	34	51
Belgrade	7				
Manchester	11	5			
Melbourne	12	21	16		
Toronto	14	17	18	22	

through private funding, attracting money from broadcast rights, corporate sponsorships, ticket sales, and merchandising.

Some journalists, such as William O. Johnson of *Sports Illustrated*, noted that two of Georgia's most illustrious citizens were not a part of Payne's campaign—TBS owner Ted Turner and former United States President Jimmy Carter. The IOC would presumably not have reacted favorably to a bid supported by either Carter, who had ordered the United States' boycott of the Moscow Games, or Turner, who had initiated the Goodwill Games. To be sure, when the IOC met in Tokyo in September 1990 to vote on where to place the 1996 Games, the Second Goodwill Games had already shown that this effort no longer constituted a challenge to Olympic competition, but, even so, the Atlantans did not want to remind anyone of past controversies.

The IOC's decision to choose Atlanta, a city of 425,000 inhabitants and a metropolitan population of 3,000,000, shocked many observers. Just two days earlier *The New York Times* had declared there was no clear favorite. Atlanta had spent nearly $7 million in its campaign, but Athens was the sentimental choice for these "Centennial Games." Athens, however, suffered from an image of political instability and security problems, and many people questioned whether it had an adequate infrastructure to host the Games. Atlanta, however, reportedly profited from its multiracial image; Andrew Young, who recruited African votes for Atlanta, played a key role in the American success. Cynics suggested Coca-Cola, which was centered in Atlanta, and the prospect of American television revenues—Atlanta is a part of the United States East Coast time zone—also contributed heavily to the IOC's considerations.

Greek officials raged at the decision. They had counted heavily on Athens' glory as the host of the first modern Games; they had also invested an estimated $25 million in making their bid. Melina Mercouri, a member of the Greek delegation at the IOC's Tokyo meeting, protested, "Coca-Cola won over the Parthenon temple." Andreas Papandreou, head of the Greek socialist party, complained, "I express my deep regret that the international community did not respect history and the spirit of the Olympic Games and, yet again, committed an injustice against Greece." Greek Deputy Prime Minister Athanasios Kanellopoulos declared the Olympics could now recover their original principles only by establishing a permanent home in Greece.

Nor did the Greek resentments die quickly. When Ailene Voisin, a reporter for the *Atlanta Journal-Constitution*, visited Athens in 1995, she found the Greeks still complaining. Greece's Deputy Minister of Sport, George Lianis, said to her, "I wonder what we missed and [why Greece] did not [host] the Olympic Games even once in the 20th century, while we were holding them for 13 whole centuries." The Atlantans, reorganized as the Atlanta Committee for the Olympic Games (ACOG), hailed the Games as Atlanta's opening to world business and tourism, an economic boon for the State of Georgia. (As a stimulus to Atlanta's visibility, the Games were part of a series of events including the Democratic National Convention of 1992 and the 1994 Super Bowl.) ACOG estimated that between 1991 and 1997 the economy of Georgia would receive an infusion of $5.1 billion as a result of the Games; moreover, the Games would produce a surplus of $156 million from a budget of $1.58 billion. The Games would leave numerous important constructions behind for future generations (table 17.2), including a dormitory and a new aquatic center for Georgia Tech University, a track for Clark Atlanta University, a baseball park for the Atlanta Braves (owned by Ted Turner), and the rebuilt house where Margaret Mitchell, the author of *Gone With the Wind*, was born. In all, these, Payne promised, would be the biggest and best Olympics ever, and he predicted that "southern hospitality" and "our friendliness" would "steal the show."

ACOG quickly lined up its set of sponsors. "Centennial Olympic Games Partners" included locally headquartered firms (The Home Depot and Delta Air Lines), food and drink concerns (McDonald's and Budweiser), and financial and business interests (NationsBank, Champion Products, IBM, Swatch, AT&T, and Motorola). "Sponsors of the Atlanta Games" included security systems, health insurance, and paper and soap providers, as well as an official television game show. The IOC would not sign up automobile manufacturers as TOP sponsors, but ACOG listed three motor vehicle manufacturers as sponsors: BMW provided motorcycles, Nissan provided the "official import utility vehicle," and General Motors was Official Sponsor Domestic Car and Truck.

Table 17.2

Atlanta Construction Projects

Sport/Venue	Estimated Cost ($ in millions)	Comments
Olympic Stadium	160-170	To be converted to a 45,000-48,000 seat baseball park and given to the city of Atlanta for use of the Atlanta Braves baseball team
Aquatic	17.5	To be given to Georgia Tech
Archery, cycling	5-6	Temporary facilities, to be removed
Basketball	7-8	To be given to Morehouse College
Equestrian	18-20	To be given to the Horse Park
Hockey	25-30	To be given to Morris Brown College and Clark Atlanta University
Rowing	10-12	To be given to the city of Gainesville and Hall County
Shooting	12-14	To be given to Fulton County
Tennis	12-15	To be given to Stone Mountain Park

ACOG Press Guide, June 1995, pp. 37-38.

NBC paid $456 million for the television rights, and in July 1995, a year before the opening of the Games, the network reported it had almost sold out advertising time for its planned 165 hours of Olympic telecasts, promising revenue of more than $615 million. The Georgia lottery began a two-dollar Olympic Gold scratch-off game. ACOG at the time claimed to have raised 76 percent of forecasted revenue, having signed more than 34 sponsors and 97 licensees. In October 1995, in his last financial forecast before the Games, Payne reported that although sponsorships had produced less money than planned, ticket sales were bringing in significantly more: "We currently have in hand or under firm contract 86 percent of the money we need." The budget included a reduced contingency fund of $30 million, which Payne insisted was adequate.

Trouble arose in September 1995 when the city of Atlanta announced its own plan to collect money from the Games. A marketing firm had offered a plan to raise $2.3 million by leasing public property to companies for retail carts and kiosks for use during the Games. Some of the Games' big sponsors complained about this "ambush marketing" by rivals, and the IOC, in the person of its liaison with ACOG, Richard Pound, immediately protested: "We do not think it is right for the host city of an Olympic Games, which is not assuming any financial risk, to be out raising money in competition with the Olympic organizing committee." Amid rumors Pound would order Payne to sue the city over the issue, Payne assured IOC officials he would resolve the matter. The multitude of street vendors in Atlanta would in fact evoke the IOC's strongest criticism of the Atlanta Games.

The efforts of the Atlanta municipal officials put the confusing economic realities of the Games into sharp relief. The IOC, the USOC, and the ACOG all sought commercial support and funds, but in protecting their investors they imposed far-reaching restrictions on others. For example, the agent of Dan O'Brien, an American decathlonist, protested bitterly when the USOC blocked Fuji Film, not an Olympic sponsor, from using his client's picture for advertising in Atlanta during the Games—because Kodak had paid a large sum to be the exclusive film supplier to the Games. During the Atlanta Games an Associated Press release suggested, "It has become easier for reporters searching for athletes' comments at the Games to track them down at private promotions arranged by agents than at team-sponsored functions." Shaquille O'Neal told reporters in Atlanta he would answer questions about his new megacontract with the Los Angeles Lakers in the "Reebok tent." No matter how one might argue the pros and cons of the case, businesses large and small wanted to improve their balance sheets by exploiting the Games, but Olympic officials, to assure the greatest possible return for themselves, wanted to bless only a few of them.

Long before the start of the Games, critics predicted economic problems (Can the Games realize their income projections?), worried about the weather (Won't it be hot and muggy?), and questioned the arrangements (Can Atlanta handle the traffic?). When it became known in the fall of 1995 that Payne was drawing a salary of $669,112, *The Atlanta Journal-Constitution* quickly pointed out this made him the most highly paid nonprofit executive in the nation. Critics of "capitalist Olympics" renewed their positions of 1984, bemoaning "unprecedented corporate involvement." Even the symbol of the Games, a computer graphic originally called "Whatzit" and then renamed "Izzy," came under attack; a writer for *The New York Times* said it resembled a "soap bubble with a thyroid condition." Atlantans had to face skyrocketing rent costs as demands for Olympic housing rose. Richard Pound, however, echoing the IOC's reaction to the financial problems of Montreal, objected to spending money to build competition venues, saying this should be the task of governments: "Revenues should pay for the party, not the banquet hall."

On a visit to Atlanta in September 1995, Samaranch seemed to approve ACOG's program. At the end of the month, however, the IOC ruled that beginning in 2004, host cities would receive only 49 percent of money generated from the sale of television rights instead of the 60 percent they were presently getting. The rest would be divided between the IOC, the IFs, and foreign NOCs. This would presumably limit an Organizing Committee's possibilities for financing new construction from their own budgets.

Meanwhile, Atlanta organizers continually had to deal with new problems. The death of a construction worker in February 1995 cast a serious pall over the excitement of the preparations, and United States President Bill Clinton made a special trip to Atlanta to offer encouraging words to ACOG. The bombing of a federal building in Oklahoma City in April 1995 sent waves of apprehension through ACOG security officials and law enforcement agencies. In May 1995, Barrow County officials in northeastern Georgia added a new twist by refusing to host Somalian athletes who had hoped to train there; the officials wanted to register their feelings about atrocities suffered by American peacekeepers in Somalia.

Nor was there any shortage of international problems. Reporters seeking controversy inquired of the United States State Department as to whether the government, in light of recent disputes with Cuba, was considering banning the Cubans from the Games; a State Department spokesman denied any such thought. Israeli officials complained that the presence of a Palestinian Arab delegation would compromise the Middle East peace process. A more difficult question arose when American horse breeders objected to permitting foreign horses infected by the equine piroplasmosis virus to compete in the Games. (Melbourne had refused to admit foreign horses in 1956.) The United States Department of Agriculture nevertheless approved a waiver allowing the horses into the country under strict quarantine.

Not the least of Atlanta's problems revolved around local crime. Some journalists called Atlanta the "murder capital of the United States"; certainly, in 1994 its violent crime rate was about four times the national average. A private survey in January 1996 called Atlanta the most dangerous United States city in terms of violent crimes. In March 1996, Georgia Attorney General Mike Bowers, a Republican, declared, "I'm willing to bet it's safer to walk the streets of Sarajevo than walk the streets of my hometown." Atlanta mayor Bill Campbell, a Democrat, called Bowers's comments "reckless, irresponsible and inaccurate." Olympic officials insisted visitors would have nothing to fear.

Some social activists in Atlanta did not accept the arguments that the Games would help the local economy. For example, local groups complained the building projects would hurt the people who most needed help. In the words of Anita Beaty, cochair of the Olympic Conscience Coalition, "The Olympics have become a commercial circus, using athletes and athletic events to make incredible profits at a cost of great human suffering." The critics pointed to social costs of the planned urban transformation and focused on the immediate disruption that would result from construction projects. The projects, they complained, were displacing poor and homeless residents of the city; the "gentrification" of neighborhoods would mean a net loss of housing for poor people; and security measures could infringe on the civil rights of the poor (*Spoilsport's Guidebook to Atlanta* 1996). City officials rejected these arguments, insisting that overall the city would realize significant benefits from hosting the Games.

Activists did not limit themselves to merely targeting the ACOG. In February 1995, the IOC refused to respond to a demand from Atlanta Plus, a coalition of women's groups, that the IOC follow the example of its past South African policy and ban Iran and other Moslem countries that "discriminate against female athletes." As Anita DeFrantz, an American woman on the IOC's Executive Board, explained this decision, since the protest was directed against a specific religion, "it doesn't seem to be in the interest of enhancing women's opportunity in sports." (Iran actually sent its first woman competitor to the Atlanta Games, Lida Fariman, in target shooting.) In September 1995, however, the IOC's Executive Board called on the world's NOCs to increase the proportion of women in their decision-making structures.

In an effort to avoid legal struggles with athletes, especially in American courts, the IOC obliged Olympic contenders to waive their own legal rights and submit to "final and binding" arbitration by a special Olympic court—the Court of Arbitration for Sport. Mindful of the Butch Reynolds case as well as of a former East German sprinter, Katrin Krabbe, the IOC, with the endorsement of the IAAF, wanted to avoid being drawn into controversies in various national courts. Some individuals, mindful of past controversies about drug enforcement, objected to the new demand, but the IOC's initiative prevailed on this point.

As journalists and athletes gathered in Atlanta for the opening of the Games on July 19, it became fashionable to emphasize the disorder and confusion one could find, even to express hopes for disasters. Bob Duff, a Canadian journalist, declared that ACOG stood for "Atlanta Can't Organize the Games," and he reported that in the American Civil War, "the Yankees lit a torch and burnt Atlanta to the ground. Another torch will be lit here Friday and some seem to be quietly hoping that history will repeat

Contrasting Views of Olympic Urban Renewal in Atlanta: Centennial Olympic Park

The Centennial Olympic Park will be a lasting legacy of the 1996 Centennial Olympic Games for the citizens of Atlanta and Georgia. An inviting gathering place in close proximity to the major activities of the Games, the Park will welcome tens of thousands of residents and visitors during the Games.

Tree-lined with landscaped topography of plazas of native greenery, flowers, paths, soothing water features and resting places, it will serve as a welcome respite for our guests. . . .

Following the Games, the park will serve as the focal point for the economic and housing development of an important but underutilized section of Atlanta. The Park will bring a renewed sense of purpose and commitment to the values espoused by the Olympic Movement.

"Who Benefits," undated press release distributed by ACOG.

But what lies buried in the dirt beneath these finely manicured lawns, these bubbling fountains, these bricks that speak of Olympic pride and corporate sponsorship?

The area was once home to three homeless shelters and service centers that constituted over ten percent of the total shelter beds in the entire city.

It also contained several small, family-run businesses which had close reciprocal relationships with the central business district. These businesses were slowly built up to serve the light industrial, distribution and service needs of the downtown area.

But with lightning speed this area became bulldozed to construct a public space with a hidden price tag. . . .

This part is destined to become a legacy of displacement and erasure. Now that's Southern hospitality!

Spoilsport's Guidebook to Atlanta (Atlanta [1996]).

---

itself" (Duff 1996). Then organizers had trouble with travel arrangements and communications on the first days. As a correspondent of *The New York Times* explained, "To IBM's misfortune, the system that failed was a complex, custom software application upon which thousands of news editors and reporters were relying for the speedy distribution of accurate results to hundreds of news organizations around the world" (Lewis 1996). The journalists were unforgiving. In the words of CNN's Bobbie Battista, "The world has come to Atlanta, and apparently the world has come to complain."

IOC leaders demanded that ACOG correct the problems immediately, while local officials tried to downplay all problems. Privately, ACOG officials groaned that the worst thing possible had happened—the media

Mission of the Court of Arbitration for Sport:

The CAS sets in operation Panels, composed of one or three arbitrators, which have the task of providing for the resolution by arbitration of disputes arising within the field of sport, in conformity with the Procedural Rules. To this end, the CAS attends to the constitution of Panels and the smooth running of the proceedings. It places the necessary infrastructure at the disposal of the parties.

The responsibility of the Panels is, among other things;

- to resolve the disputes that are referred to them through ordinary arbitration,
- to resolve through the appeals arbitration procedure disputes (including doping-related disputes) concerning the decisions of disciplinary tribunals or similar bodies of federations, associations or other sports organizations, insofar as the statutes or regulations of the said sports bodies or a specific agreement so provide,
- to give non-binding advisory opinions at the request of the IOC, the IFs, the NOCs and the associations recognized by the IOC and the Olympic Games Organizing Committees (OCOGs).

In 1996, for the first time in Olympic history, the CAS has established an ad hoc Division in Atlanta, at the site of the Games. Thanks to this arbitration structure, the CAS was able to pronounce final and enforceable decisions within 24 hours of the lodging of the request for arbitration.

The procedure was free. The ad hoc Division was composed of 12 arbitrators; 6 cases were brought to this Division during the Olympic Games of Atlanta.

IOC Web Page on the Internet.

were dissatisfied. The mayor of Atlanta, Bill Campbell, publicly proclaimed, "I tend to dismiss the critics as part of this whining syndrome that has become so pervasive in our country." At the end of the Games, Samaranch himself offered a balanced judgment: "At the beginning we had some problems with arrival of teams and transportation and technology. Bit by bit, things were controlled. In the last week, things were excellent in the organization of the games." This judgment, however, was not what the journalists chose to remember and immortalize.

In the early morning of Saturday, July 27, a bomb explosion in Centennial Park, an unsecured park created to serve ticket holders and casual visitors alike, killed one person and injured over 100 more. A reporter died of a heart attack. The bomb itself did not seem to have a specific target, and its purpose has remained obscure. After brief consideration, IOC leaders decided to go on with the Games. By Sunday the Games' festive atmosphere seemed restored, and when Centennial Park reopened, the crowds of revelers returned, albeit with a new respect for security procedures.

As the competition proceeded, American commentators rushed to speak of these as the "women's Games." The American female gymnasts won a team gold, the American women's softball, basketball, and soccer teams all won gold medals, and individual American women athletes showed remarkable competitive spirit regardless of how they finished in the standings. In contrast, United States men's soccer and baseball teams were unsuccessful, and the basketball Dream Team III failed to generate much enthusiasm among both television broadcasters and viewers. The perception of the women's Games, however, was probably distinctively American, and many of the same journalists had used the same imagery for the Los Angeles Games of 1984 (Galford 1996). (They would again revive the image for the Nagano Games of 1998.) Women's competition of itself was not new as other countries had produced women champions in the past, but for the American journalists who now noticed the women's competition, the important thing seemed to be that the American women were winning. The real test of this journalistic revelation would be the media's subsequent coverage of women's sports.

Otherwise, the competition evoked a variety of forms of international controversy. Americans suggested an Irish swimmer, who won three gold medals, had used performance-enhancing drugs; a Cuban player slugged a Russian player in a women's basketball game; and police had to separate a French fencer and his Cuban opponent when they clashed after their match. A British sprinter, Linford Christie, the defending Olympic champion was disqualified for making two false starts, and he refused to leave the track, delaying the competition.

Even before the Games had ended, many journalists, politicians, and Olympic officials had formulated their lasting judgments, repeating the critical choruses about technological breakdown in what Reuter Information Service called "Sardine City." While Atlantans congratulated themselves on having put on a good show, foreign critics, while grudgingly admitting the Atlantans themselves had been friendly, called the Games "poorly organized," focusing on traffic problems, computer glitches, and "overcommercialization." Samaranch himself abstained from his traditional formula of calling the latest Games "the best ever," instead praising the athletic competition and calling the Games "exceptional," leaving it to others to interpret his words.

The critics fired at a broad range of targets. A Hungarian official, Reszo Gallov, declared, "Atlanta, despite its goodwill, organized a very weak Olympic Games." Primo Nebiolo, President of the IAAF, complained, "I was disappointed with Atlanta. Placing one's trust in private hands is wrong." (While in Atlanta, however, IAAF officials signed a five-year contract with Adidas.) The Finnish newspaper *Helsingen Sanomat* criticized beach volleyball as an Olympic sport, but that of course was not a decision of the ACOG. A British journalist, Tony Parsons, complained of the "boorish crowds, bad losers." The German *Der Spiegel* reported that German athletes felt exploited and were complaining about their own administrators.

Some of the sharpest commentary came from Greece—before, during, and after the Games. Angry about the IOC's choice of Atlanta in preference to Athens, the Greeks had at first threatened to boycott these Centennial Games. In April 1996, Athens, with the blessings of the IOC, hosted its own centennial "Golden Games." When Atlanta ran into its problems with transportation and computer breakdowns, Greeks snorted that American know-how was not what the IOC had dreamed it was. Fani Pali-Petralia, a former Minister of Sport, declared that Atlanta "gave the impression of a cheap carnival" and commented, "It takes a lot of effort to organize the Games as badly as Atlanta did."

In their rush to judge, the critics frequently contradicted each other. They spoke of "overcommercialization," for example, in radically different ways. Did the AT&T or Coca-Cola advertising constitute overcommercialization or should this word apply only to the multitude of street vendors? Samaranch and Richard Pound objected to the "bazaar" atmosphere on the streets, where many small vendors plied their wares. Others used the term to refer to the massive presence of TOP sponsors such as Coca-Cola and AT&T in the neighborhood of the Games. For Samaranch and other IOC members, the TOP sponsors were an essential part of the Games, but even so Olympic organizers insisted that General Motors cover the name "Chevrolet" on the trucks that participated in the opening ceremonies. Olympic officials argued the IOC had to control the commercial dimension of the Games; the IOC, as the "owner" of the Games, should draw the income. As Samaranch told the press in Atlanta, "This commercialization must not run the games; the games must be run by the IOC."

For NBC, a major player in Atlanta, the Games were a resounding success. It had concentrated on what NBC Sports President Dick Ebersol called the "key sports of the Summer Olympics—track and field, swimming and diving, and gymnastics." The first seven days of competition gave the network the top seven Nielsen ratings of the week, overpowering all other networks' programming. Its Nielsen rating of 23.4 during that period was the network's highest since 1980. The network's final average of 21.6, with a 41 percent share fell second to Los Angeles's scores of 23.2 and 44, but in all, the Games' Nielsen scores stood some 25 percent above the scores for the Barcelona Games in 1992, meaning the network easily satisfied the guarantees it had given sponsors. Subsequent studies showed the Games had been a television success throughout the world. An IOC report issued in April 1997 declared that 9 out of 10 television viewers around the world had watched part of the Games. "Television continues to be the medium through which the world experiences the Olympics," Samaranch declared.

NBC officials especially welcomed the reports that over half the television viewers were women, including a healthy share of the attention of young women in the range of 18 to 34 years of age. NBC's research had suggested specific approaches in broadcasting to meet these demographic targets, and the results constituted a great success for the Games' "show business" dimension. NBC expected to make a profit of "just under $40 million" on its investment of $456 million for the broadcasting rights, and NBC officials looked optimistically at the prospect of broadcasting future Games. Even before the end of the Games, according to an unidentified NBC executive, a "half-dozen separate multinational advertisers" had indicated interest in discussing "multi-Olympic deals."

Critics of NBC, however, attacked both what NBC had done and what it did not do. They complained strongly about the network's creating a sort of virtual reality, not revealing what was taped and arranged as opposed to what was live. Many felt the network had deceived them when it showed Kerri Strug's vault on a sprained ankle without informing the audience the event was previously taped. The critics also complained about the "soap-opera" quality of human interest stories. Others criticized the network's decision to ignore women's softball or women's basketball. (Men's basketball, which had promised overwhelming victory over all opponents, probably did not seem likely to hold an audience for very long either.) Politicians chimed in with criticisms along these same lines, adding a new dimension to the mixture of politics and sport in America. *The New York Times* declared, "The Olympic Games, for all their entertainment value, are still news, not a made-for-TV movie."

As for the athletes themselves, those who won went home in glory. Greeks greeted their returning Olympians with marching bands and fireworks; Greek gold medalists were each to receive a bonus of $285,000, silver medalists $195,000. American gold medal winners received $15,000 from the USOC. Select American victors could look forward to endorsement contracts, and, for a very few, the honor of seeing their pictures on a box of Wheaties. French gold medal winners each received $68,952 tax free. A Thai gold medal boxer, Somluck Kamsing, received 32 million baht, about $1.7 million. The Lithuanian government pledged 800,000 lits ($200,000) to reward its bronze medal basketball team. Hong Kong's gold medal windsurfer, Lee Lai-shan, received a number of rewards, including a kilo of solid gold. South Korean gold medal winners were promised a monthly stipend of $1,000 for life. In Belgrade an estimated 100,000 people greeted the returning athletes. The OAU praised the general accomplishments of African athletes, singling out the gold medal Nigerian soccer team for special praise. Each soccer player also received a new home and car. Josia Thugwane, the South African black who won the marathon, dedicated his victory to South African President Nelson Mandela; Mandela in turn invited Thugwane and South African gold medal swimmer Penny Heynes to tea.

Olympians who failed to live up to the expectations of their compatriots did not fare so well. The Americans debated intensely as to why the 400-meter men's track relay had won only a silver medal, not a gold. A Greek reporter called a Greek weight lifter who had failed to win a medal a "disgrace." Kenyan officials had to defend their country's failure to live up to expectations, saying, "The fact that many Kenyan athletes win races all over the world has played in many people's minds here that we are superhuman beings, which is not the case." *The Times* of India angrily declared, "The next Olympics should also have brass, tin, wood and plastic [medals] to give our players a chance to bring glory to the nation." In Cairo, *Al-Akhbar* reported, "A lot of people suggest that we merge the sports authority with the sewer authority." Reflecting on the undistinguished performance of British athletes, Dick Palmer, secretary of the British Olympic Association, declared, "I have a message for British sports officials: We need money."

Reviews of the Olympic results offered some the opportunity to deliver strong negative feelings about the United States. The traffic problems and the computer glitches at the Games offered easy targets, but some critics were more creative. The Chinese press complained of unthinkable difficulties and unfair treatment in Atlanta, and it insisted the Americans had conspired to limit the Chinese victories. One newspaper declared the United States "cannot bravely face China, which is becoming stronger and stronger in sports." The Russian newspaper *Moskovskii Komsomolets* declared that the United States had "proved its meanness toward humanity and filled its own pockets at the same time." Linford Christie, the British sprinter disqualified for two false starts, blamed the Americans for his problems: "If it was anywhere else other than the USA, I'm sure I would have been in there." Iran's President, Hashemi Rafsanjani, praised Rasul Khadem, a gold medal wrestler, for having rubbed "America's nose in the dirt" and for having triumphed in the "house of Satan."

With time, the harsh judgments of Atlanta may soften, but on the whole the experience continued the stormy relationship that Americans, through enthusiasm, error, and passion, have shared with the Olympic Games. When it closed its books on June 30, 1997, the ACOG reported it had just broken even with its $1.7 billion budget. After renegotiating some outstanding contracts and holding back about $10 million to cover its responsibilities for lawsuits and cleanups, it did not give Payne or other top officials any bonuses. The city of Atlanta, however, was facing massive lawsuits from street vendors who claimed to have lost money. Even apart from the fact that in the last 16 years, the United States had hosted the Summer Games twice and the Winter Games once, and the fact that the Winter Games of 2002 were scheduled for Salt Lake City, the United States was unlikely to host another Summer Games for quite some time. Although there were no evident storms on the horizon for Salt Lake City yet, it seemed inevitable some would arise.

Chapter **18**

From Atlanta to Nagano

The Nagano Games (1998) introduced women's ice hockey to the Winter Olympics. The US women's team won the gold, but the men's team, made up of NHL professionals, recorded disappointing performances both on and off the ice.

Controversial as it was, the Atlanta experience colored the future of the Olympic Games. Members of the IOC carried away thoughts of what they liked and disliked, and what they disliked seemed to predominate. In June 1997, Richard Pound called Atlanta's efforts a "wasted opportunity." Echoing Killanin's explanation of the financial debacle of Montreal, Pound argued the ACOG had spent $500 million on "infrastructure" that in the long run benefited the city of Atlanta but not the Games. In essence, he agreed with those ACOG sympathizers who called the new constructions in Atlanta the Games' "real profit," but he argued the money would have been better used for actually running the Games. European officials called the Olympic Village cramped and overcrowded, the food bad, transportation a mess and the atmosphere "cheap and tawdry." Looking toward future Olympics, IOC members insisted the errors of Atlanta, especially what Pound called "junk" commercialism, must not be repeated.

Representatives of OCOGs in Nagano, Sydney, and Salt Lake City had to reflect on what they thought they had learned; hopefuls for winning the right to host future Games studied what they should emphasize or avoid. Everyone concerned with the Games also had to consider some basic questions: Was there an optimal number of spectators and athletes? What should the role of television be? How should future Olympics be financed? At the same time, it was also clear that the ending of the Cold War had not eliminated the role of states and national rivalries in the Games.

Journalists and NOC organizers had continued to calculate the achievements of participating states in terms of medal count. The IOC still refrained from endorsing any particular scoring system, and some commentators preferred to simply count gold medals instead of adding silver and bronze medals to the gold. Yet, if the old MacArthur formula were to be used, rating the teams on the basis of medals and population, the champion of the Atlanta Games was Tonga, a nation of some 100,000 people, which celebrated the single silver medal won by its superheavyweight boxer Paea Wolfgram. Perhaps more significant was the fact athletes from 79 different teams won medals, as the collapse of the East European sport superpowers had opened the way for champions from other parts of the world. In any case, medal counts as a measurement of national achievements would continue.

The United States won the most medals in Atlanta—101, including 44 gold—followed by Germany and Russia. The American medal total, including unexpected victories in some areas and disappointments in others, surprised few. The German total, 65, fewer than they had won at Barcelona, suggested the heritage of the East German program might be withering away. The Russians, as the heirs of the Soviet Union, of course now lacked the contributions of the non-Russian sources the Soviet sport program used to tap, but their athletic program was also showing signs of graying and needing financial refurbishment. France's sixth place finish in the medals table, having won 37, 15 of them gold, was by contrast an occasion for rejoicing; French Sports Minister Guy Drut spoke enthusiastically of the "dynamics of success."

Probably the most significant harbinger of future competition lay in the determination shown by the Chinese, who won 50 medals—16 gold, 22 silver, 12 bronze—which put them in fourth place in the medals count, the same place they had held in Barcelona. The Chinese gave every sign of not only becoming more competitive athletically but also more controversial politically. Beijing had bid to host the Olympic Games of the year 2000. The Chinese had hosted the Asian Games of 1990 and had been model citizens at the Barcelona Games, and PRC leaders considered it proper they should be awarded the Olympic Games. When members of the United States Congress challenged the Chinese human rights record, a member of the Chinese bid committee, Zhang Baifa, warned that in retaliation China might boycott the Atlanta Games. When the IOC then voted for Sydney, the Chinese reacted even more strongly than the Soviets had reacted to Moscow's failure in its campaign for the 1976 Games, and they considered the Americans prime culprits in their disappointment.

The possibility of a Chinese boycott hung over Atlanta until the last minute. After objecting to the reception the American government had accorded Taiwanese officials, the Chinese warned of a "strong response" should Taiwanese officials attend the Games as guests. The IOC then asked ACOG "not to do anything that would create problems," and in March 1996 ACOG President Billy Payne promised, "We will make no invitations to any political leaders from anywhere, to avoid political complications."

Controversy concerning some remarkable performances by Chinese athletes, mostly women, added to the uncertainties swirling about Chinese participation in the Atlanta Games. The Chinese spoke of special training methods and special herbal preparations, but westerners harbored suspicions of performance-enhancing drugs and pointed to the presence of former East German trainers in the Chinese Republic. Chinese women won 12 of 16 titles at the swimming world championships in Rome in 1994, but then at the Asian Games in Hiroshima, officials suspended 11 Chinese athletes, including seven swimmers. American swimming officials repeatedly pointed out that FINA officials had suspended 19 Chinese women since 1990, and some argued the Chinese should be banned from the Atlanta Games. The Chinese called western reporting biased, insisting they had rooted out abuses in their programs and now had able new athletes in their camp.

The Chinese did come to Atlanta, but once there their voices joined the chorus of complaints. Wei Jizhong, Secretary General of the Chinese

Olympic Committee, called the accusations of doping "ideological discrimination," prejudice "because China is a Communist country." Their athletes complained about their accommodations in the Olympic Village and declared "there is no comforting food for them to eat." (Some western news agencies compared this to American criticisms of the accommodations for a United Nations women's conference in Beijing in 1995.) The Chinese gymnastics coach, Lu Shanzhen, even complained that the gymnastics hall was too large: "The space is too big, my girls have not quite gotten used to it yet. . . . Even in final championship competitions, we are used to performing to crowds a third this size."

In the actual competition, the Chinese did well, although Americans barely noticed the Chinese women were their rivals in both the women's softball and the women's soccer finals. The Chinese gained a particularly sweet victory in women's singles table tennis when Deng Yaping defeated Taiwan's representative Chen Jing. Chen had won the gold medal in 1988 for China and had later defected to Taiwan, where she was now the Chinese Nationalists' best hope for their first gold medal. Taiwanese fans in the stands attempted to wave their own national flag during the competition, but security officials intervened and stopped them, because the IOC had banned the Nationalist flag at the Olympics. The table tennis match was suspended for five minutes while police handcuffed one particularly unruly fan and removed him bodily.

The Chinese women swimmers, however, performed surprisingly poorly, thereby adding to the suspicions of drug use. "They swam dirty at their trials," said one American official, suggesting that they were now swimming "clean." Canadian coach Dave Johnson added the thought, "There's not a lot of people around here feeling too sorry for them."

The Chinese reacted angrily to the negative comments. The Beijing press repeated the athletes' objections to the housing and the lack of Chinese food; commenting on the bombing in Centennial Park, the English-language *China Daily* declared, "The United States should make a thorough self-criticism over their entire organization work for the games. It is a pity that one of the world's most advanced nations cannot take preventive measures against terror under its nose." Chinese commentators also suggested transportation problems and false alarms in the Olympic Village smacked of conspiracy.

When the Games ended, the Chinese expressed triumph together with strong hostility toward the United States. Chinese commentators accused Americans of prejudicing the judging in men's gymnastics, of winning the women's softball championship as the result of an umpire's calling a foul ball a home run, and in general of creating a hostile atmosphere. Sports Minister Wu Shaozu complained of "some unfriendly US media and troubles with living conditions, security and referees." The Beijing *Youth*

Daily declared, "Now everyone who came to Atlanta is asking the question: Why choose this damn city to host the centennial Games?" The experiences in Atlanta, wrote another commentator, "have made more and more people dislike the United States, dislike Americans."

Wu Shaozu's complaints about the media had a follow-up in a campaign accusing NBC and its Olympics host Bob Costas of "ignominious prejudice" and "hostile comments" about China. In broadcasting the opening ceremonies, Costas had spoken of "problems with human rights" and other international disputes in which the Chinese were involved, and he had also referred to the controversies over performance-enhancing drugs. An ad in *The Washington Post* of August 14, signed by representatives of 78 Chinese student associations around the world, demanded an apology from both NBC and Costas. On August 16, Wei Jizhong, in a "talk to the whole world," declared, "As a socialist power, China has stood up like a giant—brave, industrious and fearless of attacks and slanders. Anyone who tries to stop its thriving cause of sport will end up—to use a Chinese proverb—'like a mantis trying to obstruct a running chariot'." The *China Daily* added its own criticism of Atlanta organizers and of the "brazenly partisan" American media.

NBC apologized. On August 22, Ed Markey, NBC Vice President for Sports, stated Bob Costas "did not intend any disrespect to the People's

---

Newspaper advertisement regarding Bob Costas' comments, August 14, 1996:

Congratulations* to TEAM CHINA!
16 Gold, 22 Silvers & 12 Bronzes

*NBC commentator Mr. Bob Costas' hostile comments against many international athletes, including Team China, had badly contaminated the spirit of the Olympics and deeply offended countless viewers worldwide. Mr. Costas and NBC should have the courage to publicly apologize for their ignominious prejudice and inhospitality. . . .

UC Berkeley Chinese Students and Scholars Association (BCSSA); UCSF CSSA; Chinese American Assoc. of Commerce; New China Education Foundation; Wu Yi Friendship Assoc.; Chinese Journal Corp., Inc.; Silicon Valley Chinese Engineers Association (SCEA); Stanford Univ. CSSA; UC Davis Chinese Students and Scholars Fellowship; Federation of Chinese Students and Scholars of Canada (FCSSC); Cornell Univ. CSSA; The Univ. of Chicago CSSA; Oxford Univ. CSSA; Network; Univ. of S. Florida CSSA; Univ. of Oregon CSSA; Nan-Hai Art Center and 55 other organizations representing approximately 70,000 members worldwide; MENG Jiulonh, GAO Yang, WANG Tieli, WANG Taiping, ZHANG Shengwei, WU Yue plus an additional 2,800 concerned individuals.

The Washington Post, August 14, 1996.

Republic of China or its citizens." Markey declared Costas's comments "were not based on NBC beliefs." Costas himself issued no public statement, although he told nighttime television host Jay Leno he had no intention of apologizing. The General Electric Corporation, which owned NBC and had significant investments in China, denied having put any pressure on the network to make a statement.

Chinese spokespersons expressed dissatisfaction with NBC's response. An official of the Chinese Foreign Ministry called on NBC to "draw lessons and make sure that there will be no recurrence," and others argued that Costas should "apologize on air during prime evening hours and in writing." In September, *The New York Times* carried another ad (costing $21,000), demanding that Costas apologize. In a separate letter to Markey, Lee Zheng, a member of the protesting group, called on NBC to "take disciplinary action against Mr. Costas." The issue soon faded from the public press, but NBC will surely remember this experience as its officials plan future Olympic broadcasts.

The Chinese protests fell into the pattern of past efforts of the world's newly emerging forces to control discussions of their domestic affairs in the foreign media. In this case, the Chinese exploited traditional sentiments for "keeping politics out of the Games," perhaps mixed in with international economic interests, and they transformed Costas's comments into racial slurs. *The New York Times* gave them a sympathetic hearing, arguing the "vigilance of some ethnically sensitive groups should not necessarily be ignored. Often they provide much-needed understanding of cultures unfamiliar to other groups. Better to learn this way than from racial inanities from Al Campanis or Jimmy 'the Greek' Snyder" (Sandomir 1996). In framing their complaints about negative foreign reporting as "racial inanities," the Chinese may well have developed a journalistic weapon Soviet propagandists had never conceived of.

The Chinese rhetoric made clear the ideological conflicts that had been a part of the Cold War had not disappeared. Beijing's image of Atlanta had much in common with Hashemi Rafsanjani's denunciation of the "house of Satan." The Russians too revived Cold War rhetoric: The newspaper *Izvestiia* insisted the Americans had twisted the medal count, weighing a bronze medal as equal to a gold, "in a way more advantageous to the hosts," and Vitaly Smirnov, an IOC member and head of the Russian Olympic Committee, accused the Americans of introducing sports such as beach volleyball simply to fatten their score. The reference to counting only gold medals recalled Doug Gilbert's (1980) lamentation after the Montreal Games, but *Izvestiia* had offered no such argument, say, after the Sarajevo Games when the East Germans had won more gold medals than the Soviets had. Smirnov's complaint about new sports resembled the American cries in Helsinki about "Kitty League" sports, and Brazilians, who won a gold and silver in beach volleyball, should perhaps have felt aggrieved by the Russian's comments.

A major theme of IOC officials after the Atlanta Games concerned lessons on "how not to put on an Olympics." It was not satisfactory that spectators, despite the bombing, spoke of having enjoyed themselves: The Atlanta Games had not been "grand" enough, and IOC officials were not sure they wanted so many spectators. "On its 100th birthday, the modern Olympics fell victim to gluttony and its own success," declared an Associated Press news release, adding, "The games can go two ways—expand and self-destruct, or contract and survive." Calling the Atlanta ambiance a "commercial carnival," IOC leaders, admitting the Games needed a great deal of money, declared that in the future they would demand a government guarantee in addition to any private funding, so as to eliminate "excessive" commercial sponsorship. They also demanded the host city and the Organizing Committee make clear their mutual responsibilities in advance. The IOC, moreover, would retain veto power over sponsors' marketing plans.

The IOC assured its own financial future by selling television rights to future Games even before it had chosen the sites. It estimated its income over the XXVth Olympiad, 1992 to 1996, at $3 billion, and in December 1996 Samaranch and Richard Pound sold the American rights to the Summer Games of 2004 and 2008 and the Winter Games of 2006, all not yet awarded, to NBC for $2.3 billion. "The three contracts guarantee financial stability for many members of the Olympic Movement, namely National Olympic Committees, International Federations, Organizing Committees, and the IOC for the years to come," the IOC declared in announcing the agreement. The European Broadcasting Union then committed $1.442 billion for the rights over the same period; a Japanese television pool agreed to pay $545 million. The IOC now had a relatively free hand in choosing the sites for future Olympic Games.

The financial problems facing Organizing Committees surfaced sooner than Olympic officials and members anticipated. Sounds of distress coming from Nagano, the site for the 1998 Winter Games, indicated there was a revenue shortfall and the hosts would not be able to live up to the promises given in 1991 when the IOC had accepted the region's bid. Nagano had originally promised to cover all transportation and housing costs of participating delegations, but in the winter of 1995-1996, the Organizing Committee announced that in the face of rising costs, it would have to withdraw that offer. To cover the financial shortfall, the IOC declared it might have to expand its TOP IV program, adding additional sponsors. Then a general financial crisis swept through Asia in the winter of 1997-1998. Nevertheless, after the Games had concluded, Nagano officials assured all parties the Games had broken even.

In the last preparations for the Nagano Games, other worries abounded. Japanese officials ignored complaints the proposed downhill ski run was too short and had long refused to extend the run up into an environmentally protected area. Ice hockey officials complained the seating capacity of their arena was too small, and organizers admitted they had not secured as many "western-style" hotel rooms as they had anticipated. IOC visitors also expressed concern about the access roads to the region. Journalists predicted trouble.

Despite all this, the Japanese presented a successful and joyful Games. The IOC took pride in the fact the athletes represented a record (for the Winter Games) 54 National Olympic Committees, and at 827 there were more women competing than ever before (table 18.1). The IOC welcomed the way in which Nagano organizers, in contrast to Atlanta, observed the IOC's contracts with sponsors. The city abounded in evidence of the presence of major sponsors such as Coca-Cola, McDonald's, and AT&T, and local businesses reportedly refused to accept American Express cards for the duration of the Games, honoring Visa's place as the official credit card of the Games. Although snow, fog, rain, and even an earthquake interfered with the staging of outdoor competition, the Games produced a number of startling results. Hermann Meier, a German, recovered from a frightening crash on the slopes to win two gold medals in skiing; Japan, the host country, won more gold medals (five) than it had in its participation in all previous Winter Games together; and the American women's hockey team won the gold in the first appearance of this sport in the Games.

On the negative side, the IOC had to face past, current, and future problems related to the use not only of performance-enhancing drugs but also of so-called "social," or "recreational," drugs. Testing revealed that a snowboarding champion had traces of marijuana in his system. The IOC first demanded the return of his medal and then gave it back after the Court for Arbitration in Sport had ruled there was no clear agreement between the IOC and the skiing federation banning marijuana use by athletes. When reports came from Canada that the traces of marijuana were considerably more substantial than first indicated, the head of the IOC Medical Commission dismissed them, declaring the case was closed. Olympic officials then ignored several more reports on marijuana use by athletes, but Samaranch insisted the IOC should ban proscribed "social drugs" whether or not they were considered to be performance-enhancing.

The flap over the use of marijuana highlighted two major problems in the IOC's drug policies: the purposes of testing and the relations of the Olympic athletes with local law authorities. Some administrators and athletes insisted since marijuana was a "social" drug, not a performance-enhancing one, the IOC had no business ruling on its use. Samaranch,

Table 18.1

Women's Participation in the Winter and Summer Games Since 1972

Summer Games	Sports	Events	NOCs	Number of Women
1972 Munich	8	43	65	1,058
1976 Montreal	11	49	66	1,247
1980 Moscow	12	50	54	1,125
1984 Los Angeles	14	62	94	1,567
1988 Seoul	17	86	117	2,186
1992 Barcelona	19	98	136	2,708
1996 Atlanta	21	108	169	3,626
Winter Games				
1972 Sapporo	3	13	27	206
1976 Innsbruck	3	14	50	231
1980 Lake Placid	3	14	31	233
1984 Sarajevo	3	15	35	274
1988 Calgary	3	18	39	313
1992 Albertville	4	25	44	488
1994 Lillehammer	4	27	44	523
1998 Nagano	6	31	54	827

IOC Web Page on the Internet.

however, insisted the IOC should ban any drugs that were considered illegal, whatever their effect on athletic performance. Conflicts with the laws of the host country, to be sure, were not new. In 1912, there had been no boxing at the Stockholm Games because the sport was not permitted in Sweden. In 1956, the equestrian competition had to be held in Stockholm because of the strict quarantine Australian officials would have demanded for foreign horses. As the IOC became more powerful, however, it could override local laws: In 1996, United States officials made concessions in their equine regulations so foreign horses could come to Atlanta. Certainly, clothed in the Games' grandeur, IOC members sometimes seemed to feel their status put them above the law.

Japanese laws posed a number of problems for the organizers of the Games. An Austrian skier who had admitted having used cocaine in the past could enter the country only after intense diplomatic negotiations had paved his way. Biathlonists complained because Japan's gun laws deprived them of the constant companionship of their rifles and required detailed accounting of the use of the bullets. When Japanese police investigated the use of marijuana by the athletes, many foreigners, both journalists and sport officials, did not seem to believe the Japanese police should concern themselves with what the athletes smoked in their spare time, but Japanese authorities objected to the cavalier attitude their Olympic guests showed toward their laws. More problems of this sort will undoubtedly arise in the future.

The participation of NHL players in the hockey tournament produced a new level of play in Nagano, as the Czech team defeated the Russians for the gold medal, but there were also complications. Olympic officials suspended a member of the Swedish team, Ulf Samuelsson, because he had given up his citizenship for an American passport, but the CAS rejected a Czech demand that Sweden be forced to forfeit the games it had won. The United States hockey team performed poorly and then caused considerable scandal by trashing a room in the Olympic Village right before their departure for home.

As ever, from the viewpoints of participants and national team administrators, the picture of the Games could be quite different. In the matter of judging, for example, Aleksandr Lukashenko, the authoritarian President of Belarus and the Chairman of the Belarussian Olympic Committee, saw conspiracy, charging that Olympic organizers took part in a "Mafia collusion" aimed at undermining the athletes from his state and also from other Soviet successor states. American commentators claimed to see signs of collusion between the skating judges from "East European states," but international skating officials and the IOC only spoke of the need to review the standards of judging. Arguments over the quality of judging remain a continuing topic for journalists and sport administrators.

The Germans came away from the Games with the most medals: 12 gold, 9 silver, and 8 bronze (table 18.2). More than half the team were products of the East German sport system, but German officials and their fans were delighted. "It was great," the *Berliner Zeitung* quoted the German Olympic Committee President Walther Träger as saying. "I return to Germany very satisfied. With this team we needn't be afraid of the future either." German fans enthusiastically welcomed the victors, but the Committee had a steep bill to pay: 20,000 DM (about $11,000) for each gold medal, 15,000 for silver, and 10,000 for bronze. Including rewards for all who finished in the top eight of their event, the total was expected to run to 1,000,000 DM, or about $550,000.

Table 18.2

Medal Results in Nagano

	Gold	Silver	Bronze	Total
Germany	12	9	8	29
Norway	10	10	5	25
Russia	9	6	3	18
Austria	3	5	9	17
Canada	6	5	4	15
USA	6	3	4	13

In all, the XVIIIth Winter Olympics vividly illustrated the evolution of the Olympic Games. Japan had last hosted the Winter Games in 1972, Avery Brundage's last year in power. Now, a quarter of a century later, Karl Schranz's clash with the IOC President seemed almost ludicrous in light of the arrival of the professional gladiators from the National Hockey League and the enormous financial rewards falling upon teenage figure skaters. Memories of Brundage's objections to skiers' displaying their skis on television interviews could only arouse a smile when the coat Samaranch wore at the opening and closing ceremonies prominently displayed the name of its maker.

Commercial symbols could now push even Olympic symbols off the television screen. CBS announcers wore jackets that carried the Nike "swoosh"; since, however, Nike had not given money as a sponsor of the Games, the jackets could not carry the Olympic rings in their CBS logos. Nor was Nike's advertising limited to the American market; the Nike symbol showed prominently on the uniforms of many competitors, and Nike had even funded the Kenyan cross-country skier who competed in Nagano.

Commercial interests, however, could control only part of the Games' worldwide image, and at the center of this festival witnessed in all parts of the globe stood Juan Antonio Samaranch, who loomed as a moral force above the daily cares of the world. *The Chicago Tribune* had called him the "shy Olympics savior" (March 1, 1996); now he had a majestic presence. At the opening ceremonies he called upon the governments of the world to observe the "Olympic truce" the United Nations General Assembly had approved the previous fall. (Observers well understood he was in fact addressing the United States government, which was then considering military action against Iraq.) In the course of the Games, Pope

The Olympic Truce

The United Nations General Assembly unanimously adopted a resolution entitled "Building a peaceful and better world through sport and the Olympic ideal" in New York on November 25 [1997]:

> This is the third time since the IOC first launched, on the occasion of the Games of the XXV Olympiad in Barcelona in 1992, its project for an Olympic truce in keeping with the ancient Greek tradition of the Ekecheiria, that the General Assembly has declared itself in favour of this initiative. The resolution invites the Member States to observe, individually and collectively, the Olympic truce from February 7-22, 1998, during the XVIII Olympic Winter Games to be held in Nagano, Japan, and to seek, in conformity with the purposes and principles of the Charter of the United Nations, the peaceful settlement of all international conflicts. . . .
>
> Our modest contribution is a symbolic one. It is the gesture that has significance and value. The representatives of our respective countries at the United Nations are well aware of this and understand it better than anyone, as does the United Nations Secretary General, Koffi [sic] Annan, with whom we have excellent relations. The International Olympic Committee, whose centennial year, 1994, was proclaimed international year of sport and the Olympic ideal by the United Nations General Assembly, is anxious to help developing countries and particularly the most disadvantaged.

IOC Web Page on the Internet.

John Paul II and UN Secretary-General Khofi Annan sent greetings and congratulations to Samaranch, and Samaranch himself stood as the ultimate judge of the Games. In the words of CBS announcer Jim Nantz, the world awaited Samaranch's "validation and approval." Would he describe these Games the "best ever" or only "spectacular" or "exceptional"? Samaranch, fully aware he commanded worldwide attention and respect, acclaimed the Nagano Games for the "best organization of the Winter Olympic Games."

In April 1998, two months after the close of the Nagano Games, the IOC awarded an Olympic Cup to the city of Nagano. According to the IOC's press release, this award served to recognize an "institution or association with a general reputation for merit and integrity that has been active and efficient in the service of sport and has contributed substantially to the development of the Olympic movement." IOC spokespersons declared this was the first such award since the Lillehammer Games of 1994. It was clear to everyone the IOC had consciously chosen to pass over the organizers of the Atlanta Games for any comparable award.

Chapter **19**

Entering the 21st Century

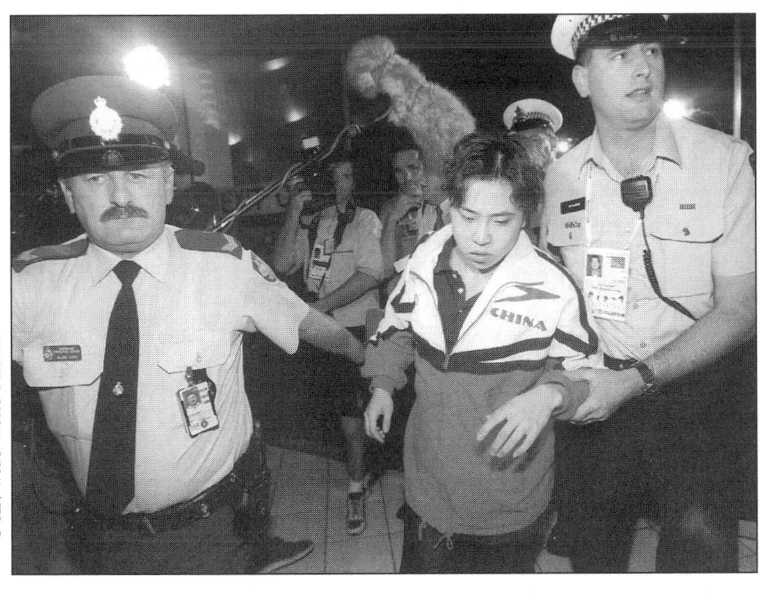

Performance-enhancing drugs are a persistent and embarrassing problem for the Olympics. In January 1998, Australian customs officials found several vials of banned human growth hormone in the luggage of a Chinese athlete coming to compete in a World Cup swimming meet. While the Australians plan tight security for the Sydney Games (2000), such scenes are a continued embarrassment for the Chinese, who are planning to bid for the 2008 Games.

As the 20th century grinds to its conclusion, the Olympic Games, already into their 2nd century, holds a firm and unique place in the consciousness of the world. The popular appeal of elite sport competition will undoubtedly continue, and theorists will always offer their interpretations of the significance and potential of the phenomenon. This largest, regularly scheduled gathering of people in the world, celebrated by the media in all nations, can expect to draw increasing attention from organizations, groups, and even individuals who want to compete or watch the competitors or somehow to enter into the celebration to send out their own messages or simply to make money.

On the surface, the special demands of various participating states, role of television, concern about drug abuse, fears about possible terrorist attacks, and intrusion of business interests or publicity seekers all might seem familiar, but new considerations keep raising unprecedented problems for Games organizers. In preparation for the Salt Lake City Winter Games of 2002, for example, Olympic organizers' security precautions against terrorist attacks will have to come to terms with Utah's liberal gun laws, which allow private individuals to carry concealed weapons.

Political maneuvers and struggles continue to run through the entire Olympic structure. Juan Antonio Samaranch's term as IOC President runs into the year 2001. He has said he plans to retire at that time, but he could change his mind. Before the Atlanta Games, American journalists speculated that Richard Pound, the IOC's liaison with ACOG, seemed to have the inside track to succeed Samaranch, but his criticism of Samaranch's decision to stay on for another term may have hurt his cause. When Anita DeFrantz, an American, became a member of the Executive Board, journalists speculated that she may soon become the IOC's first woman President. In the winter of 1997-1998, Jacques Rogge, a Belgian member of the IOC and the President of European Olympic Committees (EOC), faced the prospect of being excluded from the Board when his term as Vice President ended, but then the Committee elected him as a member at-large. When, in 1998, Rogge, an orthopedic surgeon by profession and a past rugby international, took on the job of being the IOC's liaison with Athens for the 2004 Games—this in addition to his position as liaison for the Sydney Games—observers saw his chances of succeeding Samaranch as improving.

Political turmoil plagues the work of all three OCOGs planning future Games. In the case of Atlanta, Billy Payne had provided continuous leadership for the Games from beginning to end, but the three Committees now working are experiencing considerable confusion and politicking. The Sydney Committee has seen its leadership change several times, and elections scheduled for the state of New South Wales in 1999 hold out the prospect of yet more change. The head of the Salt Lake City Committee had to resign because of personal problems, and after Athens won the right to host the 2004 Games, some time passed before politicians and sport officials could agree upon a Chairperson for the Organizing Committee.

In 1999 and 2001, the IOC will preside over the birth of two more OCOGs, first for the Winter Olympics of 2006 and then for the Summer Games of 2008. The process of choosing Athens for the 2004 Summer Games involved charges of bribery and complaints about costs, especially on the part of the losing candidates. Likewise, the campaign for the 2008 Games promises to be particularly volatile because China has been preparing to renew its bid. If the Chinese do decide to apply, they will not take kindly to another rejection. Yet in the spring of 1998, Samaranch suggested it might be premature for the Chinese to bid for the 2008 Games. And what might NBC's role in this question be?

Among the IFs, the football federation, FIFA, faced a significant succession crisis. When João Havelange, the President since 1974, announced he would retire in June 1998 on the eve of the World Cup in France, a bitter electoral campaign ensued. The first candidate to come forth was the President of the European Football Association (UEFA), Lennart Johansson, a Swede who had long criticized Havelange's leadership. Havelange then came out for Joseph S. (Sepp) Blatter, the Swiss General Secretary of FIFA. Johansson's supporters demanded Blatter resign his duties in FIFA before the voting, but Blatter hesitated. A compromise finally provided for Blatter to run for the office after giving up much of his power, and in the end FIFA elected Blatter.

Struggles also continue within various National Governing Bodies, often with commercial overtones. Nike has taken its campaign for the world athletic clothing and shoe market into the heartland of its competitor Adidas, namely the German Football Federation. Nike established ties with Borussia Dortmund, one of the most prominent teams in the Bundesliga, and Nike Sports and Entertainment (NSE), building on Nike's support of Brazilian soccer, claimed worldwide rights for the telecast of the Germany-Brazil match of March 25, 1998. Adidas managed to block NSE's claim to the rights to broadcast the game in Germany itself. "An advertising battle," *Welt am Sonntag* (March 15, 1998) called the football match.

The National Olympic Committees continue to offer a variety of political formats, just as they display varying degrees of independence from their governments. The British Olympic Committee had defied its government to attend the Moscow Olympics in 1980, while the USOC had bowed to Washington's will. Yet, some argue the United States Department of Defense was executing the will of the USOC in ordering military personnel out of the Goodwill Games in 1986.

Financing is also handled differently around the world. The USOC raises money privately; the Italian sport structure depends on the national football lottery; others, on money from their governments. The former Soviet Union offered a classic model of the outright dependence of an NOC on the governmental sport ministry, in this case known as the *Goskomsport* (State Sports Committee) and correspondingly of the role of sport as an instrument of the government's domestic and foreign policies.

Commercial considerations loom over all international sporting events. For example, the IOC had not liked the crowds in Atlanta. Sydney instead promised there would be fewer visitors—and therefore lower attendance than at Atlanta. The talk of keeping down the number of spectators, against the background of the IOC's insisting various sports make themselves more photogenic for television cameras, indicates the role of television in future Olympics will be even greater than what the pessimists were already bemoaning. In Jacques Rogge's words, "We need spectators at the Games, but the IOC does not insist on 100,000-seat stadiums. The Olympics are primarily put on for television" (Swift 1996). A USOC official went even further, saying of the Games, "This is a made-for-TV event, and there are a number of things we can do to enhance that. That's our job, to enhance the brand" (Hoffer 1998).

Emphasizing cameras instead of live spectators would guarantee the elite nature of the Games, call for attracting more wealthy spectators, and make the Games more dependent on sponsors and Nielsen ratings. NBC, moreover, had contracted to pay $705 million for rights to the Sydney Games, an increase of 50 percent over its payment for the rights to Atlanta. NBC's Nielsen ratings triumph in Atlanta had brought carryover success to other of the network's programming and offered the prospect of more subscriptions to the network's two cable channels, CNBC and MSNBC, which could be expected to offer subsidiary telecasting for the Games of 2000 and after. NBC's judgments on which sports to cover, driven by ratings and sponsors, promise to become an increasingly important factor in IOC deliberations.

Concern about reaching the East Coast market in the United States continues to dominate the television industry's calculations and raises questions about how much live competition viewers can expect to see. CBS, facing a 14-hour difference between Nagano and New York, failed to achieve the 19.3 Nielsen rating it had promised its sponsors; the preliminary rating was an average of only 16.2 percent of TV households watching the Games. CBS's broadcasts nevertheless dominated the crucial two-week period in the February "sweeps" that establishes price scales for television sponsors, and CBS executives claimed theirs had been an "upscale," educated audience.

In preparing for the Sydney Games (September 15 to October 1, 2000), where they will have to deal with a 15-hour time difference from New York, NBC officials are reportedly planning little or no live telecasting (Hoffer 1998). IOC members, however, never seem sure of the balance one should offer American television viewers. Given NBC's interpretation of its audiences in 1992 and 1996, the network will probably continue to headline women's gymnastics. Underlying the discussions are whisperings the Games need more personal clashes, as in Lillehammer. Writing in *The New York Times* of January 6, 1998, Jere Longman quoted Samaranch as joking, ". . . Maybe we could arrange something." In assessing CBS's disappointing ratings in Nagano, Richard Pound commented, "Two well-known figure skaters stayed home from Nagano and that probably had an effect." Do American viewers want women's sports, sensation, or only victories?

The emphasis on television, of course, will not mean the elimination of spectators altogether; the Olympics could never downsize to being studio sport competition with canned applause. Spectators constitute an essential part of the sport television picture; Roone Arledge established that principle 30 years ago. What, then, is the optimal size of a stadium or arena? Rogge questioned the need of a stadium seating 100,000. Neither the IOC nor NBC, it would seem, would have looked for a stadium seating 80,000 for the women's soccer final at the Atlanta Games, but spectators filled it, thrilling the players if not the NBC executive who had characterized soccer as "chess with a ball" and therefore—in his opinion—of little television value.

Running parallel to the idea of limiting spectators is the thought of limiting the number of athletes. IOC members have talked of limiting the number of participants to 10,000, but the increase in the number of recognized NOCs (there were 197 in Atlanta) and the IOC's decision to add new sports forced Sydney organizers to plan for more than the 10,000 athletes to which they had agreed (table 19.1). On the other side of this coin stands the question "Why send athletes?" Increasingly, Samaranch and others spoke of not staging the Games for "tourists," meaning individuals such as the renowned English ski jumper in Calgary who had no chance of winning. For some NOCs, this might not present a problem, but should an NOC fill every slot? An American went to court to force his way onto his country's delegation to Nagano on the grounds United States officials had chosen not to fill their complete quota of athletes in his sport.

Sydney organizers, who sent a delegation of 104 people to Atlanta, drew several key conclusions from what they had witnessed. Immediately after the Atlanta Games, the head of Sydney 2000, Mal Hemmerling, told the German magazine *Der Spiegel* he considered three things most important: Organizers should never surrender to the idea of anything's being "too early" (a reference to the computer programming glitches); organizers had to look at every venue as a separate entity; and Sydney

Table 19.1

Growth of the Summer Games

	Nations	Athletes
1972 Munich	122	7,156
1976 Montreal	88	6,085
1980 Moscow	81	5,326
1984 Los Angeles	140	7,078
1988 Seoul	159	8,465
1992 Barcelona	172	10,563
1996 Atlanta	197	10,744

The IOC Official Olympic Companion, 1996; IOC Web Page on the Internet.

must focus its attention on the athletes, "the heroes of the Games." IOC President Samaranch posed a different set of priorities for the Australians: "communications, security and transport."

First and foremost, in the aftermath of the bombing in Centennial Park, the Australians declared they would consider creating a giant security zone encompassing all main venues in the Games rather than establishing security around each of several major venues: "Anyone who goes into that zone would have to go through security checkpoints." Australia already had a variety of security problems, ranging from a heated debate about the right to bear arms to concerns about attacks on French and Indonesian diplomatic representatives over questions of ethnic and nuclear policies. Although Australians were reportedly considering new security laws, the Premier of the State of New South Wales, Bob Carr, declared, "Security will be tight in the year 2000, but it need not be intolerable. It's an Aussie Games we're planning." In 1998, fan violence at World Cup soccer games in France forced the Australians to tighten their security plans.

Sydney organizers promised they would use only computer programs that had been functioning well for more than one year; there would be no street vendors; and government officials who were members of the Organizing Committee would facilitate the resolution of any problems arising between Games organizers and local authorities. Sydney officials were working with the Greenpeace organization to ensure the Games will be "environmentally" sound, but to their distress, Greenpeace officials challenged the use of some plastic piping. In addition, Sydney organizers promised both the opening and closing ceremonies of the Games would feature Australian aborigines. As for complaints about television coverage in Atlanta, Hemmerling declared he saw "nothing bad" in television's role in the Games.

After their first optimistic statements, however, the Sydney Organizing Committee experienced a number of problems. For example, the participation of government officials in the work of the Committee actually intensified the political intrigue. In 1997, Hemmerling resigned as Chairman. Between 1994 and 1998 observers counted 17 resignations among major SOCOG officials, and the Committee went through four Chief Executives. Meanwhile, Greenpeace spokespersons challenged the quality of the water in Sydney's harbor. Samaranch protested the decision of Sydney hotels to charge a bed tax for visitors to the Olympic Games. Aborigines threatened to use the Games as a stage for protests against local laws and practices. Then organizers publicly argued over who should formally open the Games: the Queen of England or the Australian Prime Minister. In short, one might say controversy had become almost normal in the functioning of an Organizing Committee.

Apart from nationalist rivalries and the danger of terrorist violence, probably the biggest problem continuing to dog the Olympic Games is that of the use of performance-enhancing drugs. IOC, IF, NOC, and OCOG officials have exchanged heated accusations as to who was not properly enforcing antidrug rules. Meanwhile, challenges to the IOC's antidoping policies questioned the necessity of testing, ability of the testing to catch the newest drugs, and accuracy of the findings of the testing. Certainly, Olympic officials have found it much easier to denounce such practices than to ban them. Some administrators and athletes seem to think drugs play essentially the same role as a better vaulting pole, lighter running shoes, more efficient bicycles, or a swimmer's shaved head. Others suggest drug testing is as flawed and hypocritical as the old system of amateur standards the IOC has long since abandoned. Both doctors and courts question the efficiency and accuracy of efforts to control "doping" in sport.

In advance of the Atlanta Games, a British doctor, Michael Turner, had publicly declared, "If you're talking about track and field, you're talking about a situation where the percentage may be 75 or above of Olympic athletes in Atlanta will have taken some kind of performance-enhancing drug." In a news conference, Prince Alexandre de Merode, head of the IOC's Medical Commission, responded, "Let me just laugh slowly." De Merode insisted testing had improved to the point that "instead of having a shadowy area of 80 percent we have a clearly-lit zone of 80 or 90 percent and a small crescent that is still dark." In fact, Olympic officials admitted they had to be careful because of possible inaccuracies in urine testing, and they were hesitant to install a system

Drug Testing Results in the Summer Games

- Mexico 1968: 1 case of alcohol in modern pentathlon.
- Munich 1972: 7 cases—2 of amphetamines in weight lifting and judo, 2 of coramine in cycling, 3 of ephedrine in basketball, swimming and weight lifting.
- Montreal 1976: 11 cases—1 of amphetamines in shooting, 1 of fencamfamine in weight lifting, 1 of phenylpropanolamine in yachting and 8 of anabolic steroids (1 in track and field and 7 in weight lifting).
- Moscow 1980: none reported.
- Los Angeles 1984: 12 cases—1 of ephedrine in volleyball, 7 of nandrolone (5 in weight lifting and 2 in track and field), 2 of metenolone in volleyball and wrestling, 2 of testosterone in volleyball and track and field.
- Seoul 1988: 10 cases—1 of caffeine in modern pentathlon, 4 of furosemide (2 in weight lifting, 1 in wrestling and 1 in judo), 1 of propanolol in modern pentathlon, 1 of pemoline in weight lifting, 3 of stanozolol (1 in track and field and 2 in weight lifting). Four medalists were found guilty of doping and the IOC stripped them of their medals: three Olympic champions (Ben Johnson, Canada, 100-meter sprint, track and field; Mitko Grubler and Angel Guenchev, Bulgaria, weight lifting) and a bronze medalist (Kerrith Brown, Great Britain, judo).
- Barcelona 1992: 5 cases—1 of strychnine in volleyball, 1 of norephedrine in track and field, 2 of clenbuterol in track and field, and 1 of mesocarb in track and field.
- Atlanta 1996: 1 case of methandienone and 1 case of stanozolol.

IOC Web Page on the Internet.

of blood testing for the Sydney Games. In Atlanta, the CAS overturned the disqualification of several Russian athletes, thereby raising further questions about the process of identifying the drugs to be banned and then enforcing the bans.

Even a clear-cut finding can result in a troubling court case. United States courts in particular have acted to restrain what plaintiffs could call the "arbitrary authority" of sport organizations in a wide variety of

Two Problem Drugs, 1998:

Erythropoietin (EPO, rEPO)—a natural hormone secreted by the kidney. EPO stimulates the formation of red blood cells (RBC) in the bone marrow. . . .

rEPO injections have been shown to increase RBC production and hemoglobin concentration in the blood from 6-11 percent over 6 weeks. . . . In a recent review, the American College of Sports Medicine indicated that EPO administration in healthy subjects seems to provide ergogenic effects similar to those seen with blood doping. . . .

Current urine drug testing techniques may detect rEPO use for only 2-3 days following the last administration; however, the physiological effects of rEPO may last for weeks, making the drug test moot.

Human Growth Hormone (hGH, in a synthetic form rhGH)—a natural hormone secreted by the anterior pituitary gland in the brain. hGH stimulates growth of the bones, but also affects the metabolism of carbohydrate, fat, and protein. hGH is considered an anabolic hormone. . . .

When administered to subjects who are hGH-deficient, rhGH supplementation increased lean body mass and decreased body fat. When given to subjects who have normal endogenous levels of hGH, rhGH supplementation may increase lean body mass, but not necessarily muscle mass, strength, or athletic performance. . . .

RhGH use is not detectable using current drug-testing procedures.

Williams 1998, *The Ergogenics Edge.* pp. 194-195, 214-215.

cases, including drug testing as well as other demands for due procedure: Challenging suspensions for positive drug testing; questioning the choice of this athlete and not that one for competition; and blocking United States figure skating officials' efforts to respond to the attack on Nancy Kerrigan before the Lillehammer Games. In Atlanta, IAAF officials backed away from banning an Australian sprinter and an Italian high jumper in Atlanta, despite positive drug tests, for fear of litigation on the scale of the celebrated Butch Reynolds case. (IAAF officials undoubtedly breathed more easily when neither competitor medaled, just as they may have rejoiced when Reynolds failed in his effort to regain Olympic glory.) The IOC, of course, hoped its Court for Arbitration in Sport could resolve such problems, but more controversy seemed to have a sure place in the future.

Political considerations have also colored the decision making in the IOC's drug policies. In 1998, the trial of former East German sport officials charged with having given performance-enhancing substances to athletes and thereby having endangered and even damaged their health aroused considerable discussion. United States swimming officials demanded the medals won by East German swimmers in the 1970s be revoked. German Olympic officials objected to such a belated review of only the German athletes, and IAAF officials declared their opposition to rewriting the records. And while the IOC agreed to review the records of past competitions, some voices also called for taking advantage of the coming of a new century by starting with an entirely new set of records.

The East German case, however, concerned the past history of the Games, and a more immediate problem tormenting FINA and the IOC during the XXVIth Olympiad concerned the continued charges against Chinese women swimmers. In their national competition in the fall of 1997, the Chinese had set a number of new records, and United States Swimming officials in particular pressed FINA to challenge the Chinese. At the World Swimming Championship, held in Australia in January 1998, customs officials discovered human growth hormone in the luggage of one woman swimmer, and meet officials subsequently excluded four Chinese swimmers for failing drug tests. The IOC affirmed its faith in the Chinese officials. "There were only five cases," said Prince de Merode. Nevertheless, Samaranch later warned the scandals in Chinese swimming could compromise China's bid for the 2008 Games.

One other area of development to which Samaranch has given high priority was the recruiting of women for both sport competition and sport administration, including membership in the IOC. Samaranch's accomplishments in this area have been considerable, but here too new

---

IOC Rule on Gender Testing:

All competitors taking part in women's events . . . or as the female competitor of a mixed team . . . shall be subject to gender verification. Competitors who have been registered for such competitions shall report to the Gender Verification Office established for purposes of the competition. Failure to so report renders the competitor ineligible to participate in the competition.

Gender verification tests will be conducted under the supervision of a member of the IOC Medical Commission. . . .

Female competitors holding a valid certificate of femininity issued by the IOC Medical Commission will be exempted from further tests upon presentation of such certificate on the occasion of Gender Verification. For competitors who do not hold such a certificate, the IOC Medical Commission shall issue a certificate for cases in which the results of the tests are conclusive.

A screening test for purposes of gender verification prescribed by the IOC Medical Commission will be conducted. If the test is inconclusive, the competitor will be required to undergo further tests as may be prescribed by the IOC Medical Commission.

IOC Web Page on the Internet.

---

questions and challenges have developed. Opposition to the principle of gender testing has grown; at Lillehammer, Norwegian doctors refused to conduct the examinations. Some IOC leaders argued such a move would eliminate the holding of separate events for men and women, but a conference on Women and Sport, meeting in October 1996, had demanded an end to the practice. In the words of Anita DeFrantz, who chaired the conference, "Why should you have to test women to find out they're women and not test men?" The IOC agreed to consider the matter but indicated there would be gender testing in Sydney.

Despite his many successes, such as having brought the Olympic Games out of their political turmoil of the early and mid-1980s and having put the Games on a sound financial foundation, Samaranch himself has experienced growing criticism from journalists who are always looking for chinks in the Olympic armor. In connection with the Nagano Games, he agreed to an interview with CBS and then complained the interviewer, Bob Simon, had ambushed him with questions about his public life in Franco Spain and about the IOC's relationships with dictators such as Erich Honnecker of East Germany and Nicolae Ceaucescu of Romania. In response, Samaranch asserted he was proud of his past, but he then reportedly asked the President of CBS either to quash the interview or to allow him to speak Spanish in a retake. The CBS President insisted publicly he could not interfere in the work of the network's news section.

The questions Simon put to Samaranch, to be sure, were nothing the IOC President could not have expected. Frank Deford had asked basically the same questions in an HBO broadcast before the Atlanta Games. Both men had used material published by two British journalists, Vyv Simson and Andrew Jennings (1992). When the Simson and Jennings book first came out, Samaranch had denounced it as slander and had sued the authors in a Swiss court. Neither Simson nor Jennings appeared before the court, and Samaranch won a symbolic verdict, which he considered to have refuted the dark image of his having served Franco. When Simon's interview appeared on the CBS show *60 Minutes*, it included an interview with IOC Vice President Richard Pound who defended the IOC's practices in dealing with the "real world."

The fates of Ceaucescu, killed in the course of the Romanian revolution, and of Honnecker, forced into exile, brought up the additional question of what happens to "Olympians" outside of the Games. International conflicts and national revolutions could have far-reaching effects on the lives of athletes and IOC members alike. In their time, Brundage and Edstrøm had expressed their concern to Soviet officials about the internment of Carl von Halt. In August 1990, a Kuwaiti member of the IOC died in the course of the Iraqi invasion of his country. In 1996, both the IOC and NBC expressed sympathy for Mamo Wolde, a former marathon champion from Ethiopia, who was arrested in 1992 as having been associated with the former Marxist regime in Ethiopia.

The IOC has not always rallied to the support of its members, however. On the eve of the Albertville Games of 1992, Robert Helmick, who in his time had been President of FINA and the USOC as well as a member of the IOC and its Executive Board, ran afoul of charges he had taken money from organizations that had dealings with the USOC. The IOC accepted his resignation quietly. In 1996, several figures prominent in Olympic history went on trial in their homelands. On March 11, Chun Doo Hwan and Roh Tae Woo, the patrons of the Seoul Olympic Games of 1988, went before a Seoul court, charged with having massacred hundreds of protesters in 1980. In 1988, Samaranch had praised Roh for strengthening democracy in Korea (Hill 1996); in August 1997, three weeks after the conclusion of the Atlanta Games, the court decreed the death penalty for Chun and a long prison term for Roh. The sentences were later commuted.

At the close of the 20th century, the growing entertainment value of the Games, together with the accompanying contributions from sponsors, promises new dimensions to the politics of the Games. All interested parties—the IOC, sponsors, equipment makers—want sporting events to be seen by as large an audience as possible. The companies, moreover, could wield enormous power; the Nike "swoosh" had even displaced the Nagano Olympic rings on the television screen. Without a doubt, governments, politicians, businessmen, and ideologues will continue to consider what use they can make of all this. Governments, NOCs, and corporations alike will calculate which arrangements and contracts will suit them best. Those who refuse to recognize the politics of the Games put themselves at the mercy of the people and organizations who actively participate in the political competition.

List of Acronyms

AAU	Amateur Athletic Union
ACOG	Atlanta Committee for the Olympic Games
ANOC	General Assembly of National Olympic Committees
AOC	American Olympic Committee
CIS	Commonwealth of Independent States
FIBA	International Amateur Basketball Federation, International Basketball Federation
FIFA	International Association of Football (Soccer) Federations
FINA	International Amateur Swimming Federation
FIS	International Ski Federation
FRG	Federal Republic of Germany
FSU	Former Soviet Union
GAIF	General Assembly of International Federations
GANEFO	Games of the Newly Emerging Forces
GDR	German Democratic Republic
IAAF	International Amateur Athletic Federation
IF	International [Sports] Federation
IOC	International Olympic Committee
LAOOC	Los Angeles Olympic Organizing Committee
NATO	North Atlantic Treaty Organization
NBA	National Basketball Association
NOC	National Olympic Committee
OAU	Organization of African Unity
OCOG	Organizing Committee for the Olympic Games
PRC	People's Republic of China
SANOC	South African National Olympic Committee

SCSA	Supreme Council for Sport in Africa
SI	*Sports Illustrated*
USOC	United States Olympic Committee
USSR	Union of Soviet Socialist Republics

Bibliography and References

The historiography of the Olympic Games is rich and varied, including scholarly, documentary, journalistic, popular, romantic, and cynical accounts. Some concentrate on the competition and on the heroes; some on the institutions. The Games themselves are a topic within the study of the history and sociology of sport. In turn, the political history of the Games requires some familiarity with the cultural and social history of individual societies as well as with the history of international relations. Therefore, a brief bibliography such as this faces something akin to a black hole.

One might first choose from the official and semiofficial histories of the Games. To be sure, at one time the IOC refused to give its full approval to Bill Henry's history of the Games (1948), allowing it to be labeled only "approved," but in more recent times IOC officials have themselves contributed to the historiography: see especially the books by Richard Pound (1994) and Lord Killanin (1983) as well as Pierre de Coubertin's own memoirs (1979). *The Olympic Games*, edited by Lord Killanin (1976) and John Rodda, provides perhaps the best introduction. First issued in the 1970s, when Killanin was President of the IOC, the work underwent modifications for later Games, but the collection of essays in the first edition remains unsurpassed as a broad overview of the Games. The International Olympic Committee (1996) subsequently put its name on an *Official Olympic Companion*, although the book bears the note "The articles published in the IOC *Official Olympic Companion* do not necessarily reflect the opinion of the International Olympic Committee." In addition, almost every country participating in the Games has produced some account of its own achievements. Games Organizing Committees have published books, and many National Olympic Committees have published reports on specific games. The United States Olympic Committee has licensed *The Olympics Factbook* (Connors, Dupuis, and Morgan 1992). Then one can look to books published by various international sports federations. The IOC has also designated the American sport historian John Lucas (1980) as an official Olympic historian. Also deserving mention is the CD-ROM *Olympic Gold* (1995), issued by S.E.A. Multimedia Ltd., Jerusalem, and for which the United States Olympic Committee and the IOC share the copyright and to which the IOC has given a special award.

Independent studies of the Olympic Games have multiplied rapidly in the last generation. In this grouping, one should first note the works of three American writers: John Hoberman (1984, 1986), John MacAloon (1981), and Allen Guttmann (1978, 1984, 1994a, 1994b). Guttmann is perhaps the leading American theorist on sport, and his biography of Avery Brundage (1984) constitutes a major contribution to the history of the Games. MacAloon began his work on the Olympic Games with his account of the life of Pierre de Coubertin, and he has contributed richly to the study of the ceremonies and the functioning of the Games. Hoberman places his comments on the Games in the context of his studies of ideologies of sports and the social dimensions of sports. Other useful general histories include the works of David Kanin (1981), Christopher Hill (1996), and Richard Espy (1981). David Wallechinsky's (1984) *The Complete Book of the Olympics*, which has undergone several revisions, deserves special note as a reference work.

In addition to the books mentioned, much valuable material has appeared in collections of essays, anthologies, and conference proceedings. Included are *Sport and International Relations* (Lowe, Kanin, and Strenk 1978); *Sport and Society: An Anthology* (Talamini and Page 1980); *The Politics of Sport* (Allison 1986); *The Changing Politics of Sport* (Allison 1993); *Sport and Politics* (Redmond 1986); and *The Olympic Games in Transition* (Segrave and Chu 1988).

Individual Games have drawn special attention from various historians. Richard Mandell has published major accounts of the Athens Games of 1896 (1976), the Berlin Games of 1936 (1971), and the Munich Games of 1972 (1991). David Young's study of the Athens Games (1996) challenges the conventional interpretation of these first modern Games, contrasting Young's own work with Greek sources on the Games with the hitherto standard account based on Coubertin's memoirs.

Since the Munich Games of 1972, each set of Games has stimulated the formation of its own bibliography. The multivolume series entitled *The Olympic Century* (1996) promises to be a major addition to this type of literature; the volumes so far published include works by George Constable, George Daniels, Ellen Galford, and Ellen Phillips.

The works mentioned thus far are mostly by American and English authors. Histories by authors of other nationalities, however, may offer completely different perspectives and interpretations. The Germans in particular have been prolific in this regard. This bibliography lists only selected works; one might also look for studies by Hajo Bernett, Manfred Blödern, Willi Daume, Carl Diem, Karlheinz Gieseler, Arnd Krüger, Wilfried Lemke, Karl Lennartz, Karl Scherer, and Horst Überhorst. For East German accounts, one can begin with the writings of Klaus Ullrich (1979, 1980) or Doug Gilbert (1980).

The literature in French, includes, of course, the works of Coubertin himself as well as a number of works about him. See Marie Therese

Eyquem, *Pierre de Coubertin—L'épopée Olympique* (1966), Y-P. Boulogne, *La vie et l'oeuvre pedagogique de Pierre de Coubertin* (1975); Ernest Seillière, *Un artisan d'energie français: Baron Pierre de Coubertin* (1917).

Russian and Soviet authors have produced a number of significant works. Although many western writers object to their biased Soviet Marxist arguments, their output includes very useful reference works, especially in preparation for the Moscow Games of 1980: the three-volume Fizkul'tura i sport work *Vse o sporte* (1978); B. Khavin, *Vse ob olimpiiskikh igrakh* (1979); and the second edition of Fizkul'tura i sport's *MOK i mezhdunarodnye sportivnye ob"neniia. Spravochnik* (1979). Other significant works include Aleksei Romanov (1973), Valerii Shteinbakh (1980), Aleksandr Kolodnyi's account of the American boycott of Moscow (1981), and the memoir by Ignatii Novikov (1983), the head of the Moscow Organizing Committee.

One should also take note of the exposés that criticize the structure of the Olympic Games and its leaders. Some, with their own ideological agendas, aim at the very nature of international sport and international business, and others focus on personalities. One of the most significant of these works is the one by Vyv Simson and Andrew Jennings (1992), which directs its harshest salvoes at Juan Antonio Samaranch. Samaranch sued the authors in a Swiss court and won a symbolic award of four Swiss francs. The authors did not appear before the court, however, and Jennings has continued his attacks on the leadership of the Games.

In constructing this study, I began with the archive of Avery Brundage, held at the University of Illinois at Urbana-Champaign. For guidance in this enormous collection, the handbook compiled by Maynard Brichford (1977) is indispensable. Alan Guttmann's biography of Brundage (1984) also constitutes a valuable guide to Brundage's career and its significance for the Games. Other useful, special sources include the archive of German newspaper clippings in the Weltwirtschaftsarchiv (Hamburg, Germany); the archives of the Ban the Soviets Coalition (Mission Viejo, California), and interviews with the organizers of the Goodwill Games (June and August 1986, TAC headquarters in Indianapolis, IN, and October 1989, CNN headquarters in Atlanta, GA).

Periodical literature provides rich, contemporary sources for the study of the Games. The American weekly *Sports Illustrated* is a sponsor of the Games and carries many stories and reports; the IOC itself publishes the monthly *Olympic Review*. Scholarly journals that carry useful material include *Olympika*, *The Journal of Sports History*, *The International Journal of the History of Sport*, and *Stadion*. For specific Games, local newspapers can be invaluable, for example, *The Atlanta Journal-Constitution* or *The Los Angeles Times*. In the account of the

Seoul Games, I used *The Korea Herald* and *The Korea Times* for news from South Korea and *The Pyongyang Times* and *The People's Korea* from North Korea. In the modern computer world, one can also look to web pages, such as the IOC's Web Page,

http: // www.olympic.org / index.html.

References and Select Bibliography

AAU. N.d. *Minutes of the Annual Meeting 1935*. N.p.: AAU.

Allison, Lincoln, ed. 1986. *The Politics of Sport*. Manchester: Manchester University Press.

———. 1993. *The Changing Politics of Sport*. Manchester: Manchester University Press.

American Olympic Committee. N.d. *Report. 7th Olympic Games Antwerp*. N.p.: AOC.

———. N.d. *Report: Games of the XIth Olympiad*. New York: AOC.

Andrianov, K.A., ed. 1970. *Olimpiiskie Igry*. Moscow.

Ashe, Arthur R., Jr. 1988. *A Hard Road to Glory*. New York: Warner.

Atlanta Committee on the Olympic Games. 1995. *Press Guide*. Atlanta: Author.

Bamberger, Michael, and Don Yaeger. 1997. "Over the Edge." *Sports Illustrated*, April 14, 60-64.

Bear, Cecil. 1952. *Official Report of the XV Olympic Games*. London: World of Sports.

Berlioux, Monique. 1981. Letter published in *Olympic Panorama* (Moscow). No. 1.

———. 1984. "The History of the International Olympic Committee." Pp. 24-47 in *The Olympic Games 1984*, ed. Lord Killanin and John Rodda. London: Marrimack.

Blödern, Manfred, ed. 1984. *Sport und Olympische Spiele*. Reinbeck: Rowohlt.

Blume, Klaus. 1990. "Die Angst vor dem Sprint ohne Sieg." *Rheinischer Merkur*. September 21.

Booker, Christopher. 1981. *The Games War*. London: Faber & Faber.

Booth, Douglas. 1998. *The Race Game: Sport and Politics in South Africa*. London: Frank Cass.

Bose, Mihir. 1994. *Sporting Colours: Sport and Politics in South Africa*. London: Robson Books.

Boulogne, Y-P. 1975. *La vie et l'oeuvre pedagogique de Pierre de Coubertin*. Montreal: Leméac.

Brichford, Maynard, comp. 1977. *Avery Brundage Collection, 1908-1975*. Schriftenreihe des Bundesinstituts für Sportwissenschaft, no. 12. Koln: Karl Hoffmann.

British Olympic Association. 1924. *Official Report of the VIIIth Olympiad, 1924*. London: BOA.

British Olympic Committee. 1981. *Official Report of the 1980 Games*. London: BOC.

Brokhin, Yuri. 1977. *The Big Red Machine: The Rise and Fall of Soviet Olympic Champions*. Translated by Glenn Garelik and Yuri Brokhin. New York: Random House.

Brzezinski, Zbigniew. 1983. *Power and Principle*. New York: Farrar, Straus & Giroux.

Carter, Jimmy. 1982. *Keeping Faith*. New York: Bantam.

Comité Olympique Français. 1924. *Les Jeux de la VIIIe Olympiade*. Paris: COF.

Connors, Martin, Diane L. Dupuis, and Brad Morgan. 1992. *The Olympics Factbook: A Spectator's Guide to the Winter and Summer Games*. Licensed by the United States Olympic Committee. Detroit: Visible Ink Press.

Constable, George. 1996. *The XI, XII & XIII Olympiads*, vol. 11 in *The Olympic Century*. Los Angeles: World Sport Research & Publications.

Cook, Theodore Andrea. 1908. *The Fourth Olympiad*. London: British Olympic Committee.

Cosell, Howard. 1985. *I Never Played the Game*. New York: Avon.

Coubertin, Pierre de. 1979. *Olympic Memoirs*. Lausanne: International Olympic Committee.

Crump, Jack. 1966. *Running Round the World*. London: Hale.

Daly, Chuck. 1992. *America's Dream Team*. Atlanta: Turner Publishing.

Daniels, George G. 1996. *The XIX Olympiad*, vol. 17 in *The Olympic Century*. Los Angeles: World Sport Research & Publications.

Deford, Frank. 1988. "Olympian Changes," *Sports Illustrated*, vol. 69, 126-127.

Department of Information of the Republic of Indonesia. 1963. *The Birth of GANEFO*. Jakarta: Author.

Department of State Bulletin. March 1980, 50.

———. April 1980, 3.

———. June 1980, 30.

———. July 1984.

Diem, Carl. 1952. "Bilanz der Spiele." Pp. 383-391 in *Die Olympische Spiele 1952*. Frankfurt: Olympischer Sport-Verlag.

Duff, Bob. 1996. Untitled Internet communication.

Edwards, Harry. 1969. *The Revolt of the Black Athlete*. New York: Free Press.

Espy, Richard. 1981. *The Politics of the Olympic Games*. Berkeley: University of California Press.

Eyquem, Marie Therese. 1966. *Pierre de Coubertin—L'épopée Olympique*. Paris: Calmann-Lévy.

Galford, Ellen. 1996. *The XXIII Olympiad*, vol. 21 in *The Olympic Century*. Los Angeles: World Sport Research & Publications.

GANEFO. *Ekawarsa GANEFO*. 1965. Djakarta: GANEFO.

Gieseler, Karlheinz. 1966. *Sport als Mittel der Politik*. Mainz: V. Hase u. Koehler.

Gilbert, Doug. 1980. *The Miracle Machine*. New York: Coward, McCann & Geoghegan.

Graham, Paul, and Horst Überhorst. 1976. *The Modern Olympics*. West Point: Leisure Press.

Grigor'ev, E., I. Mel'nikov, and V. Chertkov. 1974. *Miunkhen: Olimpiada i politika*. Moscow: Sovetskaia Rossiia.

Grombach, John. 1975. *The 1976 Olympic Guide*. Chicago: Rand McNally.

Grot, Zdzislaw. 1973. *Zarys dziejow kultury fizycznej w Wielkopolsce*. Warsaw: PWN.

Guelke, Adrian. 1986. The Politicisation of South African Sport. Pp. 118-48 in *The Politics of Sport*, ed. Lincoln Allison. Manchester: Manchester University Press.

Guttmann, Allen. 1978. *From Ritual to Record: The Nature of Modern Sports*. New York: Columbia University Press.

———. 1984. *The Games Must Go On: Avery Brundage and the Olympic Movement*. New York: Columbia University Press.

———. 1994a. *Modern Sports and Cultural Imperialism*. New York: Columbia University Press.

———. 1994b. *The Olympics: A History of the Modern Games*. Champaign-Urbana, IL: University of Illinois.

Hay, Eduardo. 1981. "The Stella Walsh Case." *Olympic Review* no. 162: 221-222.

Hazan, Baruch A. 1982. *Olympic Sports and Propaganda Games: Moscow 1980*. New Brunswick, NJ: Transaction Books.

Henry, Bill. 1948. *An Approved History of the Olympic Games*. New York: Putnam.

Herodotus. 1972. *The Histories*. London: Penguin.

Hill, Christopher R. 1996. *Olympic Politics*. 2d ed. Manchester: Manchester University Press.

Hoberman, John M. 1984. *Sport and Political Ideology*. Austin: University of Texas.

———. 1986. *The Olympic Crisis: Sport, Politics and the Moral Order*. New Rochelle, NY: Caratzas.

Hoffer, Richard. 1998. "Putting the Gold on Hold." *Sports Illustrated*, March 2, 28.

Holmes, Judith. 1971. *Olympiad 1936*. New York: Ballantine Books

Holzweissig, G. 1981. *Diplomatie im Trainingsanzug*. Munich: Oldenbourg.

Houlihan, Barrie. 1994. *Sport and International Politics*. New York/London: Harvester, Wheatsheaf.

"India Hosts the Asian Games." 1983. *Olympic Panorama* (Moscow) (1): 42-47.

Inter-Allied Games 1919. Paris: Games Committee.

International Olympic Committee. 1996. *Official Olympic Companion*. Compiled by Caroline Searl and Bryn Vaile. London/Washington: Brassey's Sports.

International Olympic Committee *Charter*.

Iumashev, Valentin. 1988. "Na Olimp!" *Ogonëk* No. 44, pp. 26-27.

Jenkins, Sally. 1992. "New Allegiances (Eastern European Olympians at Albertville)." *Sports Illustrated*, v. 76, Feb. 24, pp. 38-40.

Johnson, William Oscar. 1987. "A Vote for South Korea." *Sports Illustrated*, v. 67, July 13, pp. 87-91.

Johnson, William Oscar, and Anita Verschoth. 1989. "Out of the Shadows." *Sports Illustrated*, 27 November, pp. 16-21.

Kanin, David B. 1981. *A Political History of the Olympic Games*. Boulder, CO: Westview Press.

Katz, Donald. 1994. *Just Do It: The Nike Spirit in the Corporate World*. New York: Random House.

Khavin, B. 1979. *Vse ob olimpiiskikh igrakh*. Moscow: Fizkul'tura i sport.

Kieran, John, Arthur Daley and Pat Jordan. 1977. *The History of the Olympic Games*. Philadelphia: Lippincott.

Killanin, Lord, Michael Morris. 1976. "Clarification by the IOC," *Olympic Review*, no. 107-8.

———1983. *My Olympic Years*. New York: Morrow.

———, and John Rodda, eds. 1976. *The Olympic Games*. New York: Collier.

Kolatch, J. 1972. *Sports, Politics and Ideology in China*. New York: Jonathan David Publishers.

Kolodnyi, Aleksandr. 1981. *"Igry" vokrug igr*. Moscow: Sovetskaia Rossiia.

Kun, Laszlo. 1982. *Vseobshchaia istoriia fizicheskoi kul'tury i sporta*. Moscow: Raduga.

Lapchick, R.E. 1975. *The Politics of Race and International Sport*. Westport, CT: Greenwood.

Lekarska, Nadejda. 1973. *Essays and Studies on Olympic Problems*. Sofia, Bulgaria: Medicina i Fizcultura.

Lenin, V.I. 1961. *Pol'noe sobranie sochineniia*, Vol. 25. Moscow: Gospolitizdat.

Lewis, Peter D. 1996. "Software Crashes and Bad Data Mar Games." *The New York Times*, July 29.

Lowe, Benjamin, David B. Kanin, and Andrew Strenk, eds. 1978. *Sport and International Relations*. Champaign, IL: Stipes Publishing Company.

Lucas, John A. 1980. *The Modern Olympic Games*. South Brunswick and New York: A.S. Barnes.

———. 1992. *The Future of the Olympic Games*. Champaign, IL: Human Kinetics.

Ludwig, Jack Barry. 1976. *Five Ring Circus*. Toronto: Doubleday Canada.

MacAloon, John J. 1981. *This Great Symbol: Pierre de Coubertin and the Origins of the Modern Olympic Games*. Chicago: University of Chicago Press.

Mahoney, Jeremiah T. 1935. "Germany Has Violated the Olympic Code!" Pamphlet. New York: The Committee on Fair Play in Sports.

Mandell, Richard D. 1971. *The Nazi Olympics*. New York: Macmillan.

———. 1976. *The First Modern Olympics*. Berkeley: University of California Press.

———. 1991. *The Olympics of 1972: A Munich Diary*. Chapel Hill: University of North Carolina Press.

Margulies, Lee. 1992. "Olympics carry NBC to victory." *Los Angeles Times*, August 12.

Martzke, Rudy. 1992. "Final Moments Leave Costas Tongue-Tied." *USA Today*, August 10.

Mayer, Otto. 1960. *A travers les anneaux olympiques*. Geneva: IOC.

Maynaud, Jean. 1966. *Sport et Politique*. Paris: P. Cailler.

Melbourne Organizing Committee. 1958. *Official Report*. Melbourne: Organizing Committee for the Games of the XVIth Olympiad.

MOK i mezhdunarodnye sportivnye ob"neniia. Spravochnik. 1979. 2d ed. Moscow: Fizkul'tura i sport.

Moragas Spa, Miquel de, Nancy K. Rivenburgh, and James F. Larson. 1995. *Television in the Olympics*. London: John Libbery.

Mzali, Mohamed. 1976. "Mr. Mzali: 'I am sorry about the boycott of the Montreal Games'." *Olympic Review*, no. 107-108, pp. 461-63.

Noel-Baker, Philip. 1978a. "V Stockholm 1912." Pp. 40-44 in *The Olympic Games*, ed. Lord Killanin and John Rodda. New York: Collier.

———. 1978b. "VII Antwerp 1920." Pp. 44-47 in *The Olympic Games*, ed. Lord Killanin and John Rodda. New York: Collier.

Novikov, I.T. 1983. *Olimpiiskii meridian Moskvy*. Moscow: Fizkul'tura i sport.

Olympic Gold: A 100 Year History of the Summer Olympic Games. 1995. Jerusalem: S.E.A. Multimedia.

O'Neil, Terry. 1989. *The Game Behind the Game: High Stakes, High Pressure in Television Sports*. New York: Harper & Row.

Österreichische Olympische Comite. 1948. *Olympia. Fest der Völker*. Vienna: Österreichische Staatsdrückerei.

Oçzdçzyânski, Jan. 1979. *Mówione warianty wypowiedzi w âsrodowisku sportowym*. Kraków: Zaklad Narodowy im. Ossoliânskich.

Pauker, Ewa. 1964. *GANEFO I: Sports and Politics in Djakarta*. Rand P-2935.

Peppard, Victor, and James Riordan. 1993. *Playing Politics: Soviet Sport Diplomacy to 1992*. Greenwich, CT: JAI Press.

Phillips, Ellen. 1996. *The VIII Olympiad*, vol. 8 in *The Olympic Century*. Los Angeles: World Sport Research & Publications.

Pope, Steven. 1997. *Patriotic Games: Sporting Traditions in the American Imagination, 1876-1926*. New York: Oxford University Press.

Popov, Sergei. 1981. "We Stand for Cooperation." *Olympic Panorama* (Moscow) (1): pp. 9-10.

——— and A. Srebnitsky. 1979. *Soviet Sport: Questions and Answers*. Moscow: Novosti Press Agency.

Pound, Richard W. 1994. *Five Rings Over Korea*. Boston: Little, Brown.

Poviliunas, Arturas. 1995. *Olimpine Ugnis Negesta*. Vilnius: LTOK.

Quanz, Dietrich. 1993. "Civic Pacifism and Sports Based Internationalism: Framework for the Founding of the International Olympic Committee." *Olympika* 2:1-24.

Redmond, Gerald, ed. 1986. *Sport and Politics*, vol. 7 in *The 1984 Olympic Scientific Congress Proceedings*. Champaign, IL: Human Kinetics.

Reich, Kenneth. 1986. *Making It Happen*. Santa Barbara, CA: Capra.

Report of the Organizing Committee on Its Work for the XIIth Olympic Games of 1940. Tokyo: Tokyo Organizing Committee.

Ricquart, Vincent J. 1988. *The Games Within the Games: The Story Behind the 1988 Seoul Olympics*. Seoul: Hantong.

Riordan, James. 1977. *Sport in Soviet Society*. Cambridge: Cambridge University Press.

———. 1986. "Elite Sport Policy in East and West." Pp. 66-89 in *The Politics of Sport*, ed. Lincoln Allison. Manchester: Manchester University Press.

Romanov, A.O. 1963. *Sovremennye Problemy Mezhdunarodnogo Olimpiiskogo Dvizheniia*. Moscow: Fizkultura i sport.

———. 1973. *Mezhdunarodnoe Sportivnoe Dvizhenie*. Moscow: Fizkul'tura i sport.

Romanov, Nikolai. 1981. "The First Step Toward the Olympics." *Olympic Panorama* (1): p. 11.

Rushin, Steve. 1994. "How We Got Here." *Sports Illustrated*, August 16, 34-42.

Ryan, Allan. 1968. "A Medical History of the Olympic Games." *JAMA* Vol. 205.

Sandomir, Richard. 1996. "Did Bob Costas Single out the Chinese?" *The New York Times*, September 6.

Scherer, Karl Adolf. 1974. *Der Männerorden: Die Geschichte des Internationalen Olympischen Komitees*. Frankfurt am Main: Limpert.

Schmidt, Paul. 1949. *Statist auf Diplomatischer Bühne, 1923-45 : Erlebnisse des Chefdolmetschers im Auswärtigen Amt mit den Staatsmännern Europas*. Bonn: Athenäum-Verlag.

Schneidman, N.N. 1978. *The Soviet Road to Olympus*. Toronto: Ontario Institute for Studies in Education.

Schöbel, H. 1968. *The Four Dimensions of Avery Brundage*. Translated by Joan Becker. Leipzig: Edition Leipzig.

Segrave, Jeffrey O., and Donald Chu. 1988. *The Olympic Games in Transition*. Champaign, IL: Human Kinetics.

Seillière, Ernest. 1917. *Un artisan d'energie français: Baron Pierre de Coubertin*. Paris: H. Didier.

Senn, Alfred Erich. 1985. "The Soviet Boycott of the 1984 Olympics: The Baltic Dimension." *Baltic Forum* (Stockholm) 2(1):88-104.

———. 1988. "The Question of a Permanent Home for the Olympic Games." *Modern Greek Studies Yearbook* 4:35-50.

Setton, Alice Ailene. 1941. *The Women's Division National Amateur Athletic Federation: Sixteen Years of Progress in Athletics for Girls and Women, 1923-1939*. Stanford: Stanford University Press.

Shaikin, Bill. 1988. *Sport and Politics: The Olympics and the Los Angeles Games*. New York: Praeger.

Shapiro, Henry. 1976. Interview, February 4.

Shirer, William L. 1941. *Berlin Diary*. New York: Knopf.

Shteinbakh, V. 1980. *The Soviet Contribution to the Olympics*. Moscow: Novosti Press Agency.

Simson, Vyv, and Andrew Jennings. 1992. *Dishonored Games*. New York: S.p.i. Books. Alternate edition published as *The Lords of the Rings: Power, Money, and Drugs in the Modern Olympics*. Toronto: Stoddart.

Smith, Red. 1983. *The Red Smith Reader*. New York: Vintage.

Sovetskii sport, July 8, 1986.

Spoilsport. 1996. *Spoilsport's Guidebook to Atlanta*. Atlanta: Spoilsport.

Sportsmeny. 1974. *Sportsmeny stran sotsializma na mezhdunarodnoi arene* (Athletes of the Socialist Countries in the International Arena). Moscow: Fizkul'tura i sport.

Steinberg, David. 1979. *Sport Under Red Flags*. Ph.D. diss., University of Wisconsin at Madison.

Stepovoi, P.S. 1984. *Sport-politika-ideologiia*. Moscow: Fizkultura i sport.

Stolbov, V.V. 1983. *Istoriia Fizicheskoi Kul'tury i Sporta*. Moscow: Fizkul'tura i sport.

Strasser, J.B., and Laurie Becklund. 1991. *Swoosh: The Unauthorized Story of Nike and the Men Who Played There*. New York: Harcourt, Brace, Jovanovich.

Sugar, Bert Randolph. 1978. *The Thrill of Victory.* New York: Hawthorne Books.

Swift, E.M. 1988. "Mandate for Barcelona." *Sports Illustrated,* vol. 69, p. 154.

———. 1996. "See Y'all in Sydney." *Sports Illustrated,* 12 August, 122-23.

Talamini, John T., and Charles H. Page, eds. 1980. *Sport and Society: An Anthology.* Boston: Little, Brown and Company.

Thucydides. 1972. *History of the Peloponnesian War.* London: Penguin Books.

Tomlinson, Alan, and Garry Whannel, eds. 1984. *Five-Ring Circus: Money, Power and Politics at the Olympic Games.* London: Pluto.

Ueberroth, Peter, Richard Levin, and Amy Quinn. 1985. *Made in America: His Own Story.* New York: William Morrow.

Ullrich, Klaus. 1979. *Kreuzritter im Stadion.* Berlin: Sportverlag.

———. 1980. *Triumph Olympia.* Berlin: Sportverlag.

Umminger, Walter. 1968. "Gedanken zur Schlussflier," in *Die XIX Olympischen . . .*

Van Rossein, G. N.d. *The Ninth Olympiad.* Amsterdam: J.H. De Bussy.

Vse o sporte. 1978. 3 vols. Moscow: Fizkul'tura i sport.

Wallechinsky, David. 1984. *The Complete Book of the Olympics.* New York: Penguin.

Wenn, Stephen R. 1994. "An Olympic Squabble: The Distribution of Olympic Television Revenue, 1960-1966." *Olympika* 3:27-48.

Whannel, Garry. 1983. *Blowing the Whistle. The Politics of Sport.* London: Pluto.

———. 1992. *Field in Vision: Television Sport and Cultural Transformation.* London/New York: Rutledge.

Williams, Melvin H. 1998. *The Ergogenics Edge.* Champaign, IL: Human Kinetics.

WWA. Welt Wirtschaftsarchiv. Hamburg, Germany. File of newspaper clippings on Berlin Olympics.

Young, David C. 1996. *The Modern Olympics. A Struggle for Revival.* Baltimore: Johns Hopkins University.

Zaseda, Igor. 1981. *Led i Plamen' Leik-Plesida.* Kiev: Zdorov'ia.

Index

Italicized page numbers indicate photographs. Tables are denoted by an italicized t following the page number.

A

Q

R

S

T

U

V

W

X

Y

Z

About the Author

Alfred Erich Senn is professor emeritus of history at the University of Wisconsin, Madison, where he has taught since 1961.

He received a PhD in East European history at Columbia University in 1958. Senn is the author of eight books, several monographs, and numerous scholarly articles. His book, *Gorbachev's Failure in Lithuania*, was awarded the Edgar Anderson Presidential Prize by the American Association of Baltic Studies in 1996.

Professor Senn lives in Madison, Wisconsin, with his wife, LaVonne.